LONDON ACCESS®

W9-ALT-124

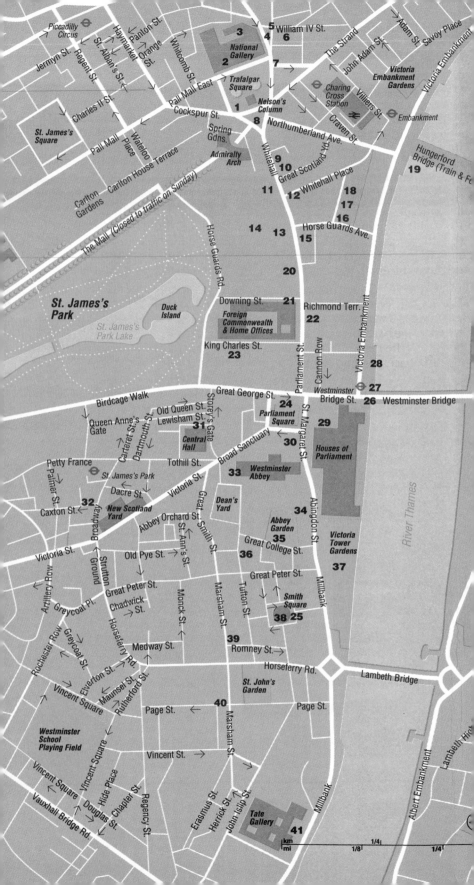

Whitehall

A walk down Whitehall from **Trafalgar Square** to **Westminster** is a kind of pilgrimage, a sleeve-shaped journey that echoes the River Thames, covers one-and-a-half acres of land,)00 years of history, and thrives as headquarters for history-in-the-making. Kings and queens are still crowned here, democracy is still guaranteed here, and in a rare mood of architectural harmony, power is still juxtaposed here. The **Houses of Parliament**, representing Temporal Power and the daily democracy of life, serves as a foil for its ancient neighbor, **Westminster Abbey**, seat of Spiritual Power and the ultimate democracy of death.

Unlike the English, Trafalgar Square is emotional and chaotic. Only partially, accidentally, and belatedly did the square come into its inspired position as gateway to democracy, a pragmatic stretch linking Whitehall with the Houses of Parliament. London's only grande place where her citizens can gather to express their joys and concerns, the square impartially upholds the ideals legislated 500 yards away by Parliament and administered in between by Whitehall. It is design justice that the square keeps an eye on both.

The walk passes the 3 most prestigious clubs in the land: the **National Portrait Gallery**, the **House of Commons**, and **Poet's Corner**, as well as 2 ancient pubs where the distinguished, and those who report on the distinguished, have been quenching their thirsts for centuries. Predictably, the concerns of the great and powerful are primarily greatness and power, so ordinary concerns—shops, banks, hotels—are in rather short supply.

You might stop for lunch on a boat moored to the Thames or for a concert at **St. John's, Smith Square**. You could have a drink in a crypt filled with those who have the ear of Parliament and perhaps even see an MP or 2. Your tour of Westminster Abbey may be delayed by a wedding or a funeral, an encouraging reminder that this magnificent and historical place is not a museum, that people still fall in love, make vows, dream, live, and die here.

The walk ends at the **Tate Gallery**, where you can be restored by tea and scones in the gallery café and be brought to life by the incandescent light in the late paintings by Turner. At the end of the walk, standing on the steps of the Tate and looking out at the Thames, Millbank, and Vauxhall Bridge Road, you may wonder if it is a day by Monet, the pre-Raphaelites, or Whistler.

On weekends, Westminster and Whitehall are abandoned to tourists. MPs return to their constituencies, civil servants stay home, and many of the restaurants, pubs, and shops that exist primarily to serve the governing elite shut as well. The ideal time for this walk is Monday through Thursday when Parliament is in session, even if you have no parliamentarian concerns. On Sunday, the most interesting parts of Westminster Abbey are closed, and the galleries (National Portrait and Tate) do not open until 2PM.

1 Trafalgar Square (1841) The square is a testament to England's victory over Napoleon's fleet in the decisive battle off the coast of Spain in 1805, the **Battle of Trafalgar**. It is even more monumental testimony to the defeat of anything like Napoleonic vision in town planning. Trafalgar Square is London's grandest place. If this were Paris, Haussmann's ruthlessness would have us looking down heart-stopping vistas of Buckingham Palace and Westminster Abbey; broad avenues would connect the square to Regent Street and the British Museum; and the square itself, instead of sunken, treeless, and confused, would be greenish, elevated, and uniform. The triumph of the English at Trafalgar, and 7 years later at Waterloo, was also a triumph of Englishness. Trafalgar Square honestly reflects the victory of democratic style over dictatorial grandeur: the military, architectural, and dramatic defeat of what the English dislike most—ostentation.

Until 1835, the site was occupied by the Royal Mews, when mews were for mewing—the shedding of old plumage and the growing of new. **Edward I** (reign, 1272–1307) kept his hawks here, and **Richard II** (reign, 1377–1399) kept his falcons and goshawks, a rather distinguished legacy for the famous pigeons and starlings who mew monotonously in the square today.

Whitehall

By the reign of **Henry VII** (reign, 1485–1509), horses were kept in the Royal Mews. In 1732, landscape gardener, architect, and painter **William Kent** (1685–1748) built the **Royal Stables** on this site, then known as *Great Mews*, *Green Mews*, and *Dunghill Mews*. The stables stood until 1830, when they were replaced by the National Gallery.

The original designs for the square were made by **John Nash** (1752–1835), who had already brought elegance and grandeur to London with Regent Street, Regent's Park, and Marble Arch, under the aegis of the Prince Regent, later George IV. With Regent Street, Nash provided the first north-south axis to connect London's 3 main east-west routes (Oxford Street, Piccadilly, and the Strand). In his early sketches of Trafalgar Square, Nash saw the site as the medieval turning-point in the road leading from Westminster Abbey to St. Paul's Cathedral. There was no open space, only a widening where the bronze statue of **Charles I** had stood since 1675, marking the spot where the 3 roads met. Nash designed the square as a grand axis connecting government (Parliament Square), finance (the City), and aristocracy (St. James's and the Royal Parks). Unfortunately, Parliament accepted Nash's site and rejected his designs.

Trafalgar Square as you see it today is the work of **Charles Barry** (1795–1860), the distinguished architect of gentlemen's clubs, including the Reform Club and the Traveller's Club in Pall Mall, and the club of clubs, the Houses of Parliament. Barry favored the Italian palazzo style for this war memorial and he created in Trafalgar Square an economic, Victorian interpretation of the piazza.

At Trafalgar Square:

Nelson's Column (1843, William Railton) Horatio Nelson (1758–1805) entered the service of his country at the age of 12, suffered from seasickness all his life, lost his right eye at the Battle of Calvi, his right arm at Santa Cruz, and his life at Trafalgar. The hero whose last words were *Thank God, I have done my duty*, is now exiled in perpetuity 170 feet overhead in a gray London sky.

Trafalgar Square

In a city where the sun is no incentive and the past is all-pervasive, there seems to be no need to rush things, and by and large, Londoners do not. From the time of Nelson's funeral at St. Paul's (1805) and the raising of his column in Trafalgar Square (1843), almost 40 years went by. Railton's design of a massive Corinthian column won the competition for the monument in 1837. The capital is of bronze cast from cannons recovered from the wreck of the *Royal George*. On the sides of the pedestal are 4 bronze bas-reliefs cast from the metal of captured French cannons, representing incidents in the battles of St. Vincent, Aboukir, Copenhagen, and Trafalgar.

The statue of Lord Nelson is by the sculptor **E.H. Bailey.** The figure of the naval hero is 17 feet high and his sword measures 7 feet 9 inches. Together with the column, the monument is as tall as an 18-story building, a satisfying reward for a man who measured just 5 feet 4 inches in real life.

Guarding the column are 4 vast (20 feet by 11 feet) and loveable lions by Queen Victoria's favorite animal painter, **Sir Edwin Landseer.** Late arrivals, it is these magnificent, tenderfaced creatures who humanize the square. When Landseer died in 1871 the public put wreaths around the lions' necks.

Four octagonal oil lamps that have been converted to electricity occupy the corners of the square. They are reputedly from Nelson's flagship, *HMS Victory*. One likes to think so.

Every year on 21 October, the anniversary of the Battle of Trafalgar, a parade and service are held in the square by members of the Royal Navy. Officers from modern ships of the fleet lay wreaths at the bottom of the column, and descendants of those who fought at Trafalgar place an anchor of laurels. Nelson, a genius for naval battle, was a hero with a gift for inspiring devotion.

The highlights of the year for the square are Christmas and New Year's Eve. A giant crib and an enormous Christmas tree, a gift from the Norwegians, are erected and carols are sung on most evenings. On New Year's Eve thousands defy death to congregate in the square and welcome in the New Year to the chimes of nearby Big Ben.

Statue of George IV Most noticeable of the many other notables in the square is George IV (reign, 1820–30), who worshipped Nelson (though the feeling was not mutual) and under whose auspices Nash first conceived the square. After the Battle of Trafalgar had estab-

lished Britain's command of the seas, George IV commissioned Turner's great battle piece, *The Battle of Trafalgar* (hanging in the National Maritime Museum, Greenwich). But George IV's great obsession was architecture. As Prince Regent he built the Brighton Pavilion; as King he rebuilt Buckingham Palace and transformed Windsor into the finest of all the palaces of the British monarchy. An expert horseman, he commissioned most of the equestrian paintings by **George Stubbs** in the Royal Collection. Therefore, it is baffling that this statue by **Sir Francis Chantrey**, commissioned by George IV to surmount Marble Arch, shows the King in Roman dress, riding bareback without stirrups. As he had not finished paying for it, the statue was not completed and placed in the square until 12 years after his death. *King George IV* had to be added because no one knew who it was.

Statue of James II Another king in Roman dress, James II (reign, 1685–88) seems less affected, mainly because he had the good luck to have **Grinling Gibbons** (1648–1720) as sculptor. Impulsive and bullheaded, James II annoyed Parliament with his pro-Catholic wife and politics. He was succeeded by his protestant daughter, **Queen Mary II**, and spent the last 11 years of his life in exile in France.

The naval influence in Trafalgar Square continues with busts of 3 modern heroes: admirals **Beatty** and **Jellicoe** of World War I, and **Admiral Cunningham** of World War II. Carved into the stone of the north wall between Jellicoe and Cunningham are the **Imperial Standards** for length, showing you the exact measurements of an imperial inch, foot, yard, rod, chain, pole, and perch.

Fountains In a city blessed with rain, fountains are few. Barry's original fountains and their large pools were part of a design to break up the large, unruly crowds that the government of the day was perceptive enough to realize would congregate. Even with the fountains and their pools, 50,000 people can and do congregate in the square when the cause of democracy calls. The original fountains designed by Barry now face Parliament in Ottawa, Canada. **Sir Edwin Lutyens** (1869–1944) designed the fountains in the square to commemorate admirals Jellicoe and Beatty. They have first-rate water power, and every morning at 10AM the mermaids and mermen respond to the repetitive booms of Big Ben in the distance by democratically christening nearby Londoners and visitors, people and pigeon.

Buildings The late **Sir John Benjamin**, poet laureate and passionate defender of Victorian architecture, saw the weighty stone buildings that surround Trafalgar Square as a historic backdrop. Looking left in the direction of Whitehall are **Herbert Baker's South Africa House** (1935), its somber classical facade indifferent to the opponents of apartheid who patrol the sidewalk night and day; the rounded **Grand Buildings** (1878) and **Trafalgar Buildings** (1881), designed by the **Francis brothers**

(refurbished instead of demolished); **George Aitchison's Royal Bank of Scotland** (1885); **Reginald Blomfield's Uganda House** (1915);

and **Canada House** (1827), the most handsome building on the square, built by **Sir Robert Smirke**. Originally the **Royal College of Physicians**, this building of warm Bath stone has suffered from conversion and extension of the upper parts but remains a dignified presence.

2 National Gallery (1838, William Wilkens) The most important building in Trafalgar Square is the National Gallery, anchoring the north side. Architects complain that the scale of the Neoclassical building is weak in relation to the square, but the blame should fall on a parsimonious Parliament, which compelled Wilkens to use the columns from the demolished **Carlton House** in the portico. The original building was only one room deep, more a facade than a gallery. But its limited size—now much expanded with an extension in progress—had no effect on its importance. Although relatively small (just over 2000 pictures), it houses one of the most comprehensive surveys of Western art. ♦ See page 45 for complete details.

3 National Portrait Gallery (1895, Ewan Christian and J.K. Colling) After getting your bearings in Trafalgar Square, this is where to begin a day in London, a stay in England, or a trip to Europe. It is not an art gallery—eminence of the sitter, not the artist, is what counts. More eloquent than words, the faces in the portraits are the history of England: history as poetry, biography, and prophecy. Resist the temptation to wander through the bookshop first or amble up the stairs. Take the slow elevator to the top floor and begin, confusingly, a few steps down on the upper mezzanine. Here you will find the first portrait to break away from the stylized representations of kings: a very natural and touching young **Richard II** (reign, 1377–99). Sensitive, cultivated, and artistic, Richard appreciated beauty and was a patron of **Chaucer**. His talents were for art and beauty and love (he was heartbroken when his wife, **Anne of Bohemia**, died); he had no talent for politics. Deposed by his cousin **Henry IV**, he was murdered at Pontrefact Castle. This painting of Richard II is a copy (the original is down the street in Westminster Abbey), but it is a moving start to a royal procession where art, history, and British civilization converge.

The great age of portraiture began with the Tudors when **Hans Holbein** (c. 1497–1543) became court painter to **Henry VIII** (reign, 1509–47). Brought to England from Holland by **Erasmus**, Holbein was the greatest 16th-century artist to work in England. His portraits

Restaurants/Nightlife: Red   Hotels: Blue
Shops/Parks: Green
                                Sights/Culture: Black

show a profound perception of character, at once powerfully direct and full of nuance. Through Holbein, Henry VIII is indelibly fixed

Whitehall

in our minds, although unfortunately for the King, the artist arrived in England after the King was no longer young, thin, and handsome.

The most celebrated, acclaimed, and painted monarch of all time is **Elizabeth I** (reign, 1558–1603), who was virtually an icon during her reign. In many of her portraits, even the decorations on her clothes are emblematic— an ermine on a sleeve symbolizes chastity, pearls represent purity. Elizabeth I's legendary ability to rule was enhanced by her being a living idol to her people, a living work of art.

Alongside the kings and queens are the writers who captured the ages for us in words: a portrait of **Shakespeare** (1564–1616) attributed to **John Taylor**, the best likeness of the playwright that exists, and **Samuel Pepys** (1633–1703) by **John Hayls**. While Elizabeth I was proclaiming herself Gloriana, more than mortal, Donne was writing of a heaven *where there shall be no darkness nor dazzling, but one equal light; no noise nor silence, but one equal music; no fears nor hopes, but one equal possession; no ends nor beginnings, but one equal eternity.* As the paintings in the 25 rooms make brilliantly clear, England would

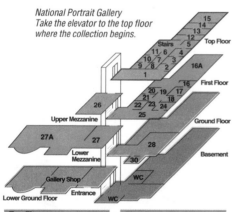

National Portrait Gallery
Take the elevator to the top floor
where the collection begins.

not come close to such a heaven on earth for several hundred years.

Don't miss:

Holbein cartoon of Henry VIII in black ink and colored washes on paper, part of a wallpainting for Whitehall Palace (now lost). Still visible are the hundreds of tiny pinpricks that the artist used to transfer his designs to the wall. ◆ Mezzanine

Elizabeth I, by Marcus Gheeraedts the Younger, done soon after the defeat of the Spanish Armada. The Queen is standing triumphantly on her kingdom of England, storm clouds behind and a brilliant sky before her. ◆ Top floor, Room 1

Charles I and Sir Edward Walker after the campaigns in the West Country in 1644–45 A look of serenity and sadness on the face of the King, as though to presage the tragic future. ◆ Top floor, Room 2

Oliver Cromwell with an unknown page by Walker (c. 1649) and miniature of Oliver Cromwell; by Samuel Cooper (1656) Both paintings show a man aware of the tragedy around him, and the miniature by Cooper, the finest miniaturist of all, shows a psychological subtlety rare in any painting. ◆ Top floor, Room 2

Admiral Horatio Viscount Nelson This unfinished study for a full-length commission is a quite brilliant portrait painted from life by **Sir William Beechey** in 1800–01, showing all the passion and fire of the hero who destroyed Napoleon's sea power and of the man, brave, tender, and honest. Opposite Nelson is **Emma Lady Hamilton** (1765–1815), done by **George Romney** in 1785. She was the great love of Nelson's life, his mistress, the mother of his daughter Horatia, and part of one of the great love stories in British history. ◆ Top floor, Room 12

The Romantics: 3 portraits, **William Blake** (1757–1827), by **Thomas Phillips** in 1807, visionary poet and artist; **John Keats** (1795–1821), by his friend **Joseph Severn** in 1821, one of England's best-loved and finest poets who died in Rome of tuberculosis at the age of 25; and **Lord Byron** (1788–1824), by Thomas Phillips in 1814, the Romantic Man—poet, lover, and revolutionary. Byron captured the poetic and romantic imagination of the age and died in Greece fighting for Greek independence. ◆ Top floor, Room 13

Jane Austen (1775–1817), by her sister Cassandra This tiny drawing is the only likeness that exists of the beloved and acute observer of the human heart. ◆Top floor, Room 15

The Brontë sisters, by their brother, Branwell (c.1835) Anne, Emily, and Charlotte looking young and serious. The ghost in the background is Branwell, who painted himself out of the portrait. Also by Branwell is the beautiful, cracked portrait of Emily Brontë. ◆ 1st floor, Room 17

Restaurants/Nightlife: Red   **Hotels:** Blue
Shops/Parks: Green   **Sights/Culture:** Black

Charles Darwin (1809–82), by John Collier A haunting, spiritual portrait of the man who used science to destroy the myth of creation. ♦ 1st floor, Room 20

Elizabeth Barrett Browning and Robert Browning painted by Gordigiani in 1858 In the same room as a portrait by **Ballantyne** of the artist **Landseer** sculpting the lions that are now outside in Trafalgar Square. ♦ 1st floor, Room 21

Henry James (1843–1916), by John Singer Sargent The American writer who loved London and settled in England, painted on his 70th birthday by the American artist who lived in London and became the most fashionable portrait painter of his generation. ♦ 1st floor, Room 25

The Twentieth Century on the Ground Floor The controversial painting *Queen Elizabeth, the Queen Mother*, by **Alison Watt**, was hung in 1989 to mixed response. You'll either love it or hate it. Royal portraits include *Prince Charles* wearing his polo clothes and *Princess Diana* when she was still plump and girlish; political portraits include **Gerald Scarfe**'s *Margaret Thatcher*, **Sargent**'s *Nancy Astor*, and **Sickert**'s *Churchill*; artist's portraits include *Delius* by **Procter**, *James Joyce* by **Blanche**, and *W.H. Auden, T.S. Eliot, Dylan Thomas*, and *Virginia Woolf.* There are also self-portraits by contemporary British portraitists **Graham Sutherland** and **David Hockney**, among others. Temporary exhibitions are held here and are almost always worth a look.

The **National Portrait Gallery Bookshop** is one of the best shops for postcards. (The bestseller is the melancholy portrait of Virginia Woolf.) All the heroes and heroines upstairs are down here in alphabetical order. Like museum shops the world over, this one has cleverly expanded. It stocks all the books you are in the mood to read after gazing at the portraits above. ♦ Ground floor

There is no café within the Portrait Gallery, but next door in the **National Gallery Restaurant** you can have a late second breakfast, lunch, or tea. Run by **Justin de Blank Ltd**, it is a cut above the usual gallery/museum fare. You can order light salads, cheeses, tempting cakes, wines, and herbal teas. Sit and write postcards from the Portrait Gallery Bookshop. ♦ Gallery free; occasional charge for special exhibitions. M-F 10AM-5PM; Sa 10AM-6PM; Su 2-6PM. 2 St. Martin's Place, WC2. 071/930.1552.

4 Statue of Edith Cavell (1920, **Sir George Frampton**) In the small island next to the National Portrait Gallery and behind Trafalgar Square is a monument to Edith Cavell (1865–1915), a nurse who was shot by the Germans in 1915 for spying and helping British prisoners escape. The statue was unveiled in 1920 by **Queen Alexandra**. Four years later, the Labor Government added her famous words, *Patriotism is not enough*, a sentiment that would have shocked Nelson, who thought patriotism was everything.

Do not criticize your government when out of the country. Never cease to do so when at home.

Sir Winston Churchill

5 The Chandos ★★$ A cooked English breakfast is served from 8 to 10:30AM in *The Opera Room* on the 1st floor of this hand-

some real ale pub across the street from the Post Office. ♦ Daily 8AM-noon. 29 St. Martins Ln (King William IV St) WC2

6 Post Office One of the liveliest buildings around Trafalgar Square, built in the 1960s. It used to be open 24 hours a day, and is still London's only post office with relatively late hours. ♦ M-Sa 8AM-8PM; Su 10AM-5PM. 24 William IV St, WC2. 071/930.9580

7 St. Martin-in-the-Fields (1726, **James Gibbs**) **John Nash**'s design for Trafalgar Square was never realized. But his role in it endures because it was his idea to open up the vista that brings St. Martin-in-the-Fields into the square. The church is not actually part of the square, but it is its single source of pure loveliness. Built by Wren's disciple, James Gibbs (1682–1754), its steeple rises 185 feet from the ground, almost the same height as Nelson's Column. The steeple atop the portico of Corinthian columns has been an inspiration for many American churches. The porch offers shelter to passers-by on rainy days, and the steps are a resting place for tired tourists. On Monday and Tuesday at 1:05PM, you can enjoy the famous lunchtime concerts of chamber and choral music in the light and airy church where **Charles II** was christened and his mistress, **Nell Gwynn**, was buried. ♦ St. Martin-in-the-Fields, Trafalgar Sq, WC2. 071/930.0089

Within St. Martin-in-the-Fields:
Field's Restaurant ★★$ Hidden within the crypt of St. Martin is this little treasure of a restaurant used by theater stars for private parties and by office workers to meet their friends for lunch and snacks. The floors (gravestones), the walls (16th-century stone), and the black furniture all are made less sepulchral by the strains of Bach and the busy clatter of china. ♦ M-Sa 10AM-3:15PM, 5:30-8:30PM; Su noon-6:30PM

London Brass Rubbing Center This has moved from St. James's Piccadilly. You can rub effigies of medieval brasses (mostly facsimiles), creating your own knight in shining armor. If you feel pressed for time, buy a readymade knight. This is a nice place to spend time with children, who love creating copies of the effigies. ♦ M-Sa 10AM-6PM; Su noon-6PM. 071/930.0089

George Bernard Shaw offered **Churchill** tickets for the first night of *St. Joan* for himself and *a friend if you have one.* Churchill replied that he was sorry he would not be able to attend and asked for tickets for the second night, *if there is one.*

Bessie Braddock, MP: *Sir, you are drunk.*
Churchill: *And you, madam, are ugly, but I shall be sober in the morning.*

Whitehall: A royal residence for 160 years, from the reign of Henry VIII to James II. The royal palace that gave the area its name

was destroyed by fire in 1698; the name White Hall was simply a term for a grand hall used for banquets and festivities. Today it is one of London's widest and busiest streets connecting Trafalgar Square with Parliament Square. Behind the high impenetrable facades and tall cupolas of its stately buildings, thousands of civil servants act on government decisions. The air of power is almost palpable. This is the road of kings and queens, who use it for coronation, marriage, and burial en route to Westminster Abbey.

8 Statue of Charles I (1633, **Hubert Le Sueur**) Whitehall physically begins at the statue of Charles I (reign, 1625–1649) on his horse, gazing onto the scene of his tragic execution at **Banqueting House** on 30 January 1649, with Parliament looming in the distance. It was his quarrel with Parliament that led to his downfall. In 1642, civil war erupted between the Parliamentarians (the Roundheads, led by **Oliver Cromwell**) and the Royalists (known as the Cavaliers) over Parliament's demand to approve the King's choice of ministers. Charles was tried for treason to the realm and died on the scaffold.

Now stranded in an islet, unreachable except by the most intrepid pedestrian, *Charles I* is the oldest, finest, and most poignant statue in London. The horse's left foot bears the date 1633 and the sculptor's signature. When the Civil War broke out in 1642, the statue was hidden in the churchyard of St. Paul's, Covent Garden. After the King's execution, Cromwell sold the statue for scrap to a resourceful brazier named **John Rivett**. A brisk trade in candlesticks, thimbles, spoons, and knifehandles, a kind of *Charles I Souvenir Shop*, thrived until the Restoration, when the statue miraculously reappeared. **Charles II** rewarded the Royalist brazier with £1600. (The Banqueting House, one of the most fabulous buildings of its time, had cost just under £16,000.) The statue finally found its home on Whitehall in 1675.

9 Silver Cross ★★$ **Charles I** licensed this as a brothel and pub in 1643. The facade is Victorian, but the building is 13th century, with a wagon-vaulted ceiling, ancient walls sheathed in lead, and, in the bar, a plaster ceiling embossed with vine leaves, grapes, and hops made while Charles I was still living down the street. For the past 250 years it has been the *local* for the Old Admiralty next door, and for nearly as long it has been the pub of journalists who report on Whitehall. It opens early and serves English breakfasts, home-cooked lunches, afternoon teas, and excellent evening buffets. A warm and special pub. ♦ M-F 8AM-11PM; Sa-Su 9AM-10:30PM. 33 Whitehall, SW1. 071/930.8350

10 Clarence ★★$ A Whitehall institution, this 18th-century pub has gaslights inside and out, oak beams overhead, sawdust on the floor, and wooden tables and pews. The old farm equipment on the beams may be in deference to the regulars from the Ministry of Agriculture next door, but this is also a pub for connoisseurs of real ale—choose among 7 served with full bar meals twice daily. ♦ M-Sa 11AM-3PM, 5:30-11PM; Su noon-2PM, 7-10:30pm. 53 Whitehall, SW1. 071/930.4808

11 Old Admiralty (1725, **Thomas Ripley**) The stone screen adorned with sea horses is by **Robert Adam** and leads into the cobbled courtyard. This is all that can be seen of the place that for 200 years ruled the waves. In the **Board Room** upstairs, a wind dial (1708) still records each gust of wind over the roof, even though no one waits here for a sign that the wind will carry the French across the English Channel. The present Admirality still meets in the building. Smoking has never been allowed, a rule that even Churchill humbly obeyed. Here **Nelson** both took his orders and returned 5 years later to lay in state, awaiting his funeral at St. Paul's. **Bailey**'s original model for Nelson's statue in Trafalgar Square is kept here. ♦ Whitehall, SW1

12 Ministry of Defense (1898, **William Young & Son**) In this more pacifist age, the Old War Office is called the Ministry of Defense. Inevitably, it lacks the romance of the Old Admirality across the street, but the Baroque domes above its corner towers, visible from Trafalgar and Parliament squares as well as from St. James's Park, have a lingering imperial grandeur. ♦ Whitehall, SW1

13 Horse Guards (1750–60, **William Kent**) The 2 troopers are magnificent and impassive on their horses, elegant concoctions of tunics and plumes under archway and clock tower. Even the twin sentry boxes are pure Gilbert and Sullivan. The *Mounting of the Guard* takes place at 11AM each morning. Don't confuse this with the *Changing of the Guard*, which happens at 11:30AM at Buckingham Palace. Londoners under the age of 12, the best judges of these things, prefer the daily cavalry show at Horse Guards to the infantry performance outside Buckingham Palace. Young would-be soldiers will also explain that the red tunics and white plumes are the Life Guards, blue tunics and red plumes are the Blues and Royals. The soldiers are not allowed to talk, and if you don't touch their swords or the velvet-soft muzzles of the horses, you can take photos or be photographed with them.

The Horse Guards have been guarding since the days of **Charles II** (1630–85), when they guarded Whitehall Palace. The palace burned down in 1698, but the guarding has continued. Horse Guards itself was rebuilt in 1760.

There are manners everywhere, but aristocracy is bad manners organized.
Henry James

Though designed by William Kent, it was built after his death by **John Vardy**. So what do they guard now? Less palatial concepts—like history, tradition, and magic. ◆ Mounting the Guard M-Sa 11AM; Su 10AM. Mounted guards on duty 24 hours. ◆ Whitehall, SW1. 071/925.2263

14 Horse Guards Parade Go through the arch at Horse Guards and you will be in Horse Guards Parade. Ignore, if you can, the cars and dwell on the white stone and splendid Palladian building with arches, pediments, and wings, architecturally one of the finest buildings in London. The parade ground, now so ingloriously used as a parking lot for Whitehall's high and mighty, used to be the Whitehall Palace tiltyard. In 1540, **Henry VIII** invited knights from all over Europe to compete in a tournament on this site.

Every year on the second Saturday in June, the Queen leaves Buckingham Palace in her carriage to drive down Horse Guards Parade for **Trooping the Color**. This is the most spectacular military display of the year in a country that has no rival in matters of pomp. An annual event dating back to medieval times, it was originally an exercise to teach soldiers to recognize their regimental flags. Now it is the sovereign's official birthday, ceremonial acceptance that English weather does not guarantee a successful outdoor occasion before June. Crowds line the Mall to watch the procession, but it is possible for the lucky few to get tickets. Write from the beginning of January to the end of February to the Brigade Major, Trooping the Colour, HQ, Household Division, Horse Guards, Whitehall SW1A 2AX. ◆ Behind Horse Guards, Whitehall, SW1

Inigo Jones

15 Banqueting House (1622, **Inigo Jones**) On a bitter winter's day in January 1649, a small procession left St. James's Palace and walked through the park to Whitehall. A king of England was going to his execution. Cross-

ing Whitehall, **Charles I** may have gotten his first glimpse of the scaffold built outside the central windows of Banqueting House and his

last look at the perfectly proportioned Palladian building commissioned by his father, **James I**.

Banqueting House and the fate of Charles I are inextricably bound. The proportions of the hall, one of the grandest rooms in England, create a perfect double cube at 110 feet long and 55 feet high. This design represents the harmony of the universe, of peace, order, and power—the virtues of divine kingship instilled in Charles I by his father. The magnificent ceiling, which Charles commissioned from **Peter Paul Rubens**, represents the glorification of James I, a visual statement of James' belief in the absolute right and God-given power of kings. If you follow the panels from the far end of the room, you see James rising up to heaven, having created peace on earth by his divine authority as King: peace reigns, the arts flourish, and the king is defender of his realm, the faith, and the Church.

When Charles I tried to impeach 5 members of Parliament, Civil War broke out between the Parliamentarians and the Royalists. Seven years later he was tried in Westminster Hall and convicted of treason to the realm.

On the day of the execution, Charles I wore a second shirt so that he would not shiver in the cold and have his people believe he was afraid. He was a king in life and a sad and courageous king in death: *I go from a corruptible to an incorruptible crown where no disturbances can be.*

With one blow, England was without a king, and severed with Charles' head was the belief in the divine right of kings. Until this moment, kings were the chosen representatives of God on earth. Now men would choose princes.

Three centuries later England still has her kings and queens, and Banqueting House still stands. In spite of being one of the most important buildings in all of English architecture, it is almost always empty. Empty but not haunted; there is no feeling that the ghost of Charles I lingers under the newly cleaned ceiling. A bust of Charles I over the staircase entrance (added by **Wyatt** in 1798) marks the site of the window through which he stepped onto the scaffold. ◆ Nominal admission. Tu-Sa 10AM-5PM; Su 2-5PM. Whitehall, SW1. 071/930.4179

Charles I, whose last word was *Remember*, is remembered every year at 11AM on the Sunday nearest to 30 January, the date of his death. Hundreds of cavaliers in full dress, members of the English Civil War Society, march to Banqueting House, where they lay a wreath at noon outside the window where Charles climbed through onto the scaffold.

Opposite the Horse Guards, at Banqueting House, is the site of the old **Whitehall Palace**, once the largest palace in all of Eu-

rope. It began in 1245 as the London residence of the Archbishops of York, called **York Place**, and acquired dimensions of grandeur when **Cardinal Wolsey** moved in (1528). The Cardinal had already begun the incomparably splendid Hampton Court, the palace outside London that rivaled Versailles in size and sumptuous splendor. Thus it was an experienced hand that created the palatial proportions in York Place, building magnificent gardens, a wine cellar, a chapel, and lavish accommodations for the lords, knights, and ambassadors of Europe. Wolsey presided over a miniature Renaissance Court that included 23 acres, 800 servants, and folie and audacity, as **Henry VIII**, his neighbor and king, lived a few yards down the road in second-rate accommodations at the Palace of Westminster. After the Cardinal's fall in 1530 (he failed to obtain papal consent for the King's divorce from **Catherine of Aragon**), Henry VIII lost no time in making York Place his. He changed the name to Whitehall, acquired the land to the west from the Abbot of Westminster and created St. James's Park, built 3 tennis courts, a tiltyard (now Horse Guards Parade), and a bowling alley. Henry VIII married **Anne Boleyn** here in 1533 and **Jane Seymour** in 1536. He died here in 1547. **Elizabeth I** was taken from the Palace of Whitehall to be prisoner in the Tower, then returned in triumph as Queen. The first performance of Othello was performed at Whitehall. After the execution of Charles I in 1649, **Oliver Cromwell** moved into the palace, with **John Milton** as his secretary. Cromwell died here in 1658, and **Charles II** succeeded him to the throne here. It remained the royal residence until the reign of **William III**, when, on 4 January 1698, a fire started by a laundrymaid burned the palace to the ground. All that remains today is the name, the wine cellar, a riverside terrace, the walls of the tennis courts, and Banqueting House.

16 New Ministry of Defense Building
(1959, **Vincent Harris**) These vast buildings were placed behind Whitehall on Horse Guards Avenue out of respect to the scale and proportions of **Inigo Jones**' Banqueting House. Started just after World War II, this is where the real problems of war and peace are handled—with a few exceptions. In the basement is all that survives of the original Whitehall Palace: **Henry VIII**'s wine cellar.
The Tudor brick-vaulted roof is 70 feet long, 30 feet wide, and weighs 800 tons. Because the wine cellar interfered with the line of the new building, it was moved 40 feet to one side, lowered 20 feet, and then pushed back

to its original site. A huge excavation was made, a mausoleum of concrete and steel built around the cellar to protect it, and a system of rollers devised that shifted the cellar a quarter of an inch at a time until it had completed its journey of 43 feet. The whole operation cost £100,000, a vast sum at the time. All the same, you can see it only on Saturday afternoon, by appointment. Apply in writing to the Department of the Environment. ♦ Horse Guards Ave, Whitehall, SW1

17 Whitehall Court (1884, **Archer and Green**) This massive Victorian attempt at a French château was a grand apartment building—both **H.G. Wells** and **George Bernard Shaw** had flats—and home of several clubs, including the **Farmers'** and the **Liberal Club**. ♦ Whitehall Ct, SW1

18 Royal Horse Guards Hotel $$$ Once the apartments of the influential, the 284 rooms and suites overlooking the Thames are now for the affluent. The reception rooms and the restaurant, **The Granby**, have the feel of a gentlemen's club, but the guest rooms are light and spacious and more feminine. At lunchtime the hotel bar fills with civil servants from the Ministry of Defense, a quieter breed than that which fills the pubs nearby. Try to sit in the outdoor courtyard, which overlooks an ornamental garden. ♦ 2 Whitehall Ct, SW1. 071/839.3400

19 RS Hispaniola ★★$$ Walk down Whitehall Place or through the gardens behind Whitehall Court to reach Victoria Embankment on the Thames and have lunch or dinner in this restaurant-ship floating on the river. The boat doesn't actually go anywhere, but watching other boats sail up and down the river makes you feel maritime. When the sun is out, sit on the upper deck and eat fresh Colchester oysters. The fish is excellent and the menu features game in season. ♦ M-F noon-2PM, 7-10PM; Sa 7-10:30PM. Victoria Embankment, Westminster Pier, WC2. Reservations recommended. 071/839.3011

20 Cabinet Office (1733–36, formerly the Treasury) Several great architects had their hands in the design, including **William Kent, Sir John Soane**, and **Sir Charles Barry**. The building exudes Victorian self-confidence and weightiness. At the north end is the office of the Privy Council, the queen's private council comprising *princes of the blood*, high officers of the state, and members of Parliament appointed by the Crown. It seems fitting that *Sir Walter Raleigh* (1959, **William Macmillan**), once a member of Elizabeth I's Privy Council, stands opposite. He may look a happy man today, but his fate was grim enough. (Raleigh exhibited a very stiff upper lip on the scaffold. Testing the ax for its sharpness he remarked, *This is a sharp medicine, but it will cure all diseases.*) ♦ Whitehall, SW1

It was the nation and the race dwelling all around the globe that had the lion's heart. I had the luck to be called upon to give the roar.
Sir Winston Churchill

Drawing Courtesy David Gentleman

control room crammed with phones and maps covered with marker pins showing the positions of military defenses. Churchill made

his stirring wartime broadcasts from the room behind the door marked *Prime Minister*. You can almost hear that steadfast, bear-like growl, *Let us therefore brace ourselves to our duties and so bear ourselves that if the British Empire and its Commonwealth last for a thousand years men will still say, this was their finest hour.* It is amazing to think that from these poky little rooms Churchill brilliantly conducted a global war. ♦ Admission. Tu-Su 10AM-5:50PM. Clive Steps, King Charles St, SW1

21 Downing Street History and television have made the street one of the most famous and familiar in the world. But modern politics and terrorism have shut it off from the public. Named after its builder, **Sir George Downing**, the street lost its quiet, residential air when **No. 10** became the official residence of the first prime minister, **Sir Robert Walpole**, in 1735. The facade is modest, but inside there is considerable grandeur. Some of the women who have lived in the house have complained about the lack of space and light. But **Margaret Thatcher**, the first female occupant to be prime minister, made few complaints.

No. 11 Downing Street is the official residence of the Chancellor of the Exchequer. **No. 12** is the office of the Chief Government Whip, the title for the member of Parliament responsible for organizing and maintaining discipline in the party ranks in the House of Commons.

22 Cenotaph (1920, **Sir Edwin Lutyens**) Rising in the center of Whitehall is this austere memorial to the dead of World Wars I and II. The simple structure of Portland stone shows no sign of imperial glory or national pride or religious symbol; it is not a monument to victory but a monument to loss. Between the wars, men would take off their hats whenever they passed. Now hats have gone out of style and memories have faded, but once a year, on *Remembrance Sunday* (second Sunday in November), a service is held to remember the dead of these wars. It is attended by the Queen, the royal family, representatives of the Army and Navy, the Prime Minister, and leading statesmen. Wreaths are placed at the monument while bands play the haunting music of **Sir Edward Elgar**'s *Nimrod*. At 11AM, a 2-minute silence is observed in memory of the dead.

23 Cabinet War Rooms Churchill masterminded the British war effort from this complex 17 feet underground, and now 6 of the rooms are open to the public. You will find the room where the War Cabinet met and the

The Battle of London

At tea time on a gloriously fine Saturday afternoon—7 September 1940—400 German planes came over London and bombed a virtually undefended city. After dark another armada of 250 bombers followed, helped to their targets by fires already blazing every mile along both sides of the Thames. By dawn, 430 civilians had been killed, and 1600 carried wounded from the debris of their homes. This was the start of the Battle of London—Goering's blow right into the enemy's heart.

For 57 nights without let-up the Luftwaffe attack continued. Every night during that September and October bombers flew over, at least 200 strong. London was caught off-balance. Defense was impossible, devastation enormous. The death toll: 9500. By this, the first mass civilian attack in history, the Germans hoped to force a surrender. It failed.

London: 2000 Years of a City and its People
by **Felix Barker** and **Peter Jackson**

24 Parliament Square (1850, **Sir Charles Barry**) Barry conceived the square as a kind of garden foreground to his new Houses of Parliament. The first monument you see is a determined-looking *Winston Churchill* standing on the corner gazing at the House of Commons, which he loved with all his heart and all his life. This 12-foot bronze statue by **Ivor Robert Jones**, unveiled in 1973, has not transformed the landscape or led to the re-naming of Parliament Square. But it is the memory of Churchill, more than that of Nelson or King Charles I, that dominates Whitehall. Among the many other brooding statesmen in the square are *Disraeli* (**Lord Beaconsfield**), by **Raggi** (1883), and *Abraham Lincoln*, tall and rumpled and looking like the man who knew too much. His statue is a copy of the *St. Gaudens* in Chicago.

Restaurants/Nightlife: Red   **Hotels:** Blue
Shops/Parks: Green   **Sights/Culture:** Black

25 Footstool $$ Rather than dive into the nearest snack bar, walk a little further along Millbank for the Footstool, which is hidden in the

brick-built crypt of St. John's. Here you can see the lobbyists at rest and play, and the powers behind the Conservative Party lunching in the restaurant. Humbler office folk nibble quiche at the cold-food counter. Open evenings when concerts are on. ♦ Restaurant: M-F 12:15-2:15PM; closed alternate Th. Cold-food counter: M-F 11:30AM-2:45PM. St. John's, Smith Sq. 071/222.2779

Earth has not anything to show more fair:
Dull would he be of sould who could pass by
A sight so touching in its majesty:
This City now doth, like a garment, wear
The beauty of the morning; silent, bare,
Ships, towers, domes, theatres, and
temples lie
Open unto the fields, and to the sky;
All bright and glittering in the
smokeless aire.
Never did sun more beautifully steep
In his first splendour, valley, rock or hill;
N'er saw I, never felt, a calm so deep!
The river glideth at his own sweet will:
Dear God! The very houses seem asleep;
All all that mighty heart is lying still!

William Wordsworth (1770–1850)
Composed upon Westminster Bridge,
3 September 1803

---

26 Westminster Bridge (1862, **Thomas Page**) Once you get this close to the Houses of Parliament, you really have to walk onto Westminster Bridge. The Gothic buildings, rising almost vertically from the Thames, are among the most famous views in the world and an inspiration for poets and painters and believers in democracy. The 810-foot cast-iron bridge is not the one that inspired Wordsworth to write his sonnet. But the view surpasses by far what **Wordsworth** saw that early morning in 1803. He would not have seen the highly wrought Houses of Parliament with the imposing Victoria Tower. He could not have set his watch by the clock lovingly, if wrongly, called Big Ben. Looking down the river, he would not have seen Whitehall Court, the Shell-Mex House, the Savoy, or Somerset House in the background. Standing on the new Westminster Bridge stirs up poetic feelings as the magnificence of Westminster and Whitehall reveals itself.

27 Boadicea (1902, **Thomas Thorneycroft**) *Queen Boadicea*, a symbol of liberty, is well placed at the Westminster end of the bridge, looking out onto the Houses of Parliament from her chariot. Under the rule of the **Emperor Nero**, a savage revolt broke out in the newly conquered province of Britain when Roman soldiers forced their way into the palace of the widowed Queen Boadicea. They flogged the Queen for refusing to surrender the lands of the Iceni and raped her 2 daughters. In her fury, Boadicea led a savage rebellion, massacring the inhabitants of the Roman capital at Colchester, then turning south to the undefended port of Londinium. No mercy was shown, and the flourishing town was quickly destroyed. Seventy thousand lost their lives. But the revenge of the Queen of Iceni was short lived. The Romans, led by **Paulinus**, met the Britains in a formal battle and annihilated them. Boadicea and her daughters took poison, ending the rebellion. In the bronze statue, Boadicea has her 2 half-naked daughters at her side, but the cause of freedom is made more difficult in a chariot that lacks reigns.

28 Westminster Pier Perhaps the only thing better than walking in London is floating along the Thames. Westminster Pier is the main starting point for boat trips downstream to the Tower of London and upstream to Kew Gardens and Hampton Court. From April to October, boats going upstream leave about every 20 minutes starting at 10AM and boats going downstream leave every 30 minutes from 10:30AM. From November to March, services to the Tower and Greenwich leave every half-hour. Full information is available from the River Boat Information Service. ♦ Westminster Pier. 071/730.4812

29 Houses of Parliament (1840–60, **Sir Charles Barry** and **Augustus Pugin**) To the modern world, no single view so powerfully symbolizes democracy as this assemblage of Gothic buildings that look as if they have been here throughout the 900 years this has been the site of English government. In fact, these buildings have been standing just over 100 years, but their Gothic style powerfully represents the aspirations and traditions of those 9 centuries. The *Symbol of Democracy*, the *Mother of Parliaments*, remains a royal palace. It is officially called the *New Palace of Westminster*, a name that goes back in history to the 11th century when this was the site of the old Palace of Westminster. First occupied by **Edward the Confessor** (reign, 1042–66), the building was the principal London residence of the monarch until 1529, when **Henry VIII** moved down the street to Whitehall Palace. Parliament continued to sit here until the palace was burned to the ground in the disastrous fire of 1834. All that is left of the ancient Palace of Westminster is the undercroft and cloisters of **St. Stephen's Chapel** and **Westminster Hall**, the long Norman hall that is the greatest window into the history of Britain's parliamentary heritage.

After the fire, it was decided to build new and enlarged Houses of Parliament on the same site. A competition was held for a building in either the Gothic or Tudor style. The winners were Sir Charles Barry and Augustus Pugin. Barry gave the buildings an almost classic body. Pugin, with his unrivaled knowledge of Gothic style, created a meticulous and exuberant Gothic design. The Houses of Parliament

Houses of Parliament

is built on an axial plan that reflects almost ladderlike the hierarchical nature of British society: House of Commons, Commons Lobby, Central Lobby, Lords Lobby, House of Lords, Princes Chamber, and Royal Gallery. The building covers an area of 8 acres and has 11 courtyards, 100 staircases, 1100 rooms, and 2 miles of passages. The House of Commons is in the northern end (MPs enter from **New Palace Yard** on the corner of Bridge Street and Parliament Square) and the House of Lords is in the southern end. (The Peers entrance is in **Old Palace Yard**, where **Guy Fawkes** was hung, drawn, and quartered in 1606 for trying to blow up Parliament, and where **Sir Walter Raleigh** was beheaded in 1618.)

Within the Houses of Parliament:

Westminster Hall (1097) Built by **William Rufus**, son of **William the Conqueror**, this vast barnlike room is where Parliament began and where **Simon de Montfort** marched in and enforced it. At the end of the 14th century, **Richard II** had the hall rebuilt (c. 1320–1400, **Henry Yevele**), adding the massive buttresses that support 600 tons of oak roof. The hall contains the earliest surviving example of an oak hammerbeam roof, which was a miracle of engineering in its day—it marked the end of supporting piers. The austere and venerable room has witnessed earthshaking moments of history almost since its beginning. Under the benevolent eyes of the carved angels in the arches of the beams, Richard II was deposed the year the work was completed and successor **Henry IV** was declared King. In 1535, **Sir Thomas More**, former speaker of the House of Commons, stood trial here for treason against his former friend and tennis partner, **Henry VIII**, and was beheaded on Tower Hill. Seventy years later, on 5 November 1605, England's most famous terrorist, **Guy Fawkes**, was accused of trying to blow up King James I and Parliament. **Charles I**, King of England, stood trial in his own hall in 1649 and was convicted

of treason. **Oliver Cromwell**, the most formidable parliamentarian who ever lived, signed the King's death warrant and had himself named Lord Protector here in 1653. After the restoration of **Charles II** to the throne, Cromwell was brought back to the hall, or rather his skull cut from his skeleton was brought back and stuck on a spike on one of the oak beams, where it rattled in the wind for 25 years until it finally blew down in a storm. And it was here, in Westminster Hall, that **Churchill** lay in state for a fortnight while a grateful nation paid its last respects.

Crypt Church Though once abused and desecrated, and even used as the speaker's coal cellar, the chapel was richly restored by **E.M. Barry** and has a wonderful pre-Raphaelite feeling. The main walls, vaulting, and bosses have withstood at least 5 fires. Members of both Houses of Parliament use the chapel for weddings and christenings.

St. Stephen's Porch The public enters the Houses of Parliament through the porch and hall. Now there is a security check with metal-detecting arches, airport-style, right next to Westminster Hall.

Central Lobby The security check is an understandable but inglorious entrance to the lobby, the crossroads of the Palace of Westminster, connecting the House of Commons with the House of Lords. Citizens meet their MPs in this octagonal vestibule. The ceiling, 75 feet above the floor, contains 250 carved bosses with Venetian mosaics that include the patron saints of England, Ireland, Scotland, and Wales. Above the ceiling is the central spire of the palace, a feature that was not in Barry's original plans, but imposed by **Dr. Reid**, a ventilation expert who insisted it be built as a shaft to expel *vitiated* air. It has never been needed or used for anything. In the floor of encaustic tiles, Pugin inscribed the Latin text from Psalm 127: *Except the Lord keep the house, they labour in vain that build it.*

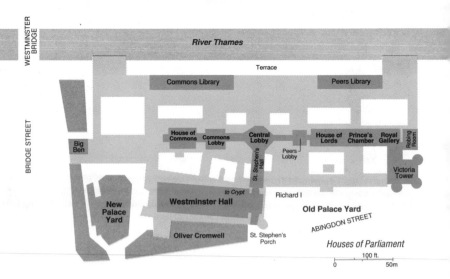

Houses of Parliament

Members' Lobby Off the Central Lobby is the members' or Commons Lobby, the Piccadilly Circus of Commons life where members gossip and talk to the lobby journalists. It is architecturally rather bleak, referred to as *neogothic*, and was never quite restored after the 1941 German bombing that left it in ruins. A more moving reminder of the destruction is the **Churchill Arch**, made from stones damaged in the fire of 1941. Churchill proposed that it be erected in the lobby in memory of those who kept the bridge during the dark days of the war. Above the main door of the Commons Chamber is the family crest of **Airey Neave**, placed here after he was assassinated by terrorists in New Palace Yard in 1979.

House of Commons The House of Commons was completely destroyed in the air raid of 10 December 1941, and was rebuilt in 1950 by **Sir Giles Gilbert Scott**, simply and without decoration and, under Churchill's influence, in the exact proportions of the prewar House. It is impressively small: only 346 of the 650 members can actually sit down at any one time, the rest crowding around the door and the speaker's chair. The smallness is believed to be fundamental to the sense of intimacy and conversational form of debate that characterize the House. Equally important is the layout of the **Chamber**, with the party in office (called the government) and the opposition facing each other, their green leather benches 2 swordlengths apart and separated by 2 red lines on the floor, which no member is allowed to cross. The **Press Gallery** and the **Public Gallery** are at opposite ends of the Chamber.

Each day the House opens with a procession in which the speaker (wearing a wig, knee breeches, and a long black gown) enters, preceded by the sergeant-at-arms, who carries a mace (the symbol of authority), and followed by the train-bearer, chaplain, and secretary. The day begins with prayers, and no strangers (journalists or visitors) are ever admitted. MPs face the seats behind them—an extraordinary sight—because in the days when they wore swords it was impossible to kneel on the floor. Therefore they turned to kneel on the benches behind them. Every member has to swear loyalty to the Crown (a problem for Irish MPs for the past 100 years), although no monarch has been allowed to enter the House of Commons since 1642, when **Charles I** burst in to arrest his parliamentary opponents. Open to the public only by prior appointment with a member of Parliament or by waiting in line, starting at about 5PM. ♦ Sessions: M-Th from 2:30PM, often until late; F 9:30AM-3PM. Prime Minister's question time: Tu, Th 3:15 PM. 071/219.4272

Queen Elizabeth arrives in the Irish State Coach at the Houses of Parliament once a year for the **State Opening of Parliament**. In a ceremony that has changed little since the 16th century, she delivers her speech (a policy statement written by the party in office) in the **House of Lords**. She enters through the **Royal Entrance**, a gate beneath the **Victoria Tower** that she alone uses. She proceeds to the **Norman Porch** and into the **Robing Room**, where she puts on the Imperial State Crown amid the astonishing splendor of Pugin's decoration. Every inch of the room is covered in gemlike Gothic and Tudor frescoes and hung with pictures depicting the Legend of King Arthur. The procession continues into the **Royal Gallery**, which is 110 feet long, 45 feet wide, and lined with paintings, including *The Death of Nelson* and *The Meeting of Wellington and Blucher at Waterloo*. Both paintings are 45 feet long and 12 feet high. They took the artist, **Daniel Maclise**, 6 years to complete, an appropriate recognition of 2 events without which this grand, Gothic, and democratic place would not exist. Finally, the Queen passes through the **Prince's Chamber**, which is the anteroom to the House of Lords and a celebration of Tudor, with dark paneling and full-length portraits of **Henry VIII**, 5 of his 6 wives, and his mother.

House of Lords This is the most elaborate part of Barry's design and Pugin's ultimate masterpiece: Victorian, romantic, and stunning. At 80 feet long, it is not grand in size, but it is extravagantly ornate. Stained-glass windows shed a dark, red light, and 18 statues of the barons of Magna Carta stare down from the walls. They look like saints, emphasizing the sacred look of the room, but the long red-leather sofas on either side suggest a chapel not really consecrated. Between the 2 sofas is a huge red pouff, the *Woolsack* (the traditional seat of the Lord Chancellor), stuffed with bits of wool from all over the Commonwealth. At the far end of the room under an immense gilded canopy is the ornate throne of the Queen. ♦ Sessions M-W 2:30PM; Th 3PM; occasionally on F. 071/219.4272

Outside the Houses of Parliament:

Big Ben The most beloved image in all of London is Big Ben, towering 320 feet over the Thames, telling time, and lighting up the London sky. Every guidebook will tell you that Big Ben is not the clock, but the bell. However, in people's hearts, the clock tower is, and always will be, Big Ben. The tower itself now leans 9^1/$_2$ inches, the clock's 4 dials are 23 feet wide. The minute hands are each as tall as a red London double-decker bus. The pendulum, which beats once every 2 seconds, is 13 feet long and weighs 685 pounds. Besides being endearing, the clock is a near-perfect timekeeper. After spending 3 years under scaffolding, the clock tower has emerged several shades lighter and glistening—4000 books of gold leaf were used to reguild the gold surfaces. Plans were made to restore the hands to their original color, but when it was found that they were blue (the color of the Conservative party), it was felt that Big Ben could not be partisan and they were painted black instead. The hours are struck on the 13 ^{1}/$_2$-ton bell, named Big Ben after the First Commissioner of Works when the bell was hung. Since 1885, a light has shined in the tower at night when Parliament is sitting.

Victoria Tower When it was built, the 336-foot tower was the tallest in the world—taller than early American skyscrapers—and it is still the world's highest square masonry tower. Barry saw the Palace of Westminster as a legislative castle and this was to be its keep, its great ceremonial entrance. The Victoria Tower, technologically far ahead of its time, later had to be massively reconstructed to save it from collapse. It is now an archive of over 3 million parliamentary documents dating back to 1497, including the death warrant of **Charles I**. During the day, the Royal Standard flies when the Queen is present and the Union Jack when Parliament is sitting. On a clear day, the flag can be seen by the naval men in Greenwich.

Statue of Cromwell (1899, **Sir Hamo Thornycroft**) Every 3 September, tribute is paid to Cromwell's memory as founder of our modern

democracy at his statue in front of the Houses of Parliament. When the statue was first erected, Parliament refused to pay for it. Prime Minister **Lord Rosebery** paid for it himself.

The **Houses of Parliament** was an inspired collaboration between 2 men of vastly different talents and visions, **Sir Charles Barry** and **Augustus Pugin**. They worked together in the fertile harmony of mutual respect, each expanding the realm of possibility for the other. Barry was a man of classical ideas and temperament. His **Traveller's Club** in Pall Mall shows his Neoclassicism at its best. Pugin was a Gothic genius, in love with tracery, foliage, bays, emblems, oriels, turrets, and paneling—a medieval world of tapestries and trumpets. Pugin's drawings won Barry the competition; Barry's solid experience and talent provided Pugin his Camelot. The 2 men combined romanticism with logic. But Pugin, under constant attack from the Parliamentary Commissions who decried his efforts and cut his salary in half, died at the age of 40 in Bedlam madhouse; Barry, whose wife had laid the foundation stone, died of worry and overwork within months after the work was finished.

30 St. Margaret (1504–23, **Robert Stowell**; original church founded in the 12th century) **Sir Walter Raleigh** was beheaded out front and is buried beneath the altar; **Samuel Pepys** married a vivacious 15 year old in the church in 1655; **John Milton** married here a year later; **Winston Churchill** married here in 1908. It has been the parish church of the House of Commons since 1614. The magnificent Flemish glass window was commissioned by **Ferdinand** and **Isabella** of Spain to celebrate the engagement of their daughter **Catherine of Aragon** to **Prince Arthur**, the older brother of **Henry VIII**. By the time the window arrived, Henry had become King and married Catherine—by then his brother's widow. On an ordinary day, this would be quite enough to get one's attention, but St. Margaret's has the bad luck of being wedged in between the Houses of Parliament and Westminster Abbey. Most people go past thinking it is an extension of the latter. Treasures in the church include stained-glass windows in the south aisle, done by artist **John Piper** in 1966; the west windows, given to the church by Americans; the **Milton window**, with the blind poet dictating to his daughter; a memorial to **Sir Walter Raleigh**, the colonizer of Virginia, with lines from the American poet **John Greenleaf Whittier**: *The New World honours him whose lofty plea for England's freedom made her own more sure;* and a tablet near the altar where Raleigh is buried urges: *Reader-Should you reflect on his* *errors Remember his many virtues And that he was a mortal.* ◆ St. Margaret, Parliament Sq, Westminster, SW1

Whitehall

31 Westminster Arms ★★$ Home-cooked steak, kidney pie, and real ale make this a popular pub with MPs, journalists, and young clerics in the neighborhood who are summoned by bells—the Division Bell in the pub and the church bells next door. A nice atmosphere. ◆ M-Sa 11AM-3PM, 5:30-11PM; Su noon-2PM. 9 Storey's Gate, SW1. 071/222.8520

32 Stakis St. Ermin's Hotel $$$ This ornate marbled hotel is within shouting distance of Westminster Abbey, Buckingham Palace, and the Houses of Parliament. Businesspeople whisper to each other that St. Ermin's really does serve London's best breakfast. The secret is out. ◆ Caxton St, SW1. 071/222.7888; fax 071/222.6914

33 Westminster Abbey (1245, **Henry of Reims**) One of the finest French Gothic buildings in the world—it is officially called the **Collegiate Church of St. Peter**—and the most faithful and intimate witness of English history. Westminster Abbey has survived the Reformation, the Blitz, and requiring even more miraculous tenacity, 9 centuries of visitors, pilgrims, worshippers, wanderers, and tourists. Today the abbey is like a medieval Heathrow, with windows, buttresses, and vaulting all heavenward, taking flight; and the traffic below, earthbound, in awe.

It is almost impossible to see the abbey without being surrounded by thousands of tourists, either moving aimlessly down the aisles or purposefully following a raised umbrella that is reeling off *Abbey Highlights*. If possible, come here for a service, when the abbey empties of tourists and regains some of its seren-

ity. In any case, try to avoid it in the morning, when all the guided bus tours in London combine Westminster Abbey with the Changing of the Guard. (Likewise, avoid St. Paul's in the afternoon before 3PM, when the tours combine St. Paul's and the Tower of London.)

Once upon a time, this really was an abbey, a monastic community designed for the monkish life of self-suffcent contemplation, with cloisters, refectory, abbot's residence, orchards, workshops, and kitchen gardens. In legend, the first church was built in the 7th century and St. Peter himself appeared at the consecration. A Benedictine abbey was also founded; it was called Westminster (west monastery) because it was west of the City of London. The existence of the abbey today is due to the inspired determination of **Edward the Confessor**, who set to work on a great monastery to promote the glory of God in 1050. In order to supervise the progress of the abbey and efficiently preside over his Kingdom of England, he moved his palace next door—hence, the Palace of Westminster—and established the bond between Church and State that has endured for more than 900 years.

Edward the Confessor was brought up in Normandy and built his abbey in a Norman style, advanced and unlike anything that had ever been seen in England. The King, ill and unable to attend the consecration of his church, died a week later on 6 January 1066. No one knows if his successor, **Harold**, was crowned here or at St. Paul's, but after Harold's death at the Battle of Hastings, **William the Conqueror** was crowned here on Christmas day 1066. The ceremony was written down in the 14th century and is preserved in the abbey. Since 1066, the kings and queens of England have all been crowned at Westminster Abbey, except for 2: **Edward V** (presumed murdered) and **Edward VIII** (abdicated).

In 1245, **Henry III** decided to rebuild the now canonized St. Edward's church in a more magnificent style. Influenced by the French Gothic style of the cathedrals of Amiens and Reims (Sainte Chapelle in Paris was being built at the same time), Henry started to build, at his own expense, the soaring and graceful church that is here today. The King's architect, **Henry of Reims**, worked with great speed in cathedral terms. By 1259, the chancel, transepts, part of the nave, and the chapter house were complete, giving the medieval church remarkable unity of style. The nave, continued in the late 14th century by **Henry Yevele** (master mason who built Westminster Hall), was built in the style originally planned by Henry of Reims.

The only important additions to Henry III's church have been the **Henry VII Chapel**, begun in 1503 and believed by many to be the most beautiful and most perfect building in England, and the towers on the west front, built in the 18th century from the designs of **Wren** and **Hawksmoor**.

The best way to enter the abbey is under the towers by the **West Door**, where you can take in the majestic height of the roof: 102 feet to the exalted vault, the pale stone touched with gold and tinted by the colored glass of the aisle windows. The eye is pulled upward in prophetic astonishment at the sheer beauty of it all, then immediately distracted groundward by the chaos of the white-marble figures. You understand at once that any tour of Westminster Abbey will have to be 2 tours, even if taken simultaneously: one, a tour of the plan and beauty of the building, serene and coherent; the other, a survey of the haphazard and wonderful confusion of the once-great and now-dead. It requires great presence of mind to deal with both at the same time.

Standing at the entrance, you see the impressive length of the stone-flagged nave, the decorated choir screen in front of the nave (too gold, too gaudy, too late), and above, the Waterford chandeliers, 16 in all, presented by the **Guinness** family in 1655 to mark the 900th anniversary of the consecration of the abbey. Criticized for being more Mayfair than Gothic, they have come under the spell of the abbey and now look superbly right.

Immediately in front of you, beyond the stone honoring **Winston Churchill**, is the grave of the **Unknown Warrior**, a nameless British soldier brought to the abbey from France on 11 November 1920. The flag that covered the coffin hangs nearby, alongside the Congressional Medal of Honor. The poppy-filled slab contains earth and clay from France, a terrible and moving reminder of a whole generation lost.

To your right is **St. George's Chapel**, the Warrior's Chapel, with an altar by **Sir Ninian Comper** and a tablet on the west wall commemorating the one million men from the Empire and the Commonwealth who died in World War I. A memorial to **Franklin D. Roosevelt** hangs here. Just outside the chapel is a haunting portrait of the young **Richard II**. It is the first genuine portrait of a king painted in his lifetime. The sad brevity of Richard's life seems to show in his face. The choir screen, designed by **Edward Blore** in 1828, jolts a bit. Its bright goldness drains the color from **Lord Standhope** and **Sir Isaac Newton**, who are framed within the arches. Near Newton, a Nobel bevy of scientists are gathered, including **Charles Darwin**, who used science to destroy the myth of creation, and **Ernest Rutherford**, who unsettled creation by his discovery of the atomic nucleus.

Behind the screen is the **choir**. The choir stalls are Victorian, but the choir itself has been in this position since Edward the Confessor's own abbey stood on the site. The organ was installed in 1730, but it has been uplifted, rebuilt, and enlarged. Organists at the abbey have been quite dis-

tinguished, including **Orlando Gibbons, John Blow**, and his pupil **Henry Purcell**.

Because the **North Transept** has one of the

main entrances to the abbey (**Solomon's Porch**), it is thick with people coming and going, adding confusion to the mixed bag of the distinguished who are here permanently. Still, persevere until you reach **St. Michael's Chapel** in the east aisle and **Roulbiliac**'s monument to **Lady Nightingale**. The poor woman was frightened by lightning and died of a miscarriage. She collapses into her husband's arms, while he, frantic and helpless with fear, watches Death, a wretched skeleton, aim its spear at his wife. Maddeningly, this aisle is frequently used for storing chairs. Ask an attendant for permission to visit.

Kings and queens have been crowned in coronation services in the **sanctuary** itself since the time of **Richard II** in 1377. A platform is created under the central space (the lantern) between the choir and the sanctuary. The **Coronation Chair** is brought from the **Confessor's Chapel** and placed in front of the high altar. Since the coronation of **Charles I**, the anthem *I was glad when they said unto me, We will go into the House of the Lord* is begun as

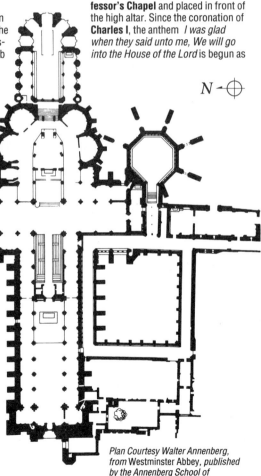

N

Plan Courtesy Walter Annenberg, from Westminster Abbey, *published by the Annenberg School of Communications, 1972*

Plan of Henry VII's Chapel

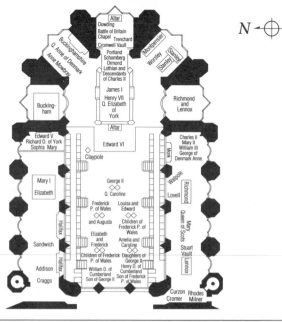

Plan of Sanctuary and Chapels

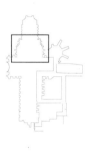

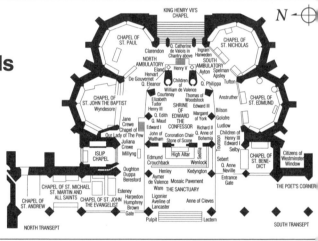

Plan of South Transept and Poet's Corner

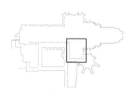

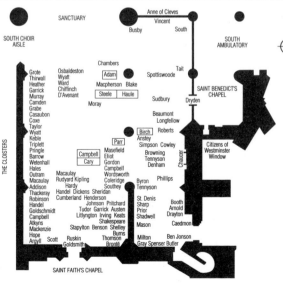

Plans Courtesy Walter Annenberg,
from Westminster Abbey,
published by the Annenberg School
of Communications, 1972

soon as the sovereign enters the West Door. When **Queen Elizabeth** entered the choir for her coronation in 1952, under the eyes of God and the television cameras, a chorus of *Vivat, vivat, vivat regina Elizabetha* rang out from the voices of Westminster School's scholars. At the sanctuary, she was presented by the Archbishop of Canterbury to the people 4 times, in turn on all sides, who then acclaimed her with loud cries of *God Save the Queen*. After an elaborate ceremony of oaths, a service of holy communion, and annointing with special oil, robed in gold and delivered of ring, sceptor, and orb, the archbishop performed the act of crowning.

To the north are the 3 finest medieval tombs in the abbey: **Edmond Crouchback**, the Earl of Lancaster and the youngest son of Henry III, and his wife, the rich and pretty **Aveline of Lancaster**. Theirs was the first marriage in the new abbey in 1269. The third grave belongs to **Amyer de Valence**, Earl of Pembroke.

Behind the high altar is the **Shrine of Edward the Confessor**. This is the most sacred part of the abbey, the destination of pilgrims. The Purbeck marble tomb contains the body of the saint. Beside the saint are Henry III, who built the church in homage to the Confessor; Henry's son **Edward I**, the first king to be crowned in the present abbey; and his beloved **Queen Eleanor**, for whom he set up the Eleanor Crosses all the way from Lincoln to the tomb where she is buried.

The **Coronation Chair**, when not in use for coronations, stands behind the high altar. Built in 1300, the chair was designed to incorporate the **Stone of Scone**. The stone, part of the Scottish throne since the 9th century, was captured and brought back from Scotland by Edward I in 1297. The **Stone in the Throne** represents the union of the 2 countries, a union that, 600 years later, is not without resistance. The stone has been stolen from the abbey by Scottish nationalists several times, most recently in the 1950s, but it has always been recovered. The graffitti on the back of the chair was done by 18th-century schoolboys at Westminster School.

If you are able to look at one and only one part of the abbey, make it the **Henry VII Chapel**. Because you pay a small admission fee, the abbey suddenly becomes quieter and emptier, a blessing as this is one of the most beautiful places you may ever see. Notice the exquisite tracery of the fan vaulting, miraculous intricacies and ecstasies of stone, Matisselike in their exuberance; the high wooded choir stalls that line the nave—and their misercordes; the carvings beneath the seats, including a woman beating her husband, and mermaids, mermen, and monkeys; the black-and-white marble floor; and throughout, the royal badges, a kind of illustrated Shakespeare of Tudor roses, leopards of England, the *fleur-de-lys* of France, the portcullis of the Beauforts, grayhounds, falcons, and daisy roots. This is the Renaissance in England, and Hea-

ven is on Earth in a world alive with confidence, harmony, beauty, and art. The chapel is the grand farewell to the great Gothic style and

the perfect setting for the **Order of the Bath**, the chivalrous knights who were installed in the 18th century and whose order still exists today. (The most recent installation of a Knight of the Bath was in 1982.) In the aisles on both sides of the chapel are a few unforgettable tombs. In the south aisle rests *Lady Margaret Beaufort* by **Torrigiani**. She was the mother of Henry VII, and was a remarkable Renaissance woman devoted to education, the arts, and the journey of her soul. Her effigy, one of the finest in the abbey, shows a delicately lined face with the gentle sensitivity that in time becomes beauty.

Having restored religion to its original sincerity, established peace, restored money to its proper value, etc.... Most world leaders would die for an epitaph like that, but it seems rather an understatement for **Queen Elizabeth I**. Her 4-poster tomb in the north aisle reflects Gloriana more gloriously, although how she feels about being buried with **Mary Queen of Scots**, whom she had beheaded, God only knows.

In **Innocent's Corner**, at the end of the aisle, are effigies of the 2 infant daughters of **James I**: **Sophia**, under her velvet coverlet, died at birth; and **Mary**, leaning on one elbow, died at age 2. Both, looking like small dolls, bring tears to parents' eyes and fascinate small children. In another tomb close by lie the bones of 2 children found in the Tower of London and brought here by order of **Charles II** in 1674. They are believed to be **Edward V** and his brother **Richard**, sons of **Edward IV** and allegedly murdered by their uncle **Richard III** in 1483.

In 1889, **Henry James** came to Westminster Abbey for the memorial service of **Robert Browning**, whose ashes were being consigned to **Poet's Corner**. Afterward he wrote that Browning stood for *the thing that, as a race, we like best—the fascination of faith, the acceptance of life, the respect for its mysteries, the endurance of its charges, the vitality of will, the validity of character, the beauty of action, the seriousness, above all, of the great human passion*. James' testimony to Browning seems a perfect testimony to Anglo-Saxon England, Westminster Abbey, and above all, to its corner of poets, where the honored are the greatest that a generous nation has to confer. All those honored here are not buried here, but among those honored are **Geoffrey Chaucer, Edmund Spenser, Ben Jonson** (who is buried upright!), **William Shakespeare, John Milton, John Dryden, Dr. Samuel Johnson, Thomas Gray, Richard Brinsley Sheridan, Oliver Goldsmith, William Blake, William Wordsworth, Samuel Taylor Coleridge, Percy Bysshe Shelley, John Keats, Thomas Babington Lord Macaulay, Jane Austen,** the **Brontë sisters, Walter Scott, William**

Makepeace Thackeray, Charles Dickens, Henry Wadsworth Longfellow, John Ruskin, Rudyard Kipling, George Gordon Lord Byron,

George Eliot, Dylan Thomas, W.H. Auden, D.H. Lawrence, Lewis Carroll, Gerard Manley Hopkins, and since 1976, **Henry James**. One of the newest stones was unveiled on 11 November 1985. It is a memorial to the poets of World War I. Among those mentioned are **Rupert Brooke, Robert Graves, Herbert Read, Siegfried Sassoon**, and **William Owen**. Above the dates 1914–1918 is the statement from Owen: *My subject is War, and the pity of War. The poetry is in the pity.* The ashes of **Sir Laurence Olivier**, Britain's finest actor this century, were buried in the abbey in the fall of 1990—a fitting tribute to this well-loved artist.

Ninety-minute **Supertours** of the nave, choir, Statesman's Aisle, Poet's Corner, the royal chapels, and the Coronation Chair are offered Monday through Saturday. (The **Jericho, Parlous**, and **Jerusalem** chambers can only be seen on the tour.) Reservations in the south aisle of the nave. ♦ Westminster Abbey: daily 9AM-4PM, unless attending a service. Holy Communion: daily 8AM, 5PM (Visitors may not walk around the abbey during services.) Royal chapels: Admission. M-Tu, Th-F 9AM-4:45PM; W 9AM-7:45PM; Sa 9AM-2PM, 3:45-5:45PM. Supertours: M 9:45, 10:15, 11AM, 2:15, 3:30PM; Sa 10, 10:45AM, 12:30PM. 071/222.5152

Around Westminster Abbey:

Chapter House (1250) From 1257 until **Henry VIII**'s reign, this exquisite octagon with Purbeck marble roof served as the Parliament House for the Commons. ♦ Daily 10AM-4PM

Chapel of the Pyx (c. 1090) Once the monastery treasury, it passed to the Crown during the Dissolution. ♦ Daily 10AM-4PM

Dean's Yard You can only gaze through the iron gate at the charming tree-shaded yard behind the abbey. The yard and the buildings of Westminster School arranged around it are not open to visitors.

Great Cloisters The courtyard offers a breathtaking view of the buttresses and flying buttresses on the south side of the **Henry VIII** Chapel. The large **brass-rubbing center** is open Monday-Saturday 9AM-5PM. ♦ 071/222.2088.

Abbey Treasures Museum This 11th-century holy **Madame Tussaud**'s is the highlight of the day for children, who definitely prefer the macabre to the historical. The wax effigies were used for lyings-in-state and funerals, and the clothes are not costumes but the real thing, including **Nelson**'s hat with its green eyepatch. The abbey represents the divine harmony of immortal man with God; the museum is an unnerving reminder of the mortal in us all. ♦ Admission. Daily 10AM-4PM

34 Jewel Tower (1366, **Henry Yevele**) **Edward III** built the tower to hold his jewels and silver. There are no jewels (not of the ruby and diamond variety, that is) in this last surviving domestic part of the royal Palace of Westminster. But you can see the drawings submitted in the competition for the Houses of Parliament. These fascinating architectural documents make you even more certain that **Barry** and **Pugin** were the right men at the right time. ♦ Admission. M-Sa 10:30AM-1PM, 3-4PM. Abingdon St, Westminster, SW1

35 Abbey Garden The 900-year-old garden (the oldest cultivated garden in England) is open to the public on Thursday. Its main attraction is lavender, which you can have shipped to the US. ♦ Th 10AM-6PM, Apr-Sep; Th 10AM-4PM, Oct-Mar. Band concerts 12:30-2PM, Aug-mid Sep

36 Whippel's The shop is the supplier to the religious trade. Bishops' purple socks are out of stock at the moment (*they're on order but hard to get nowadays*), but this is a great source for church candles. They will make beeswax candles in any size you want. ♦ M-F 9AM-1PM, 2-5PM. 11 Tufton St, SW1. 071/222.4528

37 Victoria Tower Gardens These gardens are a tranquil oasis overlapping the Thames, ideal for a picnic lunch or an afternoon nap. Two varying principles of heroism can be found in the sculpture: **A.G. Walker'**s statue of **Emmeline Pankhurst** (1858–1928), the leader of the women's suffrage movement often imprisoned for her beliefs; and a replica (1915) of **Rodin**'s *Burghers of Calais* (1895), a monument to those who surrendered to Edward III in 1347 rather than see their town destroyed. ♦ Westminster, SW1

38 St. John's, Smith Square (1728, **Thomas Archer**) **Itzak Perlman** and **YoYo Ma** have given lunchtime concerts in the church, along with the **Allegri, Endymion**, and **Amadeus** quartets. The musical reputation is high indeed, in part because each Monday the concerts are broadcast live on BBC Radio 3. You won't find this church unless you are looking for it, but it is a treasure—original, idiosyncratic, and personal. After almost being destroyed by bombs in 1941, St. John's was rebuilt but not reconsecrated. ♦ Westminster, SW1

England surely is the paradise of little men and the purgatory of great ones.
Cardinal John Newman

39 Wilkens ★$ There are not many around like this: a health-food café with delicious salads, thick homemade soups, and granary bread. Self-service, cheap, cheerful, fast. ♦ Daily 8AM-6PM. 61 Marsham St, SW1. 071/222.4038

40 Lockets ★★$$ MPs dine here regularly on the kind of food you find in English novels: roast beef, jugged hare, and when in season, pheasant and grouse. It is like eating in the Stranger's Dining Room at the House of Commons, only the food is better and the wine list is vastly superior. ♦ M-F 12:15-2:30PM, 6:30-11PM. Marsham Ct, Marsham St, SW1. 071/834.9552

41 Tate Gallery (1897, **Sidney J.R. Smith**; northwest extension, 1979 **Michael Huskstepp**; Clore Gallery, 1987 **James Stirling** and **Michael Wilford & Associates**) If you can only handle one major museum and if you like paintings, the Tate is where you will find true happiness. It houses 2 great national collections comprised of more than 10,000 works, yet it is accessible and welcoming.

The collections are an interesting mix of British mid-16th century and modern international art, including the works of living artists that are, naturally, controversial. Arguments to house the collections separately come up from time to time. But it is a singular pleasure to be able to look at **Turners** and **Blakes, Whistlers, Sargents, Rothkos**, and **Giacomettis**, all hanging happily within minutes of each other.

The gallery began life through the generosity of **Sir Henry Tate** (of the sugar manufacturer Tate & Lyle), who donated his collection of 70 "modern" British paintings and sculptures and offered to pay for a building to house it. A vacant lot on the River Thames at Milbank, previously occupied by Jeremy Bentham's Model Prison (from which less-than-model prisoners were sent down the Thames to the Colonies) was acquired, and the wedding-cake building with its majestic entrance was opened in 1897. Its formative years were spent as a kind of annex of the National Gallery. But in

1955 a formal, albeit friendly, divorce took place, and the Tate was finally independent. You will recognize and revel in the lively good

nature of this museum, a spirit that sets it apart in the world of cultural institutions and makes cultural fatigue wonderfully impossible.

The Tate Gallery issues free plans of the gallery at the entrance. Because the vast collection is changed regularly, this is an invaluable way to locate what you want to see.

The **Turner Bequest** is one of the great treasures London offers its citizens and visitors, and one of the truly remarkable collections of the work of one artist. At his death in 1851, the artist J.M.W. Turner left his personal collection of nearly 300 paintings and 19,000 watercolors and drawings to the nation, with the request that his finished paintings (some 100) be seen all together, under one roof. In spite of his staggering generosity, his wish was ignored for more than 125 years. Finally, Turner's one hope has been realized with the **Clore Gallery** extension, which makes up in concept and design for the long neglect of Turner's wish. The paintings are top-lit with daylight, the kind of light, with all its varied and changeable qualities, in which the artist expected his pictures to be exhibited. Works on paper (watercolors and drawings) are in galleries where daylight is kept out in order to prevent the fading of the images. Not only has the architect taken great care to see that the art is sympathetically displayed and scientifically preserved, he has also made it possible for visitors to glimpse the River Thames as they stroll past the pictures. The Thames played a prominent part in Turner's life and art—he painted it, and he lived and died on its banks in Chelsea. Don't miss Turner's *Views of Petworth House, Sussex*, a painting of the home of his great patron and benefactor, **George Wyndham**, 3rd Earl of Egremont; *Peace: Burial at Sea*, a memorial to his friend, the painter **Wilkie**, who died at sea off Gibraltar; or the pictures of Venice.

Other works in the Tate that must be seen are **Gainsborough**'s *Sir Benjamin Truman, Suffolk Landscape*, and his portrait of the Italian dancer *Giovannae Baccelli;* **George Stubbs**' *Mares and Foals, The Haymakers*, and *The Reapers*; the polite paintings by **Sir Joshua Reynolds, Romney**, and **Lawrence**, which give you a

Courtesy of the Tate Gallery

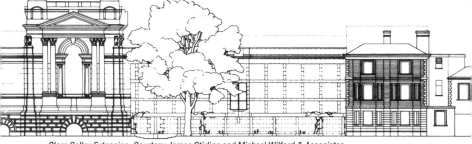

Clore Galley Extension, Courtesy James Stirling and Michael Wilford & Associates

glimpse into the serene world of the 18th century; the **William Blake** collection, the richest and most comprehensive in the world; the pre-Raphaelites, especially **Millais'** exquisite *Ophelia* and **Rossetti**'s paintings of his wife, **Beata Beatrix**; the irresistible portraits of John Singer Sargent, especially *Carnation, Lily, Lily, Rose*; and Whistler's *Little White Girl: Symphony in White No. II*. Hanging nearby are the newly appreciated paintings of **Tissot**.

The **French Impressionist** collection marks the beginning of the Tate's modern collection, and it includes **Manet**'s *Woman with a Cat*, which once belonged to Degas; **Bonnard**'s *La Table*; the brilliant Provence landscapes of **Cézanne**; and **Vuillard**'s *Seated Woman*.

Cubism is represented with some outstanding pictures by **Braque, Picasso**, and **Juan Gris**. An exciting and remarkably comprehensible outline of 20th-century art includes works by **Kokoschka, Léger, Masson, Matisse, Edward Munch** (*The Sick Child*), **Kandinsky, Mondrian**, and **Malevich. Rodin**'s large marble carving, *The Kiss*, made a few years after the version in the Musée Rodin, is one of the most popular pieces in the gallery.

The new display of the collection, the first comprehensive rearrangment in some 20 years, gives greater prominence to 20th-century British art, including **Stanley Spencer**'s 2 great Resurrection narratives set in Cookham and Port Glasgow. The story of British figure painting continues with the School of London paintings by **Francis Bacon, Lucian Freud, Frank Auerbach, Leon Kossoff**, and **R.B. Kitaj**, whose work has recently attracted increasing international attention. The grand central galleries have been restored to their original function as spaces for sculpture, and now show some of the masters of 20th-century British sculpture in the context of work by their European contemporaries. See especially work by **Richard Deacon** and **Tony Cragg**, who dominate the new generation of British sculptors. ♦ Free; admission for certain major exhibitions. M-Sa 10AM-5:50PM; Su 2-5:50PM. Millbank, SW1. 071/821.1313, recorded information 071/821.7128

You must not miss Whitehall. At one end you will find a statue of one of our kings who was beheaded; at the other the monument to the man who did it. This is just an example of our attempts to be fair to everybody.
Edward Appleton

Within the Tate Gallery:

Tate Gallery Shop Superbly printed postcards, excellent books, T-shirts with masterpieces from the Tate, the ubiquitous Tate Gallery canvas bags, prints, posters, framing facilities, and a few special made-for-the-Tate items that change frequently. ♦ M-Sa 10AM-5:30PM; Su 2-5:30PM

Tate Gallery Restaurant ★★★$$ The Tate Gallery Restaurant is known for 2 things: the romantic and beautiful **Rex Whistler** mural *Expedition in Pursuit of Rare Meats*, painted in 1926–27, and the wine list, which is unquestionably the best in town due to the sheer number of superb bottles and the amazingly low prices. The restaurant, refurnished by **Jeremy Dixon** in 1985, is frightfully chic and comfortable. A lunch here is hard to beat, surrounded by the wit and elegance of the mural. Order a 1978 *5ème cru classe* **Château Lynch-Bages** to go with your thoroughly English lunch. Your neighbors will be astute members of the wine trade, distinguished patrons of the arts, and sometimes couples who have come up from the country to compare their Joseph Wrights, Turners, and Stubbs with the Tates. Enjoy the most charming lunchtime rendezvous in the whole of London. ♦ M-Sa noon-3PM. Reservations required far in advance. 071/834.6754

Coffee Shop ★★$ Self-service and excellent, with good game pies, pâtés, salads, and wine. The cakes, pastries, coffee, and tea make this a popular afternoon eating place. It seems like a great place to meet people as well, as everyone sits at long crescent-shaped tables. ♦ M-Sa 10:30AM-5:30PM; Su 4-5:15PM

We left London on Saturday morning at half past five or six, the 31st of July (I have forgot which). We mounted the Dover Coach at Charing Cross. It was a beautiful morning. The city, St. Paul's, with the River and a multitude of little boats, made a most beautiful sight as we crossed Westminster Bridge. The houses were not overhung by their cloud of smoke, and they were spread out endlessly, yet the sun shone so brightly, with such a pure light, that there was even something like the purity of one of nature's own grand spectacles.

Dorothy Wordsworth
writing in her journal while traveling
with her brother William

Nicholas Sevota
Director, Tate Gallery

Tate Gallery Bests:
William Dobson, *Endymion Porter*
William Hogarth, *Calais Gate*
George Stubbs, *Haymakers*
J.M.W. Turner, *Snowstorm*
Dante Gabriel Rossetti, *The Annunciation*
Pierre Bonnard, *The Bath*
Pablo Picasso, *The Three Dancers*
Stanley Spencer, *The Resurrection, Cookham*
Henri Matisse, *The Snail*
Max Ernst, *Pietà*
Henry Moore, *Falling Warrier*
Ben Nichollson, *Painting 1937*
Mark Rothko, *The Rothko Room*
Tony Cragg, *On the Savannah*

Dr. Alan Kay
Apple Fellow, Computer Legend

Portobello Hotel. All the rooms are handsomely furnished, and some are beautifully decorated around different themes. The Round Room has a round bed, the Bath Room is full of antique mirrors, and the Four-Poster Room has 18th-century mahogony.

Henry Steiner
Designer, Hong Kong

Buy *Time Out* magazine as soon as you arrive at Heathrow. It is a weekly guide to London with a lively, inquiring editorial style and a permissive, poor-but-honest layout. Along with dependable listings of cinemas, theaters, and protest rallies is a short roster,constantly reviewed and amended, of good, inexpensive restaurants of varying cuisines.

You can buy picture postcards from all over at the **Postcard Gallery** on Neal Street. Owner and designer Derek Birdsall has colored the small space black and covered the walls with cards in floor-to-ceiling racks. Horror-movie stills, kitsch landscapes, etc., suitable for collecting, framing, trading, or even mailing are available here.

Lord Weidenfeld
Publisher

The library of the **House of Lords**.
The walk from the top of **Bond Street** down to **Piccadilly** and **St. James's Park** and through **Jermyn Street**.
Wilton's, the quintessentially English fish restaurant.
The **National Gallery** on Saturday morning, especially the Italian Renaissance rooms.
Royal Opera House, Covent Garden, on a gala night.
Annabel's, the enduring conventional/unconventional dinner and after-dinner meeting place.
The **Garrick Club** during the busy midweek lunch hour.

Roger Ebert
Film Critic

The walk across **Hampstead Heath** from **Parliament Hill** to the **Spaniard's Inn**, and then down the road to **Kenwood House**.
The corner table next to the fire in the front room of the **Holly Bush**, Hampstead.
The Thames-side walk from **Hammersmith Bridge** to **Chiswick House**.
Jermyn Street, particularly the **Paxton and Whitfield** cheese shop.
The **London Library** in St. James's Square.
Highgate Cemetery.
Houses: **Sir John Soane's Museum** in Lincoln's Inn Fields, **Lord Leighton's House** in Holland Park, and **Dr. Johnson's House** in Gough Square.
Bookstores: **Heywood Hill**, Curzon Street; **Fisher & Speer**, Highgate High Street; **Skoob**, Sicilian Lane; **Bernard Stone's Turret Bookshop**, Lamb Conduit Street.
Books: *Ian Nairn's London* (Penguin), the fierce, passionate, affectionate book about the best and worst things in the city, ranging from the ugliest house to the most stygian underground passage to Soane's breakfast room.
Galleries: the **Catto Gallery**, Hampstead; **Chris Beetles**, Ryder Street; **Agnew's** and the **Fine Arts Society**, Bond Street; **Abbott and Horder**, Museum Street; **Pomeroy-Purdy**, Southwark.
Restaurants: **Rules, Le Caprice, Langans, Ken Lo's Memories of China, Dino's** at the South Kensington tube stop.

Helen McCabe
Art Historian and Writer

Best paintings of London:

Claude Monet, *The Thames Below Westminster* (National Gallery)

André Derain, *The Pool of London* (Tate Gallery)

James McNeill Whistler, *Nocturne In Blue and Gold: Battersea Bridge* (Tate Gallery)

Antonio Canaletto, *View of the City of London from Richmond House* (Duke of Richmond & Gordon Collection)

Oskar Kokoschka, *View of Thames* (Tate Gallery)

Ginner, *London Bridge* (Museum of London)

Durmmond, *St. James's Park* (Southampton Art Gallery)

Christopher Wray
Owner, Lighting Emporium

Houses of Parliament
Albert Hall
St. Pancras Station
Michelin Building

Restaurants/Nightlife: Red   Hotels: Blue
Shops/Parks: Green   **Sights/Culture: Black**

Piccadilly

In this mile-long street called Piccadilly, London wears her heart on her sleeve. Like a love affair, the street begins in an atmosphere of gesture and respect at **Hyde Park Corner**, then eases gently into the intimate tranquility of **Green Park**, the *lovers only* mystique of the **Ritz**, and the exuberant vows of Wren's own favorite church, **St. James's, Piccadilly**. But as **Eros** gets closer, something happens. The grandeur begins to diminish and the street loses its dignity. Instead of coziness, it is all confusion and traffic. Everything becomes familiar and louche. By the time the God of Love is in sight, poised on one foot and aiming his arrow, there are unmistakable signs of ordinariness and doubt. This is Piccadilly Circus? This is Eros?

Piccadilly Circus will probably always baffle the attempts to render it worthy of a great city. Yet it remains surprisingly loved by Londoners and visitors, who are irresistibly drawn to the area by its one feature of distinc-

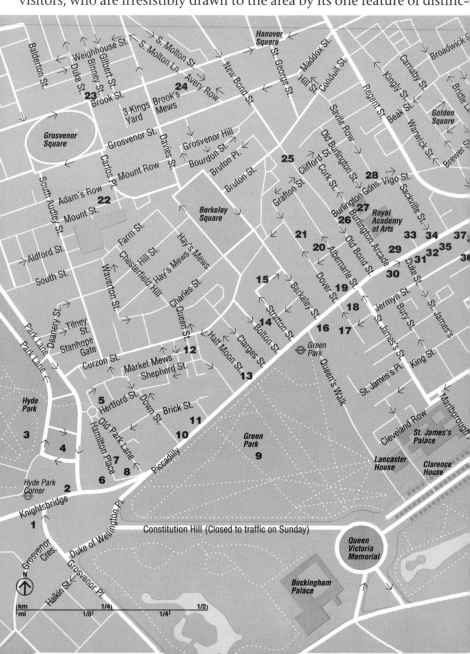

tion, the statue of Eros. A journey to Eros offers all the joys of traveling, with a perfect miniature version of the essence of London en route.

The walk ends at the God of Love, in a pedestrian precinct, and begins at the Goddess of Peace, in a quadriga. Along the way, you pass the last house in Piccadilly, known as No. 1, London (**Apsley House**); an oasis of green (**Green Park**); the longest wait for the best hamburger in London (**Hard Rock Cafe**); the headquarters for London's café society (**Langan's Brasserie** and **Le Caprice**); the most beautiful dining room in the world (the **Ritz**); a Regency shopping center (the **Burlington Arcade**); a bank by **Lutyens**; a hotel by **Norman Shaw**; and a church by **Wren**. Piccadilly is the home of one of London's favorite galleries (the **Royal Academy**) and was the home of **Lord Byron** (**Albany**). If it is raining, you can stay dry under the Rolls-Royce of umbrellas (**Swaine & Adeney**) and, in lieu of an umbrella, you can have tea at the most luxurious grocery store in London (**Fortnum & Mason**).

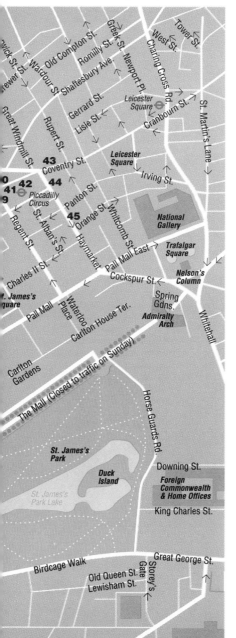

The best time to be in Piccadilly is on a weekday, when every foot of the mile-long stretch is luxuriously and romantically alive with the English gentry shopping for those expensive but vital little necessities —cashmere jumpers, Hunter Wellingtons, and Barbour jackets. It's a sign of the times, where once these shops were open just a half-day on Saturday, they are now open all day, although many restaurants don't open at all. The **Wellington Museum** at Apsley House is open Tuesday through Sunday, so ideally your walk will avoid Monday, except when there's a bank holiday and (bizarrely) it opens! Piccadilly goes past one of London's oldest West End theaters, the **Criterion**, and ends in the heart of the West End theaterland, so you could end this walk the way Londoners do, in the company of **George Bernard Shaw, Noel Coward,** or **Tom Stoppard.**

1 Hyde Park Corner *It is doubtless a signal proof of being a London-lover quand même that one should undertake an apology for so bungled an attempt at a great public place as Hyde Park Corner,* **Henry James** *wrote at the turn of this century. Many decades, improvements, and embellishments later, Hyde Park Corner is still being bungled and now suffers the ultimate indignity: it is a traffic island, albeit a grand one. In order to reach this pivotal triangular patch, you must go beneath it into a warren of underpasses, where you will best make your way by following the sounds of a forlorn harmonica and the clinks of 10-pence pieces being tossed into the player's hat by grateful pedestrians.*

In a battlefield of automobiles, the Goddess of Peace reins in the Horses of War. This beautiful and dramatic statue, placed on the corner in 1912 after the Boer War, is one of the finest silhouettes in the London sky and uniquely presents an almost identical profile from either side. Looking at her, you almost forget that 200 cars a minute are circling the corner and that with the tyranny of the auto-

mobile, cities have no hope of peace. The sculptor, **Captain Adrian Jones**, created the *Goddess of Peace* after a career of 23 years as a cavalry officer. He combined his unique equestrian knowledge with a true artistic gift to make the statue a stunning monument to peace. Tragically, World War I broke out 2 years after it was placed at Hyde Park Corner, and the monuments that surround the statue are memorials to the many thousands who would die in a world-wide stampede of the Horses of War.

The *Goddess* dominates sky and square from her position on top of the arch, designed by **Decimus Burton**, which was placed on the corner in 1828. Few arches have been pushed around as much as this impressive structure. It was originally built as a northern gate to the grounds of Buckingham Palace and surmounted with a statue of the Duke of Wellington. But now it leads nowhere. It was initially called **Wellington Arch**, but the name was changed to **Green Park Arch**, and now it is mostly known as **Constitution Arch**. Its triumphant decline seems endless; after some years as a flat and then a police station, it is now a skyward funnel for exhaust fumes from the underpass below.

A statue of **David**, with his back to the motorized world, stands as memorial to the Machine Gun Corps. It was designed by sculptor **Francis Derwent Wood** in 1925, and it bears a muscular resemblance to poet **Rupert Brooke**. You almost see Brooke's haunting words written on the battlefields of France, where he dreamt of *hearts at peace, under an English heaven.* Instead, we read that *Saul hath slain his thousands but David his tens of thousands.*

The massive monument facing the old St. George's Hospital building is the splendid *Royal Artillery Monument*, designed by **C.S. Jaeger** in 1920. It bears the sadder, more prosaic inscription: *Here was a royal fellowship of death.* Four bronze figures weighed down with the knowledge of death surround a huge gun aimed at the Somme, the battlefield in France where so many men in the Royal Artillery died in World War I.

The huge equestrian statue of the **Duke of Wellington**, which formerly surmounted the arch, was sent to Aldershot in 1883, where it still stands. The statue in Hyde Park Corner facing Apsley House is the work of **Sir J.E. Boehm** (1888). It shows the Duke on his beloved horse, **Copenhagen**, who bore his master nobly for 16 hours on that fateful day at the Battle of Waterloo. When Copenhagen died in 1836, he was buried with full military honors. The inscription on his headstone reads *God's humble instrument, though meaner clay, should share the glory of that glorious day.*

Art long ago ceased to be monumental. To be monumental, as the art of Michelangelo or Rubens was monumental, the age must have a sense of glory. The artist must have some faith in his fellow men, and some confidence in the civilization to which he belongs. Such an attitude is not possible in the modern world—at least not in our Western European world. We have lived through the greatest war in history (1914–18), but we find it celebrated in thousands of mean, false and essentially unheroic monuments. Ten million men killed, but no breath of inspiration from their dead bodies. Just a scramble for contracts and fees, and an unconcealed desire to make the most utilitarian use of the fruits of heroism.

Herbert Read, 1945
English essayist, in *A Coat of Many Colours*

The English are mentioned in the Bible: Blessed are the meek, for they shall inherit the earth.

Mark Twain, *Pudd'nhead Wilson's New Calendar*

I am a snob. Why not? The whole strength of England lies in the fact that the enormous majority of English people are snobs.

George Bernard Shaw, *Getting Married*

2 Apsley House (Wellington Museum; c.1770, **Robert Adam**) The honey-colored stone and grand proportions provide solid dignity to Hyde Park Corner, and although Apsley House never looks open and requires subterranean tenacity to reach, the effort is well worth it. Known as **No.1, London,** this was the home of the **Duke of Wellington**— the man who finally defeated **Napoleon**. The attic and basement are still the home of the present-day duke himself.

The house is a mix of flawless Adam proportions and added-on grandeur made possible by a generous gift of £200,000 from Parliament as gratitude for the defeat of that little man Napoleon. Inside the house, the loser of Waterloo looms considerably larger than life in a statue by **Canova** that augments Napoleon to an idealized 11 feet, covered not in medals but with the ubiquitous fig leaf. Napoleon commissioned the statue, then rejected it because it failed to express his calm dignity— and because the winged figure of Victory was turning away from him. It stayed packed away in the basement of the Louvre until 1816, when it was bought by the British government and presented by **George IV** to the Duke of Wellington, for whom Victory had been perfectly placed.

The museum contains a touchingly idiosyncratic collection of victorious loot, glorious batons, swords, and daggers. It's odd to think that soldiers carried off dinner plates, but they must have. There are stupendous services of Sèvres, Meissen, and Berlin porcelain, silver and gold plate (including the ultimate extravagance—a gold-plated silver dinner service). The focal point of the china collection is the Egyptian Sèvres service commissioned by Napoleon as a divorce present for **Josephine**. Together in a museum as they would never have been in life, are Wellington's sword and Napoleon's court sword (taken from his carriage after the Battle of Waterloo), as well as flags, medals, and snuff boxes.

The **Piccadilly Drawing Room**, on the 1st floor, is a jewel of a room, with wall-hangings, curtains in butter-yellow, windows that frame Hyde Park Corner, and excellent paintings, including *Chelsea Pensioners Reading the Waterloo Despatch* by **Sir David Wilkie**.

The **Waterloo Gallery**, designed by **Benjamin Dean Wyatt** in 1828, is the big draw in Apsley House. The vast 90-foot corridor is called the Waterloo Gallery because banquets were held in it each year on the anniversary of the great victory over the French. (These banquets are now held at Windsor and presided over by the present queen and the current duke of Wellington.) The room was designed to display the Duke's magnificent collection, particularly the Spanish pictures captured at the Battle of Victoria and subsequently presented to the Duke by **King Ferdinand**. The collection includes paintings by **Rubens, Murillo** (the beautiful *Isaac Blessing Jacob*), **Correggio** (*The Agony in the Garden*—the Duke's personal favorite), and 4 outstanding pictures by

Velásquez, including the early *Water Seller of Seville*. Also in the room are 2 notable **Van Dycks**, including *St. Rosalie Crowned with Roses by Two Angels*. The windows fascinate almost as much as the pictures. They are fit with sliding mirrors, which at night transform the room into an evocation of Louis XIV's *Galerie des Glaces* at Versailles.

Piccadilly

At the far end of the Waterloo Gallery is **Goya**'s *Equestrian Portrait of Wellington*. Don't worry if you find this a disappointing Goya. X-rays show the picture was originally of **Joseph Bonapart**. Last-minute political alterations called for the head to be replaced with Wellington's, who never liked the painting and kept it in storage in his country house at Stratfield Saye, Berkshire. Perhaps the most exciting painting in the collection, though, is that by **Sir Thomas Lawrence** of the Duke of Wellington, because, until June 1990, it appeared on the back of every £5 note! Last admission, 4:30PM. ♦ Admission. Tu-Sa 11AM-5PM; Su 2-6PM. Bank holiday Mondays 11AM-5PM. Apsley House, Hyde Park Corner, W1. 499.5676

3 Statue of Achilles (1822, **Sir Richard Westmacott**) Behind Apsley House in Hyde Park is the memorial to the Duke of Wellington from the Ladies of England, paid for by a women's subscription. It is cast from cannons captured at Salamanca, Vitoria, and Waterloo. The statue's flagrant nudity was once a shock, but is now a fascination.

4 Statue of Lord Byron and his Dog (1880, **Richard Belt**) The feeble and boring statue of the poet is separated from *Achilles* by Park Lane. It is all the more annoying because it was chosen by sentimental Victorians who rejected the one artist most suited to re-create Byron: **Rodin**.

5 Hilton Hotel $$$ Queen Elizabeth was not at all pleased with the view from the 28-story modern hotel when it was first built in the 1960s—guests could catch a glimpse of royal life, right over the Buckingham Palace garden wall. (She has since landscaped for privacy, but in the summer, royal spotters can still peek in and see the garden parties.) But the view of the city and Hyde Park from the high-rising hotel is marvelous. This is the archetypal Hilton, with 448 simply decorated rooms and suites with all the American-style comforts. The **Windows on the World** restaurant is modeled on the one in New York's World Trade Center. The **Brasserie** serves buffet and Continental breakfasts, snacks, and tea with pastries; attached to it is a **Godiva** chocolaterie. **Trader Vic's** cocktail bar is in the basement. ♦ Deluxe ♦ 22 Park Ln, W1. 071/493.8000; fax 071/493.4957

Restaurants/Nightlife: Red	**Hotels:** Blue
Shops/Parks: Green	**Sights/Culture:** Black

6 Inter-Continental $$$$ The English like to stay here and pretend they are in America. They are dazzled by the telephones, American showers and scales in the bathrooms, as well as the oversized everything: rooms, beds, towels, and closets. In true American style, you'll find them discussing business over breakfast in the **Coffee House**, or watching shop lovers in the **Aquascutum** and **Cartier** boutiques, who book Rolls-Royces to take them on shopping trips farther afield. The elegant women in the elegant lobby are more likely to be company presidents than the wives of company presidents. The Inter-Continental may lack English charm, but you can be certain that nothing will go wrong. ♦ Deluxe ♦ 1 Hamilton Pl, Hyde Park Corner, W1. 071/409.3131; fax 071/409.7460

Within the Inter-Continental:

Coffee House ★★$ These are the breakfasts of champions, and rated by the *Times* as among the best in London. There's a choice of 3: the basic Continental, the fruit-and-grain buffet, or the classic English breakfast with kippers, kedgeree, kidneys, et al. You can also go à la carte. Famous chefs congregate here from time to time. ♦ Daily 7AM–midnight. 071/409.3131

Hamilton's Supper Club ★★$$ Such a club is rare in London; it's so rare most Londoners don't know it exists. Come here at night; it's quite exquisite. Diners eat from a delicious menu—try the warm lobster and prawn salad with caviar—and gaze through the vast glass windows where they can see across Hyde Park Corner to the twinkling lights of the evening's traffic cutting a swath through the deepening green of the parks. ♦ Tu-Sa 7PM–1AM. 071/409.3131

Le Soufflé ★★★★$$$$ Luxe, luxe, luxe with a **Michelin** star, caviar, and cool yellow-and-turquoise pastels. Named after the specialty of chef **Peter Kromberg**, this is one of London's top restaurants. The diners sip their champagne (choose from among 15 on the wine list) with the nonchalance of film stars and tuck into their breast of pheasant wrapped in a strudel parcel with a truffle sauce with the expertise of brain surgeons. Try the daily *choix de chef* or the set menu of 7 courses for dinner. The menu changes completely every 2 weeks and has seasonal variations. This is a trend-setting restaurant, so you'll eat it here first, then find it elsewhere. The wine list is a labor of love, even though the prices are the kind usually associated with things that are

forever. Have a look at the special sommelier's choice. ♦ M-F 12:30-3:30PM, 7-11PM; Sa 7-11PM; Su noon-4PM. 071/409.3131

7 Inn On The Park $$$ The hotel was built in 1970, but it is suffused with the elegance of other eras—1930s ocean liner, first-class, with fabulous antiques thrown in. **Howard Hughes** stayed here in his declining and difficult years, so this hotel has a pretty good track record of perfect service. Afternoon tea is served in the **Four Seasons** lounge, all sweetness and light, against a background of harp or piano music. The **Inn** offers the largest choice of teas in London as well as a lethal sequence of sandwiches, scones, and pastries. ♦ Deluxe ♦ Hamilton Pl, Park Ln, W1. 071/499.0888, 071/493.1895/6629

Within the Inn On The Park:

Lanes ★★$$ The set lunches deserve their popularity. This isn't imaginative food, just very good and honest food—English roasts, Scottish salmon, game in season. ♦ Daily noon-3PM, 6PM-midnight. 071/499.0888

Four Seasons ★★★$$$ Get excited about this restaurant—the rest of London is, including people who know a lot about food. Chef **Bruno Loubet** presides over the restaurant with a long, intricate, some might say extravagant, menu. Try the filet of sea bass steamed with a blend of salt and aromatic herbs served on a bed of fresh pasta. There is a minute private garden to look at. And an extensive wine list. Customers are asked to leave their portable phones with the manager. ♦ Daily noon-3PM, 7-11PM. 071/499.0888

8 Hard Rock Cafe ★★★$ People have been waiting in line to eat here for almost 2 decades, undeterred by rain, sleet, or snow. The Hard Rock has the best hamburgers in town, and until the Los Angeles and New York branches opened, possibly the best hamburgers in the world. For Americans, it is a round-trip ticket home to the 1960s: Budweiser beer, Chicago Bears, hamburgers the size of a catcher's mitt, waitresses with name tags (Dixie, Cookie), and hot-fudge sundaes. The best time to go (dare we say?) is late afternoon, when it is neither lunch nor dinner, the music isn't brain-damaging loud, and you don't have to wait. This is the original Hard Rock; now they're everywhere. ♦ M-Th, Su 11:30AM-12:30AM; F-Sa 11:30AM-1AM. 150 Old Park Ln, W1. 071/629.0382

9 Green Park Greener than emeralds from Asprey, the 60 acres of sable-soft grass offer the kind of luxury money can't buy in a city. There are no flowerbeds in the park. Instead, ancient beech, lime, and plane trees spread their limbs like maps of the world. In spring, a tapestry of daffodils and crocuses appears. The sloping canvas chairs cost a few pence—don't worry, the chair collector will come to you and give you a little sticker as proof that you have paid. Sit down and read *English Hours* by Henry James, the morning newspaper, or just observe the perfect Englishness all around you. The noble mansions around Green Park that established the atmosphere of wealth, luxury, and society have nearly all disappeared, replaced by their 20th-century equivalent—*hôtels deluxes*. Still, the flavor of grandeur is continuous, undefeated, and immediately perceptible.

10 Athenaeum $$$ This hotel is small compared to its modern neighbors and offers the kind of service that feels more like a private house with an old-fashioned feel—towels the size of tents, monogrammed linen sheets, and telephone and switchboard services—but it is totally modern. If you like to begin the day with a jog, Green Park and Hyde Park are on the doorstep. There is a breakfast buffet, and the excellent **Windsor Lounge** restaurant is especially popular at lunchtime. If you are planning a longer stay, there is an adjoining apartment house. ◆ 116 Piccadilly, W1. 071/499.3464; fax 071/493.1860

11 Park Lane Hotel $$$ For starters, it isn't on Park Lane; it's on Piccadilly overlooking Green Park. It sounds anonymous and modern, but it is old, lovely, and full of character. The rooms are personal, the suites have their original 1920s décor and dreamy Art Deco bathrooms, and the clientele is fiercely loyal. The hotel's ballroom—a monument to the Deco period—is regularly used for debutantes and charity balls; the entrance was used for filming *Brideshead Revisited*. ◆ Piccadilly, W1. 071/499.6321

Within the Park Lane Hotel:

Brasserie on the Park ★★$ 1980s Art Deco and brasserie classics—onion soup, steaks, fish cakes, English grills, French country dishes, and slimming salads. ◆ Daily 10:30AM-12:30PM. 071/499.6321

Bracewells ★★★$$ The Louis XVI carved paneling (from the London home of American banker and philanthropist **Pierpoint Morgan**) makes this restaurant feel like a gentlemen's club, and the excellent wine list has the kind of wines and prices that are usually found only in those privileged places. But the food is definitely superior to clubland. Think about the English oysters, the poached halibut with saffron and shredded leeks, the chicken cooked with fresh ginger and lime, and the lavish trolley of desserts. This is a bargain, with set menus available at lunch and dinner. ◆ M-Sa 12:30-2:30PM, 7-11:30PM; Su 12:30-2PM, 7-10:30PM. 071/499.6321

12 Shepherd's Market The best way to reach this tiny square, filled with small white houses, boutiques, restaurants, and pubs, is from Curzon Street, through the covered passage at No. 47. This was the site of the May fairs of the 17th century and is now home to upmarket ladies of ill repute who can occasionally be seen flitting from doorway to doorway like beautiful ghosts. Two of London's best pubs are here: **Shepherd's Tavern** (50 Hertford St) and **Ye Grapes** (Shepherd's Market), with its tiny restaurant, **Ted's Pantry**. Both serve excellent pub lunches and refreshingly cold beer and ale. The market is packed with bijou restaurants and wine bars. ◆ Mayfair, W1

13 Half Moon Street Poke around the street' for a few minutes—it is home to some very distinguished ghosts. **Boswell** (1740–95) lived here, recording his walks with Johnson and taking endless cures for his gonorrhea, which he then wrote about in graphic detail in his London journal. **Fanny Burney** (1752–1840) also lived on the street, as did the essayist **Hazlitt** and the poet **Shelley**. More recently, Half Moon Street was the address of **P.G. Wodehouse**'s Bertie Wooster and his faithful Jeeves.

14 Langan's Brasserie ★★★$$$ Like the Cafe Royal and the Closerie des Lilas, Langan's Brasserie will eventually be in the literature of the age, even though the genius recalled will be of the deal-making Hollywood genre, not *The Sun Also Rises*. The beautiful, clever, rich, and promising come here to see and be seen, and it is good luck for everybody that the food is as good as it is, thanks to **Richard Shepherd**, chef and part owner. **Michael Caine** also owns a part. There has been little change in the restaurant following the untimely death of the other owner, **Peter Langan**. Dress glamorously and have a look at the pictures. (Langan's eye for 20th-century British still adorns the walls.) Start your meal with the spinach soufflé with anchovy sauce, order a plainish main course, and end with crème brûlée. Rumor has it that famous people get better seats and the lesser known get what they're given; of course, this is rigorously denied by the restaurant. Jazz bands on alternate nights. Avoid Langan's on Saturday night, when *tout-Londres* is nowhere near London and the restaurant fills with couples from the suburbs. ◆ M-F 12:30-2:45PM, 7-11:45PM; Sa 8PM-12:45AM. Stratton St, W1. 071/491.6437/8822

15 Mayfair $$$ This innocuous and unassuming sister to the Inter-Continental down the street is rather an appropriate hotel to be next to Langan's. **Michael Jackson** stayed here on his world tour, barricaded in against the press and inevitable groupies. **Neil Diamond** and **Billy Joel** have been here, too, so their 16-year-old fans who camp outside would have you believe. Be assured, rock stars wear a uniform just like everyone else and are very easy to spot, even if you don't know who they are. It's odd really, because at first glance there's nothing unusual about the place at all. The staff manages to look as if nothing strange is going on, while the bar appears to be filled with members of the secret services of various countries. ◆ Stratton St, W1. 071/629.7777; fax 071/629.1459

PICCADILLY LONDON

16 The Ritz $$$$ Two more evocative words are hard to imagine. Such is the power of the Ritz that the name can be spelled in light bulbs and still be glamorous. The hotel was built in the style of a French château with a Parisian arcade from the designs of **Mewès** and **Davis** in 1906. For ordinary, aspiring folk, this is a kind of *Brideshead Revisited*, a world of elegance, beauty, and perfection that is rooted in the past and maintained with fastidious dedication. The champagne era has little in common with the Perrier age. Men and women danced cheek-to-cheek to stringed orchestras, waiters were anonymous and moved like members of the corps de ballet, and hotels were an art, one of the civilizing forces in any capital city. The Ritz is dedicated to the memory of that bygone age, applying politeness and gallantry to modern hotel service.

A wonderful way to begin any day is with breakfast at the Ritz, more appropriate after a stroll in Green Park. The menu offers such English treats as Cumberland sausage, Lancashire black pudding, Finnan haddock kedgeree, and Scotch kippers, or there's a beautiful fruit-and-grain buffet, even eggs Benedict. But lunch may well be the Ritz's finest hour—the delicate pastel colors of the world's most beautiful **Palm Court** dining room, subtly lit by dreamy London daylight; a table by the windows overlooking Green Park; a grilled Dover sole washed down with *Krug Grande Cuvée*.

Pity about the tea at the Ritz. It is so popular that you must book ages in advance, and it is about as special as tea at Paddington Station. The staff is keen that people should not come here for tea, but that's no reason for it to be poor. Most Londoners forego this disappointing pleasure and have a better tea at **Brown's**, returning here for a glass of champagne after the tea hordes have gone. Also too bad that jackets, ties and all such formality are now required. ♦ Deluxe ♦ Piccadilly, W1. 071/493.8181; fax 071/493.2687

17 Caprice ★★★$$ London's chic set nibbles and chatters the night away while glancing around all the while to see who else is here. No paparazzi, either. It has a wide and deceptively simple menu and wine list. It is THE place to go. Just behind the Ritz. ♦ Daily noon-3PM, 6PM-midnight. Arlington House, Arlington St, SW1. 071/629.2239

18 Barclays Bank (1922, **William Curtis Green**) Influenced by a bank in Boston, this opulently designed bank is a surprise. Walk on marble floors and gaze at the Renaissance interior with its rich Venetian-red banking pillars. Sit at Japanese black-lacquer furniture as you sign your checks. It is well worth cashing them here just for the surroundings. ♦ 160 Piccadilly St, W1

19 John Murray The publisher opened his office on Albemarle Street in 1812, and went on to publish the works of **Lord Byron, Jane Austen, George Crabbe**, and a host of other literary greats. This is the place where Byron's autobiography was burned after his death because the poet's friends thought it was too shocking. His mistress, **Lady Caroline Lamb**, haunts the building. The seventh John Murray runs the firm today. ♦ 50 Albemarle St, W1

20 Granary ★★$ Simple English dishes such as lamb with mint sauce and summer pudding set out on a self-service counter. ♦ M-F 11.30AM-8PM; Sa 11:30AM-2:30PM. 39 Albemarle St, SW1. 071/493.2978

21 Brown's Hotel $$$ There is no discreet plaque saying that Henry James stayed here, and he probably didn't, but there is something perfectly Jamesian about this hotel just off Piccadilly. It is very popular with the kind of Anglophile Americans who come to England once a year to look at pictures, visit their tailor, see a few plays, and visit friends they have known since the war. **Theodore Roosevelt** spent his honeymoon with **Edith** here in 1886 (they got married a few blocks away at St. George's, Hanover Square), and **Franklin D. Roosevelt** spent his honeymoon with **Eleanor** here in 1905. You feel that it is just as intimate and democratic an English country house now as it was then. The restaurant is worthy of a presidential palate, and this is one of the most divine and quintessentially English places for tea in London. The rooms are intimate and lamplit, the sofas and chairs solid and comfy, and the sandwiches, scones, and cakes plentiful and superb. Naturally, it gets crowded, so book ahead if possible. ♦ Deluxe ♦ 22-24 Dover St, W1. 493.6020; fax 493.9381

One wonders if the English are so fond of tea because they have tried coffee.
Anonymous

English life, while very pleasant, is rather bland. I expected kindness and gentility and I found it, but there's such a thing as too much couth.
S.J. Perelman

Restaurants/Nightlife: Red   **Hotels:** Blue
Shops/Parks: Green   **Sights/Culture:** Black

Between 3 and 6PM, **Brown's** (pronounced *Brine's*, in a cut-glass accent) teatime lovers can be found ensconced around the lacy tables on comfy chairs and sofas. The sequence of events in English afternoon hotel tea is small sandwiches (the famous cucumber as well as salmon, tomato, and egg) followed by scones (on which you put a layer of butter, a layer of jam, and a layer of clotted cream —whipped cream is cheating), then toasted teacakes, and finally, pastries. It requires a certain stamina, and if all you want is a cup of tea, you will have some difficulty.

22 Connaught $$$$ Owned by the **Savoy Group**. It is easier to get into the restaurant here than into the hotel. Indeed, unless you know someone who has stayed here, it's almost impossible. For those lucky enough to secure a room, it's like staying in a deliciously comfortable English country mansion, where the sitting rooms are warmed by an open fire, all the bedrooms are different, and there are oil paintings, antiques, and flowers everywhere. ♦ Deluxe ♦ Carlos Pl, WI. 071/499.7070; fax 071/495.3262

Within the Connaught:

The Connaught ★★★★$$$$ Arrive early, with time to spare, because some of the dishes take an hour to prepare and you will have to wait in this gleaming, paneled restaurant. It's called the most consistent restaurant in town and the last bastion of traditional food, served up on crisp linen tablecloths. Here, chef **Michael Bourdin**'s Anglo/French haute cuisine shows what a master can really do with roast lamb, guinea fowl, calf's liver, and the ultimate dessert—bread-and-butter pudding. The adventurous should avoid the hot trolley and may find some of the simple dishes boring (kidneys and bacon being the least exciting), so be daring and try the dishes that change daily, like the *Duc de Crêpes de Connaught* (pancakes filled with lobster and topped with black and white truffles). The vintage ports here are truly vintage, and the wine is expensive... but for one evening... ♦ M-F 12:30-2PM, 6-10:15PM. Jacket and tie required. Reservations required. 071/491.7070

23 Le Gavroche ★★★★$$$$ This was voted one of the top 4 of London's restaurants in 1990 by *The Good Food Guide*; it was also the first London restaurant to win 3 *Michelin* stars. The justifiably famous **Albert Roux**, with his son **Michel**, can be found in the kitchens producing divine recipes based on regional French cooking. Deals worth millions are struck as property developers bargain across the lunch table, while nearby diplomats from the American Embassy can be seen whispering in the green-and-copper basement rooms. Try the boudin blanc of chicken or noisettes of lamb Provençale, followed by melon filled with red fruit, or banana soufflé with rum. The wines are fabulously expensive, and it's worth sticking

with the cheaper end. ♦ M-F noon-2PM, 7-11PM. 43 Upper Brook St, W1. Jacket and tie required. Reservations required. 071/408.0881

24 Claridge's $$$$ There is one hotel favored above all others by the royal family for functions. It is Claridge's. It is reassuringly old fashioned and unassuming, and the service is

respectful (so would you be if you dealt with as many statesmen and diplomats as they do). The drinks are brought by a liveried footman to your seat; there is nothing so vulgar as a bar. Reminiscent of the '30s, a Hungarian quartet entertains daily in the foyer with its glossy black-and-white marble tiles. Even though it's owned by the **Savoy Group**, the restaurant here is not particularly famous, but is beautiful to gaze at with floor-to-ceiling Art Deco mirrors along the walls. If you could stay in one of the huge Art Deco bedrooms, with a real log fire and a separate dressing room, you'd start to love it here, too. Failing all else, when shopping in Bond Street becomes too much, drop in for a refreshing glass of champagne. ♦ Deluxe ♦ Brook St, W1. 071/629.8860; fax 071/499.2210

Doing Bond Street in Style
If money were no object there would be only one way to see Bond Street. Stay at the Connaught, shop, take lunch at Le Gavroche, shop, champagne or tea at Claridge's, shop, supper at the Connaught.

25 Bond Street This is Fifth Avenue, Rodeo Drive, the Faubourg-St. Honoré, and one of the most expensive properties on the English Monopoly board. Imperturbably chic, Bond Street leads from Piccadilly to Oxford Street and is paved with Gold American Express Cards all the way. The legendary shopping street recently celebrated its 300th birthday, cheating only a little bit: Old Bond Street was built in 1686, but New Bond Street, which begins at Clifford Street, only dates back to 1721. You can blame the confusing street numbering system on a Parliament that, in 1762, forbade the use of hanging signs to identify shops (too many customers were being clobbered in high winds) and numbered the streets separately, first up the east side toward Oxford St and then down again on the west.

Art galleries flourish on and around Bond. You can buy a **Turner** at **Thomas Agnew & Son**, a **Francis Bacon** at **Marlborough Fine Arts**, a **Vanessa Bell** at **Anthony d'Offay**, or an unknown at **Sotheby's**, the world's largest auctioneer. If art is your style, do look on Albemarle, Dover, and Grafton streets. Antique lovers should turn left into Burlington Gardens, then left again into a maze of back streets crammed with the opulently old and unusual.

Contrary to popular belief, Englishwomen do not wear tweed nightgowns.

Hermione Gingold

Bond Street Shopping Map

OXFORD STREET

shoes **R. Cartier**

woolens **W. Bill**
restaurant **Old Vienna**

Bambino children's clothing
Cerruti 1881 men's and women's clothing

BLENHEIM STREET

shoes **Kurt Geiger**
Royal Bank of Scotland
linen and lingerie **Frette**
cashmere **Brainin of Bond St.**
shoes **Alan McAfee**
jewelry **Nawbar & Co.**
luggage, bags **Henry's**
clothing **Daniel Hechter**
women's clothing **Alexon**
men's designer clothing **Lanvin**
shoes **Russell & Bromley**

(NEW BOND STREET)

DERING STREET

Louis Féraud women's clothing

Etienne Aigner clothing, bags

Please Mum children's clothing
Escada women's clothing

Bentley & Co. goldsmith
Halcyon Days knickknacks by royal appt.

BROOK STREET

Barclays Bank
Bond St. Silver Galleries
clothing **Saint Laurent**
shoes **Kurt Geiger**
shoes **Bally**
works of art **Christopher Gibbs**
men's silk clothing **Cecil Gee**

Fenwicks dept. store

Cornelia James gloves by royal appt.

LANCASHIRE COURT

44 shops **Bond St. Antique Centre**
men's clothing **Herbie Frogg**

Midland Bank

Jason fabrics

White House linen and clothing
Chappell pianos
Magli shoes
F. Pinet women's shoes

GROSVENOR COURT

Chinacraft

men's clothing **Beale & Inman**
women's clothing **Beale & Inman**
fabrics **Simmonds**
men's clothing **Saint Laurent**
women's clothing **Robina**
women's clothing **Marie Claire**

MADDOX STREET

Rossini men's clothing and furs

Massada antique jewelry
Smythson stationers
Gorgissima women's clothing (Dior)
Mallet antiques
Herbie men's clothing
Ermenegildo Zegna men's clothing
Fogal hosiery
Sotheby's auctioneer
Bond St. Carpets
L.A. Chermann paintings
Herbert Johnson hatters
Gordon Scott shoes

BLOOMFIELD PLACE

antique jewelry **S.J. Phillips**
men's clothing **Zilli**
clothing **Polo/Ralph Lauren**
antiques **Partridge**
fine art **Wildensein & Co.**
The Fine Art Society
leather travel goods **Louis Vuitton**
luxury goods **Iseton**

Celine accessories

Tessiers antique jewelry
Russell & Bromley shoes

BRUTON STREET

clothing **Hermès**

clothing **Emanuel Ungaro**
boutique **Givenchy**
Air France
National Westminster Bank
women's clothing **Valentino**
coats, furs, bags **Revillon**
Church's Shoes
London Savoy Taylors Guild

(NEW BOND STREET)

CONDUIT STREET

Moira '30s antique jewelry
Fior bags, jewelry
Gianni Versace
Air India

CLIFFORD STREET

Watches of Switzerland
Patek Philippe watches
Georg Jensen silver and porcelain
Piaget watches
Adler jewelry
Hennel jewelry

GRAFTON STREET

Map continues on next page

Bond Street Shopping Map, cont.

GRAFTON STREET

Asprey & Co.
coats, furs **Birger Christensen**
jewelry **Collingwood**
jewelry **Bulgari**
women's clothing **Karl Lagerfeld**
jewelry **ilias LulaoUnis**
Cartier
shoes **Rossetti**
jewelry **Chaumet**
watches **Ebel**
jewelry **Boucheron**
jewelry **Tiffany**
leather accessories **Loewe**
women's clothing **Chanel**
accessories **Gucci**
woolens **William Bill**

THE ROYAL ARCADE

chocolates **Charbonnel et Walker**
silversmith **Holmes**
shoes **Bally**
shoes **Maud Frizon**

STAFFORD STREET

art gallery **Entwistle**
art gallery **Deborah Gage**
Marlborough Graphics Gallery
Lloyds Bank
art gallery **Noortman**
fine art **Thos. Agnew & Sons**
art gallery **Thos. Gibson**
amber specialists **Sac Freres**

OLD BOND STREET

CLIFFORD STREET cont.

Philip Antrobus jewelry
Adele Davis women's clothing

Anne Bloom jewelry
Ciro jewelry
Treads women's clothing
Rolex watches
Richard Green art gallery
National Westminster Bank

BURLINGTON GARDENS

Salvatore Ferragamo shoes
Chatila jewelry
Pierre Cardin clothing
Sulka men's clothing
Frost & Reed art gallery

Rayne women's clothing
Colnaghi Art Gallery
The Leger Art Galleries
Benson and Hedges
Brainin cashmere
Jindo Fur Salon

Ana House
Takashimaya luxury goods
WR Harvey & Co. antiques
Fenzi men's clothing

A.D.C. Heritage antique silver
Watches of Switzerland

OLD BOND STREET

PICCADILLY

You can shop at the almost endless number of internationally chic shops—**Gucci, Hermès, Yves St. Laurent, Cartier, Louis Vuitton, Karl Lagerfeld, Ralph Lauren, Chanel, Kurt Geiger, Magli**. The real challenge is to find something uniquely English, but it is worth the effort. To do this, turn left onto Brook Street and look at **Courtenay** with its British outdoor clothing, silky underwear, and nighties (no, the British don't wear thermals under those tweeds), or **Shirley Parker** for classic women's clothing. If, instead, you turn right onto Brook St (it cuts across Bond) you will find **Halcyon Days**—a darling little gift emporium filled with knickknacks by Royal Appointment.

On Bond Street:

Asprey & Co. Allow the doorman to welcome you to England's most luxurious jewelry and gift shop, which specializes in the finest and the rarest, from crocodile suitcases to Fabergé frames. More wedding presents for the **Prince** and **Princess of Wales** came from here than any other single source, including the engagement ring. ♦ M-F 9AM-5:30PM; Sa 9AM-1PM. 165 New Bond St, W1. 071/493.6767

Charbonnel et Walker The fabulous chocolates come in boxes that are equally sweet treasures. ♦ M-F 9AM-5:30PM; Sa 10AM-4PM. 28 Old Bond St, W1. 071/491.0939

Folio Books Located in the peach-and-apricot Royal Arcade, this bookshop makes handsome editions of all the favorite English writers—is there anything nicer than a beautifully bound and printed set of Jane Austens? ♦ M-F 9:30AM-6PM; Sa 10AM-1PM. Closed bank holiday weekends. 5 Royal Arcade, W1. 071/629.6517

William Bill Pleasantly cluttered and un-Bond Street, with heavy sweaters, cashmeres, and tartans. ♦ M-W, F-Sa 9:30AM-6:00PM; Th 9:30AM-7PM. 93 New Bond St, W1. 071/629.2837

Smythson's Very Bond Street and very English. Smythson's invitations feel like diplomas and are the most desired in town. The leather address books and diaries are equally coveted, and even though it's un peu pretentious, the address book divided into 3 sections and simply inscribed London New York Paris is extremely useful for fortunate vagabonds. ♦ M-F 9:15AM-5:30PM; Sa 9:15AM-12:30PM. 44 New Bond St, W1. 071/629.8558

There is no stronger craving in the world than that of the rich for titles, except that of the titled for riches.

Hesketh Pearson

Restaurants/Nightlife: Red   Hotels: Blue
Shops/Parks: Green   **Sights/Culture:** Black

BURLINGTON GARDENS

Irish Linen Company	N. Peal *woolens*
tobacconist Sullivan Powell	Picket *fine leather*
classic cashmere and woolens S. Fisher	Edina Ronay *women's designer clothing*
small antiques Demas	Alex Jacobson *silk ties-upstairs*
fashion jewelry Ken Lane	Armour-Winston Ltd *cufflinks*
jewelry Richard Ogden	Goldsmiths & Silversmiths Assoc. *jewelry*
jewelry, frames D.H. Edmonds	Berk *women's cashmere/dresses*
animal bronzes Christie	Tricker Shoes
hosiery Fogal	C. Barrett & Co. *Oriental antiques*
antique and modern silver Holmes	S. J. Rood & Co. *silver and jewelry*
cashmere S. Fisher	N. Peal *men's cashmere*
coats Berk	Penhaligon's *perfumers*
jewelry Bel Arte	Scott *men's ties and woolens*
Oriental antiques Suga	Church's English Shoes/A. Jones *boots*
dolls and lead soldiers Hummel	Dunhill *men's clothings*
fine art MacConnal-Mason	Zelli *fine porcelain*
women's clothing Noble Jones	Clements *men's accessories*
Chinacraft	Johnson Walker Tolhurst *antique jewelry*
women's woolens Berk	Lord *men's shirts woolens*
antiques and hairbrushes Clements	Lord *women's woolens*
clothing James Drew	
coats Wetherall	

(vertical label between columns: BURLINGTON ARCADE)

PICCADILLY

26 Burlington Arcade (1819, Samuel Ware)
The Regency promenade of exclusive shops
may be considered a forerunner to the shopping malls that bear so little resemblance to
it. The arcade was built in the years after
Waterloo for **Lord George Cavendish** and
was inspired by Continental models. Its
purpose was to provide the Regency gentry
with a shopping precinct free of the mud
splashed by carriages and carts on Piccadilly.
The top-hatted beadles who still patrol the
arcade today were originally installed to protect the prosperous shoppers from pickpockets and beggars. Now they supposedly
ask you not to whistle or run, and they lock
the gates at 5:30PM each afternoon. Burlington Arcade was badly damaged in the
Blitz, but it recovered and was rebuilt. Today
it exudes an atmosphere of intimate but not
inconceivable luxury, with 38 shops that offer
lasting treasures. Admire the glass roof and
the iridescent-green paintwork comple-
mented by gold lettering on the small, delicately
detailed shop fronts. The ostentatious facades
were added in 1911.

Within Burlington Arcade:

N. Peal The 3 shops in the arcade, 2 for men
and one for women, have the best cashmere
in London—from the addictive socks (it is the
only place you can find cashmere knee socks
for women) to the cashmere capes. Wise
Englishwomen would rather be draped in
cashmere than diamonds, and can be seen
strolling through the arcade on weekdays
wearing the clothes to prove it. The best is never
cheap and N. Peal is no exception. ◆ M-F 9AM-
6PM; Sa 9AM-5:30PM. Men's shop: No. 54.
071/493.5378. Men's and women's shops: Nos.
37-40, 71. 071/493.0714

James Drew Silk shirts, mostly with high
necks, each one a work of seamstress' art.
◆ M-F 9AM-5:30PM; Sa 9AM-4:30PM. No. 3.
071/493.9194

Clements One of the best shops for very
English presents that you can fit inside your
suitcase: silver wine coasters (real silver,
Georgian reproduction, very handsome);
silver peppermills (with initials and date, a
nice wedding present); and a large selection
of corkscrews and quality knives. ◆ M-F
9AM-5:30PM; Sa 9AM-4:30PM. Nos. 4-5.
071/493.3923, No. 63. 071/493.0997

Goldsmiths & Silversmiths Association
A golden grasshopper with a ruby eye sits next
to glowing pink-pearl stud earrings. This shop
is a delight, with the most unusual jewelry in
the arcade. ◆ M-F 9AM-6PM; Sa 9AM-5PM.
071/499.1396

S. FISHER

S. Fisher The 10-ply cable-knit cashmere
sweater will set you back a bit, but it will keep
you warm for life. The shop has a beautiful
choice of shetlands, cashmeres, and Irish
sweaters. ◆ M-F 9AM-6PM; Sa 9AM-5PM.
Nos. 22-23, 32-33. 071/493.4180

Richard Ogden Antique jewelry, with mu-
seum-quality pieces of Art Nouveau. ◆ Daily
9:30AM-5:15PM; Sa 10AM-4PM. Nos. 28-29.
071/493.9136

Irish Linen Company Linen napkins that
could sail a small ship, sheets that assume
you have a laundry service that collects and
delivers, and special cloths for drying the
Waterford crystal wine glasses that grace the

linen tablecloth can be found in this classic shop. It is all from another era and all very nice. ♦ M-F 9AM-5:30PM; Sa 9AM-4:30PM. Nos. 35-36. 071/493.8949

Sullivan Powel Havana cigars, briar pipes, Turkish and Virginia cigarettes in cedar boxes. ♦ M-F 9:15AM-5:15PM; Sa 10:30AM-2PM. No. 34. 071/629.0433

Penhaligon Very English and very special perfumes, all with the scent of an English country garden. Try *Bluebell* (people will whisper *where did you get it*?). The bottles and labels are enchanting, with a collection of antique silver perfume bottles that are truly tokens of love. ♦ M-F 9:30AM-5:30PM; Sa 9:30AM-5PM. No. 55. 071/629.1416

27 **Museum of Mankind** (1869, **Sir James Pennethorne**) If you leave the Burlington Arcade on the northern end at Burlington Gardens and turn right, you may find you are in a Bengal village or with a primitive mountain tribe in Peru. Take your chances and go to the Museum of Mankind, a department of the **British Museum** and one of London's least known and most imaginative museums. Children love the skulls, sculpture, masks, weapons, pottery, textiles, and puppets from tribes all over the world, especially the American Indian war bonnets, bows and arrows, and peace pipes. The permanent collection (in Room 8) includes a life-size skull carved from a piece of solid crystal from Mexico and a stunning Benin ivory mask from Africa. A very realistic exhibition is staged once a year. (For example, a reconstruction of a village in the Arctic with real tools used by the Eskimos, a reconstructed log cabin, igloo, and modern bungalow, and weaving and carving displays of their work.) All this is in the heart of, but light-years away from, Piccadilly. The exterior of the museum is an example of High Victorian architecture, with statues of leaders in science and philosophy punctuating the sky, and a confusion of styles—classic versus Italian Gothic—in a kind of architectural détente. The bookshop has replicas of art and artifacts. ♦ Free. M-Sa 10AM-5PM; Su 2:30-6PM. 6 Burlington Gardens, Piccadilly, W1. 071/437.2224

28 **Savile Row** Before too long, the tailors on this street, rightly famed the world over for their expertise, may have to pick up and move their shops, some after nearly 200 years at this location. Formerly, the government classified their businesses as light industrial and allowed them to occupy space in this desirable section of town, but times have changed: the government has changed the tailors' status, and developers have followed in hot pursuit of this prime real estate. Over the next decade, big business and banks will take over the tailors' premises. It is strange that the Savile Row tailors should be so poorly looked upon in their own country, for they are believed to bring in around £20 million annually to the British exchequer. Interestingly, 40 percent comes from the United States, while less (30 percent) comes from the Brits themselves.

On Savile Row:

Gieves & Hawkes Dating to 1785, this is the oldest tailor on the street. Representatives once followed the British Fleet around the world, dressing such illustrious figures as **Nelson, Wellington, Livingstone**, and **Stanley**, and the infamous **Captain Bligh**, of *Mutiny on the Bounty* . ♦ M-Sa 9AM-5:30PM. 1 Savile Row, W1. 071/434.2001

Dege (Pronounced *deejzh*) Four of the street's top tailors work under one roof. The customers include men from the military and **Lord King** from British Airways. A lady's tailor as well. ♦ M-F 9:15AM-5:15PM; Sa 9:30AM-4PM. 10 Savile Row, W1. 071/287.2941

Henry Poole & Co. Involved in gents' tailoring for 160 years and in Victoria's day dressed the French aristocracy (or what was left of it), including **Baron Meyer de Rothschild** and **Prince Louis Napoleon**. Cutters from this company visit the best hotels in the US to attend to the weathiest of American society. ♦ M-F 9AM-5PM. 15 Savile Row, W1. 071/734.5985

Tommy Nutter Mr. Nutter is the new boy made good on Savile Row. At about £1000 for a handmade suit, his fee is on par with the rest of the Row. Rolling Stone **Bill Wyman** had his wedding suit made here and rumor has it that **Mick Jagger** has been in for a fitting or 2. ♦ M-F 9AM-6PM; Sa 9AM-5:30PM. 19 Savile Row, W1. 071/734.0831

Anderson & Sheppard The tailor here, **Arthur Mortenson**, is famed for being able to sew a Sholte shoulder (otherwise known as *the American look*), which is softer and deeper than the traditional English cut. This explains why this house has dressed American ambassadors, but not why it dresses **Prince Charles**, the quintessential Englishman. ♦ M-F 8:30AM-5PM. 30 Savile Row, W1. 071/734.1420

Edward Sexton Have a classic British suit custom made in this shop that looks like a posh men's club. ♦ M-F 9AM-5:30PM; Sa 9AM-12PM. 37 Savile Row, W1. 071/437.2368

Wells of Mayfair Although not on Savile Row, it is close by and has been since 1829. Fifteen tailors work in this ornate shop, designed in 1892 as a model workplace after workers died from the fevers they picked up in sweatshops. ♦ M-F 9AM-5:30PM. 47 Maddox St, W1. 071/629.5047

29 **Royal Academy of Arts, Burlington House** The last surviving palace of 18th-century Piccadilly. The core is still 17th century, but the pure Palladian facade, built by **Colen Campbell** around 1717 and immortalized by **Hogarth** and **Gay**, was replaced with the Victorian neo-Renaissance front by **Banks** and **Barry** in 1873. The Piccadilly frontage has an imposing grandeur that is enlightened by colorful banners heralding the exhibitions inside. These—as well as the Royal Academy itself—are always worth seeing.

From an engraving by Jan Kip after Leonard Knyff, 1707

After the changes made c. 1717

The present front as developed by Sydney Smirke, 1872–74
Burlington House Drawings Courtesy Royal Academy of Arts

In the courtyard stands *Sir Joshua Reynolds*, often draped irreverently with posters or flags connected with the exhibition, a spirited inclusion he would not have objected to as the first president of the Royal Academy.

In the rooms along the quadrangle, learned societies have their headquarters: the **Geological Society**, the **Royal Society of Chemistry**, the **Society of Antiquaries**, the **Royal Astronomical Society**, and until recently, the most prestigious society of all, the **Royal Society**, which has the most outstanding scientists in Britain. Its headquarters are now in Carlton House Gardens.

The Royal Academy, founded in 1769, marked the recognition of the importance of art and artists in this country and, for better or worse, made artists members of the Establishment. Artistic temperament being what it is, many balked and refused to exhibit at this Official Marketplace for Art—**George Romney, William Blake, Dante Gabriel Rossetti**, and **Whistler** refused, while **Gainsborough** initially exhibited. The division has not really healed with time—you can be certain that **Francis Bacon** and **David Hockney** are not part of the academy. The initials RA after an artist's name (meaning he or she is or was one of the honored 50 Academicians) may add to the price of an artist's work in the salesrooms, but they do not significantly affect his reputation in the art world. In the last 10 years, the Royal Academy has entered a new phase that is livelier and more innovative.

In the center of the entrance hall are ceiling paintings by **Benjamin West**—*The Graces Unveiling Nature* and *The Four Elements*.

There are 4 paintings by **Angelica Kaufmann** at each end—*Genius* and *Painting*, near the door to the **Friends Room** on the east, and *Composition* and *Design*, on the west. Above the central staircase is a circular painting by **William Kent**—*The Glorification of Inigo Jones*. On the 1st floor is the **Saloon**, the only surviving part of Burlington House by Colen Campbell, with the ceiling by William Kent.

Exhibitions take place in the rooms on the 1st and 2nd floors. The **Summer Exhibition** is the big event of the year at the academy, and one of London's important social occasions. Fourteen thousand works by 4000 artists are submitted, with 1300 finally selected. The gala opening in June looks like a royal garden party with pictures. The academy's reputation now rests on its international art exhibitions (this is where the enormous 1990 Monet show originated). These exhibitions last for 3 months at a stretch and can get very crowded. Go early. Sadly, the permanent collection is not generally on display—which reveals a rather blasé attitude toward the great masters' works. The splendid pictures by Gainsborough, **Sir Joshua Reynolds, John Constable, Joseph Mallord William Turner, David Wilkie, Sir Henry Raeburn, Sir Alfred Munnings**, and **Walter Sickert** comprise a collection that is both personal and interesting and will be seen briefly in 1990 before being put away again for some years. The collection contains the works by past members who, upon election, deposited a work known as a *Diploma* piece. They are exhibited periodically on the top floor in the **Diploma Galleries**, which can be reached by an unnervingly slow freight elevator.

The academy's greatest treasure is a Carrara marble relief of **Michelangelo**'s *Madonna and Child with the Infant St. John*, carved in 1505. It is one of only 4 major sculptures by the artist outside of Italy. ◆ Free; admission for special exhibitions. Daily 10AM–6PM. Royal Academy, Burlington House, Piccadilly, W1. 071/439.7438

Within the Royal Academy of Arts, Burlington House:

Royal Academy Restaurant ★★$ Big and cafeterial, but a welcome refuge from the nonstop glamour of Piccadilly. Women in tweed suits and sensible shoes, in town for the day, sit in the attractive paneled room, peacefully drinking tea and eating cakes. Hot and cold lunches are served between 11:30AM and 2:30PM. There is also a good salad bar. ◆ Daily 10:30AM–5PM. 071/439.7438

30 Piccadilly Arcade (1910, Thrale Jell) An extension of the Burlington Arcade built a century later, this charming, relaxed collection of shops connects Piccadilly to Jermyn Street.

Within Piccadilly Arcade:

Waterford Wedgwood The China specialists have a complete and tempting collection of Wedgwood and Spode. All the price lists include the import price and the amount in dollars. ♦ M-F 9AM-6PM; Sa 9AM-4PM. Nos. 173-174 Piccadilly Arcade. 071/629.2614

Armory of St. James's Decorations and medals for the otherwise unrewarded. ♦ M-F 9:30AM-5:30PM. No. 17 Piccadilly Arcade. 071/493.5082

Benson & Clegg The tailors to **George VI** will make you a suit or provide you with a set of dazzling buttons and hand-embroidered crests for your own blazer. ♦ M-F 7AM-5PM; Sa 8AM-noon. No. 9 Piccadilly Arcade. 071/491.1454

New and Lingwood Located on the Jermyn St side, this is one of the best and somehow least-known shops in the arcade. It started as the London branch of the **Eton** shop, where New and Lingwood has outfitted Etonians for many decades. The shop has beautiful ready-made shirts and a small but choice selection of sweaters, including a forest-green cable-knit cashmere sweater that is a lifetime commitment but worth every pound and pence. You can also have shirts made to order. Upstairs, incorporated within the shop, is **Poulsen and Skone**, makers of fine shoes that require another serious commitment, but in this instance they share the burden, providing care and service for your shoes for life. The ready-made shoes are pretty wonderful, too. ♦ M-F 9AM-5:30PM; Sa 10AM-3PM. No. 53 Jermyn St. 071/493.9621

Fortnum & Mason

31 Fortnum & Mason This is one of the world's most magnificent grocers and oldest carry-out stores. Inside, the crystal chandeliers reflect in the polished mahogany, highlighting temptations of caviar, truffles, marrons glacés, hand-dipped chocolates, Stilton cheeses, teas, honeys, champagnes, and foie gras. On the hour, the clock chimes sweetly and 2 mechanical figures emerge from the miniature doors. Dressed in livery of 18th-century servants, Mr. Fortnum and Mr. Mason turn and bow to each other while the bells chime the Eton school song. The clock is a relatively recent addition to this wonderful store, placed here in 1964, but it says everything: this 18th-century treasure house is ready to serve you most excellently, as it has been serving the privileged since 1707.

The luxurious hampers filled with gourmet foods, so common at Ascot and Glyndebourne, began in 1788 as packed lunches (known as *Concentrated Lunches*) for hunting and shooting parties and members of Parliament who might have been detained. The fortunate recipients would lunch on game pies and boned chickens and lobster and prawns. During the Napoleonic Wars, officers in the **Duke of Wellington**'s army ordered hams and cheeses. Baskets were sent to **Florence Night-**

ingale in the Crimea, to **Mr. Stanley** while he was looking for **Mr. Livingston**, and to suffragettes imprisoned in London's Holloway jail, who shared their hampers from Fortnum & Mason with fellow prisoners. If you are lucky enough to have tickets for Glyndebourne, Wimbledon, or Ascot, or if you just feel like a luxurious picnic in St. James's Park, Green Park, Kensington Park Gardens, or Regent's Park, indulge in a hamper worthy of the occasion. Make sure you ask for the *Picnic Hamper* the day before you want it, and choose from the cold selection, which includes Parma ham and melon, smoked salmon cornettes, fresh-roasted *poussin*, ox tongue, salad, profiteroles, cheeses, champagne, and chocolate truffles. Add a thermos of coffee and have a lordly repast under an English sky for less than you would pay in most terrace restaurants.

If you choose, while shopping at Fortnum's you can be assisted by gentlemen in morning coats who accompany you from department to department, write down your choices and requests, and advise with knowledge, patience, and charm. The teas are famous and the blue-green tins are as much a sign as a guarantee of good taste. Try the Finest Broken Orange Pekoe, a delicious everyday tea. (You will be encouraged to put less tea in the pot and drink it without milk in order to appreciate the true flavor.) Also try the Paulliac of teas: Formosa Oolong Peach Blossom. If you provide a sample of your local water, the store will carefully match it with one of its 68 varieties of tea. There is even a New York blend. The cakes and Christmas puddings are bought by those in the know. (Mrs. Thatcher bought her son's wedding cake here.) Not only are the luxury fruitcakes in a class of their own, they are (strangely) cheaper than those found in similar stores in London. Tastes are available in the cake shop's café at the back of the store. Fortnum's is also one of the very few stores in England where some American produce is available. After you have wisely invested a fortune in English honeys, Fortnum's own marmalades, teas, a game pie or 2, a tin of English biscuits, a couple of pottery crocks of Stilton, and a jar of Gentlemen's Relish (a very special anchovy paste) decorated with pheasants, consider lunch at Fortnum's. ♦ M-F 9AM-5:30PM; Sa 9AM-1PM. 181 Piccadilly, W1. 071/734.8040

Restaurants/Nightlife: Red   **Hotels:** Blue
Shops/Parks: Green   **Sights/Culture:** Black

Within Fortnum & Mason:

Fountain Restaurant ★★★$$ Underneath Fortnum's with a separate entrance on Jermyn St. Sadly, the interior was redecorated in neutral dove grays and recessed lights, which make it look anonymously like New York. Everyone misses the 1950s aqua room with its

Piccadilly

seaside mural behind the counter. Still, the food is the same, and there is a new counter for those who pop in alone and want a delicious and uncomplicated meal. Surprisingly, this restaurant is also open in the evening, so besides breakfast, lunch, and tea, you can come here for dinner, before and after the theater. The grills are first-class, the pies (game, steak, and kidney) are excellent, and if you just want something light, the sandwiches are fit for Ascot. The ice-cream sundaes are famous, and this is one of the only restaurants in London where you can get fabulous coffee, espresso, or cappuccino—again, at the counter. The Fountain is a favorite place for tea, and a number of writers, artists, and other London figures use this as their club. (That's **J.P. Donleavy** sitting in the corner.) It is without a doubt the best place in the area for breakfast. But if you have already eaten, come for what the English call *elevenses*—coffee and a Danish. ♦ M-Sa 9:30AM-11:30PM. 071/734.4938

St. James's Restaurant ★★★$$ This 4th-floor restaurant is far less known than the Fountain, hence quieter and ideal for exchanging confidences over roast beef and Yorkshire pudding. Your neighbors look like they have come to London to bid on a little something at Christie's or Sotheby's—very tweed suit and proper. ♦ M-Sa 9-11:30AM, noon-2:30PM, 3-5PM. 071/734.8040

32 Swaine & Adeney As one of London's oldest and most traditional family-run businesses, it is graced with 2 Royal Warrants: Whip and Glove Makers to the Queen, and Umbrella Makers to the Queen Mother. In a country where rain is a national preoccupation, umbrellas are serious business, and

Swaine & Adeney makes the Rolls-Royce of umbrellas. Go in and look around. In the **Gun Room**, in the basement, you will find the finest in country clothing, including the whole range of the dark-green, waxy raincoats (**Barbours**) worn by the landed gentry, and everything to do with the sartorial side of riding, horses, and hunting. Ask one of the salespeople to explain the difference between the traditional and the classic umbrella, examine the runners, open caps and ferrules, and the hand and top springs. You will be given a wide choice of handles—crooks steamed and bent by hand; woods, including malacca, whangee, congo, chestnut, cherry, hickory, ash, and maple; or if you prefer a leather handle, choose from handsewn calf, morocco, pigskin, ostrich, lizard, or crocodile. Then there's the selection of fabrics, which includes a wide variety of nylons or the best English silk. If in the end you choose the classic Brigg umbrella with the best English black-silk cover, Malacca crook, and gold collar engraved with your name and address, be assured that waiters will understand when you say you wish to keep your umbrella. There are also walking sticks, some sinister, but all remarkable. ♦ M-F 9AM-6PM; Sa 9:30AM-5:30PM. 185 Piccadilly, W1. 071/734.4277

32 Hatchards The 18th-century bookshop still has the rambling charm of that age, but it has moved into the paperback era with considerable booksmarts. Now it is a book emporium, with an excellent selection of children's books (2nd floor), art books (1st floor), and reference books, including dictionaries, Bibles, and the Oxford companions to music, literature, etc (ground floor). In the literature department (2nd floor) you can buy all 12 volumes of **Byron**'s *Letters and Journals*, edited by **Leslie Marchand**, or you can settle for the single volume of Byron's biography (all published by **John Murray**, a few yards down the street). You'll find the complete works of just about all of your favorite English writers as well as secondhand and rare books. As you enter from Piccadilly, have a look at the recent hardcover fiction. In the modern annex, a travel section with guides, literary and otherwise, will keep you going for years. The shop assistants seem to be employed here because they are charming and know about and love books. They can trace any book you care to name if it's still in print. If books are your thing, this is paradise. ♦ M-F 9AM-6PM; Sa 9AM-5PM. 187 Piccadilly, W1. 071/439.9921

33 Albany (1770–74, **Sir William Chambers** and **Henry Holland**; 1804) The building looks across Piccadilly at Fortnum from its little courtyard, and is like a Parisian *hôtel particulier* done in English Palladianism. Originally built for **Lord Melbourne**, it was converted to chambers for bachelor gentlemen in 1803. The Albany has been home to **Lord Byron**, **Thomas B. Macaulay**, **Lord Gladstone** and more recently, **J.B. Priestley** and **Graham Greene**. ♦ Albany Courtyard, W1

34 Sackville Street Take a quick look at this almost (almost) pure Georgian street, which is imbued with a confident modesty that evokes sense and sensibility, pride and prejudice.

35 Midland Bank (1922, **Sir Edwin Lutyens**) This charming neighbor of St. James's Church is worth a glance. The architect kindly deferred to St. James's by creating a bank in domestic scale in brick and Portland stone. ◆ 196A Piccadilly, W1

36 St. James's, Piccadilly (1676–84, **Sir Christopher Wren**) The church is the favorite of the man who gave us St. Paul's Cathedral and some 50 other London churches, but you have to go inside to fully understand why. The newly pointed brick, the replaced and restored spire, and the crafts market in the courtyard give no clue of the miracle inside. But miracle it is—the wide-open spaciousness, the barrel-vaulted roof, the rows of five 2-tiered windows, the Corinthian columns, the brass, the gilt, the paint. It has always been a fashionable church, especially created for large weddings. The organ was built for **James II**. The wonderful white-marble font with figures of Adam and Eve and the Tree of Life, carved by **Grinling Gibbons**, was the site of many christenings, including that of **William Blake**, in 1757. Of his church Wren said, *There are no walls of a second order, nor lanterns, nor buttresses, but the whole rests upon pillars, as do also the galleries, and I think it may be found beautiful and convenient; it is the cheapest form of any I could invent.* Ah, the economy of genius. The church is also a moving tribute to its congregation. Almost completely destroyed in the bombing of 1940, it was restored with determination and dedication. The spire was completed in 1968 by **Sir Albert Richardson**. This is an active church running lectures on various aspects of faith most evenings. ◆ Daily 10AM-6PM. Services: Su 8:30, 11AM, 5:45PM. Lunchtime concerts: Th-F 1:10PM. 197 Piccadilly, W1. 071/743.4511

The English country gentleman galloping after a fox—the unspeakable in full pursuit of the uneatable.

Oscar Wilde

Within St. James's Yard:

The Wren at St. James's ★★$ A cheerful place to come for homemade soups (thick vegetable soups served with thick slices of wholemeal bread), herbal teas, and healthy, delicious salads, as well as cakes, fruit tarts, and coffee. ◆ M-Sa 10:30AM-6PM; Su 10AM-4PM. 071/734.7449

Piccadilly Market This lively crafts market always attracts large crowds on Friday and Saturday. There is usually a good selection of pottery, hand-knit sweaters, carved-wood children's toys, enameled jewelry and boxes, all at very modest prices. ◆ F-Sa 10AM-4PM

37 Le Meridien Hotel $$$ (Formerly the New Piccadilly Hotel) In 1908, this was London's newest and most elegant hotel, built by one of the leading Edwardian architects, **Norman Shaw**. He combined dazzling opulence with architectural perfection. Throughout the 1920s and '30s, the hotel's reputation held fast. But after WWII it began a major decline. In 1983, **Gleneagles of Scotland** bought the hotel. Sixteen million pounds and a few sell-offs and acquisitions later, it came into the hands of Air France's company Le Meridien. It is once again one of the showcases of Piccadilly and a generous and sorely needed physical and psychological facelift to Piccadilly Circus. What Norman Shaw created has been preserved (by a protection order as well as by good sense). But late 20th-century notions of essential luxury are found in the golf-practice area, health club with squash courts, solarium, swimming pool, Nautilus gym, Turkish baths, sauna, Jacuzzi, beauty salon, and fitness-cuisine brasserie. The glamour is in the facilities; the rooms are comfortable and pleasant, but not remarkably grand. ◆ Piccadilly, W1. 071/734.8000; fax 071/437.3574

The grand Baroque facade of the **Le Meridien Hotel** (originally called the Piccadilly Hotel) is without a doubt the most handsome part of the present quadrant around Piccadilly Circus. The tragedy is that it was built here, and that it was done at the terrible expense of John Nash's original quadrant, which was destroyed to make way for the hotel. Nash's elegant and ceremonial conception was shattered, for once not out of the greed of business and the indifference of the public, but due to the architectural citadel itself, which purposely and purposefully ignored Nash's grand and remarkably fine plan. The guilt does not rest on Sir Norman Shaw, who genuinely attempted to restore the graciousness of this area and produced magnificent plans that respected the genuis of Nash. But Shaw was defeated and withdrew his name from the Piccadilly Development of 1912, and died soon after. The ghost of Nash has haunted this site ever since, making it almost impossible to successfully resurrect and restore the dignity that would make Piccadilly Circus worthy of a great city.

Within Le Meridien Hotel:

Oak Room Restaurant ★★$$$ The original pale oak-paneled elegance looks like a set

from *Edward VIII and Mrs. Simpson*. Chef **David Chambers** prepares such lunch and dinner creations as *Le Gaspacho de Langoustines à la Crème de Courgette, La Noisette de Chevreuil Grand Veneur*, and a delicious *Le Bar Légèrement Fumé à la Crème de Caviar*. The street of Piccadilly has become a battle ground for chefs determined to create centers of excellence and make a little part of London a gourmet delight. They have succeeded here. ◆ Daily noon-10PM. 071/734.8000

Terrace Garden Restaurant ★★$$$ This stunning brasserie in a conservatory still feels undiscovered, and it is a nice way to begin or end a theater evening. The crab soup, served with Roville, Gruyère, and croutons, is delicious. There is also a daily 3-course *table d'hôte*. Afternoon tea is served from 3-5:30PM. Business London eats its power breakfasts here—it really is a lovely way to start the day. ◆ Daily 7-11AM, 12:30-2:30PM, 3-5:30PM, 7-10PM. 071/734.8000

37 **Cording's** If London weren't a Dickensian tangle of ground leases, this shop would have been abolished and the grandeur of the Piccadilly Hotel extended. Only the web of London's property laws would enable the ceremonial designs of Nash to be destroyed and this little shop to remain. Cording's has been here since 1839, and has kept its character in an ever-changing world. You can get terrific raincoats, waterproof boots, country wools and tweeds, all high quality and costing somewhat less than next door at Burberry's and Simpson's. ◆ M-Sa 9AM-5:30PM. 19 Piccadilly, W1. 071/734.0830

38 **Simpson's** (1935, **Joseph Emberton**) The ultramodern building is a case of *if you wait long enough you'll get used to it*. It was one of the great pioneering store designs, with lavish use of materials, including glass lifts, travertine floors, space, and light. But does it belong to Piccadilly? Fifty years later, Londoners completely accept the store (and its very high-quality clothing under the **Daks** label). Visitors complain that it is an eyesore. But architects admire what they see, especially when lit at night, and what they don't see—the welded-steel structure (the second in England) with massive girders on the 1st floor. Simpson's now has an impressive women's department, with 3 floors of French, English, and American designer fashion rubbing shoulders with the tweedy country suits. But it is known mainly for its men's clothes, with the highest quality suits, tweed jackets,

overcoats, and raincoats. The service is slow, courteous, and intelligent. Within Simpson's are a barbershop and **Jeeves**, specialist drycleaners. ◆ M, W, F-Sa 9AM-6PM; Tu 9:30-6PM; Th 9AM-7PM. 203 Piccadilly, W1. 071/734.2002

Within Simpson's:

Simpson's Wine Bar ★★$ This light, airy slip of a wine bar overlooks Jermyn St. It is pretty basic—coffee, croissants, and Danish pastries in the morning and quiche and salad at lunch, when it gets crowded with well-dressed people who want to eat simply and quickly. ◆ M, W, F-Sa 9AM-5:15PM; Tu 9:30AM-5:45PM; Th 9AM-6:45PM. 071/734.2002

Simpson's Restaurant ★★$$ This restaurant provides the odd combination of English restaurant and Japanese sushi bar (with matching décor). Diners wear the kind of clothes sold in the store (smart, traditional, English) and eat the kind of food that they have in their own country houses, or so it seems. The restaurant serves proper English breakfasts (not the croissant lark, but eggs, bacon, sausage, kidneys, and kippers). At lunch, choose from either sushi or roast joints—beef and lamb—carved from the trolley, English cheeses, and trifles and syllabubs for pudding. Then top it off with a proper English tea. Quite agreeable all around. If you sit at the sushi bar you will be entertained by the chef in action. ◆ M, W, F-Sa 9AM-5:15PM; Tu 9:30AM-5:45PM; Th 9AM-6:45PM. 071/734.2002

39 **Regent Street** Signs of the grand designs of **John Nash** are quite apparent, with Regent Street (in fact, this is Lower Regent Street) at your right, running southward to Waterloo Place and the Mall, and northward to Oxford Street and Regent's Park; and Shaftesbury Avenue on the northeast, leading to Soho and the heart of theaterland. But what you see and what Nash actually created are, sadly, 2 different things. Nash planned Piccadilly Circus as an elegant square with a long arcade, very much like the Rue de Rivoli running alongside the Tuileries in Paris. The **Quadrant**, an even larger version of the crescent at Regent's Park, was the very essence of the scheme, and so crucial that Nash financed its construction out of his own pocket, persuading his builders to take leases instead of payment when his own money ran out.

Completed in 1819, it must have been very handsome, indeed. Destruction of the Quadrant began in 1848, with serious obliteration in 1905. Since then planners have tried with monotonous regularity to restore and re-create Piccadilly Circus. The latest attempt is the 1986 effort you see today: a pedestrian precinct that one can only hope won't succumb to the shabbiness to which the area is prone.

For sightseeing on Regent Street go when the shops are closed; it is quite beautiful and deserted. Remember to look up—a lot of fine detail can be found on the tops of the buildings. For shopping, the street is lacking, considering its central position and length, with

Regent Street Shopping Map

OXFORD STREET

Oxford Circus Tube	**Oxford Circus Tube**
	Wedgewood Gift Centre
	Bally *shoes*

PRINCES STREET

REGENT STREET

National Westminster Bank

HANOVER STREET — **LITTLE ARGYLL STREET**

Dickins and Jones *dept. store*

GREAT MARLBOROUGH STREET

Liberty and Co. *clothing/dept. store*
Barclays Bank

MADDOX STREET

FOUBERT'S PLACE

hairdressers **R. Fielding**

Jaeger *clothing*
Chinacraft
Hamley's *toys*
Ciro *pearls*
Berk The Scottish Shop

CONDUIT STREET

fine leather **Henry's**
Scotch House

TENISON COURT

Mappin and Webb *jewelry*

NEW BURLINGTON PLACE
Noble Furs

NEW BURLINGTON STREET

Waterford Wedgewood *china*

Burberrys

china **Villeroy & Boch**

NEW BURLINGTON MEWS

BEAK STREET

Woollen Centre

Lawleys *china and glass*
Bally *shoes*

HEDDON STREET

Viyella *women's clothing*
Country Casuals *clothing*
Reject China Shop

Scottish Woollens

porcelain and glass **Wilson & Gill**
Midland Bank

Lloyds Bank

REGENT PLACE

HEDDON STREET

Garrard & Co. Ltd. *jewelry*

pen specialists **Pencraft Ltd.**

VIGO STREET

GLASSHOUSE STREET

men's clothing **Austin Reed**

Aquascutum

SWALLOW STREET

Mitsukiku *Japanese gifts*
Scotch House *woolens and tartans*

REGENT STREET

QUADRANT ARCADE

MAN IN THE MOON PASSAGE
Chinacraft

AIR STREET
Cafe Royal

AIR STREET

Café Nicols *coffeeshop*
Barclays Bank

Piccadilly Circus Tube

Piccadilly Circus Tube

PICCADILLY

more than its fair share of airlines and ordinary chain stores. However, there are some notable exceptions. Start with **Acquascutum** (reputed to be the **Mrs. Thatcher**'s outfitter) at the Piccadilly Circus end, followed by **Garrard** (the **Queen**'s jewelers), then walk purposefully up to **Mappin & Webb**—another high-class jewelry store. If you feel the urge to buy china,

Piccadilly

wait until you've seen **Liberty**—an extraordinary and eclectic department store, much loved by the English gentry. It has an eccentric collection of china from all over the world in the basement. (Although Liberty looks Elizabethan, it was built out of timbers from 2 men'o war in 1925.) Don't forget to look in **Hamleys**, but be prepared for a long stay if you have children because they'll never want to leave.

To the right of Regent street is **Waterloo Place**, presided over by the *Duke of York Column* (1834, **Benjamin Wyatt**). The street was supposed to mark the southern end of Nash's triumphal way from Carlton House Terrace to Regent's Park. In the distance you can see the Victoria Tower at the Houses of Parliament.

40 Eros After a rest-cure of almost 2 years, during which he was treated for a near-century of exposure to the elements, the **God of Love** has returned and once more reigns over Piccadilly Circus. London's best-loved statue rises lovingly to the occasion, symbolizing London itself to millions of people all over the world. The statue is a memorial to **Lord Shaftesbury** (1801–85), a man of great virtue and a tireless reformer and educator. The

sculptor, **Alfred Gilbert**, was no less idealistic. He believed that Shaftesbury deserved something that would represent generosity of spirit and love of mankind, and would symbolize, according to the sculptor, *the work of Lord Shaftesbury, the blindfolded Love sending forth indiscriminately, yet with purpose, his missile of kindness, always with the swiftness the bird has from its wings, never ceasing to breathe or reflect critically, but ever soaring onwards, regardless of its own perils and dangers*. A prophetic statement of an artist's intent.

Gilbert created his statue in aluminum, the first time the material had been used for such a structure. As a result, the 8-foot figure is so light that it sways in the wind. Gilbert was paid £3000 for his work, even though it had cost him £7000 to build it. His eventual and inevitable bankruptcy left him with little alternative but to leave the country, living first in Belgium, and then in Italy. Lord Shaftesbury himself died lamenting *I cannot bear to leave this world with all the misery in it*. One cannot but feel he would have been sadder still to know what misery had afflicted the artist who tried to honor him. The creator of Eros was rejected, but the statue found an enduring place in the hearts of Londoners. ♦ Piccadilly Circus, W1

41 Criterion Theatre (1870, **Thomas Verity**) Tawdry signs have long buried the French-château facade of this theater. It is London's only underground theater in the physical sense of the word—you go down a series of steps, even for the upper circle. The lobby is decorated with Victorian tiles. Closed until 1992. ♦ Piccadilly Circus, W1

42 Criterion Brasserie The restaurant was designed by **Thomas Verity** in 1870, along with the Criterion Theatre, when Piccadilly was the hub of the Empire. As Piccadilly's fate declined and the area filled up with junkies, derelicts, boarded up buildings, sex cinemas, and kabob houses, the Criterion sank to a new low as the fastest cafeteria in London, serving 20 meals a minute. In 1983, thanks to the kiss of life the Greater London Council and the refurbished *Eros* were bringing to the area, **Trusthouse Forte** decided to rehabilitate the Criterion. Behind decades of plywood and formica and grease and smoke, they found pure gold, or at least the closest thing: shimmering, dazzling, gold-mosaic Byzantine vaulted ceilings and marble walls. Now elegantly restored to its former Victorian splendor, it is the prettiest brasserie/café outside of Vienna. Closed until 1992. ♦ 222 Piccadilly, W1

43 Trocadero The *Troc* has a long history on this site, going back to the 1740s, when it was a tennis court. In the 19th century, it went from circus to theater to music hall to restaurant. In the 1920s and '30s, the *Troc* flourished under **Charles Cochran**'s *Supper Time Revues*. Now it is what is apparently called an entertainment complex, filled with shops and restaurants; the first **Guinness World of Records Exhibition**; **Star Tracks**, where the starstruck come and make their own pop videos with back tracks and instruments; a terrific record shop (**HMV**); a large bookstore (**Athena Books**); a nightclub (**Shaftesbury on the Avenue**); and the **Golden Nugget Casino**, with 14 roulette wheels, 10 blackjack tables, and one *punto banco*. (All casinos in England require membership—apply in person, produce your passport, then wait 48 hours.) This 200,000-square-foot mixed bag of shops, restaurants, and entertainments is made for tourists and is especially popular with English visitors from the provinces, families, and young people. The Trocadero is doing its best with its restaurants, located on **Food Street**, where you can sample delights from around the world. There are also individual designer shops with fashion shows. Restaurants and shops are open daily until late. ♦ Golden Nugget Casino: daily 2PM-4AM. Guinness World of Records and Star Tracks: daily 10AM-10PM. Shaftesbury on the Avenue: daily 9:30PM-3AM. Coventry St, Piccadilly Circus, W1. 071/439.4938

44 Design Center A fabulous showplace for the best of British design, from toys to tackle, cars to cards, and woolies to *Wellies*. The government-sponsored **Design Council**, originally the **Council for Industrial Design**, has been providing changing exhibitions of the latest innovations in British domestic design since 1956. If you have any questions about where to find something, the experts in the center offer free and helpful advice, and the selective *Design Index* lists approximately 7000 manufacturers of well-designed goods. After looking at what is on display, you can browse in the bookstore or refresh yourself at the coffee bar. ♦ M-Tu 10AM-6PM; W-Sa 10AM-8PM; Su 1-6PM. 28 Haymarket, SW1. 071/839.8000

45 Burberrys This raincoat manufacturer, famous for quality and its signature plaid, has been protecting the British from the elements for over 150 years. Aviators like **Sir John Alcock** used Burberrys' gabardine to keep him-self warm and dry on his first flight across the Atlantic, and soldiers in the First World War wore Burberrys' trenchcoats. Today, the liveried commissionaire opens the door and you enter a world of old-fashioned charm and grace. Either climb the wooden staircase or risk the ancient lift in this glorious shop, which rambles gracefully from floor to floor.

♦ W, F-Sa 9AM-5:30PM; Th 9AM-7PM. 18 Haymarket, SW1. 071/930.3343. Also at: 165 Regent St, W1. 071/734.4060; 6-10 Victoria St, EC4. 071/236.0022

Bests

Sheila Hicks
Farbric Designer

Camden Lock Market and all the small and large markets on the edge of Regent's Canal. They are filled with crafts, second-hand clothes, jewelry, and foods from all over the world. The kids can watch puppet shows on an old barge that has been turned into a small theater.

Eating lunch at **Le Routier** at Camden Lock and watching the boats along the canal as well as the crowds. The restaurant is medium priced and serves standard, old-style French cooking, but excellent fish.

Walking along the canal path at **Camden Lock** to **Little Venice** and passing 19th-century industrial buildings, 18th-century houses, and Regent's Park. There are no cars along this quiet quarter of the busy city. If you are lazy, try the same journey by canal boat and watch the scene in comfort.

Eating lunch at a funky restaurant like **Diwani Bhel Poori**. It is frequented by middle-class intellectuals and students who enjoy excellent food at amazingly low prices. The stuffed *dosa* is wonderful. How do they manage that thin, firm, crispy pancake?

Lunch or dinner at **Nontas**. It has a pleasant atmosphere, good service, and reasonable prices. Try the fish kabob or hummus! They don't hurry you out when you are finished, except on Friday and Saturday.

English breakfast at the **Savoy**. It is maddeningly expensive, but it has a great atmosphere. The service is superb, if clearly snotty. Gaze at the amazing views of the South Bank, the Thames, and the Art Deco décor. Then pay the bill with the aplomb of one used to such indulgences!

Sharon Lee Ryder
Editor, *SF Magazine*

Chiang Mai is a must for aficiandos of Oriental Food. The menu offers items not found in more typical Thai restaurants, most of them flown in fresh from Bangkok. This is no hole-in-the-wall ethnic establishment, as its prices will attest. Its décor is well-designed and understated, and the prices are moderate by established standards. Although it is tempting to overeat, save room for fresh lychees and other exotic fruits.

I am leaving because the weather is too good. I hate London when it's not raining.

Groucho Marx

St. James's

St. James's is all about mystery and magic, royalty and aristocracy, pomp and civilized circumstances, and kings, queens, and gentlemen. In this elegant heart-shaped enclave, gentlemen's London has long been a tightly knit purlieu of royal London, an anachronistic neighborhood of refinement where time has stood still. Gentlemen still go to their clubs, that unchallenged English invention with its air of infinite mystery; shoes are still made with painstaking care for royal feet; hats are still sewn seamlessly for aristocratic heads; and when the Queen is home at **Buckingham Palace**, the Royal Standard flies. This is one of the most agreeable walks in London, a cameo portrait of England and Englishness utterly unchanged by time, wars, developers, mass production, pollution, the weak pound, or the European Community. Here daylight—if daylight be reality—has been kept at bay, preserving for us the England we secretly yearn for: the England of history books and literature, heros and heroines, Meredith and Oscar Wilde, *Ravenshoe*, *Can You Forgive Her*, and Vivien Grey. St. James's is history and address book, champagne and syllabub. It is also—egalitarians and feminists be warned—what remains of 2 ancient British ideas: the segregation of the classes and the segregation of the sexes.

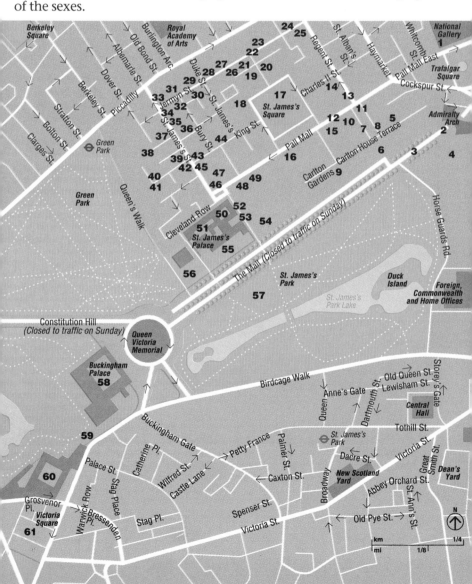

You can begin the journey in the presence of Nelson at **Trafalgar Square** and in the company of Gainsborough and Constable, among 2000 others, at the **National Gallery**, one of the richest and most extensive collections of paintings in the world. After regarding esthetic perfection, you can contemplate the material artifacts on **Jermyn Street**, where window-shopping is museumlike and the prices can reach old master figures.

In an area no larger than a football field, you can have a pair of shoes made to fit your own feet, design your own family crest, and be measured for custom-made shirts (with a minimum order of 6 and a minimum wait of 6 weeks). You can buy cheddars, Stiltons, Wensleydales, and Caerphilys in a shop that may convince you that the French are the second-best cheese producers in the world (**Paxton and Whitfield**). You can choose wild-hyacinth bath oil from a famous perfumer (**Floris**) or Ajaccio Violet from a regal barbershop (**Ivan's and Trumper's**); find refuge in a Victorian pub (the **Red Lion**) or surrender for a couple of hours in one of the best English restaurants in London (**Wilton's**). You will see where kings and queens lived before they moved to Buckingham Palace, and where the Queen lives now, although like 99 percent of Her subjects, you will have to be satisfied with gazing at facades. You can have a look at some of the treasures from the **Royal Collection**, check out the royal horses and coaches, and end the day by the shimmering lake in **St. James's Park**—London's oldest and most romantic park, where Charles II walked with his spaniels.

St. James's on a Saturday feels like a Sunday. The streets are empty, few gentlemen can be seen going into their clubs, and while most of the shops are open, you never know which ones. The National Gallery is always best on weekday mornings. If you want to see the **Changing of the Guard** at Buckingham Palace (11:30AM daily, alternate days in winter), do the second half of the walk first and get there at least half an hour early. Few of the interiors of the royal palaces are open, so good weather is desirable for the part of the walk from the bottom of St. James's Street (Marlborough Road) to Buckingham Palace and St. James's Park. Otherwise, an umbrella is essential. The **Queen's Gallery** is open Tuesday through Saturday, and Sunday afternoon; and the **Royal Mews** is open Wednesday and Thursday afternoon. Services are held in the **Queen's Chapel** on Sunday morning in the summer and in the **Chapel Royal** on Sunday morning in the winter. At 3PM each afternoon in St. James's Park, the pelicans emerge stiffly from their sanctuary by the lake and have a tea of whiting and other whole fish.

1 National Gallery (1838, William Wilkens)
In fact, there are 3 national galleries in London—the National Gallery, the National Portrait Gallery, and the Tate Gallery. Together they contain some of the finest art treasures in the world. The National Gallery is one of the very smallest picture galleries, with no vast collection of any one school or any single painter and no vast cellar of pictures in storage. Almost all of the 2050 pictures are on view, and virtually all of them are worth seeing.

Unlike most of the great national galleries of Europe, the National Gallery is not built upon the foundations of a former royal collection and did not inherit a nationally based collection. Its beginnings were late; in 1824 **George IV** persuaded the government to buy 38 paintings from the collection of Russian émigré and marine insurance underwriter **John Julius Angerstein**. The government paid £57,000 for the pictures—which included 5 paintings by **Claude Lorraine, Hogarth**'s *Marriage à la Mode* series, and works by **Raphael,**

St. James's

Reynolds, and **Van Dyck**—then opened the gallery to the public in Angerstein's former town house at 100 Pall Mall.

Two other collectors, **Sir George Beaumont** and the **Rev. William Howell Carr**, promised important collections of paintings to the nation if a suitable building were provided to house them. In 1838, the National Gallery opened. The Beaumont and Howel Carr paintings, along with Angerstein's, formed the nucleus of the national collection.

The building must certainly have influenced the early character of the collection. It was built on the site of the former Royal Mews, but the stables with barracks to the rear of the site could not be built upon, so the design could

only be one-room deep. This resulted in a stage-set of a museum with a long, drawn-out facade. But the restrictions on the architect weren't limited to size: Wilkens was also forced to incorporate into the portico the 8 columns salvaged from the demolished Carlton House, a precedent of compromise that has dogged extensions and additions to the National Gallery ever since.

The limited size of the gallery led to a purchasing policy that now makes it the envy of museums throughout the world: buy the best works of the greatest masters. For 150 years, the National Gallery had one invaluable resource for its purchasing: the English aristocracy who had been shopping on the Continent for masterpieces to add to their private collections for 400 years.

As the collection grew, so did the National Gallery. The dome and additional rooms were added in the 1870s, followed by the central staircase and further additions in 1911. In 1975, the excellent northern extension was opened, providing space for temporary exhibitions.

The pictures in the National Gallery are predominately and supremely by the old masters. They present one of the finest histories of Western European painting in existence, from **Duccio** in Italy (c. 1300) up to **van Gogh, Cézanne**, and **Klimt** in the early 20th century. Even in their native countries, painters such as **Holbein, Van Dyck**, and **Velásquez** are not represented with masterpieces of such greatness.

When the Tate Gallery opened in 1897, it took on the dual role of modern art museum and home of British art. Many of the British paintings in the National Gallery were transferred to the Tate, leaving the National with a small but choice British collection. It consists of 2 paint-

National Gallery

ings by **Stubbs**, *The Milbanke* and *Melbourne Families*; 6 by **Reynolds**, including *General Banastre Tarleton*, a portrait of the young general during the American War of Independance; 5 by **Constable**, including the evocative *The Haywain*; 10 by **Gainsborough**, including *Mr. and Mrs. Andrews* and *The Morning Walk*; 7 by **Hogarth**, 6 of which are part of the *Marriage à la Mode* series about a marriage based on money and vanity; and 8 **Turners**, including *Rain, Steam and Speed—the Great Western Railway*.

There is no substitute for looking at the pictures, and one of the bonuses of a free museum is being able to look at only a few at a time, guiltlessly. No one has to see it all in one go, and no one should. A lifetime spent looking at these paintings seems about right, starting with old favorites and acquiring new loves along the way. If you are daunted by the size of the collection or pressed for time, the National Gallery has made a kind of *Top of the Pops* of the 16 most famous pictures. The *Quick Visit Guide* describes them and is well worth its small price. The 16 masterpieces:

1 *The Wilton Diptych* (c.1395). ♦ Room 1

2 *The Battle of San Romano*, **Paola Uccello** (c. 1397-1475). ♦ Room 2

3 *The Baptism of Christ*, **Piero Della Francesca** (active 1439, died 1492). ♦ Room 4

4 *Cartoon: The Virgin and Child with Saint Anne and Saint John the Baptist*, **Leonardo Da Vinci** (1452-1519). ♦ Room 7

5 *The Doge Leonardo Loredan*, **Giovanni Bellini** (active c. 1459, died 1516). ♦ Room 10

6 *Bacchus and Ariadne*, **Titian** (active before 1511, died 1576). ♦ Room 9

7 *Equestrian Portrait of Charles I*, **Anthony Van Dyck** (1599-1641). ♦ Room 21

8 *Le Chapeau de Paille (The Straw Hat)*, **Peter Paul Rubens** (1577-1640). ♦ Room 22

9 *Giovanni Arnolfini and his Wife*, **Jan Van Eyck** (active 1422, died 1441). ♦ Room 24

10 *The Ambassadors*, **Hans Holbein the Younger** (1497-1543). ♦ Room 25

11 *Self Portrait at Age 63*, **Rembrandt** (1606-1669). ♦ Room 27

12 *A Young Woman Standing at a Virginal*, **Jan (Johannes) Vermeer** (1632-1675). ♦ Room 28

13 *The Haywain*, **John Constable** (1776-1837). ♦ Room 35

14 *The Fighting Temeraire*, **J.M.W. Turner** (1775-1851). ♦ Room 35

15 *The Toilet of Venus (The Rokeby Venus)*, **Diego Velásquez** (1599-1660). ♦ Room 41

16 *Bathers, Ansnières*, **Georges Seurat** (1859-1891). ♦ Room 45

On the lower floor of the gallery is an art lover's dream attic, with stacks of minor masterpieces, damaged paintings by great artists, and good fakes. It is fun to try and figure out what's what.

The **National Gallery Mosaics**, by Russian-born artist **Boris Anrep**, on the floors of the vestibules and halfway landing are works of art that usually go unnoticed. In the west vestibule, the theme is *The Labors of Life*, with 12 mosaics completed in 1928, including *Art*, which shows a sculptor at work; *Sacred Love*, which depicts a father, mother, child, and dog; and *Letters*, which shows a child's slate with 2 favorite children's books, *Robinson Crusoe* and *Alice in Wonderland*. In the north vestibule, the theme is *The Modern Virtues*, with

15 mosaics completed in 1952. *Compassion* shows the Russian poet **Anna Akhmatova** saved by an angel from the horrors of war; *Compromise* has the actress **Loretta Young** filling a cup with wine, symbolizing American and British friendship; *Defiance* shows **Winston Churchill** on the white cliffs of Dover, defying an apocalyptic beast in the shape of a swastika; and *Leisure* is **T.S. Eliot** contemplating both the kindly Loch Ness monster and Einstein's formula. In the east vestibule are 11 mosaics completed in 1929 representing *The Pleasures of Life*: a Christmas pudding; a conversation, with 2 girls gossiping; *Mudpie*, with 3 mud pies, a bucket, and a spade; and *Profane Love*, showing a man and 2 girls with a dog. In the halfway landing is *The Awakening of the Muses*, an illustrative archive of London's beau monde in the '30s. It shows the **Hon. Mrs. Bryan Guinness** (one of the Mitford girls and later Lady Diana Mosley) as Polyhymnia, Muse of Sacred Song; **Christabel, Lady Aberconway** as Euterpe, Muse of Music; **Clive Bell** as Bacchus, God of Wine; **Virginia Woolf** as Clio, Muse of History; **Sir Osbert Sitwell** as Apollo, God of Music; and **Greta Garbo** as Melpomene, Muse of Tragedy.

Recent acquisitions include 3 firsts for the gallery—**Købke**'s *Drawbridge to the Citadel*, **Friedrich**'s *Winter Landscape*, and **Davide**'s *Portrait of Jacobus Blaun*, plus new acquisitions of works by **Van Dyck, Poussin**, and **Cuyp**.

Special exhibitions at the National Gallery include the **Artist's Eye**, an annual event in which a well-known artist selects a number of pictures from the gallery and displays them in a setting of his own design, along with a couple of his own works. Artists who have acted as *Eye* include **Anthony Caro, R.B. Kitaj, David Hockney**, and **Francis Bacon**. The **Art in Focus** exhibition provides an in-depth analysis and presentation of a major work, usually a new acquisition. **Art in the Making** is a new exhibition in which different artists explain the technical side of their work. Guided tours leave from the vestibule weekdays at 11:30AM. ♦ Free. M-Sa 10AM-6PM; Su 2-6PM. Trafalgar Sq, WC2. 071/839.3321

Restaurants/Nightlife: Red   Hotels: Blue
Shops/Parks: Green   **Sights/Culture:** Black

Within the National Gallery:

St. James's

National Gallery Restaurant ★★$ Cheerful, cafeteria-style service, with healthy soups and salads, hot meals at lunchtime, wine and cheese, coffee, tarts and cakes, and Indian, Chinese, and herbal teas. ♦ M-Sa 10AM-5PM; Su 2-5PM. 071/839.3321

At long last, the empty space to the left of the **National Gallery** is going to have its much debated **extension**. Considerable controversy has surrounded the extension (expected completion, 1991), especially when gallery trustees decided that they could get the new space free by offering the site to a developer who would incorporate the extension into an office complex. The developer was found, and 79 architects submitted designs, but then **Prince Charles** stepped in. He called the intended design *a carbuncle on the face of Trafalgar Square* and criticized the shameful scheme of getting a building for the nation's art treasures for free. The Prince of Wales' protests resulted in the rejection of the office block extension and ultimately led to the present plan. The **Sainsbury** family, owner of the Sainsbury supermarkets, is making a gift of the building to the nation, and the Philadelphia firm of **Robert Venturi, John Rauch, and Denise Scott Brown** will design it. The new building will house the Early Renaissance, Italian, and Northern European collections, provide space for temporary exhibitions, replace the exisiting National Gallery Shop, and provide 2 additional restaurants. The architects plan to maintain the height-line of the William Wilkens National Gallery and to match its Portland stone.

2 Admiralty Arch (1911, **Sir Aston Webb**) Somehow the inglorious race of traffic around Trafalgar Square doesn't prepare you for this magnificent arch, really a screen with 5 arches: the center arch, which opens its iron gates for ceremonial processions, 2 side arches for traffic, and 2 smaller arches for pedestrians. Its very monumentality is a surprise because it is so un-London. The grand Corinthian structure in Portland stone marks the first part of the royal processional route from Buckingham Palace to St. Paul's Cathedral. Admiralty Arch isn't very old and isn't even Victorian. It is Edwardian, part of **Edward VII**'s tribute to his mother, although the King himself was dead before the memorial was completed. ♦ Trafalgar Sq, WC2

3 The Mall Two double rows of plane trees line this royal processional road, which is London's only planned avenue, sweeping rhetorically to a splendid, monumental climax. Laid out after the Restoration in 1660, the regal stretch from Trafalgar Square to Buckingham Palace was originally an enclosed alleyway for playing *paille maille* (a game similar to croquet) during the days of Charles II. It was transformed into a formal vista of Buckingham Palace by **Aston Webb** in 1910 as part of a memorial to **Queen Victoria**. On Sunday, the Mall is closed to traffic and becomes a promenade.

4 Citadel The curious historical monument has an air of mystery because it is completely covered in climbing ivy. It is actually a bomb shelter that was built in 1940 for members of the Admiralty and was never demolished. Perhaps it is kept (and scrupulously maintained by the Parks Department, which mows the acre of grass lawn on top) as a reminder of better times, when shelters like this could conceivably provide protection from bombs. ♦ The Mall, SW1

5 Carlton House Terrace (1827–32, **John Nash**) These high-gloss creamy-white buildings with their formal facades facing the Mall are the last contribution Nash made to London before his death in 1835. The 1000-foot-long terrace is a stately confection of Doric columns and human-scale arches. The upkeep is considerable, but the clean outline, intercepted by the **Duke of York Steps**, is a splendid contribution to the Mall: an impressive backdrop for royal processions by day, a royal wedding cake when floodlit at night.

Carlton House Terrace replaced **Carlton House**, the palatial home purchased by **Frederick, Prince of Wales** in 1732, subsequently owned by **George III**, then by his son, the **Prince Regent**. The Prince Regent transformed it at staggering expense into what was considered the most beautiful mansion in England, but when he became King George IV he grew bored with his treasure and demolished it in 1829. The columns were saved and recycled into the portico of the National Gallery, and Nash was asked to build Carlton House Terrace. Originally the terrace was to line both sides of the Mall in the style of Regent's Park, providing grand town houses for the aristocracy, but only one side was built.

Englishman—a creature who thinks he is being virtuous when he is only being uncomfortable.

George Bernard Shaw

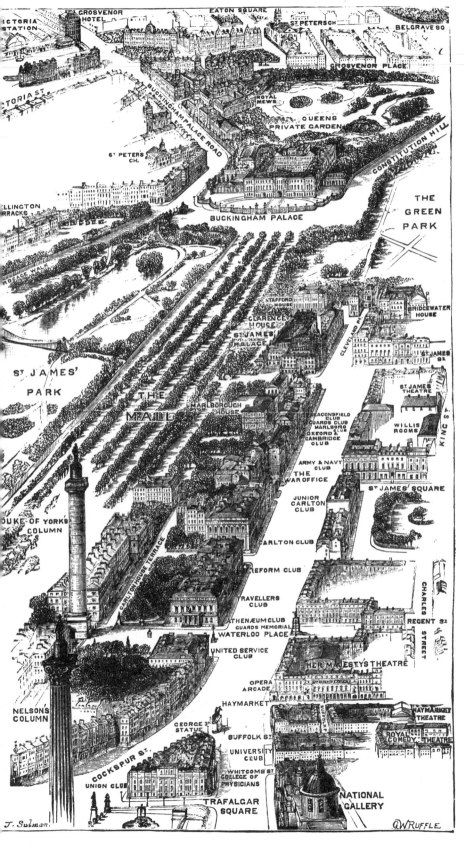

VICTORIA STATION

GROSVENOR HOTEL

EATON SQUARE

ST PETERS CH

BELGRAVE SQ

VICTORIA ST

GROSVENOR PLACE

BUCKINGHAM PALACE ROAD

ROYAL MEWS

QUEENS PRIVATE GARDEN

ST PETERS CH.

CONSTITUTION HILL

BUCKINGHAM PALACE

THE GREEN PARK

WELLINGTON BARRACKS

BIRDCAGE WALK

STAFFORD HOUSE

BRIDGEWATER HOUSE

CLEVELAND PL

CLARENCE HOUSE

ST JAMES PALACE

ST JAMES ST

ST JAMES' PARK

THE MALL

ST JAMES' THEATRE

KING'S ST

MARLBOROUGH HOUSE

BEACONSFIELD CLUB

GUARDS CLUB

MARLBORO CLUB

OXFORD & CAMBRIDGE CLUB

WILLIS ROOMS

ARMY & NAVY CLUB

THE WAR OFFICE

ST JAMES' SQUARE

JUNIOR CARLTON CLUB

DUKE OF YORK'S COLUMN

CARLTON HOUSE TERRACE

CARLTON CLUB

REFORM CLUB

CHARLES STREET

REGENT ST

TRAVELLERS CLUB

ATHENÆUM CLUB

GUARDS MEMORIAL

WATERLOO PLACE

UNITED SERVICE CLUB

HER MAJESTY'S THEATRE

OPERA ARCADE

NELSON'S COLUMN

HAYMARKET

HAYMARKET THEATRE

GEORGE 3RD STATUE

SUFFOLK ST

UNIVERSITY CLUB

ROYAL COMEDY THEATRE

COCKSPUR ST

WHITCOMB ST

COLLEGE OF PHYSICIANS

UNION CLUB

TRAFALGAR SQUARE

NATIONAL GALLERY

J. Sulman

G.W.RUFFLE.

Within Carlton House Terrace:

Mall Galleries Traditional paintings by members of the **Royal Society of Portrait Painters** and the **Federation of British Artists**, as well as occasional degree shows from the various art schools, are exhibited in the galleries. It is a good place to find English landscapes, watercolors, and oils that are Turner-ish, Constable-ish, and affordable—the kind of pictures that look wonderful when you cart them home. ◆ Nominal admission. Daily 10AM-5PM. 071/930.6844

St. James's

Institute of Contemporary Arts (Founded 1947) The **ICA** is a lively arts center, with 3 exhibitions running at any one time in its 3 galleries. Both British and foreign photography, architectural drawings, paintings, and event-art all take place in an atmosphere of industrious punk avant-garde. In the evening, the cinema shows good foreign and cult films and runs excellent film series. Experimental films, videos, and films by new filmmakers are screened in the cinémathèque. There is a children's cinema club with performances at 3pm every weekend. See films in the video library, experimental drama in the theater, or visit the bookshop, which has all the latest art books as well as magazines, postcards, and Virago novels. There is a bar and an adjoining restaurant, which serves healthy, filling food—vegetarian moussakas, wholemeal lasagne, thick mushroom soups, brown bread, and salads—followed by a selection of luscious cheesecakes, apple pies, chocolate cakes, tea, and coffee.

In order to see the exhibitions or even have a cup of coffee, you must take out a day membership, which is a good value if there is a lunchtime event that appeals to you. The events are worth checking into, as they sometimes have well-known writers interviewing other well-known writers and artists interviewing artists with questions from the public. ◆ Galleries: daily noon-8PM. Restaurant and bookshop: daily noon-9PM. Nash House. 071/930.0493, recorded information (box office) 071/930.3647

Sir Isaac Newton

The Royal Society Founded by **King Charles II** in 1660, the Royal Society is one of the most distinguished scientific bodies in the world. In the 17th century, the society was the hub of scientific discovery. **Newton, Halley, Dryden**, and **Pepys** chatted about inventions although Pepys, then president, never understood Newton's *Principia*. Past presidents include **Wren, Davy, Huxley, Thomson, Rutherford**, and **Fleming**. The society moved to Carlton House Terrace in 1966 after nearly 300 years in Burlington House on Piccadilly. Not open to the public.

6 **Duke of York Steps and the Duke of York Monument** (1834; column, **Benjamin Wyatt**; statue, **Sir Richard Westmacott**) The dramatic column in front of the steps of Carlton House Terrace dominates Waterloo Place and seems pretty serious for a man immortalized in a nursery rhyme. The Duke of York was the second son of **George III**. His 7-ton bronze statue was financed by withholding one day's pay from all soldiers. The Duke's impressive distance from it all (137 feet in the sky) was necessitated by his debts—he died owing £2 million, the pink-granite column reputedly the only means of keeping him out of reach of his creditors.

O, the Grand Old Duke of York, he had ten thousand men, He marched them up to the top of the hill and he marched them down again, And when they were up, they were up, and when they were down, they were down, And when they were only halfway up, they were neither up nor down!

Popular during the Duke's lifetime but first published in **Arthur Rackham**'s *Mother Goose* in 1913

7 **Waterloo Place** One of the few and most impressive pieces of town planning in London, Waterloo Place marks the beginning of **John Nash**'s triumphal route from Carlton House Terrace to Regent's Park. Carlton House Terrace frames Waterloo Place, which intersects Pall Mall on its way north into lower Regent Street and Piccadilly Circus.

8 **Statue of Edward VII** (1921, **Sir Bertram Mackennal**) In front of the Duke of York Steps and facing Waterloo Place is *Edward VII*, looking beefy and well. The King gave us the Edwardian age: a secure, elegant world for the rich and aristocratic, where to amuse and to be amused were raisons d'être. Because of the long life of his mother, **Queen Victoria**, he only reigned for 9 of his 69 years. He brought color and pageantry to the monarchy, but also a sense of serious commitment toward such issues as the quality of workers' lives and the treatment of Indians by English officials. Edward was aware that beyond Europe lay his empire, the largest the world had ever known. As king, he created the entente cordiale with France and used all of his considerable diplomatic skill and charm to ease the conflicts between Germany and England, conflicts that were tragically too deep for any monarch to bridge. But it is his voracious appetite for which he is remembered: at his last formal dinner at Buckingham Palace, 5 March 1910, he made his way through 9 dishes, including salmon steak,

grilled chicken, saddle of mutton, and several snipe stuffed with foie gras. His death 2 months later signaled the end of the Edwardian Age, although souvenirs of that elegant way of life can be found tucked away in the small streets behind the statue.

9 Carlton House Gardens During World War II, the Free French occupied No. 4, where de Gaulle's message to his countrymen is recorded in the plaque on the wall. ♦ Just behind Carlton House Terrace, the Mall, SW1

10 Athenaeum Club (1830, **Decimus Burton**) This is the most august of the gentlemen's clubs and one of the most distinguished buildings in London, designed by the man who gave London Constitution Arch and the Screen at the entrance to Hyde Park. The elegant cream-stucco facade is pure architectural dignity. A Wedgwoodlike frieze wraps around the building above the 1st-floor windows, while a large gilded figure of **Pallas Athene**, goddess of wisdom, practical skills, and prudent warfare, graces the porch and accurately sets the requirements for those who enter: bishops, scientists, and the top brains of the Civil Service and Foreign Office.

Inside, the atmosphere is one of intimidating wisdom. **Darwin** broods over the living eminent and distinguished. The **Royal Society Dining Society**, an elite group within the formidably elite **Royal Society**, meets here, and members of that clever and select circle are de facto members of the Athenaeum. If you meet an Englishman who is a member, you can be suitably impressed. Not open to the public. ♦ 107 Waterloo Pl, SW1

11 Institute of Directors (1828, **John Nash**) For 150 years, the building was the home of the **United Service Club**, known as the **Senior**, which was founded in 1815 for the triumphant officers of the Napoleonic wars. The building, the first commissioned by a club, was originally built by John Nash. But what you notice most are the alterations by **Decimus Burton**: the Doric columns and the Corinthian portico. While it is not as unforgettably beautiful as the Athenaeum, opposite, it is handsome. The granite mounting block outside on Waterloo Place was put there by **Wellington** to help short men get on their horses.

Lifestyles, incomes, and Labor governments do not lend themselves to a world of expensive exclusiveness, and in 1974, when most clubs were enjoying a comeback, the Senior collapsed. Now it is a business center for the **Institute of Directors**. By appointment, you can go inside and see the original 19th-century furniture designed for the club, including the 15-foot chandelier presented by **George IV** to commemorate the Battle of Waterloo, and the inimitable masculine tonality of mahogany and leather that is a gentlemen's club. ♦ 116-119 Pall Mall, SW1. 071/839.1233

If one must have a villa in summer to dwell,
Oh, give me the sweet shady side of Pall Mall.

Charles Morris

12 Pall Mall Americans pronounce it *Paul Maul*, like the cigarettes, but the upperclass English who have their clubs here say *Pel Mel*. Named after the ball game imported from France that was played in the Mall, which runs parallel, this is the ancient road from the city to St. James's. Pall Mall is lined with gentlemen's clubs and a few appropriately exclusive shops, but the residential character of Pall Mall has now given way almost entirely to offices. It is a stately boulevard by day, but a windy, monumental wasteland by night. A word of warning: traffic

tears down this broad one-way avenue with terrifying speed, so cross carefully.

13 Crimean War Memorial (1862) *Florence Nightingale* (by **Walker**), one of the few women represented in this masculine part of London, holds her famous lamp. Standing next to her is *Sidney Herbert* (by **John H. Foley**), secretary for war during her days of devotion to her country. *Honour*, on the other side, cast from captured Russian cannons, seems to have her eye on the bear-skinned guardsmen below. ♦ Foot of Lower Regent St, SW1

14 Crafts Council This is an oasis and palace for British craftspeople and a showcase for architectural design. There are 2 galleries displaying crafts, a bookshop, an information desk, and a slide library. If there were more British design like this, the Italians would be given a run for their money. ♦ Tu-Sa 10AM-5PM; Su 2-5PM. 12 Waterloo Pl, SW1. 071/930.4811

Gentlemen's Clubs

At lunchtime, taxis and modest chauffeur-driven Jaguars draw up in front of the palazzi of Pall Mall and the 18th-century houses on St. James's Street. Men wearing pin-striped suits enter buildings with no names that are distinguished by large 1st-floor windows that look onto the street below. These are gentlemen's clubs, an invention and all-pervasive image of the English. **Parliament** is a club, and the **Army** (officers only, of course) is a club. **Whitehall** is a club, and the men's colleges at **Oxford** and **Cambridge** have always had the mystique of a club. St. James's is clubland, a chain of palaces where like minds and like interests can meet—or not meet, as the clubs are as much for the reclusive as the gregarious. They began in the 18th century as coffeehouses and chocolate houses, then became exclusive casinos where whole estates were often gambled away in a night. After World War II, the clubs went into a serious decline, and like so many institutions, seemed on the verge of collapse. A number sold off their palatial premises and split the money among their members. But in the current conservative climate, the clubs are thriving again, with waiting lists of 8 to 10 years for the more popular ones. Women are now allowed in as guests in certain dining rooms (rarely the nicest rooms), although die-hard misogynists claim this is the beginning of the end of a club's reputation. Whether or not major policy decisions are still made over port and Stilton is hard to say, but when the pinstripes emerge an hour and a half later it certainly looks as though an important vote has been taken.

15 Travellers' Club (1832, **Charles Barry**) The Travellers was founded in 1819 by the **Duke of Wellington**, whose portraits loom

St. James's

throughout the club. One of the requirements for membership is to have traveled at least 500 miles from London, although the candidates' book shows that the present membership has gone somewhat farther afield. The special handrail on the staircase was put there to assist **Napoleon**'s foreign minister, the lame **Talleyrande**, up the stairs. The plain-stucco Neoclassical design shows the architect Charles Barry (Trafalgar Square and the Houses of Parliament) doing what he loved best. ◆ 106 Pall Mall, SW1

15 Reform Club (1839, **Charles Barry**) Members must subscribe to the *Reform Bill* of 1832 in order to be accepted into this absolutely stunning club. It looks like a film set, and a few films have been made here, but so great is the discretion or indifference that no one who belongs knows just which films. The design is Classicism Without Bounds: a huge indoor courtyard with marble pillars and balconies, a vast library with leather chairs, library tables, and real fires in the enormous fireplaces—and not a sound. The kitchen is the size of a ballroom and has a good reputation. This is the club of economists, members of the Treasury, and increasingly, writers and television executives. Reform does not seem a major concern here. It is one of the few London clubs with women members. Not open to the public. ◆ 104 Pall Mall, SW1

16 Royal Automobile Club (1911, **Mewès and Davis, with E. Keynes**) Here is a club that takes members more readily than most. The opulent Edwardian building with rooms in grand Louis XVI style was designed by the Frenchmen whose earlier contribution to London was the Ritz. But more enticing are the squash courts, Turkish baths, solarium, and the marble swimming pool, which is the most beautiful in London, with Doric columns covered in fish-scale mosaics. **George Bernard Shaw** swam in it in the past and **J.P. Donleavy** swims in it today after games of *de Alfonse* when he is in London. Many of the 12,000 members live abroad and use this as their London address. Unlike other clubs, no one seems to know anyone else, which probably explains why **Guy Burgess** and **Maclean** met here just before defecting to Russia in the '50s. There are 3 dining rooms, a bar, and bedrooms, which are modest, comfortable,

and considerably cheaper than a hotel. In spite of its democratic outlook, the only women you see are wives and daughters of members. ◆ 89 Pall Mall, SW1. 071/930.2345

17 St. James's Square The fine 17th-century square was laid out in the 1660s by **Henry Jermyn**, first Earl of St. Albans and friend of the widow of Charles I, Henrietta Maria, and her son Charles II. The King gave the land to the Earl in gratitude for his faithful devotion while the King was in exile in France. The square was designed with mansions on all sides for the nobility who wanted or needed to be near the palace. **Sir Christopher Wren**, who designed the church for this noble suburb (St. James's, Piccadilly), probably had a say in the elegant and dignified shape of the square.

The gardens in the square's center are open to the public, which is unusual in leafy, residential London squares where residents have keys to carefully locked gates. The handsome bronze statue of **William III** on horseback (1808, **John Bacon the Younger**) includes the molehill on which the horse stumbled, throwing the King and causing his death. During World War I, a rustic building resembling a country inn was erected in the center of the square for American officers. Called the **Washington Inn**, it stood until 1921. At No. 32, in the southeast corner, the allied commanders under **General Eisenhower** launched the invasions of North Africa (1942) and northwest Europe (1944). On the north side of the square at No.10 is **Chatham House**, the residence of 3 prime ministers: the **Earl of Chatham** (1759–61), the **Earl of Derby** (1837–54), and **W.E. Gladstone** (1890). At No. 16, **Wellington**'s dispatch announcing his victory at Waterloo was delivered by the bloodstained **Major Percy** to the **Prince Regent**, who was dining with his foreign secretary, **Lord Castlereagh**. Included with the dispatch were the captured French eagle standards, which can be seen in the Wellington Museum at Hyde Park Corner.

St. James's Square became known worldwide overnight when the **Libyan People's Bureau** at No. 5 was besieged on 17 April 1984. Gunmen within the building fired on demonstrators outside, killing young police officer **Yvonne Fletcher**. Because diplomatic immunity made it impossible for the police to enter the building, the siege went on for 10 days, and the suspects were deported instead of arrested. Fresh flowers are placed on a memorial in the square opposite No. 5 year-round in honor of Yvonne Fletcher. The building is no longer empty but filled with opulent furniture, and yet, somewhat mysteriously, no name plate appears on the door.

To be an Englishman is to belong to the most exclusive class there is.

Ogden Nash

Restaurants/Nightlife: Red   Hotels: Blue
Shops/Parks: Green   **Sights/Culture:** Black

18 London Library (c. 1760s, **James Stuart**) *It is not typically English. It is typically civilized*, wrote **E.M. Forster** in an essay devoted to this private subscription library, founded in 1841 by **Thomas Carlyle**. Inside, the London Library looks like a down-at-heel club, with worn leather chairs in the reading room, Victorian portraits on the walls, and high windows looking over the square. Past members include **Lord Tennyson, Wiliam Ewart Gladstone, Henry James, Thomas Hardy, H.G. Wells, E.M. Forster, Aldous Huxley, Virginia Woolf**, and **Edith Sitwell**. Present members are historians, biographers, critics, novelists, philosophers, playwrights, and scriptwriters.

Unlike clubs in the neighboring precincts, the London Library doesn't suffer from undaunted misogyny, although the equal numbers of men and women you're likely to see in the reading room are fairly recent, and the carpet on the stairs stops one flight before the ladies' loo. Annual membership is inexpensive, life membership isn't—there are special, shorter memberships available for visiting academics, writers, and literary Anglophiles. ♦ 14 St. James's Sq, SW1. 071/930.8873

19 Colombina ★★$ A refreshingly simple, delicious, and inexpensive trattoria with a Neapolitan chef. The deep-fried mozzarella in breadcrumbs served with a sauce is a favorite, along with the excellent fish dishes and grills. It is popular with writers doing all-day stints in the London Library. ♦ M-Sa noon-3PM, 6-11PM. 4-6 Duke of York St, SW1. 071/930.8279

20 Wheelers in Appletree Yard ★★$$ It is easy to miss this tiny restaurant tucked in between St. James's Square and Duke of York Street. It is the smallest member of a 125-year-old chain of restaurants. The menu offers No. 1 oysters and its famous Colchester specials, available around November. Try the grilled Dover sole or poached Scottish salmon, washed down with the house white wine. They have never figured out vegetables. ♦ M-Sa 12:15-2:30PM, 6:15-10:45PM. Duke of York St, SW1. 071/930.2460

21 Red Lion Pub ★★★$ A Victorian jewel with mahogany paneling and beautiful old mirrors, each engraved with a different British flower. Come early for the delicious sandwiches and beers, or better still visit the excellent restaurant. Later it becomes crowded and smoky. ♦ M-Sa 11AM-11PM. 2 Duke of York St, SW1. 071/930.2030

22 Jermyn Street Named after the Earl of St. Albans, **Henry Jermyn**, the narrow street runs parallel to Piccadilly and connects the Haymarket with St. James's Street. It is only a few blocks long and the architecture isn't remarkable (the west end of Jermyn was badly damaged during the October 1940 raids, when all but one of the buildings between Duke Street and Bury Street were destroyed). But Jermyn is the essence of St. James's, an exclusive shopping club for traditional well-to-do Englishmen who dress like the Duke of Edinburgh and Prince Charles. The shops rely on quality and specialized knowledge. Shopping here—browsing and buying—is educational and sensual, expensive and worth it.

23 Simpson's The main entrance of the department store is on Piccadilly, but there are 2 entrances on Jermyn, and the steps of the store offer a good view of this once-and-now neo-Georgian street. (See page 40 for a complete description.) ♦ M, W, F-Sa 9AM-

6PM; Tu 9:30AM-6PM; Th 9AM-7PM. Main entrance 203 Piccadilly, W1. 071/734.2002

24 Hawes and Curtis Check out this shiny green-and-white shop if you are looking for a bargain on Jermyn Street (almost a contradiction in terms); there is usually a selection of items on sale, including shirts from **Turnbull & Asser**, which owns this shop. Be careful if you want to order anything special; they won't be hurried. ♦ M-F 9AM-5:30PM; Sa 9AM-1PM. Jermyn St, SW1. 071/734.1020

BATES *the* HATTER

24 Bates The tiny gentlemen's hat shop looks undaunted by the 20th century, and time seems to be on its side. Hats are reappearing, with felt low-crown fedoras selling more briskly than in the 1940s. You will pay less here than at the famous **Lock's** on St. James's Street. Be sure to admire **Binks**, the huge tabby cat who lived here between 1921 and 1926. He was so beloved that a taxidermist was enlisted after his death.... ♦ M-F 9AM-5:30PM; Sa 9:30AM-1PM, 2-4PM. 21A Jermyn St, SW1. 071/734.2722

24 Ivan's and Trumper's Ivan's, barbers to very distinguished heads (with Royal Warrants from Edward VII, George V, and George VI), was taken over by Trumper's, which still has a shop in Mayfair. Trumper's hairbrushes, shaving brushes, soaps, hair tonics, and aftershaves are irresistible. Their Ajaccio Violet smells like violets, comes in old-fashioned bottles, and is appreciated by women as well as men. ♦ M-F 9AM-6PM; Sa 9AM-5PM. 20 Jermyn St, SW1. 071/734.1370

The well-bred Englishman is about as agreeable a fellow as you can find anywhere—especially, as I have noted, if he is an Irishman or a Scotchman.

Finley Peter Dunne, *Mr. Dooley Remembers*

Jermyn Street Shopping Map

REGENT STREET

Barclays Bank	**Plaza Cinema**
men's clothing **Toby Frogg**	
hairdresser and perfumer **Trumper**	**Rowley's** English restaurant
hatters **Bates**	**Van Heusen** men's shirts
shirtmakers **Hawes & Curtis**	**Church's** men's shoes

EAGLE PLACE — **BABMAES STREET**

National Westminster Bank	**Astleys** Briar pipes
Simpsons	**T.M. Lewin** women's clothing
	N. Peal men's clothing
	GoldPfeil leather luggage
	T.M. Lewin shirtmakers
	Cesar woman's shoes
	Baresi men's clothing
	Oggetti designer accessories
CHURCH PLACE	**Kensington Carpets**
St. James 's Church	

JERMYN STREET

DUKE OF YORK STREET

Harvie & Hudson shirtmakers

Russell & Bromley men's shoes

Robin Symes antiquities

Paxton & Whitfield cheesemongers

Edwin R. Cooper chemist

shirtmakers **Hilditch & Key**　　**Ormond Restaurant**

M. Ekstein Ltd antiques

Floris perfumers

PRINCESS ARCADE

antiques and art **Mayorcas**　　**James Bodenhan** gifts

fine gifts **Von Posch**　　**Hilditch & Key** shirtmakers
　　Trevelyan shirtmakers
toiletries **Czech & Speake**　　**Jules Piano Bar & Restaurant**
　　Foster & Son bootmakers
nightclub **Tramp**　　**S. Franses** antique textiles
　　Cavendish Hotel
restaurant **Fortnum & Mason**　　**S. Franses** antique tapestry gallery

DUKE STREET

clothing/tobacco **Dunhill**　　**Arthur Davidson** European art

Harvie & Hudson shirtmakers

PICCADILLY ARCADE　　**Trevor Philip** scientific antiques

men's clothing **New & Lingwood**　　**Ultimo** men's clothing

restaurant **Wiltons**　　**Waterman** fine art

Victor Franses Gallery　　**Taylor of Old Bond St** hairdressers

old master paintings **Heim**　　**Hilditch & Key** shirtmakers

JERMYN STREET

men's clothing **Vincci**　　**BURY STREET**

　　Turnbull & Asser hosiers and glovers
Mokaris Espresso Bar　　**Vincci** men's clothing
　　R.E. Tricker shoes
Italian restaurant **Franco's**　　**Vincci** women's clothing

National Westminster Bank　　**Davidoff** tobacco

ST. JAMES'S STREET

25 Rowley's ★★$$ This small and special steak house serves only charcoal-grilled steaks with butter. The set lunch and dinner menu is reasonably priced and very good. ♦ Daily noon-3PM, 6-11:30PM. 113 Jermyn St, SW1. 071/930.2707

26 Oggetti This designer gift store is expensive and fashionable and quite unlike anything else in the street. Its art ranges from **Bauhaus** to plain weird and is worth a look if you like the supramodern. ♦ M-Sa 9:30AM-5:30PM. 100 Jermyn St, SW1. 071/930 4694

26 Harvie and Hudson The fabrics used by these third-generation shirtmakers are of the finest quality cotton poplin, designed, colored, and woven just for them. The Windsor collars are slightly wider spread and the prices for the tweed jackets and overcoats are extremely reasonable. ♦ M-Sa 9AM-5:30PM. Nos. 77, 96, 97 Jermyn St, SW1. 071/930.3949

26 Paxton and Whitfield Mr. Paxton became the partner of Mr. Whitfield 150 years ago. Their shop is in a house built in 1674, and at any one time you can find 300 cheeses from 11 countries in it. English cheeses are finally being acknowledged for the outstanding cheeses they are, and for being ideal partners with wine. When you taste the golden cheddars, the peach- and ivory-colored Cheshires, the russet Leicesters, the marbled green Sage Derby and the blue-veined Stilton, and England's first soft cheese, Lymeswold, you will never think about French cheeses in quite the same way. The shop also has fabulous game pies, hams, pâtés, and every kind of cheese biscuit and bread. This is a perfect place to put together a picnic to take to St. James's Park. Stop at one of the wine merchants nearby to find the perfect young claret to go with it. Salespeople here are very nice about giving tastes of the cheeses. ♦ M-F 9AM-6PM; Sa 9AM-4PM. 93 Jermyn St, SW1. 071/930.0250

26 Floris Since 1730, the Floris family has been creating delicious scents, bath oils, and soaps from the flowers of the English garden. Jasmine, rose, gardenia, lily of the valley, and one of the newest, wild hyacinth, all smell fresh and clean and as close to the real thing as you can imagine. **Jacqueline Onassis** favors the sandalwood fragrance, and **Nancy Reagan** started ordering the bath soaps after visiting Buckingham Palace. You will also find large natural sponges, bone and ivory combs, fine English brushes, antique objects for *la toilette*, and a line of scents for men. The perfumer is the manufacturer of toilet preparations to **His Royal Highness the Prince of**

Wales, who has given the shop the seal of excellence called the Royal Warrant. ♦ M-F 9:30AM-5:30PM; Sa 9:30AM-4PM. 89 Jermyn St, SW1. 071/930.2885

27 Hilditch and Key Made-to-measure shirts for men and women, including royals and politicians. Good gracious, they are far too discreet to say whom. The shirts are all cut by hand—the bodies with shears, the collars with a knife. The collars, always considered the most important part of a shirt, are turned by hand and have removable stiffeners that

you must remove for laundering. The buttons are real shells, never synthethic. Besides the fine English cotton poplins, H&K carries a good selection of Viyella, a soft, warm half-cotton-half-wool mixture. The women's shirts come in many of the same colors and fabrics as the men's, but with an additional choice of bright, clear colors and the added bonus of being designed by **Bruce Oldfield**. The nightshirts (for men and women) and pajamas are quite wonderful. ♦ M-W, F 9:30AM-6PM; Th 9:30AM-7PM; Sa 9:30AM-5PM. Nos. 87, 73, 37 Jermyn St, SW1. 071/734.4707

28 Fortnum & Mason The rear (Jermyn St) entrance of the store known fondly as the *Queen's Grocer* is located on Jermyn Street. It is the best place in St. James's for breakfast, and one of the best places in London for things epicurean. The quickest route to the ice-cream concoctions at the **Fountain** is also from this side of the store. (See page 37 for a complete description.) ♦ M-F 9AM-5:30PM; Sa 9AM-1PM. 181 Piccadilly, W1. 071/734.8040

29 Dunhill It was on this very site in 1907 that **Alfred Dunhill** opened his small tobacconist shop. The philosophy that made his lighters, watches, fountain pens, and pipes famous throughout the wealthy world—*It must be useful, it must work dependably, it must be beautiful, it must last, it must be the best of its kind*—is the motto of a new generation of ambitious consumers. Dunhill has expanded to meet their every need, having dropped only the *It must be useful* as a strict requirement. ♦ M-F 9:30AM-6PM; Sa 9:30AM-5:30PM. 30 Duke St, SW1. 071/499.9566

Nearly all people in England are of the superior sort, superiority being an English ailment.

D.H. Lawrence, *The Last Laugh*

Restaurants/Nightlife: Red   Hotels: Blue
Shops/Parks: Green   **Sights/Culture:** Black

30 Green's Champagne and Oyster Bar

★★$$$ Green's is a gentlemen's club that is open to the public and filled with **Berter Wooster** lookalikes, although the waiters aren't as deferential as Jeeves. It has a bar with booths for the secretive and an open restaurant for rubbernecking. The food, though very English, is better than you will find in any club. By all means, have champagne, then choose from a mountain of lobsters, crabs, oysters, and salmon, all fresh, simply prepared, and outstanding. Or try the excellent game (when in season) because you can get

St. James's

grouse, pheasant, wild duck, and partridge, hung properly and roasted perfectly. The puddings are all English favorites—treacle tart, gooseberry fool. Crowded at lunchtime, less so at night. ♦ M-F noon-3PM, 5:30-11PM. 36 Duke St, SW1. 071/930.4566

31 Wilton's ★★★$$$ During **Johnny Apple**'s long reign as *The New York Times* bureau chief in London, he wrote with care and affection about food and wine, nourishing along the concept of good English cuisine as surely as the English scene nourished him. One of his favorites was Wilton's. It changed locations during his stay, but took its glass screens, polished mahogany, and clublike atmosphere with it, so you would never know you aren't still on Bury Street. The fish is innocently swimming in sea or stream only hours before it is placed in front of you. The smoked salmon, oysters, and game are excellent. The ingredients are prime, English, and wisely and simply prepared. In fact, it is considerably better than during its Bury Street days. ♦ M-F 12:30-2:30PM, 6:30-10:15PM; Sa 6:30-10:15PM. 55 Jermyn St, SW1. 071/629.9955

32 Turnbull & Asser One of our favorite English shopping experiences. The name is familiar to Americans who wear English custom-made shirts, especially now that there is a Turnbull & Asser club in New York, as well as appointment weeks in department stores throughout the country. But it isn't the same as coming into the solemnity of this dark wood-paneled shop where you can't be certain if the man next to you is a duke or the salesman. The store's made-to-measure service takes 6 weeks, with a minimum of 6 shirts after you approve the first. There is a lot to think about when you embark on made-to-measure shirts: the shape of the collar, the length of the points, pockets, monograms, the shape and color of buttons, a 2- or 3-button cuff. You must also be patient. First you are measured and a sample shirt is made, which Turnbull will send to you. Then you must make a set of fastidious and obsessive notes and return the shirt. This routine can go on for quite some time before you get a shirt that is perfect, and **Mr. Williams**, the managing director, cheerfully acknowledges that *Turnbull & Asser shirts know their own way*

across the Atlantic. If you can't be bothered, choose from the large selection of ready-mades. The store's clients are not all male and include **Candice Bergen** and **Jacqueline Bisset**. Turnbull & Asser reflects Jermyn Street's **Beau Brummel** legacy rather more faithfully than the other shirtmakers on the street, with daring colors and stripes that the Regency dandy would have found impossible to resist. It is worth noting that the fine craftsmanship, simple, elegant lines, and exquisite colors appealed to Beau Brummel, who emptied his pockets on many a stroll down the street and died penniless and in impoverished exile in France. ♦ M-F 9AM-5:30PM; Sa 9AM-4:30PM. Nos. 70, 71, 72 Jermyn St, SW1. 071/930.0502

32 James Drew The firm hands that create luxurious men's wear at Turnbull & Asser do the same for the ladies next door under the name James Drew. The styles are usually flirtatious translations of men's wear, served up in lavish silk blouses, dresses, pajamas, and skirts, as well as heavy crepe de Chines and jacquards in rich Gainsborough colors. ♦ M-F 9AM-5:30PM; Sa 9AM-4:30PM. 69 Jermyn St, SW1. 071/839 5133

33 St. James's Street The elegant street connecting Pall Mall with Piccadilly serves as compass for this royal and aristocratic quartier. At the bottom of the street is **Henry VIII**'s gatehouse to St. James's Palace, with a sentry on duty. Pall Mall enters the street just in front of the palace, continuing its tradition of gentlemen's clubs, although the 18th-century clubs here are considered more social and arrogant than the clubs a minute away on Pall Mall. There are no signs to indicate which club is which—if you are a member, you know, and if you aren't, you don't need to know. If you are meeting someone for lunch at his club, you could cross the street several times before getting it right.

33 White's (1788, **James Wyatt**) No. 37 St. James's Street is London's oldest, most famous, and still most fashionable club. This is where the late **Evelyn Waugh** sought *refuge from the hounds of modernity*, and where **Prince Charles** had his stag party the night before he married **Princess Diana**. If you are sufficiently well-connected to be proposed and accepted for membership, there is a waiting list of 8 years. ♦ 37 St. James's St, SW1

You ask, what was that song they sang at the opening—that's God Save The King. *You thought it was* Sweet Land of Liberty? *So it is. You Yankees took it from us and put new words to it. As a matter of fact we took it from the Ancient Britons—they had it,* England-may-go-to-hell—*and the English liked it so much they took it over and made it* God Save the King.

Stephen Leacock
Welcome to a Visiting American

Restaurants/Nightlife: Red	Hotels: Blue
Shops/Parks: Green	**Sights/Culture:** Black

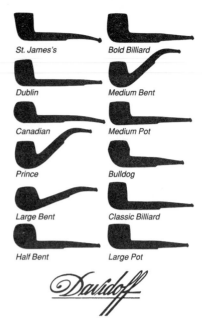

St. James's   Bold Billiard

Dublin   Medium Bent

Canadian   Medium Pot

Prince   Bulldog

Large Bent   Classic Billiard

Half Bent   Large Pot

Davidoff

34 Davidoff Using 3 recipes for flavor, **Zino Davidoff** has created a cigar and pipe smoker's heaven, with the finest Havana cigars, presumably even more plentiful now that Castro has given them up personally. The shop has an ineffable masculine pull—the handmade wooden humidors, the matchboxes, the cigar cases in leather and crocodile, the cigar holders. The sweet, leathery smell of unsmoked cigars evokes a sense of order, prosperity, and calm masculinity, which for the nonsmoker, vanishes with the first puff of smoke. But this is a new era. ♦ M-F 9AM-5:45PM; Sa 9:30AM-5.45PM. 35 St. James's St, SW1. 071/930.3079

35 Boodle's (1775, **John Crunden**) One of the best examples of club design with the central arched Venetian window in the upper room of the club. Two Rolls-Royces ferry the members back and forth from their offices at lunch, a recent development that some members believe bodes badly for the future. Until recently, Boodle's was the club for fashionable men about town and the kitchen was reputedly the best in clubland. ♦ 28 St. James's St, SW1

35 Economist Building (1964, **Alison & Peter Smithson**) The Economist complex is laughingly considered one of the few examples of successful modern architecture in London. The architects designed a group of buildings that are compatible with the 18th-century scale of St. James's Street, but maintain their 20th-century integrity. The complex provides a public open space, offices for *The Economist* magazine, a bank, and apartments. In the forecourt are **Henry Moore**'s *Reclining Figure* (1969) and **Michael Sandle**'s *Der Trommler* (1985). ♦ 25 St. James's St, SW1

36 Longmire This delectable treasure trove is the only jewelry store in St. James's and much patronized by royalty and the international upper crust. Alongside tempting displays of 19th- and 20th-century jewelry is representational and animal jewelry. **Mr. Longmire** keeps a book for clients searching for more precious creatures to add to their collections. His regal displays shimmer with the stones of each month—September is for sapphires. Heraldic work is engraved on signet rings and on one of the largest collections of cufflinks in the world, which can even be custom-enameled to clients' original designs. ♦ M-F 9:30AM-5PM or by appt. 12 Bury St, SW1. 071/930.8720

St. James's

37 Brooks' (1778, **Henry Holland**) The inveterate gambler **Charles James Fox** was a famous member of this club, founded in 1762, and **Beau Brummel** won £20,000 in one night when this was a great gambling club for Whig aristocrats. Now its members are far less reckless country gentlemen who wouldn't consider gambling away their land. ♦ 61 St. James's St, SW1

38 St. James's Club $$$$ Here is a club unlike any other in the neighborhood and it's one of our favorite places to stay. You can stay once during the off-season (August, and November through April) before applying for membership. When Hollywood comes to London—**Steven Spielberg, Cher, Natassja Kinski, Angelica Houston, Chevy Chase, Liza Minelli**, and **Dudley Moore**—it stays here. The inside has tented ceilings, Jacuzzis (well, 2 Jacuzzis), lots of mirrored walls to augment the rather small size of the rooms, Art Deco furnishings, towels as thick as sable pelts, and a piano bar that feels straight out of *Casablanca*, with mirrors. If luxury without the language barrier has a certain appeal, St. James's is the club for you. American Express Centurion Club members have reciprocal privileges here. Affiliated with the St. James's Clubs in Los Angeles, Antigua, and Paris. ♦ 7 Park Pl, SW1. 071/629.7688

39 St. James's Sandwich Company ★★★$ Blue Ball Yard was built in 1742 as stables for the mansions on St. James's Square. Now it is the home of this sandwich shop, where you can stop for delicious and uncomplicated homemade picnic meals on your way to St. James's Park. All the sandwiches are served in granary baps, which are flat, brown rolls made with whole grains. Try the smoked salmon and cream cheese, smoked-salmon pâté, avocado and prawns, turkey and blue Brie, smoked mackerel pâté with tuna, or homemade quiches, salads, and cakes. ♦ M-F 7:30AM-2:45PM. 23 Blue Ball Yard, St. James's, SW1. 071/499.1516

40 Stafford Hotel $$$ Located in a quiet cul-de-sac, this hotel is virtually a club for its loyal guests—the **Marquess of Bath** stays here when he is in London, not at his clubs. The feeling that this is an English hotel run for the English is a relief after the anonymous, international luxury hotels. The 55 rooms and 7 suites are large and comfortable and have been redecorated recently. The Stafford dining room has a wine list that resembles that of a fine club. (Two hundred labels are housed in the cellars that once belonged to St. James's Palace.) It serves a truly delectable lunch to English businesspeople who lunch frequently and know their palates won't be jaded here. Ah, but tea at the Stafford ranks high on the list of London's best teas, served in a large room filled with antiques, silver teapots, Wedgwood china, and real fires in the fireplaces at

St. James's

each end of the room. It's the next best thing to staying in the hotel. ◆ 16-18 St. James's Place, SW1. 071/493.0111; fax 071/493.7121

41 Spencer House (1752–54, **John Vardy**) The entrance to this beautiful Palladian mansion faces St. James's Place, with its finest facade facing Green Park. The house was built for the **Earl of Spencer**, ancestor of **Princess Diana**, and has stayed in the family, although it is no longer used as their town residence. The interior of the house has been well preserved, including a painted room by **James Stuart**, and the exterior has changed little since Vardy built it. ◆ 28 St. James's Place, SW1

41 Dukes Hotel $$$ This hotel in a gaslit courtyard behind St. James's Place is a kind of miniature palace, with 53 rooms, 14 suites, an elevator that descends with the stateliness of a dowager duchess, and a loyal clientele that relishes the location, tucked away in the heart of St. James's, and the extreme courtesy of the staff. It seems churlish to mention that late at night you can hear taxis turning around in the cul-de-sac courtyard, but if noise is your problem, simply ask for a room in the back. The dining room is small and produces excellent English food. Try the bread-and-butter pudding. Tea is served until 5PM. The clublike atmosphere is fitting to the neighborhood. ◆ 35 St. James's Place, SW1. 071/491.4840; fax 071/493.1264

42 The Carlton (1827, **Thomas Hopper**) This club of Conservative politicians is for men only, but, of course, **Margaret Thatcher** is allowed in, and a larger-than-life portrait of her hangs at the top of the double staircase inside. The large drawing room overlooking St. James's Street is filled with ambitious young men dressed like Sir Anthony Eden. ◆ 69 St. James's St, SW1

Popular consensus maintains that the **Carlton Club** *thinks* it runs the country, **Boodle's** runs the country, and **White's** owns the country.

It is the proud perpetual boast of an Englishman that he never brags.

D.B. Wyndham Lewis

Restaurants/Nightlife: Red
Shops/Parks: Green

Hotels: Blue
Sights/Culture: Black

42 Suntory ★★$$$$ The restaurant is one of 10 in the world owned by the **Suntory Japanese Whiskey Company**, and the standards are as high as the prices (well, almost). In the *teppan yaki* room, you can watch the chefs dissect pieces of beef and seafood with mesmerizing skill. Everything gleams and sizzles and startles with freshness, but unfortunately, there is no sushi bar. Specialities are *shabu shabu* and sukiyaki. Excellent service. ◆ M-Sa noon-2:30PM, 7-10:00PM. 72-73 St. James's St, SW1. 071/409.0201

43 King Street King Street connects St. James's Square via St. James's Street. Once its greatest claim to fame was the St. James's Theatre, which premiered **Oscar Wilde**'s *Lady Windermere's Fan* and *The Importance of Being Earnest*, **Pinero**'s *The Second Mrs. Tanqueray*, and later, **Terence Rattigan**'s *Separate Tables*. Unfortunately, the theater was demolished, even though **Vivien Leigh** interrupted a Parliamentary session in an attempt to save it. A few old residents do remain.

44 Christie, Manson and Woods Ltd. Better known simply as Christie's, one of the world's leading auction houses. In the art and antiques trade, Sotheby's, the largest auction house, is said to be run by businessmen trying to be gentlemen, while Christie's is run by gentlemen trying to be businessmen. You can safely count on both houses to employ gentlemen and businessmen and knowledgeable experts, too. Founded in 1766, Christie's has occupied this address on King Street since 1823, except for a period during and after the war when the building was being repaired from damage it suffered during the Blitz. (There is a charming **Thomas Rowlandson** print of **Christie's Auction Room**, c.1808, from the series *A Microcosm of London* by **Rowlandson** and **Auguste Pugin**.) If you come here in the morning when the sales are generally held, you may see millionaires in battle over a painting by **van Gogh** or **Picasso**, an emerald necklace, or a famous pop star's worldly goods. If it is a very important sale of paintings, representatives from the world's museums will be here, enigmatic and determined, the atmosphere a cross between a Broadway opening and an operating theater, with the auctioneer both leading actor and surgeon. Have a look in the various rooms and galleries around the auction room where items to be sold are on view. It is like being in an informal museum, with the added bonus that if you lose your head over the 17th-century carpet or the sentimental Victorian watercolor of the girl and the rabbit, you can attend the sale and bid on it. Art and antiques aren't the only items to come under the hammer: since 1766, Christie's has been selling wine at auction. It also sells vintage and collector's motor cars. The auction houses now have premises that specialize in non-masterpieces, such as ordinary paintings, furniture, and carpets, all of which can be great fun. ◆ M-F 9AM-4:45PM. 8 King St, SW1. 071/839.9060. Also at: 85 Brompton Rd, SW7, South Kensington. 071/581.7611

The Antique Trade
by **Lennox Money**
President, Lennox Money Antiques Ltd.

The 3 principle auction rooms in London are within easy walking distance of each other, with **Phillips** at the Oxford Street end of Bond Street, **Sotheby's** midway down Bond, and **Christie's** across Piccadilly on King Street near St. James's Palace.

All the salesrooms compete with each other through a network of local agents and roadshows to attract a constant flow of antiques. The auction houses divide the goods into specialty sales groups, cooperating with each other to ensure that similar items are on sale at all the houses during the same period to attract overseas buyers. Catalogs are available weeks in advance and monthly lists of sale dates are available on request.

Most of the goods on sale are bought by antique dealers, unlike in New York, where private buyers predominate. The salesrooms try to attract their private buyers through lush cataloging in order to bid up the dealers. But dealers seldom look at the catalogs, preferring to use their own judgment. Sotheby's and Phillips charge a 10-percent premium plus VAT on the premium on top of the price at which an object is knocked down in the sale, while Christie's charges 8 percent.

Another house that attracts a fashionable crowd of pedestrian shoppers is **Bonham's** on Montpelier Street, within 200 yards of Harrods. The themes of the sales usually coincide with the current social events, such as Cruft's Dog Week, Valentine's Day, the Oxford and Cambridge Boat Race, Derby Day, and the Chelsea Flower Show.

Bonham's also owns the **Lots Road Galleries Auction Room**, a favorite with young people, more because of the personality of the auctioneer and the hours (sales start after work, at 6:30PM on Monday evening) than the offerings.

Christie's, Phillips, and Bonham's have secondary salesrooms in London, while Sotheby's has moved one that specializes in fine art to Billingshurst in Sussex, a 90-minute drive from London. Collector's items and a wide variety of less important furniture and pictures are offered in the secondary rooms. They are useful for those trying to furnish their homes or for those with a specialist's interest trying to collect on a budget.

Christie's secondary salesroom at 85 Old Brompton Road has a particularly wide range of specialist sales. Phillips has a general sale at the Salem Road room in Bayswater every Thursday, and Bonham's room on Lots Road has one on Tuesday. Even the wives of Sotheby's directors can be found here looking for furniture for their country cottages. Because the salesroom experts have not sorted the goods into categories, those with eclectic tastes may find

them more fun than the auctions in the West End. They are full of surprises, often depending on the taste of those who have just died. Catalogs are available only a few days before the sales. Christie's doesn't charge a buyer's premium, but Phillips and Bonham's still charge 10 percent. Salesroom goods are seldom in fit condition, and with the difficulty of finding restorers, you may want to buy from dealers who offer goods in presentable order, but those who over-slick things up should be avoided.

St. James's

44 Spink and Son These art dealers are reputed to be the largest in the world, specializing in coins, medals, Oriental and English art, fine silver and jewelry. The rooms have the atmosphere of a museum, but many of the treasures are affordable. The exhibitions by living English artists in the gallery are worth a look. ◆ M-F 9:30AM-5:30PM. 7 King St, SW1. 071/930.7888

45 Lobb's Four generations of Lobbs have shod the rich and famous since **John Lobb** walked from Cornwall to London to set himself up as a shoemaker. The list of distinguished feet is considerable: the royal feet of **Queen Victoria**, **Mountbatten**, **King George VI**, and of course, **Her Majesty the Queen**, the **Duke of Edinburgh**, and the **Prince of Wales**; the less royal feet of **Cecil Beaton**, **Winston Churchill**, **Lawrence**, **Lord Olivier**, **Groucho Marx**, **Frank Sinatra**, **Cole Porter**, and **Katherine Hepburn**; together with the less loyal feet of spy **Guy Burgess**. In the basement of the shop, the wooden lasts of customers are kept until they die—and some for long after that. The method of making the shoes is almost the same as in Queen Victoria's day. They draw an outline of your foot in their book, look at it from every angle in search of fallen arches or other flaws, and then, on a long slip of paper folded in the middle, take a series of measurements, which are marked by snips in the paper. The drawing is converted into wooden models of your feet, around which the leather is molded. After a few days of walking the streets of London, the hefty price tag may seem reasonable for shoes that fit perfectly. ◆ M-F 9AM-5:30PM; Sa 9AM-1PM. 9 St. James's St, SW1. 071/930.3664

45 Lock & Co. The house of Lock has been covering the heads of the great and the good since 1700, and moved to this building in 1764. **Lord Nelson**'s cocked hats were made here, and the **Duke of Wellington, Beau Brummel**, and all the American ambassadors to the Court of St. James's also covered their heads with hats from Lock & Co. The first bowler hat was made here in 1850 for the gameskeepers of a **Mr. William Coke**, and the shop still refers to the style as a *Coke*. There are about 16,000 hats in stock, but you can have one made-to-measure with the French *conformateur* that has been used to determine head measurements for 150 years. In England, only the vicar carries an umbrella in the countryside, so the flat tweed caps are a bestseller for country-lovers—**J.P. Donleavy**, the **Royal Princes**, and all **Sloanes** may buy their tweed caps here, but they jostle with

St. James's

Donald Sutherland, **Elliott Gould**, and **Larry Hagman**, who are customers as well. ♦ M-F 9AM-5PM; Sa 9:30AM-12:15PM. No. 6 St. James's St, SW1. 071/930.8874

When It's Warranted: Suppliers to the Royal Household

Only the **Queen**, the **Queen Mother**, the **Duke of Edinburgh**, and the **Prince of Wales** can grant the elegant and coveted **Royal Warrant**. To qualify, a business has to supply the royal household directly with services or goods for a minimum of 3 years. The list of Royal Warrant holders is published on the first day of January in the *London Gazette*. The **Princess of Wales**, the most famous royal shopper, apparently hasn't been supplying the royal household long enough to issue her own warrant. If you want to consume royally, here are some of the choices of the royal family:

The General Trading Company, where the Prince and Princess of Wales had their wedding list, holds all 4 Royal Warrants. ♦ 144 Sloane St, W1. 071/730.0411

Hatchards Ltd. Holds all 4 Royal Warrants. Books on the royal family are only outsold by books on roses. What the royals read is a mystery (although Charles read Jung). Each year the National Book League puts together a panel of famous literary folk who choose for the royal family which books to take to Balmoral. Whether they read them or not is another matter. ♦ 187 Piccadilly, W1. 071/437.3924

R. Twining and Company Ltd. Suppliers of tea and coffee to the Queen, although rumor has it that weak Typhoo is used at the Palace Garden parties. There is a museum at the back of this sweet little slither of a building and although it's address is the Strand, it's opposite the Law Courts. ♦ 216 Strand, WC2. 071/353.3511

Truefitt & Hill Provided George IV with wigs and now cuts what still grows for the Duke of Edinburgh. The cutting is slow; shoes are cleaned free. ♦ 23 Old Bond St, W1. 071/493.2961

Hardy Brothers Ltd. London's finest fishing-tackle shop. Queen Victoria had a Hardy rod, as has every Prince of Wales this century. It was Hardy who developed a big-game reel for **Zane Grey**, which now goes for $7000. You can buy a pair of Hunter green *Wellies* for considerably less. ♦ M-W, F 9AM-5PM; Th 9AM-6PM; Sa 9AM-4PM. 61 Pall Mall, SW1. 071/839.5515

45 Overton's ★★$$ This old-fashioned bow-windowed restaurant and oyster bar appeals to an affection for Englishness and a fondness for fish. It serves the English classics: smoked Scotch salmon, whitebait, and potted shrimps to begin, followed by Dover sole, turbot, halibut, salmon trout, and Scotch salmon. Stick to the grilled or poached dishes. The restaurant serves theater dinners and suppers from 6-11PM. ♦ M-F 12:30-2:45PM, 6:30-10:45PM; Sa 6:30-10:45PM. No. 5 St. James's St, SW1. 071/839.3774

45 Pickering Place (1731) The 18th-century alleyway still has timber wainscoting for the first 6 feet from the ground. Halfway along the alley on the right is a plaque, *The Republic of Texas Legation 1842–45*, which commemorates the days when Texas was an independent republic and this was its legation. It was rented to the Texans by Berry Bros. during a time when the wine business was in a serious slump. At the end of the alley is a court surrounded by houses that looks more like a cul-de-sac in a cathedral town than the center of London. ♦ St. James's St, SW1

45 Berry Bros. and Rudd The shop looks much as it did in the 18th century. It's a wonderful crumbling pile of a wine shop, with exquisite, strangely shaped black windows. The austere interior defies all but the bravest to enter, but those who do step back in time to a long, dark room, a large oval table, a few chairs, antique prints, a few bottles of wine, and a pair of enormous scales embossed with *The Coffee Mill*, acquired from the grocer who originally occupied the site. Since the 1760s, clients have been weighing themselves on the scales, and their weights are recorded carefully in the shop's ledgers. Weight-watching was serious business even in the days when corpulence signified prosperity. The **Duke of York**, who led his men up the hill and down again, weighed 14-and-a-half stones (a stone is 14 lbs), but the weight of his brother, **King George IV**, famous for his large girth, is not recorded. The life-loving poet **Lord Byron** was obsessed with his weight, periodically depriving himself of all but a biscuit a day to try and scale down. Records show him at 159 pounds with boots in 1824 and at 180 pounds without them in 1846. But it is the wine that marks Berry Bros. and Rudd for posterity. The distinctive black-and-white labels have been appearing on bottles of claret for over 200 years, and the cellars contain bottles that many a Frenchman would be in awe of. Consider a Julienas or a Moulin-a-Vent for the picnic in St. James's Park. ♦ M-F 9:30AM-5PM. No. 3 St. James's St, SW1. 071/839 9033

46 Crown Passage A little haven of ordinariness, an escape from elegance. The sandwich bars serve ordinary sandwiches and awful coffee, and there are a few antique and coin dealers. ♦ Pall Mall-King St, SW1

47 Red Lion ★★$ A popular pub, with the same name as the pub on Duke of York Street on the other side of St. James's Square. It has good homecooked food for lunch and dinner—shepherd's pie, steak-and-kidney pie—and a lunchtime wine bar upstairs. ♦ M-F 11AM-11PM; Sa 11AM-3PM; Su noon-2PM. Crown Passage, SW1 (Pall Mall-King St) 071/930.8067

48 Oxford and Cambridge Club This is the last club on Pall Mall and more democratic and less misogynistic than the others, although women aren't entirely equal: out of a total membership of 4000, they number only 500. They are called *women associate members* and cannot have lunch in the coffee room or read in the upstairs library or morning room bar. It is as though the club hasn't been in touch with the goings on at Oxford and Cambridge, where distinctions of this kind have long been obliterated. Still, there is a lot to be said for the club. It offers reciprocal membership with numerous clubs in America, including the **University Club**, and you can stay here for a fraction of the price of hotels. The dining rooms are not High Table, but the wine lists really are. ♦ 71 Pall Mall, SW1. 071/930.5151

49 Schomberg House (c. 1698) This house at the St. James's Street end of Pall Mall is a rare example of Queen Anne architecture. Its warm brown-red brick, tall Dutch windows, and human scale are a relief after the imposing Italianate stones and stucco. **Gainsborough** lived here in his later years and died here in 1788, after finally reconciling with his old friend and enemy **Joshua Reynolds**. His parting words were *We are all going to Heaven and Van Dyck is of the company*. After World War II, the house was completely gutted and filled with modern offices. ♦ 80-2 Pall Mall, SW

Next door to **Schomberg House** is the house of the famous and pretty orange seller **Nell Gwynn**. All the property on Pall Mall belongs to the Crown, with the exception of No. 79, because Nell Gwynn refused to live in a house that she did not own.

Drawing Courtesy David Gentleman

50 St. James's Palace The whole area of London we call St. James's (pronounced by Londoners with 2 syllables as *Jameses*) owes its genesis to the Palace of St. James's. The name comes from the hospital that sheltered leprous women on the site in the 13th century. **Henry VIII** purchased the land in 1532 to build a small royal palace for **Anne Boleyn**. He had made Whitehall Palace the chief royal residence after the fall of **Cardinal Wolsey**, channeling his great energy and Renaissance imagination into enlarging it even further. But he regarded the rambling brick mansion called St. James's Palace with affection. The feminine nature of the palace is seen in its history of royal births—**Charles II** (1630), **James II** (1633), **Mary II** (1662), and **Queen Anne** (1665) were all born at St. James's. Charles II never liked Whitehall, so he spent time, energy, and money building up St. James's. But it did not become the official residence of the sovereign until 1698 when Whitehall Palace burned down. It remained the monarch's London residence until **Queen Victoria** ascended to the throne in 1837 and moved the court, under strong pressure from her prime minister, to Buckingham Palace. Its presence in modern British life has never completely vanished. To this day, all foreign ambassadors present their credentials to the Court of St. James's. It is now occupied by the **Gentlemen and Yeomen at Arms** and the **Lord Chamberlain**.

The palace had 4 courts, but fire, rebuilding, and time have cut the number in half. The state rooms, which can be seen over the wall toward the Mall, were rebuilt by **Sir Christopher Wren** in 1703. Not a lot remains of the Tudor palace, but the most charming surviving part is the **Gatehouse** and **Clock Tower**, which face St. James's Street. The tower of worn red brick has 4 stories and sits astride a pair of vast and worn gates. The turrets crowned with battlements and the sentry box manned by a handsome soldier from the Guards seem too Gilbert and Sullivan to be true, but their anachronistic presence is a heartening reminder that this is why St. James's exists. ♦ Pall Mall, SW1

51 Chapel Royal (1532) This chapel, west of the gatehouse at St. James's Palace, was built by **Henry VIII**. It is one of the great gems of Tudor London and a treasure of any epoch. The beautiful coffered ceiling was painted by **Hans Holbein**. Married beneath it were **William III** and **Mary II** (1677), **Queen Anne** (1683), **George IV** (1795), **Queen Victoria** (1840), and **George V** (1893). But what stirs the memory most is not the royal weddings, but **Charles I**, the sad, brave king who took Holy Communion in the chapel on the morning of his execution, 30 January 1649. You

St. James's

can attend services in the chapel every Sunday until the Sunday before Easter. ♦ Courtyard and chapel Su 11:15AM, Jan-Good Friday, Oct-Dec. Ambassadors' Court, St. James's Palace, Pall Mall, SW1

52 Queen's Chapel (1627, **Inigo Jones**) This architectural gem was the first church built in the classical style, and like Banqueting House in Whitehall, also by Inigo Jones, the interior is a perfect cube. The chapel was originally built for the **Spanish Infanta**, intended bride of **Charles I**, and then became the chapel of his wife, **Henrietta Maria**, also a Roman Catholic. Now it is a part of the Chapel Royal. Services are held every Sunday from Easter until the end of July. The gold-and-white coffered ceiling is original. On summer Sundays the chapel is marvelously lit by light from the wide Venetian window, which occupies the entire east wall. ♦ Services Su 11:15AM, Easter-July. Marlborough Rd, SW1

53 Friary Court The changing of the rather small guard at St. James's Palace takes place here daily at 11AM, and afterward you can usually enter the courtyard and look around. Every new sovereign is proclaimed from the balcony in this courtyard, and it was from here that 18-year-old **Queen Victoria** wept when she heard the cheers of her subjects. The **State Apartments**, through the door in the northeast corner, are open only on special occasions, usually when royal gifts are on display, and the wait can be considerable. Inside is the **Amoury Room**, lined with ancient weapons, and the **Tapestry Room**, with tapestries woven for **Charles II**. The last hand at decorating these rooms was **William Morris'** in the 1860s, an inspired choice by someone in the Queen's household. The Morris genius was perfectly suited to the Tudor proportions. ♦ St. James's Palace, Pall Mall, SW

54 Marlborough House (1710, **Sir Christopher Wren**) The house was built for **John Churchill**, first Duke of Marlborough, but more for the Duchess than the Duke. Formidable, turbulent, brilliant, and beautiful, **Sarah Churchill**, first Duchess of Marlborough (pronouced *Mawlborough*) and lady-in-waiting to **Queen Anne**, laid the foundation stone that survives within the house and reads *Laid by Her Grace The Dutches of Marlborough May ye 24th/June ye 4 1709*.

The Duchess hated the monumental palace of Blenheim, which was built for the Duke by Queen Anne after his victory at the Battle of Blenheim. So she chose Sir Christopher Wren to build her London mansion, instructing him to make it strong, plain, and convenient, which he did. The Crown acquired the house in 1817. Unfortunately, the pure perfection created by Wren has been much disguised by the additions and enlargements made in 1861–63 by **James Pennethorne**. **Edward VII** lived here while he was Prince of Wales. **George V** was born in the house, and his consort, **Queen Mary**, lived here during her widowhood. In 1959, **Queen Elizabeth** presented the house to the nation so that it could become the Commonwealth Conference Center in London.Tours by appointment weekdays 11AM or 3PM, depending on availability. ♦ Adjacent to St. James's Palace, Pall Mall, SW1. Details: London Tourist Board 071/730.3488

55 Clarence House (1829, **John Nash**) The house was built for the **Duke of Clarence**, later **King William IV**. Until **Queen Elizabeth**'s accession to the throne in 1952, she and **Prince Philip** lived here. Now it is the home of the **Queen Mother**. When she is in residence, a lone piper plays his bagpipes in the garden at 9AM, a gentle Scottish alarm clock for one of the best-loved members of the royal family. ♦ Attached to W side of St. James's Palace, Pall Mall, SW1

56 Lancaster House (1827, **Benjamin Wyatt**) Originally called **York House** and later called **Stafford House**, Lancaster House was built in light Bath stone for the **Duke of York**, of the column and the nursery rhyme, who extravagantly commissioned it but died before paying for it, whereupon it was sold to the **Duke of Sutherland**. **Charles Barry** designed the interior in 1840. **Chopin** played for **Queen Victoria** in the **Music Room** and the **Duke of Windsor** lived here when he was the Prince of Wales (1919–30). Since being restored from war damage, the building has been the setting for state banquets and conferences. The Louis XV interiors are among the most sumptuous in London. ♦ Admission. Sa-Su 2-6PM, Easter-Nov. Stable Yard, The Mall, SW1. Details: London Tourist Board 071/730.3488

57 St. James's Park Henry VIII created this, the oldest and most perfect of royal parks, with 93 acres and an enchantment of water, birds, views, gaslights, and Englishness, even though the French landscape gardener Lenôtre played a part in creating the formality and flower beds. It is a royal park in the best sense of the word: monarchs have lavished all that monarchs have to lavish in expense and ingenuity to make it the graceful, contemplative place it is today. Henry VIII drained the marshland between the 2 palaces at St. James's and Whitehall to make a deer forest and hunting park. **Charles I** created the formal walks, and walked formally and bravely across the park to his execution. His son **Charles II** created what you see today, an exotic oasis of trees, flowers, ducks, geese, and pelicans. It was Charles II who, soon after the Restoration, opened the park to the public. **George IV** got Nash to reshape the canal and create the meandering lake, crossed by the bridge that grants magical views of Whitehall and Buckingham Palace. At 3PM each afternoon, the pelicans appear for a high tea of whiting and other aquatic delicacies as though they are aware of their distinguished lineage—they are direct descendants of the pair given to Charles II by a Russian ambassador.

A wonderful bird is the pelican
His beak can hold more than his belly can
He will hold in this beak
Enough food for a week
Well I'm demmed if I know how the helican

Anonymous

A family on the throne is an interesting idea also. It brings down the pride of sovereignty to the level of petty life. No feeling could seem more childish than the enthusiam of the English at the marriage of the Prince of Wales. They treated as a great political event, what, looked at as a matter of pure business, was very small indeed. But no feeling could be more like common human nature as it is, and as it is likely to be.

Walter Bagehot, 1867
The English Constitution

The peerage—is the best thing in fiction the English have ever done.

Oscar Wilde

58 Buckingham Palace (1913, **Sir Aston Webb**) The Royal Palace is the most gazed at building in London, not because of its magnificence, because it is not very magnificent, or its great age, because what one is gazing at is a somber facade of Portland stone and French pilasters built in the early 1900s. The gazes are inspired by the magic and the mystique of the monarchy—and like Maude informed her young lover in *Harold and Maude*, we may not believe in monarchy but *we miss the kings and queens*.

St. James's

This is the oldest monarchy of all, and it is in the last country in the world where monarchy exists on a grand and sanctified scale, with religious processions, a titled and healthy aristocracy, and as the Prince and Princess of Wales prove, hysterical adulation from the country's—and world's—people that transcends nationalities, classes, and parties.

Her Most Excellent Majesty Elizabeth the Second, by the Grace of God, of the United Kingdom of Great Britain and Northern Ireland and of her Realms and Territories Queen, Head of the Commonwealth, Defender of the Faith, Sovereign of the British **Orders of Knighthood**, is the 40th monarch since the Norman Conquest, descended from **Charlemagne** and **King Canute**. Her accession in 1952 coincided with the beginning of the end of the Empire, and she has presided over its dissolution with noble queenship. She is probably one of the best-informed diplomats in the world today, having had continuous access for 38 years to world leaders. She has known **Churchill, Khrushchev**, and **Eisenhower**, and knows every major head of state in the world today. Every Tuesday night when the Queen is in London, the prime minister goes to Buckingham Palace for a talk with her. The Queen's concerned involvement, excellent memory, and sharp insight have been appreciated by almost all the prime ministers of her reign.

Buckingham Palace

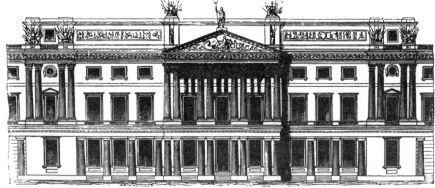

Buckingham Palace

Will she retire, step down, and turn the monarchy business over to her eldest son? The answer is no. The Queen is Queen for life, and the monarchy's continuity and survival depends on adherence to the spiritual laws of the monarchy: under the hereditary system, the last intake of breath by the dying sovereign coincides absolutely with the next intake by the living sovereign, hence the ancient cry, *The King is dead—Long live the King.*

When the Queen is in residence at Buckingham Palace, the Royal Standard waves above. The visitor's viewpoint is the rather dour eastern facade, completely rebuilt by **Sir Aston Webb** in 1913. The front western facade, visible only from a helicopter, is by **John Nash**. The main building is flanked with 2 classical pavillions and overlooks an immense sweep of lawn, 45 acres of private gardens, expanses of woodlands, giant trees, over 200 species of wild plants, a lake graced with pink flamingos, an herbaceous border, and tennis courts. This is where the Queen's garden parties are held each summer.

The original house, built for the Duke and Duchess of Buckingham in 1703, was bought by **George III** some 60 years later for his beloved **Queen Charlotte**, who filled it with children and made it into a family house, then known as **Queen's House**. **George IV** commissioned Nash to make it into a more worthy home of a monarch, but the plans became grander and more difficult to execute with time. The transformation process had many of the elements of a Laurel and Hardy film, not

the least being the scheme to surround the palace with scaffolding to disguise the fact that a new palace was being constructed, whilst the permission had been granted only for renovations and repairs. When the King died, Nash, who had transformed London into a royal and elegant city, was dismissed by an angry Parliament. An investigation into the palace's spiraling costs revealed financial irregularities. Publicly disgraced, Nash died in 1835.

William IV was not pleased with the achievements of Nash's successor, **Edward Blore**, and offered the palace to Parliament as a permanent home following the fire that destroyed Westminster in 1834, but the government refused. William IV, claiming the air was better for his asthma, stayed at Kensington Palace until his death.

Buckingham Palace became the official town residence of the sovereign in 1837, when **Queen Victoria** moved in. The Royal Standard flew here for the first time, and the dance-loving Queen and her consort **Prince Albert** extended the palace, building the **State Supper Room** and the **Ball Room**. The Queen also removed the marble arch from the front of the palace and had it placed at its present site on the north side of Hyde Park.

Sir Aston Webb, architect for **George V** and his popular wife, **Mary of Teck**, transformed the facade of Buckingham Palace, replacing the flaking Caen stone with Portland stone and adding the French-inspired pilasters. George V also saw the unveiling of the *Victoria Memo-*

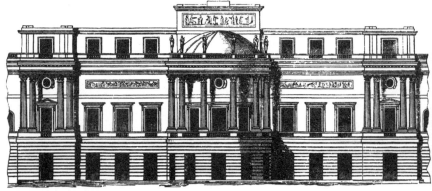

Buckingham Palace, Garden Front

rial in front of the palace, a sentimental wedding cake of a sculpture by **Sir Thomas Brock** (1911), with a seated Queen Victoria (13 feet high) facing the Mall, surrounded by the figures of Truth, Justice, and Motherhood—all dear to the Queen's heart. At the top, glistening in gold, Victory is attended by Constancy and Courage. It may suffer from the defects of Victorian sentimentality and excess, but it is hard to imagine Buckingham Palace without it. The palace is not open to the public. **Changing of the Guard** takes place in the forecourt. Arrive early, it gets crowded, even out of season. ♦ Changing of the Guard daily 11:30AM, Apr-Aug; alternate days only, Sep-Mar

59 Queen's Gallery (1830, **John Nash**) This royal treasure chest was originally a conservatory and then a chapel. In 1963, it was established as an art gallery by Her Majesty. There are continuous exhibitions, imaginative and scholarly, of the gifts to—and royal treasures of—the British monarchy, including paintings, drawings, sculptures, silver, cutlery, and furniture—a collection unparalled in magnificence and variety. The exhibitions change every 18 months. ♦ Admission. Tu-Sa 10:30AM-5PM; Su 2-5PM. Buckingham Gate, Buckingham Palace Rd, SW1. 071/930.4832

60 Royal Mews (1825, **John Nash**) Probably the finest and most valuable collection of state coaches in the world. The coaches from all periods are on display, including the state coach acquired by **George II** in 1762 that is still in use today. The coach looks like it's right out of a *Cinderella* design, with elaborate carvings representing 8 palm trees, branching at the top and supporting the roof, and 3 cherubs, representing England, Scotland, and Ireland. It is 24 feet long, 8 feet wide, 12 feet high, and weighs 4 tons. The Royal Mews is also the home of the **Royal Horses**, who may be seen pulling carriages in Hyde Park around 10AM each morning. The Royal Mews also has a shop. ♦ Admission. Royal Mews: W-Th 2-4PM. Shop: Tu-Sa 10AM-5:30PM; Su 10AM-2PM. Buckingham Palace Rd, SW1. 071/930 4832

61 The Goring $$$ Just behind the queen's house is another family-run hotel, albeit on a smaller scale. The Goring family has owned and managed this old-fashioned hotel for nearly 80 years and regularly receives plaudits for its good value, central location, and high standards. There is a beautiful private garden and the rooms have been stylishly furnished and have solid marble bathrooms. The lobby areas are classically decorated and welcoming. The restaurant is of a reasonable standard—not too expensive and serves good clarets and coffee. Try the guinea fowl with stir-fried vegetables. ♦ 17 Beeston Pl, Grosvenor Gardens, SW1. 071/834.4393

veryone likes flattery and when you come to royalty ou should lay it on with a trowel.

Benjamin Disraeli to Matthew Arnold

David Levin
Director, Capital Hotel

Any of the suites with a view on the park side of the **Hyde Park Hotel**.

The restaurant on the 4th floor of **Fortnum & Mason** for the tea, tranquility, and touch of yesteryear.

Robert Gould, the head hall porter at the **Capital Hotel**. He is the kindest and most considerate of men. In 15 years, no one has ever had an adverse

St. James's

comment about him. The Capital Hotel is my favorite small hotel because of the very high standards of food, wine, and service.

The **Connaught Hotel** is my favorite deluxe hotel.

Attending auctions at all the very fine sale rooms in town: **Sothebys, Christies, Bonham-Phillips**. No other city in the world can offer such enjoyment.

Edward Sexton
Savile Row Tailor

Bespoke Tailors:

Edward Sexton, 37 Savile Row, London, W1. 071/437.2368

Anderson & Sheppard Ltd., 30 Savile Row, W1. 071/734.1420

Malcolm J. Plews, 10 Savile Row, W1. 071/287.2941

Shirts and Hosiery:

Woods & Brown, 7 Sackville St, W1. 071/734.3821

Hilditch & Key, 73 Jermyn St, SW1. 071/930.5336

Turnbull & Asser Ltd., 71 Jermyn St, SW1. 071/930.0502

Gentlemen's Hatters:

Herbert Johnson, 30 New Bond St, W1. 071/408.1174

James Lock & Co. Ltd., 6 St. James's St, W1. 071/930.8874

Bates, 21 Jermyn St, SW1. 071/734.2722

Umbrellas:

Swaine & Adeney, 185 Piccadilly, W1. 071/734.4277

Shoes:

Alan McAfee, 17-18 Old Bond St, W1. 071/499.7343

J. Lobb, 9 St. James's St, SW1. 071/930.3664

H. Maxwell, 11 Savile Row, W1. 071/734.9714

Hairdressers:

Michael John, 23a Albemarle St, W1. 071/629.6969

Ivans and Trumper's, 20 Jermyn St, SW1. 071/734.1370

Restaurants/Nightlife: Red **Hotels:** Blue
Shops/Parks: Green **Sights/Culture:** Black

Cromwell & Brompton Roads

Cromwell and **Brompton** roads gently embrace in front of the flamboyant Baroque **Brompton Oratory**, uniting at that almost imperceptible angle: 2 roads, 2 villages (Kensington and Knightsbridge), and 2 different worlds. It seems an unlikely union. **South Kensington**, with its nexus of museums, is Victorian and high-minded, evidence of one man's grandiose vision of the educational and moral value of art, while luxe and high-spirited **Knightsbridge** is home ground for the chic, sophisticated, and fashionable. But like

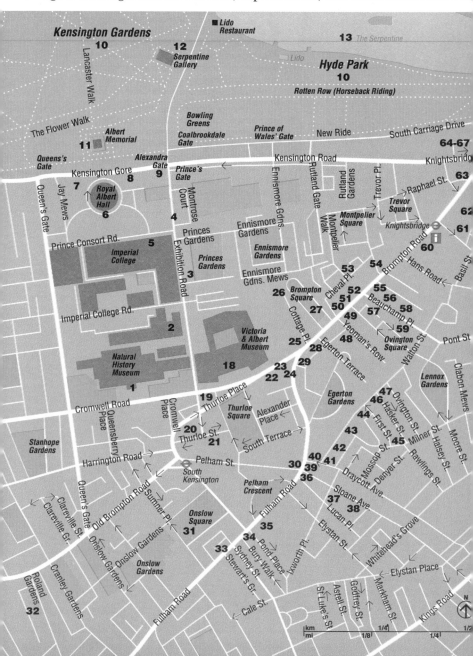

Kensington Gardens

10

Lancaster Walk

12
Serpentine Gallery

Lido Restaurant

13 *The Serpentine*

Lido

Hyde Park
10

Rotten Row (Horseback Riding)

The Flower Walk

Albert Memorial
11

Bowling Greens
Coalbrookdale Gate

Prince of Wales' Gate

New Ride

South Carriage Drive

64-67

Queens's Gate

Alexandra Gate
9

Prince's Gate

Kensington Road

Knightsbridg

Kensington Gore
7   8

Montrose Court

Ennismore Gdns.

Rutland Gate

Rutland Gardens

Trevor Pl.

Raphael St.

63

Queen's Gate

Jay Mews

Royal Albert Hall
6

4

Ennismore Gardens

Montpelier Walk

Montpelier Square

Trevor Square

Knightsbridge

62

61

Prince Consort Rd.
5

Princes Gardens

Ennismore Gardens

Brompton Road

Hans Road

Basil S

60

Imperial College

Princes Gardens

Ennismore Gardens

53   54

Knightsbridge

Exhibition Road

3

Ennismore Gdns. Mews

26

Brompton Square
27

Cheval Pl.

52
51
50

55

Beauchamp Pl.

56
57
58

Hans Road

Basil S

Imperial College Rd.

2

Cottage Pl.

49

Yeoman's Row

48

Ovington Square
59

Walton St.

Pont St

Natural History Museum
1

18

Victoria & Albert Museum

25

28

Egerton Terrace

Egerton Gardens

47

Ovington St.

Lennox Gardens

Clabon Mews

Cromwell Road

Queensberry Place

Cromwell Place

19

Thurloe Place

23
22 24

29

Thurloe Square

46

Hasker St.

First St.

44
45

Mossop St.

Denyer St.

Milner St.

Moore St.

Halsey St.

Rawlings St.

Stanhope Gardens

20
21

Thurloe St.

Alexander Place

South Terrace

43

42

Harrington Road

South Kensington

Pelham St.

Pelham Crescent

30 39
40 41
36

Draycott Ave.

Sloane Ave.

Queen's Gate

Old Brompton Road

Summer Pl.

Onslow Gardens

Onslow Square
31

35

Fulham Road

37 38

Lucan Pl.

Elystan St.

Whitehead's Grove

Clareville St.

Clareville Gr.

Onslow Gardens

34

Pond Place

Bury Walk

kworth Pl.

Elystan Place

Cranley Gardens

Roland Gardens

32

33

Sydney St.

Stewart's Gr.

Onslow Gardens

Fulham Road

Cale St.

St. Luke's St.

Astell St.

Godfrey St.

Markham St.

Kings Road

N

km
mi
1/8   1/4   1/4   1/

ll successful unions, the 2 bring out the best in one another, and a day spent in the company of both is unimaginably satisfying.

This walk includes dinosaurs and their living relatives; an earthquake; a launch pad and the actual *Apollo 10* capsule; an 11-foot bed for weary travelers mentioned in *Twelfth Night*; the art of China, Islam, and the Italian Renaissance; a quarter of a million butterflies; 10 acres of the greatest collection of antique furniture and decorative art in the world (not for sale); and 15 acres of fabulous furniture and just about everything you could conceivably desire (all for sale).

The walk begins at the **Natural History Museum**, a building that exudes Victorian confidence, worthiness, and grandeur, and looks more like an ecclesiastical railway station than a museum that houses more than 50 million items from the natural world. The walk culminates at **Harrods**, whose motto is no less modest: *Omnia, Omnibus, Ubique—All Things, For All People, Everywhere*, a claim now, sadly, untrue; Harrods has shifted way upmarket to exclude more than it includes. Still, if the magnitude of merchandise leaves you feeling muddled and breathless, a detour into **Hyde Park** and **Kensington Gardens** will help you recover from the pursuit of material matters. If you go around 10AM you can see the Queen's horse drawn carriages travel down **Serpentine Road**; in May or June watch the soldiers practicing with their horses for *Trooping of the Colour* on **Rotten Row**. The **Hyde Park Hotel**, at the end of the walk, is a worthy shrine for any Anglophile pilgrim who thinks tea in the late afternoon is as necessary as it is civilized. Nearby is one of London's best wine bars, **Le Metro**, for displaced Francophiles, and a special pub, the **Grenadier**, which was once the Officer's Mess for the Duke of Wellington's soldiers.

This is a Monday-through-Saturday walk if you want to include shopping at Harrods. But if you are primarily a museum-trotter, this could be your perfect Sunday in London, beginning with lunch at a French restaurant (the excellent **Bibendum**, noted for cuisine, is a 5-minute walk away) and finishing in time for the museum opening at 2:30PM. Because much of the walk is spent indoors, it is ideal for a rainy day, except for the detour into Hyde Park and Kensington Gardens.

The mathematicians worked out that the **Crystal Palace** *must collapse after the first strong wind; the engineers claimed that the galleries would break up and crush the visitors; the economists predicted that prices would rise drastically as a result of the vast influx of people, while doctors warned of a reappearance of the black death of the Middle Ages as a result of these crowds, which reminded them of the Crusades. The moralists predicted that England would become impregnated with all the evils of the civilized and uncivilized worlds, while the theologians argued that this second Tower of Babel would also incur the vengeance of an insulted God.*

Prince Albert, in a letter to
Frederick William IV of Prussia

On a perfect spring day, 1 May 1851, at noon, the *Great Exhibition on the Works of Industry of All Nations* was opened by **Queen Victoria** and **Prince Albert**. The name that people took to their hearts was the Crystal Palace, the gigantic and revolutionary greenhouse designed by **Sir Joseph Paxton**. It covered 19 acres and was a marvel of delicate cast-iron ribbing, with 300,000 panes of glass. The length was 1848 feet, 3 times the length of St. Paul's, and the height of 108 feet was so high that 3 elm trees on the site could be incorporated into it. Paxton was not an architect, but a creative and brilliant gardener who worked for the Duke of Devonshire. His building was as futuristic in concept as it was revolutionary in design, with prefabricated, standardized, and interchangeable units that were erected by 2000 men in just 22 weeks. The building was taken down in 1852 and reerected in Sydenham. Only the gates remain.

The main impetus of the exhibition was to raise the standard of the industrial design of goods that were being mass produced by machines. Some 14,000 exhibitors from 40 countries demonstrated the latest developments in technology and the arts. Six million people attended, many traveling on the railway for the first time. The popular and innovative exhibition made a profit of nearly £200,000, which the Prince wanted spent on a permanent center for education, museums, and learned societies. By 1856, a total of 87 acres had been purchased and roads were being built—the new Cromwell Road, a westward extension of Brompton Road, joined with Kensington Road via Exhibition Road and Prince Albert Road (now Queen's Gate), forming a complex of museums and colleges, a monument to Victorian curiosity and industry. The trend of pushing new design frontiers continues today with the newly opened **Design Museum**, which reveals British innovations and others at their very best. It is appropriately located in the ultramodern **Docklands** area (see page 168).

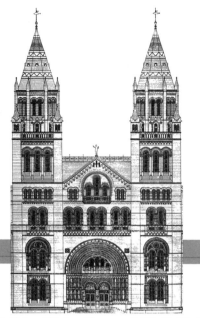

1 Natural History Museum (1873–80, **Alfred Waterhouse**) If you take a taxi into London from Heathrow, the twin-towered, Byzantine, terracotta and slate blue museum is the first real feast for the eye. It looks superb in sunlight and breathtaking when lit up against a night sky. Animal figures grace the outside of the building, and inside, painted panels of wild flowers decorate the high curved ceiling. As you enter the navelike central hall, you expect to see a high altar (or a diesel engine). But in this holy terminus dedicated to the wonders of Creation, rising high above the ordinary human figures below, is the 85-foot-long skeleton of **Diplodocus Carnegii**, the 150-million-year-old dinosaur believed to be the largest flesh-eating land animal to have ever existed. Off to the left side of the hall are push-button computer games where you can trace the evolution and extinction of the species, which dominated the earth for about 140 million years and died off about 65 million years ago.

The Natural History Museum used to be part of the **British Museum**, which was founded by an Act of Parliament in 1753. It houses the national collections of zoology, entomology, paleontology, minerology, and botany. With 4 acres to cover and some 50 million possible items to see, you may have to choose among dinosaurs, humans, whales, birds, and mammals. But be sure to see the excellent display on the origin of the human species on the 1st floor, including specimens from **Darwin**'s historic voyage on the *HMS Beagle*. Also stop by the **Whale Hall** to gaze at the overwhelming model and skeleton of a blue whale. In the bird display, in the west wing, parents linger in front of the extinct dodos, those giant pigeons who couldn't fly, and flightless emus and ostriches, while children race ahead to the penguins. The mammals exhibition shouldn't be missed, especially the rare giant panda **Chi-Chi**, who having confounded early attempts at *glasnost* by refusing to mate with Moscow

Zoo's **An-An** in the '60s, died of old age at London Zoo in 1972. She now permanently munches bamboo in the north mammal hall. The **Human Biology** exhibition features the story of fertilization and birth and the story of hormones and cells, an encouraging follow-up to **Man's Place in Evolution**. ♦ Admission. M-Sa 10AM-6PM; Su 11AM-6PM; free M-F 4:30-6PM, Sa-Su 5-6PM, bank holidays. Cromwell Rd, SW7. 071/938.9123

Within the Natural History Museum:

The Natural History Museum Shops
These are terrific! The postcards in the first shop are the best bargain in town, with gentle gorillas, gory bugs, lavish butterflies, and fleas in costume. The shop next door carries pocket-money items like plastic dinosaurs, while the gift shop has more deluxe merchandise like fossils, jewelry, minerals, replicas of skulls, and crystal goblets etched with endangered species. But the best shop is the **bookshop**, which has an excellent collection of gardening books, beautifully illustrated guides to wildflowers, and more specifically, **Hugh Johnson**'s *Encyclopaedia of Trees*, the *Catalogue of the Rothschild Collection of Fleas* in 5 weighty volumes, and a replica of Darwin's journal of the *Beagle*, all well worth the detour.

There are 3 places to eat here: a large restaurant sells hot and cold meals, salads, and health foods; a juice bar serves healthy snacks and fruit juices; and a snack bar serves those things children love that they aren't allowed to have at home.

You will not find the **Geological Museum** (1935, **John Markham**) anymore because the Natural History Museum has engulfed it and a gallery now connects the 2 sites. It was wedged in between the 2 giants, the Natural History and **Science** museums. Even on a Saturday, you can gaze peacefully at rubies, emeralds, sapphires, and diamonds, including a model of the Koh-i-noor diamond, cut under the supervision of **Prince Albert** and first shown at the *Great Exhibition of 1851*. Don't miss *The Story of the Earth*, which is entered by way of a 25-foot-high *cliff* from the Highlands of Scotland. You will be taken on a journey through the first billion years on earth, complete with an erupting volcano and earth-shaking earthquake.

The exhibitions get more didactic as you go up, culminating in the world's largest display of metalliferous ores and a model of **Stonehenge** on the 2nd floor. ♦ Free. M-Sa 10AM-6PM; Su 2:30-6PM. Exhibition Rd, SW7. 071/589.3444

Restaurants/Nightlife: Red	**Hotels:** Blue
Shops/Parks: Green	**Sights/Culture:** Black

2 Science Museum (1913, **Sir Richard Allison**) This inspired tribute to science couldn't be more appropriately located than in the nation that gave us **Newton, Darwin, Davy, Huxley, Thomson, Rutherford,** and **Fleming**. A visit here leaves you with the inevitable realization of just how many fundamental scientific discoveries have been British. The museum is especially enjoyable for the young, who can push, pull, and test the countless knobs, buttons, and gadgets. Exhibitions change regularly, so pick up a map from the **museum shop**.

The lower ground floor is heaven for the small and curious. It is filled with such items as a burglar alarm to test, a model lift to operate, a take-off and landing simulator for would-be aviators, a periscope for spying on the floor above, and many more gadgets, all to be tried and tested. For the more domestic, there is an authentic Victorian kitchen and a large collection of appliances.

The emphasis on the ground floor is on power, transport, and exploration, with the **Foucault Pendulum** demonstrating the rotation of the earth on its own axis. Also on display are *Puffing Billy* (1813), the oldest locomotive in the world; the **Boulton and Watt** pumping engine (1777); the first diesel engine made in England; 8 fire engines; full-scale models of a submarine and a moon lander; and most popular of all, the actual *Apollo 10* capsule.

A star dome in the astronomy section dominates the 1st floor. But you will also find everything you ever wanted to know about mapmaking, time measurement, iron, steel- and glass-making, agriculture, meteorology, and telecommunications. Don't miss the display on computer technology, *The Challenge of the Chip*.

The 2nd floor deals with the more didactic subjects of chemistry, atomic physics, nuclear power, and computers. Be sure to see the models of sailing ships and warships and the equipment from *Gipsy Moth IV*.

The art of flight is explored on the 3rd floor, from the hot-air balloon to the Concord. Of special interest is the *De Havilland Gipsy Moth*, used by **Amy Johnson** on her flight to Australia in 1930; a replica of the craft built by **Orville** and **Wilbur Wright** in 1903; and WWII aircraft. The aeronautics section shares the floor with a history of photography and cinematography from 1835.

The **Wellcome Medical Museum**, on the 4th and 5th floors, contains 40 tableaux and dioramas depicting medical history, from trepanning in neolithic times to open-heart surgery in the 1980s. Clever, often spine-chilling displays cover tribal, Oriental, classical Greek, Roman, medieval, and Renaissance medicine. The vast collection of curiosities includes **Florence Nightingale**'s moccasins, a microscope made for **Lister, Dr. Livingston**'s medicine chest, and **Napoleon**'s beautiful silver toothbrush.

The museum shop offers a few booklets and postcards; the **snack bar** on the 3rd floor is only for the hungry. ◆ Free. M-Sa 10AM-6PM; Su 2:30-6PM. Exhibition Rd, SW7. 071/589.3456

Dr. Neil Chalmers
Director, Natural History Museum

Breathe deeply, pause to shudder momentarily, then step briskly into the **Creepy Crawlies** exhibition. Laid out before you is the world of arthropods, the Latin name for spiders, scorpions, crabs, and centipedes. Try not to get too upset as you enter the full-size house and discover the full range of creepy crawlies that share our daily lives, including those popular cat lovers—fleas and carpet beetles. The aim is to persuade visitors that these insects are industrious creatures to be admired, not feared.

Discovering Mammals shows the spectacu-

Cromwell & Brompton Roads

lar variety and complexity of the mammal world, with giraffes, elephants, and hippos filling the gallery.

Discovering how we view and react to the world around us has been the eternal inner quest of man. In **Human Biology**, an award-winning exhibition on the human body, this is explained using interactive displays, videos, and computers. Here we see the different ages of man as well as explanations of the senses, memory, and the brain.

Frighten yourself in the earthquake machine, part of the **Story of Earth** exhibition, which traces the history of the planet, its structure and geology. The section on earthquakes and volcanoes graphically describes these natural phenomena.

Neil Cossons
Director, Science Museum

The great sequence of steam engines in the **East Hall**, the first thing visitors see when entering the museum. Here are the pioneer contributions of Newcomen, Watt, Trevithick, and Parsons.

Puffing Billy, built in 1813, and the oldest surviving steam locomotive in the world.

Philip de Loutherbourg's dramatic painting *Coalbrookdale by Night* in the **Iron and Steel Gallery**.

The engine of Henry Bell's steamer *Comet* and the collection of marine steam-engine models.

The *Orrery*, named after the Earl of Orrery, for whom it was made in 1716.

The **Vickers Vimy** aircraft in which Alcock and Brown made the first nonstop crossing of the Atlantic in 1919.

The **Portsmouth blockmaking machinery** built by Henry Maudslay to the designs of Sir Marc Brunel.

The **George III Collection** of scientific apparatus.

Launchpad, a hall full of interactive exhibitions demonstrating principles of science and technology.

The ingenious **automatic teamaker** of 1904.

3 Ognisko Polski ★★★$ In fact, this is a Polish club, but nonmembers are welcome. It is a favorite and supposedly secret haunt of many of the museum and South Kensington bohemians and intellectuals. The bar and restaurant are sort of elegant now that they have been renovated, the food very *zrazy, kasza*, and *pierogi*, and the atmosphere unbeatable. It is a kind of poor man's Russian Tea Room, with a set lunch and dinner that often includes stuffed goose and *bigos* (chopped beef or pork, cabbage, sauerkraut, and onions simmered in a spicy sauce). ◆ M-Sa 12:30-2:30PM, 6:30-11PM; Su 12:30-3:30PM, 6:30-11PM. 55 Exhibition Rd, SW7. 071/589.4670

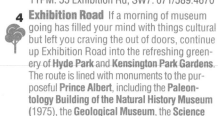

4 Exhibition Road If a morning of museum going has filled your mind with things cultural but left you craving the out of doors, continue up Exhibition Road into the refreshing greenery of **Hyde Park** and **Kensington Park Gardens**. The route is lined with monuments to the purposeful **Prince Albert**, including the **Paleontology Building of the Natural History Museum** (1975), the **Geological Museum**, the **Science Museum**, and the **Henry Cole Wing** of the **V&A**. The road culminates in the gargantuan **Albert Hall**, which, along with Kensington Park Gardens, is presided over by the **Albert Memorial**.

5 Royal College of Music (1894, **Sir Arthur Blomfield**) Inside the elaborate building is a remarkable collection of more than 500 musical instruments, ranging from the earliest known stringed keyboard instruments to some wonderfully bizarre concoctions of the 19th and 20th centuries. There is also a portrait collection with more than 100 paintings and several thousand engravings and photographs, including **Burne-Jones'** portrait of **Paderewski** (1890) and **Epstein's** bust of **Vaughn Williams.** ◆ Admission. Music collection: M, W 2-4:30PM, Sep-July. Portrait collection: M-F by appt. Prince Consort Rd, SW7. 071/589.3643

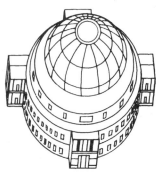

6 Royal Albert Hall (1871, **Fowke**) This stupendous piece of Victoriana is a memorial to **Prince Albert**, ordained and encouraged by **Queen Victoria.** The vast 735-foot red-brick elliptical hall with its glass-and-iron dome can hold 8000 people. Apparently, the Prince approved of the design (although he wanted this site to be for another National Gallery), and it is a fitting climax to the cultural complex honoring the education of the mind and spirit in which he so strongly believed.

Albert Hall still operates under a Royal Charter and is the venue for sporting events, beauty contests, pop concerts, military tatoos, and most famous of all, the **Henry Wood Promenade Concerts**, performed daily between mid July and mid September. Known as the *Proms*, these performances of classical music have an informal atmosphere and are packed with sincere lovers of music. The last night of the Proms is famously emotional and tickets are by lottery. ◆ Kensington Gore, SW7. Information 071/589.3203, tickets 071/589.8212

7 Royal College of Organists (1875, **H.H. Cole**) This eccentric 4-story building was designed by a soldier in the Royal Engineers, a policy consistent with **Prince Albert's** preference for engineers and artists over architects. It delights passersby with its euphoria of decoration and colors—blues, reds, and yellows—and its frieze of musicians. What's missing from this picture? Well, there is no organist...and no organ. ◆ Kensington Gore, SW7

8 Albert Hall Mansions (1879–86, **Norman Shaw**) The warm-brick mansions were one of the earliest blocks of flats in London. If they weren't so utterly English—the style is Queen Anne Revival with oriels, gables, dormers, and arches—they would seem almost European in their scale and grandeur. The flats are extremely desirable because of their superb location and palatial-size rooms. They are occupied by an appreciative elite, including the English designer **Jean Muir**, whose flat is decorated entirely in white. ◆ Kensington Gore, SW7

9 Royal Geographical Society (1873–75, **Norman Shaw**; formerly Lowther Lodge) The statues outside the informal Dutch-style building are of **Sir Ernest Shackleton**, who commanded 3 expeditions to the antarctic and discovered the location of the south magnetic pole in 1909, and **David Livingstone**, who discovered the Zambezi River, the Victoria Falls, and the source of the Nile, and was famously rescued by the journalist **H.M. Stanley.** Inside is an outstanding map room with a collection of more than 500,000 maps and a model of Mount Everest. The society sponsors monthly exhibitions (mainly photographic) of travel and travelers throughout the world. ◆ Free. M-F 10AM-5PM. 1 Kensington Gore, SW7. 071/589.0648

10 Kensington Gardens and Hyde Park Of all the features that make London the most liveable city in the world—the innate courtesy of the English, the civilized lay of the land with its squares and humane, domestic architecture, the thick layers of sympathetic history—it is the parks, the vast oases of green, that give the city an almost unique supply of urban oxygen and humanity.

It is inconceivable to know London without spending time in the parks, and for many Londoners and visitors, the vast, natural wonderland of Hyde Park and Kensington Gardens in the heart of the city is not only a favorite part of London, but a compulsory stopover.

Even a half-hour here is like a day in the country—walking across grass, sheltered by trees, with a soundtrack of birds and a cast of exuberant dogs, placid dog owners, joggers, pinstriped businessmen, nannies with prams the size of economy cars, children briefly angelic in their school uniforms, and lovers who stroll in their own pool of private peace. The English, unlike the French and the Italians, don't look very impressive walking along city streets. But in their parks they become distinguished, their features enhanced by the blue of the sky, the green of the grass. They thrive in natural settings, even those surrounded on every side by busy roads and the relentless noise and movement of city life.

Kensington Gardens is the *My Fair Lady* of London parks—elegant, charming, and romantic, merging as seamlessly as a silk dress into the vaster green of Hyde Park. The difference between the 2 parks and just where they do merge is a mystery to many. But true lovers of London earth and sky can define perfectly the area that begins at Kensington Palace and extends to Alexander Gate on the south and Victoria Gate on the north, with the connecting Ring Road as boundary.

The gardens, which were laid out by **Queen Anne**, were originally the private property of Kensington Palace, and they still have a regal air, enhanced by the presence of the royal home. They were opened to the public in the 19th century on Saturday only, and became a fashionable venue for promenades. Many English writers, among them **Thackeray** and **Matthew Arnold**, have praised their *sublime sylvan solitude*, as **Disraeli** put it. The **Round Pond**, constructed in the 18th century, was originally octagonal, and the **Broad Walk**, leading from the pond to the palace, was once lined with magnificent elm trees.

11 Albert Memorial (1872, **Sir Gilbert Scott**) A little to the west of where the Crystal Palace once stood sits **Prince Albert**, holding the catalog of the *Great Exhibition of 1851* and gazing down on the museums, colleges, and institutions that his vision, energy, and endeavor inspired. His throne,

Albert Memorial

crowned by a spire of gilt and enameled metal that ends in a cross rising 180 feet high, is an imposing piece of Victorian art made loveable by its sheer excess. The monument was commissioned by the Prince's mournful widow, **Queen Victoria**, and unveiled by her in 1876. Below the bronze statue of the Prince Regent are marble statues of animals representing the 4 continents, while allegorical figures representing Agriculture, Commerce, Manufacture, and Engineering stand at the 4 angles. On the pedestal is a magnificent procession of reliefs of the greatest artists, writers, and philosophers of the Victorian era. The memorial is a gift to Londoners and London-lovers, but it was never a gift to the Prince, who pleaded against such a remembrance. *It would*

Cromwell & Brompton Roads

disturb my quiet rides in Rotten Row to see my face staring at me, and if (as is very likely) it became an artistic monstrosity like most of our monuments, it would upset my equanimity to be permanently ridiculed and laughed at in effigy, wrote the Prince, prophetically. Indeed, for many years the monument was denounced as an example of the worst of Victorian sentimentality and ugly excess. But time, on our side and the Prince's, has brought the memorial and the Prince into deserved veneration. ♦ Kensington Gore, SW7

12 Serpentine Gallery Once the **Kensington Gardens Tea House**, the beautiful building is now the ideal art gallery and ambitiously provides a setting for monthly exhibitions of contemporary art. Gallery talks Sunday at 3PM. ♦ Free. Daily 10AM-dusk. Kensington Gardens, W8. 071/723.9072

Ever since **Egon Ronay** complained bitterly about the ghastly quality of foods served in motorway, general, and tourist restaurants, the standard of cooking has improved enormously. It is now quite hard to have a bad meal in the London parks. The **Dell Buffet** (at the Hyde Park Corner end of the Serpentine) and the **Lido** (it looks like a boathouse) are beautifully located and the food is simple and good. You will not find Londoners eating at the **St. James's Park Buffet**; they have yet to realize that the capitol's parks now serve delicious, uncomplicated grub to all.

13 The Serpentine This 40-acre artificial lake was formed by damming the West Bourne, a stream that no longer exists. The riverlike lake is London residence to a vast range of waterfowl. But the swimming hole, the **Lido**, was closed due to a health hazard, although there is a small kids' paddling pool in summer. In 1816, **Harriet Westbrook**, first wife of the poet **Shelley**, committed suicide by drowning in the Serpentine. Nearby is the **Boathouse**, where rowboats may be hired by the hour for a perfect afternoon by Renoir.

Along the **Long Water** is *Peter Pan* (1912, **Sir George Frampton**), the most popular figure in Kensington Park Gardens. The statue is almost rubbed smooth by adoring little hands. Just beyond him are the **Tivoli Gardens**, 4

Cromwell & Brompton Roads

ornate shimmering fountains bedecked with flowers that make you wonder whether you are really in Italy or France, they are so out of character in London. ♦ Hyde Park, W8

Restaurants/Nightlife: Red	**Hotels:** Blue
Shops/Parks: Green	**Sights/Culture:** Black

If you don't take a stroll around Kensington Gardens, you will miss 2 of London's hidden jewels—**White's Hotel**, which has been put on a par with the Savoy, but is nowhere near as well known, and the latest restaurant in town, **Kensington Place**. The walk is a long one, though, so be prepared.

14 White's Hotel $$$ Squirrels will run up your legs to be fed with nuts as you stroll along the North Flower Walk toward Lancaster Gate. Here, just across Bayswater, is one of London's most exclusive yet virtually unknown hotels. It is a shade less expensive than the Savoy or the Inn on the Park, with which it has been ranked. The building looks like the London home of an earl, and the interior wouldn't disappoint him, either—it is filled with crystal chandeliers, white marble, and the shades of old English roses. The Jeeveslike service does not disappoint and the restaurant is rather good, too. ♦ 90-92 Lancaster Gate, W2. 071/262.2711; fax 071/262.2147

15 Kensington Place ★★★$$ In a city chockfull of antiques and history, the residents go the opposite way and favor the minimalist bare-wood-and-glass look in this, the trendiest of London's brasseries. A *Times* Restaurant of the Year (1989); its chef, **Rowley**

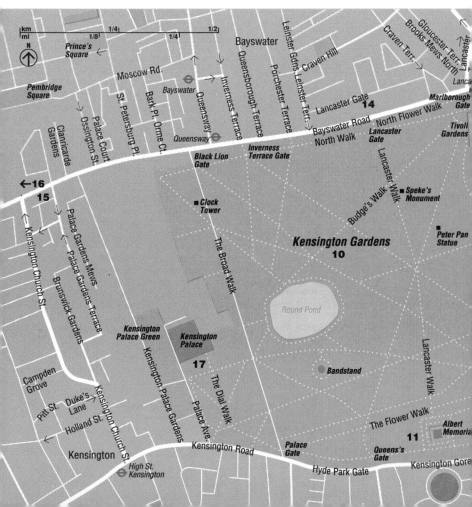

Leigh, is feted by London foodies. The seats may not be that comfy, but it is always packed. And you may be expected to hurry through your delightful goat-cheese mousse with olives, followed by a grilled rump steak with salsa verde, or perhaps steamed John Dory with tomato and cucumber, and as you get to the finishing line—the obligatory baked tamarillos with vanilla ice cream. (Chocolate lovers should try the *marquise*). ♦ M-Sa noon-11:45PM; Su noon-10:15PM. 201 Kensington Church St, W8. 071/727.3184

16 Geales ★★$ Geales was 50 years old in 1990, and its cottage dining room and rustic furniture remain loved by all who come here. The fish is fresh from Billingsgate and Grimsby, and the batter, which coats it, has beer in it. Try the crab soup before you tuck into a large cod and chips. If you think that's fattening, ask for the apple crumble for dessert and then try to stand up. Beer, wine, and champagne are available. No good fish shop is open on Monday (the fish would be over a day old), and Geales is no exception. ♦ Tu-Sa noon-3PM, 6-11PM. 2 Farmer St, W8. 071/727.7969

The stately homes of England
How beautifully they stand
to prove the upper classes
Have still the upper hand.

Noel Coward

17 Kensington Palace It looks more like a grand English country house than a palace, and that is the essence of its charm. Known in royal circles as *KP*, it is very much a living palace. Present residents include the **Prince** and **Princess of Wales** and the 2 little princes, who occupy the largest apartment, with 3

Cromwell & Brompton Roads

floors on the north side; **Prince** and **Princess Michael of Kent**; the **Duke** and **Duchess of Gloucester**, their 3 children, and his mother, **Princess Alice**, who have 35 rooms at their disposal; and **Princess Margaret**, who has a mere 20 rooms but the best views. The **Duke** and **Duchess of York** have a place in the country and live at Buckingham Palace when they're

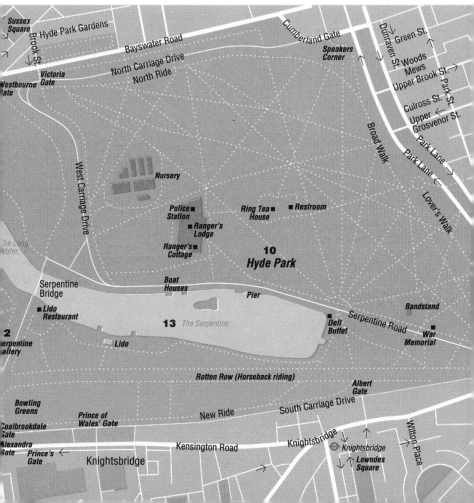

in town. The **Queen** decides who lives in the palace, and no one pays rent. But the residents are responsible for alterations and decorating, and their own electricity, telephone, and heating bills.

The palace's historical claims are quite considerable, dating back to 1689, when **William III** commissioned **Sir Christopher Wren** to build a palace out of the existing **Nottingham House**, away from the damp conditions of Whitehall Palace, which aggravated his asthma. Past residents include 5 monarchs: **William** and **Mary, Anne, George I,** and **George II. Queen Victoria** was born here and stayed until she became Queen and moved into Buckingham Palace. But it was in this nonpalatial palace, then known as Kensington House, that she was awakened with the news

Cromwell & Brompton Roads

that she was Queen, and it is here that the present Queen occasionally comes to visit her grandchildren.

In 1899, on Queen Victoria's 80th birthday, the **State Rooms** were opened to the public and in 1975 more rooms were opened.

A visit to the palace starts at the small entrance in front of the **Queen's Staircase**, where you buy tickets, guides, and cards. The steps lead to the **Queen's Apartments**, looking much as they did when Sir Christopher Wren decorated them for William and Mary. Next door to the **Queen's Gallery**, with fine carvings by **Grinling Gibbons**, is the **Queen's Closet**, which is anything but a closet. It was the setting for the famous and final quarrel between Queen Anne and the **Duchess of Marlborough**. After you pass the **Queen's Bedchamber**, with its tempting fourposter bed, the rooms become grander. The **Privy Chamber** has Mortlake tapestries by **William Kent** on the ceiling and overlooks the state apartments of Princess Margaret. Beyond are the **Presence Chamber** and the **King's Staircase**. One of the most stunning rooms is **King William's Gallery**, designed by Wren with woodcarvings by Gibbons and an Etruscan ceiling painted by Kent. This room leads into the **Duchess of Kent's** drawing room and its ante room, which contains Queen Victoria's Georgian dollhouse and her toys. But perhaps the favorite room is **Queen Victoria's Bedroom**, where the young princess received the news of her accession. It is now filled with mementos of the long-reigning queen, including the curtained cradle where her babies, and those of queens **Alexandra** and Mary, slept.

The **Council Chamber** contains souvenirs and artifacts from the *Great Exhibition,* including the painting over the mantelpiece of **Prince Albert** holding the plans of the Crystal Palace. Also look for the extraordinary ivory throne from India, the lavish silver-gilt table pieces, some of which were designed by Prince Albert, and the centerpiece with 4 of Queen Victoria's dogs. There is an excellent

exhibition of **Court Dress** on the ground floor. Princess Diana loaned the **Emanuel** wedding dress to the collection in 1987. This dress sums up everything about the story of her romance with Prince Charles— a fairy tale. More than any other, it has profoundly influenced the style of wedding dresses ever since.

British cook **Prue Leith** sometimes gets into action in the kitchens at Kensington Palace and produces delicious lunches and teas for the visitors in the **Orangerie** between July and September; do ask, it may be open. ♦ Admission. M-Sa 9AM-5PM (last admission 4:15PM); Su 1-5PM (last admission 4:15PM) Kensington Gardens, W8. 071/937.9561

18 Victoria and Albert Museum (Main quadrangle, 1856–84, **Fowke, Sykes**, and others; Cromwell Road entrance, 1909 **Sir Aston Webb**) If you have a curious mind and a receptive heart, and if you like *stuff,* the Victoria and Albert Museum will become one of your favorite places on earth. It is one of the most addictive and rewarding museums in the world, covering 12 acres of enchantment and delight. The museum is the prodigious offspring of the *Great Exhibition of 1851,* opening a year later as the **Museum of Manufactures**, with a collection of objects purchased from the exhibition. The initial intent was to display *manufactured* art, but when great works of art were bequeathed to the museum (including the permanent loan of the **Raphael Cartoons** and the largest collection of **Constables**), the scope expanded and the intention and name were changed to the **Museum of Ornamental Art**. In her last major engagement, **Queen Victoria** laid the foundation stone for the buildings that face Cromwell Road, and at her request the museum was renamed once again in 1899. The Victoria and Albert Museum, affectionately known as the **V&A**, is eclectic, idiosyncratic, and immense, yet accessible and humane, a museum that is worthy of the vision and energy of its founders.

If there is such a thing as the *South Kensington Style,* the V&A is its finest example. The massive building is a concoction of red brick, terra cotta, and mosaic, with assertions of Victorian confidence towering beside Victorian gloom. **Henry Cole**, the museum's first director, preferred engineers and artists to architects. The resulting cast-iron structure with corrugated-iron facings built by **William Cubitt** in 1855 looked more like a decorated factory and quickly became known as the *Brompton Boilers.* The building was removed in 1867 to form the Bethnal Green Museum. Sir Aston Webb's Cromwell Road facade, begun in 1891 and completed in 1909, evokes the Victorian ethos of pomp and imperial importance. It is flanked by statues of Queen Victoria and **Prince Albert** by **Alfred Drury**, and **Edward VII** and **Queen Alexander** by **Goscomb John**. On top of the great central tower is the figure of *Fame* resting upon a lantern shaped like an imperial crown.

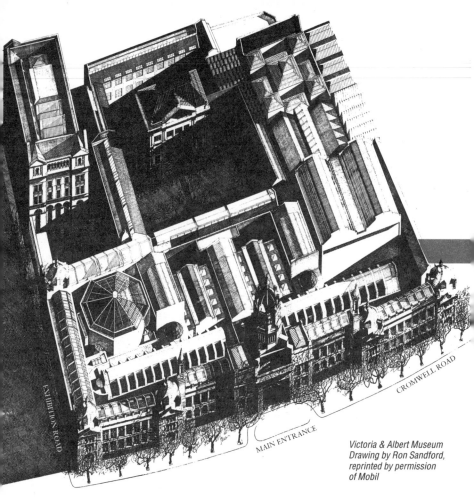

*Victoria & Albert Museum
Drawing by Ron Sandford,
reprinted by permission
of Mobil*

Entering the museum is like embarking on a great, extravagant, and wonderful expedition. You will get lost in the more than 150 rooms; not only is the V&A the best place in town to be lost, they actually suggest that's what you do in the guide book, for every cul-de-sac then becomes a treasure trove of discovery. The museum is now run by the firm hand of **Elizabeth Esteve-Coll**, but even the best-laid plans of museum curators are no substitute for a little aimless wandering. The maze of galleries and labyrinthine passages is still a wonderland where masterpieces hide behind idiosyncrasies.

There are 2 types of galleries within the museum. The **Art & Design Galleries** contain masterpieces grouped around a style, nationality, or period, while the **Materials & Techniques Galleries** revolve around a type of object, like silver or ceramics.

The V&A publishes an earnest guide that contains interesting bits of historical information on everything from the Renaissance to William Morris and divides the museum into 4 walks. The collections are vast, so be warned! If you are suffering from museum-lag and want to narrow down your looking, here is a list of some of the must-sees in the V&A.

Great Bed of Ware (c. 1590, English) The huge Elizabethan Bed of Ware was said to have been occupied by 26 butchers and their wives on 13 February 1689. In the 1830s, **Charles Dickens** tried to purchase the bed. It is easily the most famous bed in the world, mentioned by **Shakespeare** in *Twelfth Night* and by countless writers and historians. It is nearly 9 feet high, 11 feet long, and $10^1/_2$ feet wide, a size that sometimes distracts from the beauty of the carved, painted, and inlaid decoration. ◆ Room 54

Raphael Cartoons The cartoons, works of art in their own right, were drawn with chalk on paper and colored with distemper by Raphael and his scholars in 1513 as designs for tapestry work for **Pope Leo X**. The tapestries are still at the Vatican. Three of the original cartoons are now lost; the others are here because **Rubens** advised **Charles I** to buy them for the newly opened tapestry factory at Mortlake. After Charles' death, **Cromwell** bought them for £300 and they remained at Whitehall until **William III** moved them to Hampton Court. They have been on permanent loan at the V&A since Queen Victoria ruled Britain. ◆ Room 48

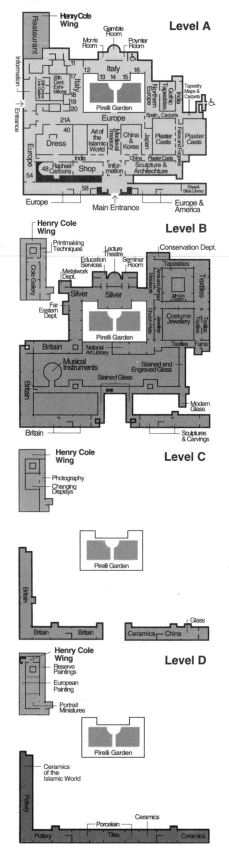

Norfolk House Music Room (c. 1753, English) This Baroque gold-and-white room was once in a grand London house on St. James's Square. The overmantel features a carved and gilded cluster of musical instruments. ♦ Room 58

Morris, Gamble, and Poynter Rooms The original tearoom, café, and restaurants in the museum occupied this space until 1939, and having been recently restored, they almost knock you sideways with longing for those esthetically elaborate and civilized days. The **Green Dining Room**, decorated for the museum by **William Morris** and **Philip Webb**, features Burne-Jones stained glass and painted panels representing the months of the year. The wallpaper and furniture are by William Morris. The chimney piece in the **Gamble Room** came from Dorchester House on Park Lane. It is surrounded by pillared and mirrored ceramic work and a ceiling of enameled iron plates that incorporates a quotation from *Ecclesiastes*. The dazzling materials were chosen not so much for their beauty but because they are fire resistent and easy to clean! The **Grill Room**, designed by **Sir Edward Poynter**, still has the original grill, set in a Dutch dream of Minton blue-and-white tiles representing the seasons and the months. The 3 rooms form a first-class example of Victorian design. ♦ Rooms 13-15

The Dress Collection The recently enlarged and expanded room houses a collection of fashion dating from around 1580 to the present and draws more crowds than any other exhibition in the V&A. The English and Continental male and female fashions, with outfits from the 1960s and early '70s, are strangely exotic and many are still eminently fashionable. ♦ Room 40

Fakes and Forgeries Even the floor has criminal undertones; it was laid by the women inmates of Woking Prison. In here are housed the best fakes of their kind from the hands of master forger **Giovanni Bastianini**, whose work is displayed among a host of other bogus objects purporting to be something they are not. ♦ Room 46

Sculpture The Renaissance in Italy. **Donatello** breathes life into stone in his marble relief, the *Ascension and the Madonna and Child*. Few can match his mastery, though **Rodin** does with the *St. John the Baptist*. ♦ Rooms 11-21A/48, Exhibition Rd entrance

British Art and Design, **1900–1960** Huge sealed glass rooms have been built to house the objects that trace British design from the Arts and Crafts movement started by William Morris in the 19th century to the new functionalism of the 20th. You will find furniture by **Charles Rene Mackintosh** and **Edwin Lutyens** and almost everything from the **Omega Workshops** (the decorative arts movement of Bloomsbury from 1913–1919), including sculptures by **Henri Gaudier-Brzesca**. ♦ 20th Century Exhibition Gallery

Restaurants/Nightlife: Red   **Hotels:** Blue

Shops/Parks: Green   **Sights/Culture:** Black

Henry Cole Wing This splendid addition opened in 1984 and houses the **Constable Collection**, which was presented to the museum by the artist's daughter. It provides a trip to the English countryside through the eyes and genius of one of England's most beloved painters. Especially appealing are the *Haywain* and *Salisbury Cathedral*. This painter, like no other, has captured the English countryside the way the English would like to believe it still could be. ♦ Exhibition Rd entrance

Free hour-long guided tours meet at the main (Cromwell Road) entrance of the V&A Monday-Saturday at 11AM, noon, 2, and 3PM. ♦ Voluntary contribution. M-Sa 10AM-5:50PM; Su 2:30-5:50PM. Cromwell Rd, SW1. Information 071/938.8441, main switchboard 071/938.8500

Within the Victoria and Albert Museum:

V&A Restaurant ★★$$ The restaurant on level A of the Henry Cole Wing is one of the best museum restaurants in town, with imaginative salads, first-class hot foods like crab pie, light, fluffy mousses for dessert, and excellent ordinary wines, including an English white wine. The restaurant is good for lunch, snacks, or afternoon tea. ♦ M-Sa 10AM-5:30PM; Su 2:30-5:30PM. 071/938.8500

V&A Shop Located to the left of the entrance, the shop is run separately from but for the museum by **V&A Enterprises**. The profits are all ploughed back into the V&A. Exclusive to the museum are the replicas of individual works of art within the V&A. These include the *Statue of Shakespeare* in terra cotta, and the ceramic alphabet tiles from the **Gamble Room**, known as the *Kensington Alphabet*. There is a vast range of stationery, diaries, and William Morris needlepoint cushions. The choice of postcards, books, and publications is outstanding. Just inside is the **V&A Crafts Shop**, a showcase for British craftspeople, with original objects in pottery, silver, gold, and glass—future treasures for the museum itself. ♦ M-Sa 10AM-5:50PM; Su 2:30-5:50PM. 071/938.8500

19 Ismaili Center (1983, **Casson, Conder & Partners**) The controversial modern building opposite the V&A is a religious and cultural center for the Islamic community. Prayers 8PM. Within the building is the **Zamana Gallery**, with an entrance on Cromwell Gardens. ♦ Free. Tu-Sa 10AM-5:30PM; Su noon-5:30PM. 1 Cromwell Gardens, SW7. 071/730.4830

20 Hoop & Toy ★$ The name of the pub refers to the game of metal hoop and wooden stick, which is now only featured in illustrated children's books. The pub has the atmosphere of days gone by, with gaslights outside, dark wood, polished brass, Edwardian drawings on the walls, and a menu with 18th-century dishes like beef-and-ale pie. A *Free House* that offers a large choice of beers and 7 real ales. ♦ M-F 11AM-11PM; Sa 11AM-3PM, 5:30-11PM; Su noon-3PM, 7-10:30PM. 34 Thurloe Pl, SW7. 071/589.8360

21 Daquise ★★$ For V&A regulars, the routine often includes lemon tea and apple strudel at this Polish café. Nothing has changed since WWII: the look of the Polish waitresses—young, pretty, and efficient; the menu of *golubcy* (stuffed cabbage), *kasza* (boiled buckwheat), *zrazy* (beef rolls stuffed with cucumber, bacon, and mushrooms). Polish émigrés meet here for morning coffee, lunch, afternoon tea, or dinner. ♦ Daily 10AM-11:30PM. 20 Thurloe St, SW7. 071/589.6117

22 Rembrandt Hotel $$ This appropriately named hotel facing the V&A has welcomed guests since the turn of the century. It is part of the **Sarova** group and offers the kinds of facilities that some travelers find very reassuring: fax, direct-dial telephones, and 24-hour

food and porterage service. The jewel in the hotel's crown is access (at extra cost) to the incredibly posh **Aquilla** health club, located within the hotel. The club is a conscious attempt to re-create a Roman spa. It is a marbled world of tiles, pillars, arches, and murals, complete with a gymnasium, a 50-by-20-foot pool with a Jacuzzi, a fountain, music, a grotto, a sauna, a solarium, and a salad bar. The hotel itself is more down-to-earth and present day, with 2 restaurants. **Masters** serves a buffet lunch and an à la carte dinner (with hotel classics like tournedos and scampi). The **Conservatory** offers light meals and sandwiches throughout the day and afternoon tea. You can get a traditional English breakfast here, including grilled kidneys, kippers, and smoked haddock, or try the buffet. ♦ 11 Thurloe Pl, SW7. 071/589.8100; fax 071/225.3363

22 Period Brass Lights An antique shop specializing in cast brass and Ormulu wall lights, chandeliers, Tiffany lamps, and English cut-glass lead crystal. ♦ M-F 9:30AM-5:30PM; Sa 9:30AM-6PM. 9A Thurloe Pl, SW7. 071/589.8305

23 M.P. Levene Ltd. This much-respected silver shop is a favorite with the diplomatic community in London. It carries an impressive choice of old Sheffield plates and silverware and a beautiful selection of silver frames and objects that are the epitome of the English country house. If you ask, the salespeople will patiently explain the markings on the English silver. ♦ M-F 9:30AM-6PM; Sa 10AM-1PM. 5 Thurloe Pl, SW7. 589.3755

24 Felton & Sons Ltd. One of the many joys of life in London is that flowers don't cost the earth. This florist has been here since 1900 and is known for its sumptuous and rare blossoms. ♦ M-F 8:30AM-5:30PM; Sa 8:30AM-noon. 220 Brompton Rd, SW3. 071/589.4433

24 The Wine Gallery ★★$ The vast majority of wine bars in London sell substandard wine, slabs of defrosted quiche, and salads straight from plastic tubs, delivered (one hopes) daily. But the Wine Gallery—or Galleries, as there are now 3 in London—serves good, honest wines and fresh food prepared with care and imagination. Try the salads, fishcakes, steamed mussels in season, and grills. ♦ M-F 12:30-3PM, 6:30-11PM. 234 Brompton Rd, SW3. 071/584.3493. Also at: 294 Westbourne Grove, W11. 071/229.1877

25 London Oratory of St. Philip Neri

(1880–93, **Herbert Gribble**) Better known as the **Brompton Oratory**, it is the first important Roman Catholic church to be built in London after the Reformation. There are few beautiful Catholic churches in London, but this one is sensational. The smell of incense greets you upon entering the High Roman oratory, with domes and vaults, a domed nave, and Italian ornaments and statues, including the Carrara marble statues of the **apostles**, carved by

Mazzuoli, a disciple of **Bernini**, which stood for 200 years in Siena Cathedral, and the altar in the **Lady Chapel**, constructed by **Corbarelli** and sons in 1693, which came from Brescia in northern Italy. In ecclesiastical and liturgical terms, an oratory is a congregation of secular priests living together without vows. The Fathers of the oratory are not monks, and thus are not bound together by the 3 religious vows but by the internal bond of charity and the external bond of a common life and rule.

The Oratorian Movement in England came about as the result of the conversion of **John Henry Newman**, a Victorian whose conversion to Catholicism shook the Anglican establishment. Don't miss the paintings of saints **Thomas More** and **John Fisher** by **Rex Whistler** in **St. Wilfred's Chapel**, and the dome, designed by **G. Sherrin**, with wooden ribs faced with 60 tons of lead. At 11AM on Sunday the church is packed with nearly 2000 people, both parishioners and visitors, for High Latin Mass with a full choir after the Italian manner. Every week you can hear work from the great composers, including **Dvorák** and **Bach**. The choirmaster, **Mr. Hoban,** works for the BBC, so the singing is perfection. ♦ Daily 6:30AM-8PM. Mass: M-Sa 7, 7:30, 8, 10AM, 12:30, 6PM. Benediction: Tu, Th 6:30PM. Latin sung High Mass: Su 7, 8, 9, 10, 11AM, 12:30, 3:30 (Vespers), 4:30, 7PM. Brompton Rd, SW3.

26 Holy Trinity (1829, **Donaldson**) In marked and very English contrast to its neighbor, the Brompton Oratory, Holy Trinity is Victorian Gothic. There is no smell of incense here. Holy Trinity is an Anglican Church with an active congregation involved in healing, movements for peace, and the Alternative Service. If women are ever ordained as priests in Britain, this church will be one of the first at which they can serve. The choir is exceptionally good. ♦ Cottage Pl, SW7

27 Brompton Square London excels at creating pretty squares, and it is hard to imagine a more humane design for urban planning. This early 19th-century square, which is not square or even rectangular but horseshoe shaped, is home for prosperous, house-proud Londoners whose only concessions to the 20th century are the burglar alarms mounted on the perfectly maintained houses and the BMWs that line the square. A plaque at **No. 6** honors the French poet **Stephane Mallarme**, who came to London to learn English and lived here in 1863. A chronically impoverished poet, however great his talent, would be unlikely to reside in this handsome square today.

28 James Hardy and Co. Ring the bell first and you will be warmly welcomed by these silversmiths, who have been here since 1853 and still have the original storefront to prove it. The shop carries silver frames, jewelry, antiques, and silverware. ♦ M-Sa 9:30AM-5:30PM. 235 Brompton Rd, SW3. 071/589.5050

28 Sun and Snow A smart (in the English sense) sportswear shop, with the latest in fashionable ski gear, including a good selection for kids. In summer, it carries everything you need for squash, tennis, swimming, and running. ♦ M-Sa 9:30AM-5:30PM. 229 Brompton Rd, SW3. 071/581.2039

29 St. Quentin ★★★$$$ *The Good Food Guide,* England's *Michelin,* wrote its 1986 entry for the Brasserie St. Quentin entirely in French, the first and only time the guide has done so. And this restaurant has stayed in the guide's top 10 restaurants ever since (albeit in English). Even though this *Frenchest* of restaurants is owned by

an Irishman, you are probably better off if you are unperturbed by Gallic manners. The food is extremely good but variable and you can expect no more nouvelle cuisine. Classic food is in—beef Bourguignon and steak *au poivre* deserve every star available, even if you have to complain to get served. You also won't find better cheeses or French bread. (The delicatessen at 256 Brompton Road has the best croissants, *pain aux* raisins, and other French treasures in town.) The décor is traditional brasserie, with a long zinc bar, mirrors, brass, glass, and waiters dressed the part. The tables along the banquette are uncomfortably close together, and you can't help but wish this were a real brasserie open all day long. **Café St. Quentin**, next door, offers café *complet* on weekends, an ideal start to a Saturday morning dedicated to the V&A. ♦ M-F noon-3PM, 7PM-midnight; Sa noon-4PM, 7PM-midnight; Su noon-4PM, 7-11:30PM. 243 Brompton Rd, SW3. 071/589.8005

30 La Brasserie ★★$ It has become a permanent fixture and it looks every bit the French brasserie you'd expect to find in Paris. The waiters are friendly, the food is so-so, but London Sloanes sob here, lovers eat breakfast here, and married couples steadfastly read the proffered papers here munching their croissants and sipping hot coffee. Great for snacks and watching London's glamorous residents gird their loins for an onslaught on Harrods and Beauchamp Place. ♦ Daily 8AM-midnight. 272 Brompton Rd, SW3. 071/584.1668

31 Number 16 $$ Even though the Victorians did everything in the grand manner, when 4 Victorian houses are knocked together it doesn't necessarily mean that the resulting hotel is large or spacious. But nostalgia buffs will forgive the occasional tiny room because, from the pretty morning room onward, all are lovingly furnished with antiques. In summer, it's bliss to sit out in the garden. ♦ 16 Sumner Pl, SW7. 071/589.5232; fax 071/584.8615

32 Blakes $$$ When actress **Anouska Hempel** became an interior designer, she knew how to emphasize the dramatic in her own extraordinary hotel. Black walls, natural leather, and bamboo furniture are enlivened by brilliantly colored parasols and flowers. Each opulent bedroom is individually styled with matching marble bathrooms; the lounge is decorated with Chinese panels, and a life-size model of **Marlene Dietrich** has been seen decorating the bar. The black-and-white restaurant has caged birds and loud music, and is expensive but very good. ♦ 33 Roland Gardens, SW7. 071/370.6701; fax 071/373.0442

Fulham Road Antiques

Antique lovers will perk up at the prospect of a long stroll down the Fulham Road. Furniture is expensive, but it is good quality and, in some cases, unique. The **Pelham Galleries** carries a range of English and European furniture from the 17th-19th centuries, clocks and Oriental lacquerware, and eye-wateringly expensive musical instruments. Some of the *objets d'art* are quite reasonably priced. At **Michael**

Lipitch (who also has a shop in New York), there are 5 floors of 18th-century English furniture, together with prints and watercolors. Then there's **Clifford Wright** for fabulous Regency gilt mirrors and furniture. For the truly daring, the sofa built for the Maharajah of Mysore and a French bedroom suite inlaid with mother of pearl can be found at the unconventional **Valerie Wade Antiques**, a shop usually associated with English or Kashmiri 19th-century papier-mâché trays and lamps and tables. Walnut lovers should try **Richard Courtney**, who specializes in this beautiful dappled wood, while the conventional may prefer to stare blissfully into the windows of shops like **Apter Fredericks**, with its fine 18th-century English furniture and exquisite Regency pieces.

Cromwell & Brompton Roads

33 San Frediano ★★★$$ London's favorite Italian restaurant is packed, relaxed, and fun. There's everything here, from good old minestrone and, of course, spaghetti, to the very un-Italian-sounding Barbary duck with wine and mango and reasonably priced wines. But you do have to book. ♦ M-Sa 12:30-2:30PM, 7:15-11:15PM; Su 12:30-3PM, 7:15-11:15PM. Fulham Rd, SW3. 071/584.8375

34 Souleiado This store is somehow reminiscent of the Mediterranean. Brightly colored materials from 200-year-old designs are printed from original wooden blocks and sold with TLC in this French-owned shop. ♦ M-F 9:30AM-5:30PM; Sa 10AM-5PM. 171 Fulham Rd, SW3. 071/589.6180

35 Butler & Wilson But why should I detour up this street? **Prince Charles** probably asks **Princess Diana** the same question, for en route to an official function she has been known to stop the royal entourage, nip into Butler & Wilson for a little bauble to match her latest creation, and then purr off in the royal limo. Fake jewelers to, well *dahlings*, everyone (who counts, that is). ♦ M-Sa 10AM-6PM. 189 Fulham Rd, SW3. 071/352.3045

36 Bibendum ★★★$$$ This spectacular Art Deco building was once owned by **Michelin**, the tire company. The company mascot was an unlikely bespectacled chap made entirely of white tires, who can still be seen occasionally gracing the top of truck cabs. His name was Bibendum and the restaurant is named after him. The food here will not give you a spare tire, and it is not rubbery. To the contrary, Bibendum is one of London's top 14 restaurants according to the 1990 *Good Food Guide*. The best ingredients go into every dish and the food is cooked to perfection on an ever-changing menu. On Sunday you will find mink-coated churchgoers walking through the door for lunch. Lunchtime is recommended; it is cheaper and less ostentatious than at dinnertime. There is an oyster stall outside every day that sells oysters whether there is an R in the month or not. Make a reservation when you book your flight. ♦ M-Sa 12:30-2:30PM,

7-11:30PM; Su 12:30-3PM, 7-10:30PM. Reservations required for dinner. Michelin House, 81 Fulham Rd, SW3. 071/581.5817

36 The Conran Shop Above, around, and to the side of Bibendum is **Sir Terence Conran**'s personal apotheosis, The Conran Shop. A legend in his lifetime, Conran brought style to London in the shape of his **Habitat** chain shops back in the '60s and '70s. The shop, Conran, is an extension of this. Perhaps he no longer needs to alter the style consciousness of the masses, for he now seems content to offer chic gewgaws to the rich. You can buy everything from leather-encased pencil sharpeners to bedspreads and furniture. But remember, the emphasis is on style first, quality second. ♦ M, W-Sa 9:30AM-6PM; Tu 10AM-6PM. 81 Fulham Rd, SW3. 071/589.7401

Cromwell & Brompton Roads

37 5151 ★★$$ **Giorgio Armani**, better known for his clothes, decided to buy this upmarket restaurant with Cajun cooking from the American south. They're so keen to be American here that they fly in Cajun spices and fresh fish daily! Testing out the authenticity is great fun, with blackened dishes like rib steak coated in a dark sauce, Louisiana jambalaya, shrimp creole, and good ol' pecan pie.♦ M-Sa noon-3PM, 6:30-11:30PM; Su 11:30AM-4PM, 6:30-10:30PM. Chelsea Cloisters, Sloane Ave, SW3. 071/730.5151

38 Zen ★★$$ Although it has been fashionable for many years; Zen gets the worst reviews, not because it's bad but because it varies. If you like Chinese cooking à la nouvelle, it is well worth the risk. However, regular diners and food lovers swear that the food here is excellent, and that the fish is superb. Try the steamed sea bass with ginger and onions, with, perhaps, the spiced braised eggplant. ♦ M-F noon-3PM, 6-11:30PM; Sa-Su noon-midnight. Chelsea Cloisters, Sloane Ave, SW3. 071/589.1781

39 Joseph The minimalist décor—black leather and white walls—gives a clue as to the goods on sale here. **Joseph Ettedgui**'s 2-floor department store contains a selection of everything that is designer chic in furnishings. Occasional tables, chairs, a sofa—some of the large goods are only available on order and can be found dotted about the women's department. There are vases everywhere, even in the men's clothing section. ♦ M-Tu, Th-F 10AM-6:30PM; W 10AM-7PM; Sa 9:30AM-6PM. 77-79 Fulham Rd, SW3. 071/823.9500

40 Joe's Cafe ★★$$ Owned by **Joseph Ettedgui** (of **Joseph** shops fame), this is a pretentious, style-conscious brasserie; if you have bought clothes at his store across the street, you will sit with an easy conscience. If not, you will succumb to the inexorable pull drawing you over to buy a little something for $200 or more. Resist just long enough to nibble on the pasta and swish down some of the delicious coffee. ♦ M-F noon-3:30PM; Sa noon-5PM; Su 11:30AM-3:30PM. 126 Draycott Ave, SW3. 071/225 2217

41 Walton Street Walton Street is a street in transition. Fashionable shops have pushed out the neighborhood hardware stores on this quiet street just steps away from the bustle of Brompton Road. Only the elegant window displays on the rather bare facades of the buildings at the lower end of the street reveal the array of goods inside: antique Rolex watches at **Van Petersen**; Lalique crystal vases at **Saville-Edells**; hand-knit sweaters by **Moussie Sayer** at **Moussie**. Members of the royal family decorate their nurseries with furniture made by the carpenters at **Dragon's**, and their heads with hats from **John Boyd**. Two 19th-century brick ovens turn out cookies, cakes, croissants, and even pizza at **Justin de Blanc Hygienic Bakery**. Restaurants such as **Ma Cuisine**, **San Martino**, and **Waltons** have loyal followings, and the only pub, **The Enterprise**, is a Walton Street institution. As you wander toward Beauchamp Place, the street's domestic side becomes apparent. The shops are less frequent and the facades grow brighter, turning into noble townhouses guarded by iron gates at the more affluent top end of the street.

41 Waltons ★★$$$ Brompton Cross is quite a little enclave of good places to eat, which is hardly surprising when you consider that this is the most exclusive area in London. At the height of the housing boom someone with more money than sense paid £36,500 for what turned out to be a cupboard! Their excuse was that they wanted a London address. Dress for the occasion, because everyone else does here. Rich up-to-the-minute cookery and opulent surroundings have contrived to keep this pricey but much-loved restaurant going for years. Try the poached veal with creamed parsley and morels to see just how delicious the cooking can be. ♦ M-Sa 12:30-2:30PM, 7:30-11:30PM; Su 12:30-2:30PM, 7:30-10:30PM. 121 Walton St, SW3. 071/584.0204

42 Van Petersen A bijou shop in a bijou street, Van Petersen sells original '30s jewelry and Georg Jensen silver, old Rolex and Cartier watches, and up-to-date jewelry. The quality is excellent, and it is not as expensive as might be expected for the area. ♦ M-Tu, Th-Sa 10AM-6PM; W 10AM-7PM. 117 Walton St, SW3. 071/589.2155

43 The Walton Street Stationery Company While your sheets are being stiched, pop across the street to this exquisite shop, which offers a similar service for your writing paper or invitations. If you have a style in mind, just tell them and it will be engraved or printed to your specifications. ♦ M-F 9:30AM-5:30PM; Sa 10AM-5PM. 97 Walton St, SW3. 071/589.0777

44 The Monogrammed Linen Shop This is where the cognoscenti come to buy Irish linen monogrammed sheets, duvet covers, dressing gowns, and handkerchiefs. Everything here has initials tastefully embroidered onto it. ♦ M-Sa 10AM-6PM.168 Walton St, SW3. 071/589.4033

London is a splendid place to live in for those who can get out of it. **Lord Balfour of Burleigh**

Walton Street Shopping Map

DRAYCOTT AVENUE

English restaurant **Waltons**
jewelry **Van Peterson**
French restaurant **Ma Cuisine**
Oriental knickknacks **Eastern Accents**
handknit sweaters **Moussie**
realtor **Maskells**
Concord Dry Cleaners
Italian restaurant **San Martino**
antique and modern lamps **Wonderful Lamps**
Walton St. Stationery Co.
dress agency **Pamela**
hatter **John Boyd**
French restaurant **Turners**
Knightsbridge Hand Laundry & Dry Cleaning
children's interior design **Nursery Window**
interior design **The Design Gallery**
women's clothing **Breeze**
maternity and kid's wear **Balloon**
hairdressers **Ellis/Helen**
fine art **Walker Bagshawe**
estate agent **Janet Osband**
estate agent **Halifax**

S.D. Fine Paintings *antique dog paintings*
Andrew Martin *interior design*
Oasis *artificial flora*
Stephanie Knight *gallery*
Carew Jones *custom-made furniture*
Percy Bass *eccentric interior design*
Merola *decadent jewelry*
Austen *sweaters*
Malcolm Innes *paintings*
Oliver Swann *paintings*
Monogrammed Linen Shop
Chesterfield *estate agents*
John Campbell *framing and restoration*
Maria Andipas Icon Gallery
Clarges Gallery
Mansfield *leather goods*
Arabesk *African jewelry*
Violy *women's clothing*
Susanne Garry *interior design*
Danielle *interior design*

WALTON STREET

FIRST STREET

public house **The Enterprise**
fine gifts **Saville-Edells**

HASKER STREET

kid's furniture **Dragons 1**
kid's designs **Patrizia Wigan**

antique prints **Stephanie Hoppen**

antiques **H.W. Newby**
maternity wear **Maman**

OVINGTON STREET

wine merchants **Threshers**

interior design **Nina Campbell**

horse paintings **The Walton Gallery**

deli **La Picena**

Italian restaurant **Scalini**

LENNOX GARDENS MEWS

Italian restaurant **Totos**

GYNDE MEWS

La Reserve *wine merchants*
Tapisserie *sew it yourself*

Wm. Hawkes & Sons *silversmith and jeweler*

Forty Eight Walton Street *antiques*

Justin De Blanc Hygienic Bakery

LENNOX GARDENS

OVINGTON SQUARE

WALTON STREET

BEAUCHAMP PLACE

PONT STREET
St. Columba's Church

45 English House ★★$$$ When you walk in, it feels as if you're in a private room in someone's home with mirrors, dark wallpaper, and *objets d'art*. Cooking extends from 18th century to Victorian, and there are some divine dishes like home oak-smoked chicken, turbot and scallop creams, and for dessert, walnut pie. ♦ M-Sa noon-2:30PM, 7:30-11:30PM; Su 12:30-2PM, 7:30-10PM. 3 Milner St, SW3. 071/584.3002

46 Saville-Edells A tiny shop stuffed to the gills with beautiful, expensive, and fascinating gifts that you won't find elsewhere. It is so cramped that every time you turn around, another piece of Lalique glass or piece of Limoges will present itself. Impossible to refuse. ♦ M-Sa 9:30AM-6PM. 25 Walton St, SW3. 071/584.4398

Cromwell & Brompton Roads

47 Dragons This shop is for grownups who want to give their children the childhood they never had. Until Dragons opened, no one could have had that kind of childhood anyway! The exquisite hand-painted children's furniture is made for the royal children and other fortunate young ones; there are children's fabrics, tiny seats, and even some toys (to keep the kiddies amused while their parents choose). ♦ M-F 9:30AM-5:30PM; Sa 10:30AM-4:30PM. 23 Walton St, SW3. 071/589.3795

48 Luba's Bistro ★★$ A fixture in the neighborhood since before WWII. Nothing has changed in the last 30 years, including the menu and, truly, the prices. Russian classics such as borscht, *kapoostniak* (braised cabbage with prunes and sour cream), blinis, and *vereniki* all make good beginnings. Follow them with the *kooliebiaka* (salmon trout pie), buckwheat piroshki, or chicken Kiev. Bring your own wine for tremendous savings. If you are watching your budget, the bistro might become a regular haunt. ♦ M-Sa noon-3PM, 6PM-midnight. 6 Yeoman's Row, SW3. 071/589.2950

49 Bunch of Grapes ★$ Once upon a time, a glass snobscreen separated the upstairs and downstairs bars in this authentic Victorian pub with its mirrors and glass screens. Now only the downstairs is in use and all is convivial and democratic, with tourists and locals alike welcomed and served delicious homemade food at lunchtime, snacks in the evening, and 4 real ales. ♦ M-Sa 11AM-11PM; Su noon-3PM, 7-10:45PM. 207 Brompton Rd, SW3. 071/589.4944

50 Crane Kalman Gallery Good 20th-century British and European paintings, with works by **Degas, Dufy, Nicholson, Moore,** and **Sutherland**, to name a distinguished few, exhibited in the gallery. ♦ M-F 10AM-6PM; Sa 10AM-4PM. 178 Brompton Rd, SW3. 071/584.7566

51 Alistair Sampson Go to the vast room in the back of this small antique shop to find early English pottery, oak furniture, brass, primitive paintings, and unusual decorative pieces. ♦ M-F 9:30AM-5:30PM. 156 Brompton Rd, SW3. 071/589.5272

52 Khun Akoran ★★$$ It's difficult to spot, b once you are inside this restaurant there is a lon and impressive list of classic Bangkok specialtie Try the *toong ngern yejyeung* (minced prawns and baby corn in a spicy sauce) and finish with the steamed whole banana with coconut cream. ♦ Daily noon-3PM, 7-11PM. 136 Brompton Rd, SW7. 071/225.2688

53 Shezan ★★$$ This Indian restaurant, in a quiet mews just off Montpelier Street, steadfastly maintains its reputation for outstanding Northern Punjabi haute cuisine. The décor is chic and minimal, allowing all attention to be focused on the delicately spiced food, which can be magical. Try the *murgh tikka Lahory*, the Khyberi chicken, or the butter *poussin*. A bottle of *Gewürztraminer* goes well with the food. ♦ M-Sa noon-2:30PM, 7-11:30PM. 16 Cheval Pl, SW7. 071/589.0314

54 Montpelier Street This Regency village between Brompton Road and Knightsbridge boasts some of the most expensive real estat in London. Check out the oils and watercolor carpets, clocks, porcelain, furniture, wine, sil ver, and jewelry offered at **W& F.C. Bonham Sons, Montpelier Galleries** (071/584.9161). Find out the time of the sale for the treasures that interest you. Silver is sold on Tuesday mid-monthly, furniture on Thursday once every 2 weeks, and antique jewelry and ceramic go under the hammer the last Friday of the month. If paintings interest you, watercolors are sold monthly on a Wednesday and oils monthly on a Thursday. When the big shows are on in London, like **Cruft's**, the **National Ca Show**, the **Chelsea Flower Show**, or the **Boat Show**, Bonhams has a painting auction to match it. And very popular they are, too. If yo like cats, dogs, flowers, or boats, this could b the time to stock up on the flat, oily variety.

55 Emporio Armani Mr. Tailored Jacket himse now owns 2 stores in London. When the Bon Street shop closed, the Italian clothes mogul couldn't resist opening up 2 new stores, but i the far more exclusive preserves of Knightsbridge and Sloane Street. It's a grand name for an Italian store on the grand scale, with sections for every kind of clothing— men's, women's, and *bambinis*, together with every accessory they'll need to get through life. After allowing your imagination, and perhaps your wallet, free rein, risk a healthy lunc of *pollo con radice di sedano* (strips of chicke with celeriac), followed by *semi freddo* (icecream cake) and a cup of delicious coffee. Emporio Armani has a coffee machine that makes up to 400 cups an hour! ♦ M-Tu, Th-S 10AM-6PM; W 10AM-7PM. 191 Brompton Rd, SW3. 071/823.8818

We don't bother much about dress and manners in England because, as a nation, we don't dress well and we have no manners.

George Bernard Shaw, *You Never Can Te*

Restaurants/Nightlife: Red   Hotels: Blue
Shops/Parks: Green
                                     Sights/Culture: Black

56 Beauchamp Place (Pronounced *Beecham* Place) Treat jostles with treat on this Regency street, where you can easily spend a whole day or a whole week shopping in the boutiques and smart shops. You will find the best of British designer clothes, old maps and prints, reject (not that you will ever find the flaw) china and crystal, antique silver, made-to-measure shoes, and lingerie fit for the Princess (who buys it here). While struggling to resist or not to resist the many covetables on the street, you can eat in restaurants that are equally smart, fun, and delicious.

56 Reject China Shops These are dotted along the street now and carry the finest porcelain, crystal, and stoneware. A certain energy and dedication is required to find the real bargains; there is a lot of truly awful stuff and the prices seem far from rejected. But if you have the stamina, you might be eating off the finest English, French, or Italian dinnerware the rest of your days, toasting with Baccarat or Waterford crystal, and gloating besides. **Beauchamp Place Corner** (34 Beauchamp Pl) carries bone china;

34-35 **Beauchamp Place** carries pottery, crystal, and gifts. ♦ M-Tu, Th-Sa 9AM-6PM; W 9AM-7PM. 071/581.5190/0737

56 Janet Reger If you are looking for crêpe de Chine pajamas and the kind of silk lingerie that the finest fantasies are made of, this is the only address you'll ever need. The brassieres are brilliantly designed, amplifying or diminishing with seductive perfection, as required. ♦ M-F 10AM-6PM; Sa 10AM-5PM. 2 Beauchamp Pl, SW3. 071/584.9360

57 The Map House Antique, rare, and decorative maps, botanical prints, lithographs, and aquatints line every inch of this tiny townhouse with honest prices. ♦ M-Sa 9:45AM-5:45PM. 54 Beauchamp Pl, SW3. 071/589.9821

Cromwell & Brompton Roads

57 Caroline Charles Recently moved across the street to larger premises, but this top English designer still sells only the finest silks

Beauchamp Place Shopping Map

BROMPTON ROAD

BEAUCHAMP PLACE (left)	BEAUCHAMP PLACE (right)
leather goods **Henry's**	**Reject China Shop**
Kinghtsbridge Furniture Co.	**Pasta Prego** *Italian restaurant*
Cushions & Covers	**Wedgewood at Chinacraft**
Shirtmakers **Valbridge**	**Janet Reger** *lingerie*
	Chinacraft
extravagant jewelry **Monty Don**	**Adele Davis** *women's clothing*
women's clothing **Caroline Charles**	**Sava** *women's clothing*
women's clothing **Beauchamp Place Shop**	
antique prints **The Map House**	**Shahzada** *Indian restaurant*
women's clothing **Monsoon**	**Jacquie** *women's clothing*
	Kanga *women's clothing*
jewelry **Annabel Jones**	**Yeldizlar** *Lebanese restaurant*
Pizza Pomodoro	**The Emanuel Shop**
cashmere **Shirin**	**Nakano** *Japanese restaurant*
jewelry **Ken Lane**	
women's clothing **Ci Bi**	**Caroline Charles** *women's clothing*
Portuguese restaurant **Ofado**	**Christina Stambolian** *evening wear*
women's clothing **Panton**	**13½** *Italian restaurant*
men's clothing **Huxley**	**Eyecompany** *optician*
Russian restaurant **Borscht n' Tears**	**Whistles** *women's clothing*
jewelry **Folli Follie**	**Ménage a Trois** *restaurant*
The Grove Tavern	**Stanley Leslie** *antique silver*
shirtmakers **Hilditch & Key**	**Paddy Campbell** *women's clothing*
handmade shoes **Deliss**	**Old England** *woolens*
	Delia Collins *beauty salon*
hairdresser **Edmonds**	**Clarabelle** *women's clothing*
Sonny's Coffee House	**San Lorenzo** *women's clothing*
Portuguese restaurant **Caravela**	**Video Shuttle**
Lebanese restaurant **Maroush II**	
women's clothing **Beachamp Place Shop**	**Maison Panache** *women's clothing*
	Sylvia's *novelty gifts*
women's clothing **Harabels**	**Scruples** *women's clothing*
Reject China Shop	**Bruce Oldfield** *women's clothing*
women's clothing **Spaghetti**	**McKenna** *antique jewelry*
oyster bar **Bill Bentley**	**Margaret Howell** *men's and women's clothing*
	Verbanella *Italian restaurant*

WALTON STREET

and linens. Caroline Charles' style is very English, but never without her own brand of sophisticated elegance. She creates clothes that you will want to wear for a lifetime.♦ M-Sa 9:30AM-5:30PM. 56-57 Beaucham Pl, SW3. 071/589.5850

58 Ménage à Trois ★★$$$ Popular with the **Princess of Wales**, whose eating habits once obsessed the press. The concept here is to serve first courses and desserts, but no main courses, so you can have a series of luxury dishes and a selection of desserts, yet still feel virtuous. The ingredients are truly palatial—salmon, scallops, langoustine, lobster, and caviar—all served with artistic verve. Even the matches are well-designed. You might walk past several times without seeing this base-

Cromwell & Brompton Roads

ment restaurant, but it is worth finding, a perfect place to celebrate an extravagant commitment at Caroline Charles, Janet Reger, or Bruce Oldfield, with the added bonus that whatever you bought will still fit after a meal here. ♦ M-F 11:45AM-3PM, 7-11:45PM; Sa 7-11:45PM; Su 7-10:30PM. 15 Beauchamp Pl, SW3. 071/589.4252

58 San Lorenzo ★★★$$$$ One day, **Princess Diana** was spotted having lunch here with some chums. It's nice to think that the royal family shops and eats locally. (After all, KP is just up the road.) This first-class Italian restaurant attracts the kind of people who appreciate carpaccio prepared 3 ways, fresh game in season (pheasant with chestnuts), and tripe with Parma ham. The staff seems to know all the glamorous hairdos and suits personally, but service to unknowns is just as attentive and courteous. ♦ M-Sa 12:30-3PM, 7:30-11:30PM. 22 Beauchamp Pl, SW3. 071/584.1074, 071/589.4633

58 Bruce Oldfield What do **Joan Collins** and **Princess Diana** have in common? A passion for Bruce Oldfield, who creates evening dresses that cling to the wearer and linger in the memories of everyone else. If you have what it takes to wear his creations (the figures in every sense) you are lucky, indeed. ♦ M-F 10AM-6PM; Sa 11AM-5:30PM. 27 Beauchamp Pl, SW3. 071/584.1363

59 Deliss Come here if you do not have neutral feet—that is, if you suffer from chronic footache because you are impossible to fit. Among the sizeable feet shod here are those belonging to **Keith Richards, Princess Michael of Kent, Jesse Norman**, and **Marvin Mitchelson**. The shoes are beautiful and at prices you can actually consider. The shop will also make shoes from your own design or copy a pair of old favorites—many make a special trip just for this service alone. ♦ M-F 9:30AM-5:30PM; Sa noon-4PM. 41 Beauchamp Pl, SW3. 071/584.3321

Restaurants/Nightlife: Red   Hotels: Blue
Shops/Parks: Green   **Sights/Culture: Black**

59 Bill Bentley's ★★$$ Sit at the bar, order a dozen oysters and a half bottle of Muscadet, and thank your lucky stars you are in London. The proper restaurant upstairs serves British fish dishes such as Dover sole and salmon trout. ♦ M-Sa 11:30AM-2:30PM, 6:30-10:30PM. 31 Beauchamp Pl, SW3.Reservations required for dinner. 071/589.5080

60 Harrods (1901–5, **Stevens and Munt**) In the past, man's desire for greatness led to the creation of cathedrals and palaces. Today, it leads to department stores, and Harrods is Notre Dame, the Taj Mahal, and Blenheim. Even if the argument Bloomingdales vs. Harrods rages over dinner tables, and even if the silk-scarf ladies of England vow that Harrods has gone downhill, the fact remains that this cathedral of consumerism is hard to beat.

Behind the solid and elegant Edwardian facade, 4000 employees in 230 departments stand ready to fulfill your every request. You can hire a chauffeur, organize a funeral, open a bank account, book a trip around the world, reserve all your theater and concert tickets, get your lighter repaired, your clothes dry-cleaned, and your nails built up in the beauty salon. There's even a special long-hair department in the salon. And, of course, you can buy just about everything your heart desires, including a yellow labrador from the pet department, a pair of Rayne pumps (preferred by the **Queen** and **Mrs. Thatcher**), a dress by **Zandra Rhodes**, a £1m Baccarat crystal table, a set of pale-blue Egyptian cotton sheets, and a bottle of Krug Grand Cuvée to be delivered to your hotel and drunk whilst adding up the bills. If you are afraid that this palace of temptation will make you lose sight of the exchange rate, plan your visit around the January sale, the most famous event of the year. It is a true test of consumer stamina, but if you are tenacious and strong you will be rewarded with real bargains.

Above all, don't miss the **Food Halls**, with their stunning mosaic friezes and fabulous displays of food. (The wet-fish display is a masterpiece!)

For a sociological study of one of the purest slices of English life, go up to the kennel, where English ladies up from the country for the day leave their labradors and Jack Russells.

Harrods has 5 restaurants and 5 bars, including a health juice bar and a wine bar. The **Georgian Room** is always *full up* for tea. People start lining up outside the elegant double-banquet room around 3:15PM, hoping to sit on the green-velvet furnishings and sip tea at the tables covered with pink linens and an array of buns, pastries, salads, butters, creams, and jams. ♦ M-Tu, Th-Sa 9AM-6PM; W 9:30AM-7PM. 87235 Brompton Rd, SW1. 071/730.1234, theater tickets 071/589.1101

61 Le Metro ★★★$$ The only drawback to this wine bar is its popularity; if dozens were to pop up all over London, the quality of life would be immeasurably improved. The restaurant serves the best of things French—salad *frissée aux foies* *de volailles*, cheeses that are fresh and ripe, good soups, casseroles, and tarts, and a choice of first-rate, carefully chosen wines, with a special selection of important *crus* by the glass, made possible by the *cruover* machine. Le Metro now stays open in the afternoon, when one would dearly love a cup of good coffee and a *croque-monsieur*. And it opens early in the morning for genuine espresso or frothy café crème and croissants. ♦ M-Sa 7:30AM-11PM; Su 7:30AM -11AM. 28 Basil St, SW3. 071/589.6286.

61 L'Hotel $$ A small country inn—the kind you never seem to find—located right in the heart of Knightsbridge. There are only 12 rooms, so you have to book well in advance in order to have pine furniture, Laura Ashley fabrics, twin beds, color TV, and clock radios, all at a reasonable price. This is the stepchild of the elegant **Capital Hotel** 2 doors down. It is extremely popular with discriminating Americans who aren't on expense accounts. The front door is locked at 10PM during the week and 6PM on weekends, but you pick up your key from the Capital, which adds to the sense of adventure. And then there is Le Metro wine bar next door, which can be entered from L'Hotel. For the lone traveler, this is one of the best places in London to stay and feel at home. A Continental breakfast is included in the price. ♦ 28 Basil St, SW3. 081/590.6286; fax 071/225.0011

61 Capital Hotel $$$$ **David Levin**, the darling of London, is a first-class hotelier, and when he decided to open his own hotel he went about creating the very best. The Capital is small, modern, sophisticated, personal, attractive, and one minute from Harrods. The 48 rooms are packed with as many of the creature comforts as could fit into the rather small dimensions, including bathrobes, toothbrushes, and roses for every lady. If you consider the elegant surroundings, perfect location, and standard of service, even the price seems reasonable. ♦ Basil St, SW3. 071/589.5171; fax 071/225.011

Within the Capital Hotel:

Capital Hotel Restaurant ★★★$$ With its own *Michelin* star and plaudits from *The Good Food Guide*, the restaurant has put the Capital Hotel on the map. Accolades for the chef, **Phillip Britten**, appear with delicious regularity in the British press. Decorated in delicate pinks, this is a luxury restaurant without the asphyxiating atmosphere of deluxe. The menu changes every few months but the fish soup or filet of steak on wild mushrooms are always good choices. The chocolate mousse is justly famous, and the French wine list draws serious winelovers from far and wide. ♦ M-Sa 12:30-2:30PM, 6:30-10:30PM; Su 12:30-2PM, 7-10PM. 071/589.5171

62 Basil Street Hotel $$ Traditional English charm abounds at Basil Street, which has been owned by the same family since it was built in 1910. It rambles eccentrically from floor to floor and is stuffed full of antiques—the place is an old-fashioned delight. It has a

loyal clientele of English country folk who make twice-yearly trips to London to shop and see plays. The prices appeal to the British sense of economy, the location is ideal, and the service is proper. Afternoon tea in the lounge is an institution and served in a room that looks like a setting for an Agatha Christie novel, with the characters and the tea seemingly untouched by the passage of time. Also popular with the frugal English is the restaurant upstairs. The salad bar, buffet, and selection of hot dishes are almost in the category of English school food, but a cut above. ♦ 8 Basil St, SW3. 071/581.3311; fax 071/581.3693

63 Scotch House Believe it or not, if you want a cashmere sweater or scarf, you will do better here in terms of quality and price than at

Cromwell & Brompton Roads

Harrods. The shop has a huge choice of the best Scottish woolens, including 300 kilts and a book that can match names with patterns. There's also a good children's department with kilts and jumpers and even those unfortunate, tiny Burberrys that make kids look like dwarves. The French, astute shoppers that they are, come here as soon as they arrive in London. ♦ M-Tu, Th-Sa 9AM-6PM; W 9AM-7PM. 2 Brompton Rd, SW1. 071/581.2151

63 Mr. Chow ★★★$$$ The restaurant's popularity goes back to the '60s, when the owner decided to combine the style and exuberance of an Italian restaurant, complete with Italian waiters, with the innate nouvelle cuisine of the finest Chinese cooking. The décor is chrome and dimmed glass with the chic of another era, and the inventive menu is explained in down-to-earth language: drunken fish (sautéed with consommé and Chinese wine), gambler's duck (like Peking Duck but better), and jade noodles with pork and prawns. The perfect choice from the wine list is a bottle of *Gewürztraminer*, which goes well with the subtly spiced food. ♦ Daily 12:30-2:45PM, 7-11:45PM. 151 Knightsbridge, SW1. 071/589.7347/8656

64 Hyde Park Hotel $$$$ More a stately home than a hotel, the Hyde Park is as much a Knightsbridge institution as the Horse Guards who trot past it each day. The Edwardian splendor of the magnificent marble entrance hall, gilded and molded ceilings, and Persian carpets the size of cricket fields leaves you wondering how Buckingham Palace can hold a candle to it, and one suspects that the service is far better here. Guests who have delighted in the pampering include **Winston Churchill** and **Mahatma Gandhi**, for whom a goat was milked each day. In the last few years, the hotel has been completely refurbished with no expense spared. Although you no longer see the maharajahs and sultans who occupied whole floors in the days before WWI, you do see the soignée jet set who are impossible to tie to a nationality, and even Armani-clad

only find designer labels here. Men's wear in the basement, fashionable accessories on the ground floor, big-name designers on the 1st. Then watch the prices drop marginally as you ascend the moving stairs. On the top, the beauty department will restore your ailing spirits. ◆ M-F 10AM-8PM; Sa 10AM-6PM. 109 Knightsbridge, SW1. 071/235.5000

65 Sheraton Park Tower $$$$ The modern exterior looks like a brick ear of corn, and it hasn't improved with age. But this circular luxury hotel offers that marvelously egalitarian notion of equal-size rooms with a view (the higher up the 17 stories you go, the better the room and the view), and you can absolutely count on spacious comfort and reliable service. There is even a complimentary valet who will unpack your suitcase. ◆ 101 Knightsbridge, SW1. 071/235.8050; fax 071235.8231

Within the Sheraton Park Tower:
The Bar, Champagne Bar, Rotunda, and Restaurant ★$$ French-influenced gourmet menus, à la carte lunches and suppers, and snacks. Service is as simple as the names of the establishments, with a useful range of buffets and prix-fixe pretheater menus. ◆ Daily 7AM-11:30PM

66 The Berkeley $$$$ It is pronounced the *Barkly*, and despite the overall theme of rich elegance, it has a personality of its own. The hotel is known for providing service to suit every whim, including a rooftop indoor-outdoor swimming pool where **Jesse Norman** takes an occasional plunge, a sauna, a small, exclusive cinema (the **Minema**), and a florist. Such distinguished luxury is usually associated with things of the past. But this Berkeley is relatively new, built in 1972. The old Berkeley, which sat on the corner of Berkeley Street and Piccadilly, wasn't left behind; the charming reception room, complete with paneling, designed by a young and unknown architect named **Sir Edwin Lutyens**, was reerected here. It is this obsessive attention to detail that makes the hotel one of the most popular in London. ◆ Deluxe ◆ Wilton Pl, SW1. 071/235.6000; fax 071/235 4330

Within the Berkeley:
Berkeley Restaurant ★★$$$ Bartolozzi's 18th-century reproductions of the Queen's **Holbein** collection adorn the paneled walls of this very Engish room furnished in Colefax and Fowler chintzes and lime-oaked paneling, with a portrait of **Sir Thomas More** observing the elegant surroundings. The food is English and Continental and very good indeed, with skillful handling of baby spring lamb, game in season, and the best fish. ◆ M-F 1-2:30PM, 7-11PM; Su 12:30-2:30PM, 6:45-10:45PM. 071/235.6000

Buttery ★$$ Named after the restaurant that stood on the corner of Berkeley Street and Piccadilly for 60 years, the new Buttery doesn't quite attract the beau monde of its namesake, but it has other merits. Chief among them is the magnificent fresh fish

Italian football managers sitting in the bar. The rooms and suites are country-house size and furnished with silk curtains, brass beds, and good antiques, recalling the tranquility of a country château. ◆ 66 Knightsbridge, SW1. 071/235.2000; fax 071/235.4552

Within the Hyde Park Hotel:
Park Room ★★$$ This grandly proportioned restaurant overlooks the greenery of Hyde Park's Rotten Row. Underneath the crystal chandeliers of this enormous room decorated in gold leaf, a new style of Northern Mediterranean cooking has been introduced, avoiding butter and cream. At midday, a sumptuous self-service luncheon is laid out in the center of the room, with layers of tender, cold roast beef, chicken-liver pâté, and salads amid the silver and fine china. It is just enough delicious nourishment for an afternoon of shopping at Harrods. The Park Room is also open for breakfast (try the scrambled eggs wrapped in smoked salmon), morning coffee, afternoon tea, and dinner. ◆ M-Sa 7:30AM-11PM; Su 8AM-11PM. 071/235.2000

Grill Room ★★$$$ The quintessentially English menu comprises roasts and grills, and a very good wine list with a large selection of first-grove clarets to complement the fine Scottish beef or rack of lamb, all served in an intimate oak-paneled room. ◆ M-F 12:30-2:30PM, 7-11PM; Su 12:30-2:30PM, 7-10PM. 071/235.2000

65 Harvey Nichols Like 2 guards at each end of Sloane Street, the General Trading Company at Sloane Square and Harvey Nichols at Knightsbridge are the arbiters of London's jet set chic. *Harvey Nix*, as it's lovingly called, is a department store devoted solely to fashion—you'll

display that allows you to choose the fish of your choice from the menu. At lunchtime, there is a tempting Italian hot-and-cold buffet, as well as à la carte. In the evening, there are excellent steaks, pasta dishes, and more seafood. ♦ M-Sa 12:30-2:30PM, 7:30-11PM. 071/235.6000

Perroquet Bar ★$$ This bar is open late for theater and clubgoers to relax in after the lights have dimmed elsewhere. ♦ M-Sa 11AM-12:30AM. 071/235.6000

Minema The unique cinema has regular film showings (well-chosen foreign films in particular) and is available for private showings. It is comfortable, small, and much-loved by cinema buffs. ♦ Seats 68. 071/235.6000

67 Grenadier ★★★$ The atmosphere of this pub is as old and military as in the days when it was the officer's mess for the **Duke of Wellington**'s soldiers, complete with a ghost of an officer who was flogged to death for cheating at cards. The excellent officer's fare in the finest British tradition is highly thought of, so if you want to have lunch or dinner it helps to book. But if at the end of a long day spent in South Kensington and Knightsbridge all you want is a bitter, you can count on the best, and a warm welcome as well. ♦ M-Sa 11AM-3PM, 5:30-11PM; Su noon-3PM, 6-10:30PM. 18 Wilton Row, SW1. 071/235.3074

Portobello Road Market
London has nearly 60 street markets, and Portobello Road Market in Kensington is among the most intriguing. Every Saturday thousands of bargain-hunting tourists and collectors converge on the narrow mile-long stretch of road in search of that one-of-a-kind souvenir or long-lost silver teapot. You can find a little of everything in the 2000 stalls lining Portobello Road, from antiques and silver (for which the market is especially well known) to coins, kitchenware, rugs, bicycles, records, and secondhand clothes. Real treasures—and bargains—are rare, and there is a lot of junk, but the fun is in the search, and if you are dedicated you will find dealers with interesting things at reasonable prices. You can lunch on delicious savory and sweet crêpes at Obelix, located in the middle of the market, or stop for a snack at the food stalls at the north end of the road. Take the underground to Notting Hill Gate and walk up Pembridge Rd, W11. ♦ Antique market: Sa 8:30AM-5PM. Some shops: M-F 9AM-5PM

Tea Trivia
Green Gunpowder is a full-leaf tea rolled into a little ball; it was named by sailors who were reminded of a ball of lead shot.

Brewing up:

1 min for tea bags

3 min for Assam and small-leaf teas

4-5 min for Ceylon, Darjeeling, and medium-leaf teas

7 min for large-leaf teas like Green Gunpowder .

A Chinese Mandarin was so delighted with the 2nd Earl Grey's praise of his tea that he made a special blend and named it after the Earl.

Jim Dine
Artist

South Kensington. The tube station and the beautiful early 19th-century streets and squares around my studio.

Victoria and Albert Museum. I have spent many, many years learning there. I go to see the ceramics in the Shriber Collection. I have a big collection of 18th-century English pottery called Wheildon, and they have marvelous examples of 19th-century English pottery and ceramics. You never can miss at the V&A—there is always something great.

Pontenuovo, near where I live off Fulham Road. A man called Mr. Pasquale is the co-owner or head

Cromwell & Brompton Roads

waiter or whatever he is, but I have known him for many years at other restaurants, too.

Wilton's. It never changes, and it is always great.

British Museum. I always go to see the antiquities in the Egyptian room, which is just grand. I don't always see the Elgin Marbles—they are too much for me sometimes, so I save them for every 2 or 3 years. I always hit the room with just Etruscan bronzes in the cases that are endless, and I sit there and draw a little drawing.

National Gallery. It is fabulous, but I don't go there all the time, partly because of how you get there. To me, Trafalgar Square is inaccessible—you can't park, and I drive or take my bicycle almost everywhere.

Harrods, to get my hair cut.

Lou Klein
Designer, Alexandria, Virginia

Go to the **Food Hall** in **Harrods Department Store** to look at the amazing fish sculpture, which could be an enormous lobster with a trout in each claw and millions of anchovy around it, a cluster of huge Dover soles surrounded by prawns and kippers, or a manta ray formed in the shape of a tulip surrounded by countless sardines and shrimps, all constantly being cooled with a fine spray of water from a tiny fountain that is hidden in the middle.

Alan Fletcher
Designer, London

Anything Left Handed, whose motto is *our customers are never right*, carries scissors, pens, rulers, corkscrews, and other practical items for lefties.

Evan Hunter
Author

Hyde Park on a Sunday. The music from the bandshell. People renting chairs. Lovers holding hands and strolling. For me, it's always sunny on a Hyde Park Sunday.

Restaurants/Nightlife: Red   Hotels: Blue
Shops/Parks: Green   Sights/Culture: Black

King's Road & Chelsea

The **King's Road**, romantic, free, and fitful, runs the entire length of a territory known as **Chelsea**, synonym for swinging London in the '60s, now a chiaroscuro stageset for '50s lovers, punks, and Sloane Rangers. Chelsea is the most authentic village left in London. The neighborhood nestles against the River Thames, south of Westminster and Hyde Park, and has a glowing riverside personality. King's Road, parallel to but out of sight of the river, is Chelsea's main street, a long, straight, and irresistible thoroughfare that flows through—and animates—the ancient and modern neighborhood.

Spending a day in Chelsea, strolling down the King's Road and wandering down the side streets, is one of the best ways to feel like you are on a first-name basis with London. The streets, the architecture, and the history have a sympathetic and humane dimension, crowned by **Christopher Wren**'s magnificent **Royal Hospital**. For many Londoners, this is the most beautiful

building in the city, and it still provides shelter to war veterans whose distinguished scarlet-and-blue uniforms are part of the iconography of Chelsea life. It is here, in Chelsea, in houses that have become grand in our inflationary age, that **Oscar Wilde, Whistler, Sargent, Thomas Carlyle**, and **Turner** lived in an atmosphere of all-pervasive coziness. History feels oddly personal here, as though the ghosts of **Henry James, Augustus John**, and Wilde walk the streets in their dressing gowns. The atmosphere of bohemian nonchalance survives in spite of the high cost of property and the cruel clog of cars.

The King's Road, however, has a personality all its own. This vital highway, created by **Charles II** as his *Route de Roi* to Hampton Court, is the backbone of Chelsea, and it is avant-garde, unpredictable, ever changing, anarchic, life-loving, decadent, visual, and overtly self-conscious. Chelsea, in sharp contrast, is profoundly residential, a village of prosperous residents who pay dearly to live in desirable houses in a maze of narrow, well-kept streets. Chelsea dwellers are stylish Londoners who appreciate the potent legacy of their *quartier's* past: riverside town, royal suburb, and artists' colony of London. They enjoy the domestic, relaxed scale of the streets lined with trees and privilege and

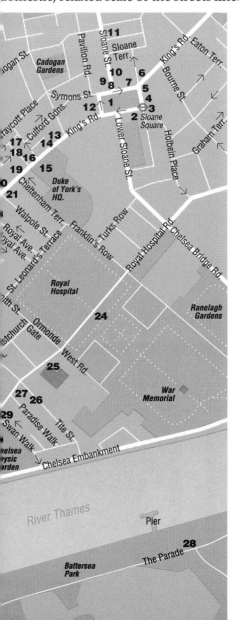

family houses (there are relatively few apartments in this area), and they endure with confident humor the King's Road, confining their regrets to the little fishmonger, the greengrocer, and the local baker, most of whom have been replaced by boutiques and antique markets.

Even if the area no longer vibrates with the fashions of **Mary Quant** or provides domiciles for **The Rolling Stones**, it has an innate vitality and a tantalizing variety of styles and beliefs. Until 1985, this was **Margaret Thatcher's** private London address; it is where punk began and survives; and it is the original home of the **Designer's Guild.** Currents of illustrious history flow like clear streams in the little side streets. The King's Road may seem tame and peaceful now, but dotted along the way, in shops no wider than a king-size bed, the fashions of the future, for better or for worse, are being scissored today.

This walk features a long thoroughfare, but ideally it should be explored in a circular manner, leaving the King's Road at **Royal Avenue** to enjoy the dense history, neighborhood pubs, and riverside easiness of Chelsea, then returning to the King's Road at **Beaufort Street** and going back in the direction of **Sloane Square.** The ideal day to be here is on a Saturday, when the King's Road is in full bloom, complete with poseurs and weddings, residents and visitors.

1 Sloane Square (c. 1780, Henry Holland) Chelsea begins here, under a tent of young plane trees and with a soundtrack of cars and taxis that drowns out the watery music of one of London's rare fountains (by **Gilbert Ledward**, presented to Chelsea by the Royal Academy in 1953). Nothing grows in the square, save the trees, but color is provided by the flower seller who is here, day in and day out, year-round. The square was named after one of Chelsea's most distinguished residents, **Sir Hans Sloane**, a wealthy physician at the beginning of the 18th century, president of the Royal Society, and at one time, owner of practically all of the village of Chelsea. Sloane lived in **Henry VIII**'s former manor house, and his vast collection of plant specimens, fossils, rocks, minerals, and books formed the foundation of the British Museum.

2 W.H. Smiths This ubiquitous bookseller—70 branches within London—located on the south side of Sloane Square is a good place

King's Road & Chelsea

to acquire maps, guides, writing paper, pens, magazines, newspapers, and paperbacks. There is also a large selection of international periodicals. ♦ M-Sa 8:30AM-6:30PM. Sloane Sq, SW1. 071/730.0351

3 Sloane Square Tube Station (District and Circle lines) The underground station was built over one of London's streams (the Westbourne), which is carried in a cast-iron conduit above the trains. In 1940, a German bomb hit the station, fracturing a gas main and injuring and killing scores of staff and passengers. This is the only tube station that serves Chelsea. ♦ Sloane Sq, SW1

4 Royal Court Theatre (1888, **Walter Emden** and **W.R. Crewe;** remodeled 1965, 1985) *Look Back in Anger* put the 1950s, Chelsea

playwright **John Osborne**, and the Royal Court Theatre on the map. After the dramatic explosion of the angry young men, things were never quite the same. Postwar England had to make way for a new aristocracy of bitter talent, relinquishing the stronghold of the duller, safer aristocracy based on class. In fact, the message had been preached at the Royal Court for decades, when **Harley Granville Barker** was producing (1904–7) the early plays of **George Bernard Shaw**. Now this is the resident theater for the **English Stage Company**, and productions are invariably original, controversial, and well worth taking a chance on if you want to see the best in London theater. ♦ Sloane Sq, SW1. 071/730.1745

5 Oriel Grande Brasserie de la Place ★★★$$ Still looking good, this relative newcomer to Sloane Square is a French café, with most of the advantages of a French café—good coffee and croissants served early in the morning, *croque-monsieurs* served all day, good wine by the glass, newspapers on sticks, attractive cane chairs, and marble-top tables. But you will long for the speed and professionalism of French waiters, sadly lacking in their English counterparts. It is the best place in the area for breakfast, and good for lunch and dinner as well. Fits in perfectly with an evening at the Royal Court Theatre. (Dickensian warning: it gets crowded at lunch and late afternoon—watch your belongings.) ♦ M-Sa 8:30AM-11PM; Su 8:30AM-9PM. 50-51 Sloane Sq, SW1. 071/730.2804

6 David Mellor Outstanding contemporary design for the kitchen and dining room. Handmade wooden salad bowls and pottery bowls and glassware—the best from British craftspeople—along with a superb choice from France. Friendly and helpful staff, which can mean a wait! The specialty here is cutlery designed by the great man himself, who,

Sloanedom

You don't have to be in London long before you hear the word Sloane, referring not only to the square but to a group of people identified by the name and its appendage, *Sloane Ranger*. It all began when 2 clever journalists, **Peter York** and **Ann Barr**, decided to call a certain class of Englishmen *Sloanes*, and their girlfriends, sisters, mothers, and wives, *Sloane Rangers*. Sloane Ranger-land is briefly defined as the postal districts SW 3, 5, 7, and 10, known to the public as Knightsbridge, South Kensington, and Chelsea, although in these inflationary times the Sloanes extend south of the river as far as Battersea and Clapham (**Sarah Ferguson** had a flat on Lavender Hill before marrying the Duke of York), Wandsworth and Putney. Sloane is not the English equivalent of preppy because the layers of class and tradition are too deep and inimitable. You can identify Sloanes by their speech (eavesdrop at the **General Trading Company**) and by their dress (silk Hermès headscarfs tied under the chin, strings of pearls—even with sweatshirts from Benetton—gold signet

rings on the little finger, *puffa* ski jackets, Labradors never far behind). The best Sloane of all is the **Princess of Wales**, but to really understand Sloanedom you have to remember those pictures of her when she first got engaged: ruffled shirt with ribbons at the neck, round cheeks, and flat shoes. She had a Sloane job (working in a kindergarten—Sloanes have the minimum formal education, and the Princess of Wales does not even have the English equivalent to a high-school diploma) and Sloane instincts (a love of home, animals, the countryside, and children). The Sloane world is the English world of nannies, private schools, church weddings, Ascot, the Chelsea Flower Show, pheasants (which they raise, shoot, and eat), Christmas, and dogs. And if this all sounds incomprehensibly vague, buy the *Sloane Ranger Handbook*, a thorough and amusing sociological survey of a single class that became a bestseller, available at the General Trading Company or **W.H. Smith**—for those who prefer to read about them rather than view them in action.

incidentally, is no relation to the Tory MP David Mellor—they just share the same name. ♦ M-F 10AM-6:30PM; Sa 10AM-6PM. 4 Sloane Sq, SW1. 071/730.4259

7 Royal Court Hotel $$ No matter how much they fix this place up, it still has the atmosphere of a provincial English hotel located near the train station. The 101 rooms have all the modern comforts, including 24-hour room service. Gold-and-black braid decorates the top-hatted doorman who, in his ornate dress, has become a fixture in the square. ♦ 12 Sloane Sq, SW1. 071/730.9191; fax 071/824.8381

Within the Royal Court Hotel:

No. 12 ★★$ Numbers are big in London right now as far as restaurants' names are concerned, and the **Old Poodle Dog**, as this was once known, is no exception. The name change and refurbishment herald yet another attempt to help the place become a cut above provincial. Frequented by quiet, well-to-do Chelsea types, it is especially good for an early English breakfast. ♦ M-Sa 7-10AM, noon-2:30PM, 6:30-10:30PM; Su 7:30-10:30AM, noon-2:30PM, 6:30-10:30PM. 071/730.1499

8 Sloane Street What Bond Street was 30 years ago. Sloane Street has quietly become one of the smartest streets in London, taking its lead from **Harvey Nichols**—by far the most stylish department store in London—**Valentino, Ungaro, Bruno Magli,** and such fashion innovators as **Joseph Brown** and **Chanel**. The fashion world can be found sipping cappuccino at **L'Express** in the basement of Harvey Nichols and run by **Joseph**, of course.

9 General Trading Company The GTC is just off Sloane Square, but it is the personification of everything Sloane—and if you still aren't sure what that means, come here and look around. It is a Sloane-size country house of a store, with irresistible objects that fit into English country life, from Chatsworth to Battersea. Check out the china department, the antiques upstairs, the garden department, and the children's toy department, which is open only between September and December. This is where **Princess Diana** had her wedding list, a fact uncovered by the brilliant sleuthing of reporter **Maria Brenner** (everyday china—Royal Worcester's Eversham; glass pattern—Apollo by Royal Brierly). Once nice young girls (pronounced *gels*) worked in florists in the hope that they might meet a prince. Now the princes are all but gone—**Prince Edward** is the only one left—and the *gels* can be found working in estate agencies or in the GTC. As most of them are waiting for lords to whisk them off their feet, the service is rather uninvolved. The café downstairs serves Sloanish foods like lasagne and salad, lemon syllabub, and chocolate cake. Expect long lines at lunchtime (excellent for observing Sloane accents and sartorial habits and Sloanedom in general). ♦ M-Tu, Th-F 9AM-5:30PM; W 9AM-7PM; Sa 9AM-2PM. 144 Sloane St, SW1. 071/730.0411

10 Holy Trinity (1888–90, **J.D. Sedding**) This church is a euphoric ecclesiastical homage to the Arts and Crafts Movement—in spite of the destructive effects of German bombs in WWII, which destroyed the vault over the nave. The stunning east window was made by **William Morris and Company** to the designs of **Burne Jones**; the grill behind the altar is by **Henry Wilson**; and many other pre-Raphaelite artists contributed to the Gothic glorification that abounds. The church also has an excellent example of a Walker organ. Check notices on the church door for lunchtime concerts. ♦ Sloane Sq, SW1

11 Hotel Wilbraham $$ One of the rare hotels that offers the atmosphere of shabby-genteel country England in the heart of London, and at refreshingly fair prices. The hotel is privately owned and unashamedly old fashioned. The 50 rooms all have telephones and room service. Ask for a largish room with your own bath and you will be extremely pleased; be warned—the single rooms are small. There

King's Road & Chelsea

is a small restaurant . The hotel is nearly always full, so book at least 2 months in advance. ♦ 1 Wilbraham Pl, Sloane St, SW1. 071/730.8296

12 Peter Jones Department Store (1936–38, **Slater** and **Moberly** architects; **W. Crabtree**, associate; **C.H. Reilly**, consultant architects) A much acclaimed piece of modern design that still succeeds 50 years after it was built. The architects followed the curve of the King's Road and created a building that has the grace and shapeliness of an ocean liner. Duchesses and secretaries shop here, and Sloanedom buys school uniforms here. (Great stuff to take back for the kids: well-made, classic English children's clothes at very reasonable prices.) The china and glass department has a superb selection of English patterns, and the linen department offers beautiful Egyptian cotton sheets, Scottish woolen blankets, Irish linen tablecloths, and napkins. On the 1st floor, you will find ladies' leather gloves lined in cashmere, Sloanish leather picture frames, and sensible country shoes, all at a lot less than you would pay anywhere else. Members of the helpful sales staff are all called partners (at the end of the year they get a share of the profits). ♦ M-Tu, Th-Sa 9AM-5:30PM; W 9:30AM-7PM. Sloane Sq, SW1. 071/730.3434

13 Body Shop You might easily get hooked on these beauty products, all made from natural ingredients that stimulate the appetite—rosemary, jojoba, cocoa butter, honey, orange blossom. They are sold in refillable plastic bottles at reasonable prices and tested without cruelty to animals. The shop now offers a range of perfumes that have a remarkable resemblance to the big names, but are offered here at everywoman prices. New lines include vegetable-based soaps, face masks, shower gels, and aromatherapy oils. ♦ M-Sa 10AM-6PM. King's Rd, SW3. 071/225.2568

Sloane Street Shopping Map

SLOANE SQUARE

National Westminster Bank	**Midland Bank**
Holy Trinity Church	
	General Trading Co. *department store*
jewelry **Cobra & Bellamy**	**GTC Café**
pharmacy **Andrews**	**Jane Churchill** *fabric and wallpaper*
SLOANE TERRACE	**Partridges** *deli*
	Coles *shirtmaker*
interior design **Colefax & Fowler**	**Presents** *gift shop*

SLOANE STREET

WILBRAHAM PLACE

Cadogan Travel
food store **Europa**

CADOGAN GARDENS

ELLIS STREET

CADOGAN PLACE   **CADOGAN GATE**

PAVILION GARDENS
Cadogan Hotel
National Westminster Bank

PONT STREET

HANS STREET

CADOGAN PLACE
Coutts & Co.
restaurant **Rib Room**
clothing **Jaeger**
men's clothing **Nicholas of London**

Ivor Gordon *fine jewelry*
Stephanie Kelian *shoes*
De Havilland *antiques*
Jean Claude Jitrois *women's clothing*
New Art Center
Bleyle *German women's clothing*
Ungaro *jewelry*
Emanuel *women's clothing*
Maria Saba *jewelry*
Fendi *leather goods*
Designer's Annexe *women's clothing*
Walter Steiger *shoes*

COTTAGE WALK
kid's clothing **Sonia Rykiel**
chemist **Moore**
women's clothing **Birger Christensen**
dry cleaner **Sketchley**
supermarket **Sloane Street Superstore**
clothing **Valentino**
hairdresser **Neville Daniel**
men's and women's clothing **Giorgio Armani**

HANS CRESCENT
YSL *designer women's clothing*
Max Mara *designer women's clothing*
Chanel *clothing*
National Bank of Pakistan
Bank of Credit and Commerce
Joseph

clothing **Hermès**
florist **Pulbrook & Gould**
hairdresser **Cadogan Club**

North Beach *men's and women's clothing*
Issey Miyake *women's clothing*
Katherine Hamnett *women's clothing*
Holiday Inn

clothing **Daks**
National Westminster Bank
public house **The Gloucester**

Kenzo *women's clothing*
Joseph *clothing and interiors*
Alexander Kenel *women's clothing*
Pied a Terre *shoes*

lingerie **Courtenay**
silversmith **Dibdin**

SLOANE STREET

HARRIET STREET
Map continues on next page

14 **Blushes** ★$ Popular bistro/wine bar with a few tables on the sidewalk year-round. It is an agreeable place to have a salad, a slice of game pie, and a glass of wine while you watch a rarefied bit of the world go by. ◆ M-Sa 8:30AM-midnight. 52 King's Rd, SW3. 071/589.6640

15 **Duke of York's Headquarters** (1801, **John Saunders**) Behind the iron railings are the barracks for several London regiments of the **Territorial Army**. The handsome Georgian brick building with its central Tuscan portico (best viewed from Cheltenham Terrace) was originally built in 1801 as a school for the orphans of soldiers. The children's bright red-and-blue uniforms were present in Chelsea until 1909, when the school was moved to Dover and Southampton. ◆ King's Rd, SW3

16 **Next** These started out 4 years ago as shops for women's clothes, with emphasis on workable and matching clothes at approachable prices arranged in an attractive setting. Then came a men's Next, with a look for the jazzier executive. Next but probably not last is a home furnishings shop with clean, attractive and affordable linens, fabrics and furniture designed by Tricia Guild. It is all so imaginative, liveable and reasonable, that it is bound to be the success story of the 90s. ♦ Tu, Th-Sa 10AM-6PM; M 10:30AM-6PM; W 9:30AM-7PM. 76-78 King's Rd, SW3. 584.5269. Also at: King's Road: No. 69, Shoes and Accessories; No. 72, Interiors; No. 76, men's clothing; No. 102, women's clothing

17 John Sandoe Books Just off the King's Road is the best literary bookshop in London, beloved by readers and writers. Although John Sandoe has now retired, his staff has a knowledge of books that would put many an Oxford don to shame. The shop gives patient credit to writers, has a devoted clientele of literate aristocrats, and will send your books anywhere in the world. ♦ M-Tu, Th-Sa 9:30AM-5:30PM; W 9:30AM-7:30PM. 10 Blackland's Terrace, SW3. 071/589.9473

18 English Garden ★★$$ A plant-filled conservatory at the back of a dark, heavily draped front room, and a scrumptious English menu. Try the Brie in filo pastry to start, grilled lobster and scallops in herb-hollandaise sauce, or the watercress-mango salad. The wines are jolly good, too. Lunch is a lot cheaper than supper here. ♦ M-Sa 12:30-2:30PM, 7:30-11PM; Su 12:30-2PM, 7:30-10PM. 10 Lincoln St, SW3. 071/584.7272

19 G&D Boulangerie ★★$ A quick coffee and croissant, standing or sitting on a stool. Good to know about. ♦ M-Sa 8AM-7PM; Su 9:30AM-4:30PM. 74 King's Rd, SW3. 071/584.1873

20 Hobbs Comfortable shoes with great style and a look definitely all their own. They are designed by **Marilyn Anselm**, are made in Italy, and are wonderfully affordable. If you like them this will be *your* shoe store. The clothes are interesting but less reliable. ♦ M-Tu, Th-Sa 10AM-6PM; W 10AM-7PM. 84 King's Rd, SW3. 071/581.2914

20 Chelsea Kitchen ★$ Cheap and honest, and after 3 decades, a King's Road institution. Everything is fresh and homemade, including the breads, scones, and pastries. The menu changes twice daily and regulars play *spot the cuisine*, which is an eclectic mixture of Italian, Spanish, French, and English. Popular for English and Continental breakfasts. ♦ M-Sa 8AM-11:45PM; Su noon-11:30PM. 98 King's Rd, SW3. 071/589.1330

21 Pied à Terre High-fashion French and Italian shoes in great colors and first-rate designs that allow you to foot the bill without serious mishap. In winter, the boots are handsome, indeed. One of 9 shops in Lon-

King's Road & Chelsea

don. The 14 Sloane St shop has handmade shoes a cut—and price—above. ♦ M-Tu, Th-Sa 10AM-6.30PM; W 10AM-7PM. 33D King's Rd, SW3. 071/730.9240

22 Monkeys ★★$$ Tucked away in a back street, this restaurant is a real find, decorated with cartoons and paintings of monkeys. You'll find yourself surrounded by pine paneling and London's chic set, all nibbling on the stuffed breast of chicken with foie gras and truffles, or *carré d'agneau diable*. There's a treacle tart and real custard for pudding. ♦ Daily 12:30-2:30PM, 7:30-11PM. Closed 3 wks in August. 1 Cale St, Chelsea Green, SW3. 071/352.4711

Sloane Street Shopping Map, cont.

HARRIET STREET

women's clothing **Cecil Gee**

women's clothing **Nicole Farhi**
women's clothing **Monsoon**
chocolate **Bendicks**
men's and women's shoes **Fratelli Rossetti**
linens **Descamps**
luggage **Louis Vuitton**

men's and women's clothing **Henry Cotton's**
Gucci
Midland Bank
clothing **Leather Rat**
shoes **Bruno Magli**

department store **Harvey Nichols**

SLOANE STREET

HANS CRESCENT, cont.

Sloane's Pizzeria
Oilily designer kid's wear
Bally shoes
The Coach Store leather goods
Bertie shoes
New Man clothing
Brown's women's clothing
La Cicogna maternity and children's clothing
Esprit women's clothing

BASIL STREET

Alfred Dunhill luxury goods

Banco de Bilbao

Barclay's Bank

Knightsbridge Tube Station

KNIGHTSBRIDGE

Chelsea Flower Show

The English are not considered a passionate race, but when it comes to their pets and their gardens, they show all the fanatical emotionalism and commitment of which the human spirit is capable. One of the great events on the English calendar, guaranteed to cause English hearts to beat quicker, is the Chelsea Flower Show, the largest, most popular, and most prestigious flower show in the world. For 4 days during the third week in May (Tuesday-Friday), a flower-lover's paradise covers 22 acres of the **Royal Hospital** grounds in Chelsea. Inevitably, the rain falls and a gallant attempt to protect the glorious flowers is made by the great marquee, which provides protection for 3 ½ acres of blooms and bloom lovers. In 1989 the sun shone gloriously, taking the exhibitors and visitors alike by surprise. Both the flowers and the guests faded rather badly in the heat.

For 40 days and 40 nights—21 to put up the show, 4 days for the show itself, and 15 to take it down—the

Royal Horticultural Society concentrates on this immense and increasingly international event. Amateurs and professionals as well as the nonhorticultural come to look, learn, judge, and buy everything from Georgian roses to Gothic garden benches and plants from all over the world.

The English class structure is evident at this most English event, beginning with a special preview for the flower-loving royal family. The first 2 days are for members of the Royal Horticultural Society, only. On Thursday and Friday members of the public are allowed. In recent years up to 70,000 people a day came to see the show, but in 1987 it was decided that such crowds were no longer tolerable, and since then numbers have been restricted to an average of 48,000 daily.

After 5PM on Thursday the cost of admission is reduced by half, as the show goes on until 8PM. On Friday, all the plants are sold off at closing.

Large marquees reflect English class and taste, and you can have anything from champagne and strawberries to beer and sausages to tea and scones. There is wonderful shopping, too, with

---

23 Royal Avenue A triumphal route intended to connect **Sir Christopher Wren**'s Royal Hospital with Kensington Palace. The ambitious design, conceived by Wren for **William III**, never got beyond the King's Road, but the majesty of the 4 rows of plane trees, lined by 18th- and 19th-century houses, makes a magnificent impression. The avenue is also James Bond's London address. You can see Chelsea Hospital in the distance as it leads to **St. Leonard's Terrace** on the north of **Burton's Court**, a large playing field with an 18th-century gate that was the original entrance to the hospital. Open-air art exhibitions are held on Saturday in the summer.

24 Royal Hospital (1682, **Sir Christopher Wren**) Guidebooks perpetuate the emotional myth that **Nell Gwynn**, mistress of **Charles II**, was so moved when a wounded soldier begged for alms that she persuaded the King to build the Royal Hospital. The more likely truth is that Charles was impressed and inspired by reports of Louis XIV's Hotel des Invalides. In 1682, diarist **Sir John Evelyn** and Army Paymaster General **Sir Stephen Fox** drew up plans for a hospital and residence for pensioners of the army, and Charles II commissioned Wren, who chose the magnificent river site. After St. Paul's, this is Wren's masterpiece of beauty. This glorious old people's home still provides shelter to 400 war veterans known as

the **Chelsea Pensioners**, and there's a waiting list to get in. (The original brief was to provide shelter for 476 men.)

On 7 June (or thereabouts) each year, the pensioners celebrate **Founders Day**, in memorial to Charles II's escape from Cromwell's troops—he hid in an oak apple tree after the Battle of Worcester—by placing a wreath of oak leaves around the neck of the bronze statue of Charles II in the **Figure Court** (carved by **Grinling Gibbons**). On this day, the pensioners change from their blue winter uniforms, designed in the time of the Duke of Marlborough, to their scarlet tunics for summer, and receive double rations! This is a magnificent ceremony, not open to the public, but parties who write well in advance are sometimes admitted. You can see the pensioners proudly walking the streets of Chelsea at all times of year resplendent in their uniforms, and even the King's Road trendies make way for them to pass.

The hospital consists of a central block, which houses the chapel and the main mall, connected by an octagonal vestibule. The pensioners live in the twin galleries, or wings, which run at right angles to the river. The small **museum** in the **Secretary's Office Block** on the east side of the hospital contains prints, uniforms, medals, and photographs associated with the hospital and its

stands selling everything from handmade wicker baskets and English *Wellies* to priceless botanical prints, floral tea towels, bowls of potpourri, and rare gardening books. But the great attraction is the gardens planted for the occasion. There are magnificent creations of flowers, shrubs, garden seats, stone paths, arbors, sunken ponds, and gazebos, with the emphasis on flowers. Every inch is jam-packed with pink and white lupins, blue phlox, pale-green bells of Ireland, white and pink poppies, pale-green tobacco plants, pink foxgloves, white snapdragons, creamy-green mignonettes, pale-blue Canterbury bells, lavender, intoxicating pink stocks, an honor guard of delphiniums—and everything is bestowed with its Latin name. Statuary is back again in classic stone foxes, nymphs, and Neptunes. The genius of these gardens is that, in spite of the unreliable and unpredictable nature of plants, they all look perfect and as though they have been in existence for ever and ever. Fifty-six Gold Medals were awarded in 1990. The top prize of **Best Garden** was won by **B & Q Retail** for their *Garden of Roses.*

Unless your heart's desire is to go on the opening 2 days, in which case you must become a member of the Royal Horticultural Society, the best thing to do is to telephone the Flower Show Information Line (071/828.1744). This number operates from the beginning of February onward each year until the show itself, and an operator will tell you exactly how and where to get a ticket in advance. Standing in line outside is definitely *outre*, although some people will always do it.

history, including 2 large paintings in **Wellington Hall**—the *Battle of Waterloo* by **George Jones**, and **Haydon**'s *Wellington Describing the Field of Waterloo to George IV.*

The pensioners have their meals in the **Great Hall** under the *Triumph of Charles II*, a huge wall painting of the King on horseback trampling over serpents, with the Royal Hospital in the background. Around the hall are portraits of British kings and queens from Charles II to Victoria. When Wellington was laid in state here in 1852, several mourners were trampled to death by the crowds.

The **chapel** is pure Wren, with his signature black-and-white marble floor, fine carved paneling, and altar rail. The glass case beside the altar contains a prayer book, placed there in 1690, opened to a prayer of thanksgiving for the Restoration, without which there would be no Royal Hospital. Visitors are welcome to attend services on Sunday. The best way to see the Royal Hospital is with a Chelsea Pensioner as your guide, and there is almost always one around who is willing to provide this service. (A gratuity is usually welcome.)

In the 18th century, the **Ranelagh Gardens** of the Royal Hospital were vast pleasure gardens open to the public, complete with a gilt amphitheater and a site for eating, drinking, music, masquerades, fireworks, and balloon flights. **Canaletto** painted them, **Mozart** played in them, the royal family enjoyed them, and all levels of London society loved them—all before 1803, when they closed their doors. Now this part of the Royal Hospital grounds is the site of the **Chelsea Flower Show**, and for 4 days in May some of the exuberance and pleasure of those early times is relived. The grounds, chapel, and **Great Hall** are open to the public, as are the **State Apartments** at certain times (ring first to check). ♦ Free. M-Sa 10AM-noon, 2-4PM; Su 2-4PM. Chapel services Su 8:30, 11AM, noon. Royal Hospital Rd, SW3. 071/730.0161

25 National Army Museum The Royal Hospital doesn't feel like a hospital, nor does it exude an atmosphere of military history, though many of the pensioners are important war heroes. Just next door, however, is this museum, which covers the history of the British Army from 1485 to the present day, including the Falklands War. The museum houses 3 galleries—the **weapons gallery, uniform gallery**, and **art gallery**—plus the history of the army, beginning with the yeoman of the guard in 1485. There are lots of models and dioramas of battles, and a fascinating skeleton of **Napoleon**'s horse **Marengo**. Originally founded at Sandhurst in 1960 and opened here in 1971, the museum is a must for students of military history and little children who stare transfixed at the longbow retrieved from **Henry VIII**'s ship, the *Mary Rose*, and who don't mind the sound of rifle fire that ricochets around the gallery. There is a permanent exhibition of the **Battle of Waterloo**, which includes a 400-square-foot model of the battle itself—for children and soldiers to marvel at. Artists represented in the art gallery include **Reynolds, Romney, Lawrence** and **Gainsborough**. ♦ Free. M-Sa 10AM-5:30PM; Su 2-5:30PM. Royal Hospital Rd, SW3. 071/730.0717

The English have an extraordinary ability for flying into a great calm.

Alexander Woolcott

Restaurants/Nightlife: Red   Hotels: Blue
Shops/Parks: Green
Sights/Culture: Black

95

26 Tite Street A kind of distilled essence of Chelsea life—can be found in this little triangle of streets—Tite Street, Dilke Street, and Swans Walk—connecting the Royal Hospital Road with Chelsea Embankment. Tite Street was the favored haunt of artists and writers in the late 19th century. The brilliant and eccentric **Oscar Wilde** lived at **No. 16** with his wife from 1884 until 1895. The study where he wrote *Lady Windemere's Fan, An Ideal Husband,* and *The Importance of Being Earnest* was painted buttercup-yellow with accents of red lacquer. The dining room, in shades of ivory and pearl, symbolized tranquility, the one quality that eluded Wilde permanently, and fatally. Wilde was arrested and imprisoned for homosexual offenses, declared bankrupt, and his house was sold while he was in Reading Jail. When he was released, he moved to France, where he died in 1900. The plaque on Wilde's house was unveiled in 1954, on the centenary of his birth, by **Sir**

King's Road & Chelsea

Compton MacKenzie before an audience of Chelsea artists and writers.

The American artist **John Singer Sargent** lived at **No. 31** in one of those studio houses that are pure Chelsea. Here he painted his portraits of the rich and famous and often beautiful, including the actress **Ellen Terry**, who lived close by on the King's Road, and the American writer who lived around the corner on Cheyne Walk, **Henry James.** Sargent died here in 1925.

The bohemian portrait painter **Augustus John** had his studio at **No. 33.** Just next door at **No. 35,** a house that is now cruelly modernized and out of place, is the former home of one of America's greatest painters, **James McNeill Whistler.** The house was cursed long before **Colin Tennant** (now **Lord Glenconner**) transformed it into *Monte Carlo modern.* Whistler built the house, using white brick and green slate, to the designs of **E.W. Godwin** in the 1870s, intending it to be his home, studio, and school. A libel suit he brought against the critic **John Ruskin** left Whistler with huge and unpayable legal costs, and he was forced to sell the house in 1879.

27 Foxtrot Oscar ★★★$ The international phonetic language is in use here—ask an airman or sailor what the restaurant's name stands for. Despite its name, this restaurant, owned by an old Etonian, is very popular. Grilled steaks, terrific salads (seafood and smoked goose), imaginative and tasty versions of English classics like kedgeree and steak-and-kidney pie, and a creative wine list. Full of Sloanes wearing bright colors, with suntans and loud voices. When they get very loud the English nickname them *Hooray Henrys.* So inexpensive, clever, and relaxed that it is well worth a meal. ♦ Daily 12:30-2:30PM, 7:30-11:30PM. 79 Royal Hospital Rd, SW3. 071/352.7179

28 Japanese Peace Pagoda If you walk to the end of Tite Street on the Embankment and look across the River Thames, you can see the newest addition to the London riverside—the Japanese Peace Pagoda. The 100-foot bronze-gold-leaf Buddha looking out over the river was inaugurated in May 1985. This temple of peace was built in 11 months by 50 monks and nuns, mainly from Japan. It is the last great work of the **Most Venerable Nichidatsu Fujii,** the Buddhist leader who died at the age of 100, one month before his temple was completed. The temple sits majestically, nobly, and peacefully in **Battersea Park** and is a great gift to Londoners and visitors alike. ♦ Daily 7:30AM-dusk. Battersea Park. 081/871.7530

29 La Tante Claire ★★★★$$$ If you have to choose between the Tower of London, Westminster Abbey, the British Museum, or a meal at Tante Claire, strongly consider going for the latter. French, yes, but it is an outstanding treasure in London's considerable firmament and a perfect place to stop for lunch (with a very generous fixed-price luncheon menu) while strolling through Chelsea. It was voted one of the top 4 London restaurants by *The Good Food Guide* in 1989. The décor is as chic and impressive as the cooking has always been. **Pierre Koffman** is that rare being—a modest genius. A meal here combines deceptive simplicity with astounding imagination. The ingredients are treated with great respect, so you can choose from first-class game, beef, fish, lamb, and vegetables in season, knowing that you will experience a revelation. The *salade savoureuse* of partridge is a good example; the foie gras, in its various guises, is equally memorable; follow it with the turbot with cinnamon and lemon as a main course. The cheeses are from **Olivier** and are perfection; and the desserts, even though you may feel that it simply isn't possible, are a tour de force and must be had. If you really have no room left you'll be able to squeeze in a sorbet, for which Koffman is renowned, even by the most seasoned diners. The set menu at lunch is an outstanding value. Do dress smartly, everyone else does. Reserve your table when you book your flight. ♦ M-F 12:30-2PM, 7-11PM. 68 Royal Hospital Rd, SW3. 071/352.6045

30 Chelsea Physic Garden Walk through **Dilke Street** onto **Swan Walk,** with its row of 18th-century houses, and you will reach the handsome iron gates of the second oldest surviving botanical garden in England, founded by the **Worshipful Society of Apothecaries** in 1673 (100 years before Kew) on 4 acres of land belonging to **Charles Cheyne.** In 1722, **Sir Hans Sloane,** botanist and physician to George II, as Lord of the Manor granted a continuous lease, requiring the apothecaries to present 50 items a year to the Royal Society (of which Sloane succeeded Isaac Newton as president) until some 2000 had been acquired. After the **Wardian** case was invented, a method of carrying seeds that prevented them from perishing, the Physic

Garden's staff became instrumental in changing the face of the world's staple crops. In 1733, the first cotton seeds were exported to a garden in Georgia, US, from the South Seas. **Robert Fortune**, a curator of the garden, carried tea to India from China, and Malaya got its rubber from South America. In 1983, the Physic Garden opened its doors to the public for the first time in 300 years. Now, on 2 afternoons a week from spring until fall and under the watchful eye of Sir Hans Sloane himself (statue by **Michael Rysbrack**), you can examine some of the 7000 specimens of plants that still grow here. The magnificent trees include the 30-foot olive tree that bears fruit each year, the Golden Rain tree, and the exotic cork oak. Plants and seeds are for sale. ♦ Admission. W, Su 2-5PM, Apr-Oct. 66 Royal Hospital Rd, SW3. 071/352.5646

Henry VIII is indelibly engraved on the memory as a robust man who had 6 wives—and went to excessive lengths in order to do so. A truer picture is of a brilliant, gifted, scholarly, athletic, musical, and devout man who was handsome in youth—over 6 feet tall with blond hair—and who had a great appetite for life. **Sir Thomas More** described him as a man *nourished on philosophy and the nine muses*. He is also the monarch who, more than any other, created the look of central London, even more than George IV and his architect John Nash.

31 Chelsea Embankment This unbeatably beautiful walk along the river suffers from the noise and anxiety of relentless traffic. Still, it is worth making every effort to transcend the motorized roar to see this miraculously unchanged patch of bohemian London. Chelsea Embankment begins at **Chelsea Bridge** (1934, **Forrest and Wheeler**), a graceful suspension bridge that edges up to the massive,

dramatic **Battersea Power Station**. The station's 4 chimneys are a vital part of London's industrial archeology as well as the Thames riverline, and have successfully resisted all attempts at demolition, even when they ceased to function. (In fact, only 2 ever functioned; the front 2 were added purely for esthetic reasons, to provide a sense of balance.) It currently stands empty and Londoners fear the worst.

32 Cheyne Walk Where the **Royal Hospital Road** and **Chelsea Embankment** converge, the elegant Cheyne Walk begins. The embankment protects the single row of houses from traffic (somewhat), and through a row of trees, the lucky residents have a view of the Thames. Some of the happy few who have lived in these priceless Georgian brick houses include Rolling Stones' guitarist **Keith Richards**, the illustrious publisher **Lord Weidenfeld** (still a resident), the recently knighted **Paul Getty, Jr.**, and **Mick Jagger** (**No. 48**). But it is the past resi-

dents who haunt the high windows. **George Eliot** lived at **No. 4** for 19 days after her late-in-life wedding to Johnny Cross, and died here. The pre-Raphaelite painter and poet **Dante Gabriel Rossetti** lived at **No. 16**, the finest house on the street. He led an eccentric *vie de bohème* here while mourning the loss of his wife, **Elizabeth Siddal** (the model for **Millais'** painting of the dying Ophelia and the deadly beauty in *Beata Beatrix* by **Rossetti**—both in the Tate Gallery). Rossetti's Chelsea ménage included a kangaroo, peacocks, armadillos, a marmot, a zebu, and frequent visits from fellow pre-Raphaelites **William Morris** and his wife, **Janey**, who inspired great passion in Rossetti. No. 16 is known as *Queen's House*, the name inspired by the initials RC on the top of the iron gateway, long assumed to be CR, standing for **Catherine of Braganza**, Queen of Charles II. In fact, the initials stand for **Richard Chapman**, who built the house in 1717. Opposite the house in the Embankment Gardens is the *Rossetti Fountain*, a memorial to the artist from his friends, including **John Everett Millais** and **G.F. Watts**, unveiled in 1887 by **William Holman Hunt**. The fountain is by **J.P. Seddon**, and the bust of Rossetti is by **Ford Madox Brown**. Unfortunately, the original bronze bust was stolen and replaced by this fiberglass copy. The plaque on **No. 23** Cheyne Walk commemorates the site of **Henry VIII's Manor House**, which stood where Nos. 19 to 26 Cheyne Walk are now. Henry VIII became fond of the Chelsea riverside during his many visits to his friend **Sir Thomas More**, and the year after More's death, he built a palace along the embankment. Before he died, he gave the house to **Catherine Parr**, his last wife. One hundred

Restaurants/Nightlife: Red	Hotels: Blue
Shops/Parks: Green	
	Sights/Culture: Black

years later, the house was purchased by **Lady Jane Cheyne**, and in 1737 **Sir Hans Sloane** bought Henry VIII's old manor. More's own house was demolished a few years later. The gateway by **Inigo Jones** was given to the Earl of Burlington, who erected it in the gardens of Chiswick House, where it still stands.

33 Cadogan Pier Every July, the pier just east of Albert Bridge is the finishing point of one of England's oldest contests, the **Dogget's Coat and Badge Race**. The race began in 1715 to celebrate the accession of **George I** to the throne, and was sponsored by **Thomas Doggett**, who awarded a coat and badge to the winner. A moving ceremony reenacting the final journey of **Sir Thomas More** from his home here on the river to the Tower of London where he was executed also takes place at the pier in July.

The pier is now a stopping point for *Thamesline*, London's half-hourly river-bus service running

King's Road & Chelsea

from Chelsea Harbour to Docklands and Greenwich. ◆ Cheyne Walk, SW3

34 Albert Bridge (1873, **R.M. Ordish**) Lovers propose here and tired commuters refresh themselves just by looking at it. This is the bridge Londoners love the most. In 1973 the bridge was strengthened but still has a weight limit, so red London buses and lorries never darken its tarmac. The latticework suspension bridge is painted in ice-cream pastels—a pale peach, pistachio, and cream—and at night it is illuminated with strings of peachy lights. Best time to see it is at dusk from Chelsea Bridge (downriver), when the sun sets behind it and the bridge takes on a fairy-tale quality. At night, see it from Battersea Bridge (upriver); the red lights of Chelsea Bridge glow behind it for a really pretty effect.
◆ Cheyne Walk, SW3

35 Carlyle's House It's a short walk up Cheyne Row to **No. 5** (now known as **No. 24**), one of the most fascinating houses in Chelsea and one of the few that is open to the public. One of a terrace of red-brick houses built in 1708, the house was the family home of the writer **Thomas Carlyle** and his wife, **Jane**. The rooms are almost exactly as they were 150 years ago when *The French Revolution* made its author famous, and **Dickens, Tennyson**, and **Chopin** were visitors. Most of the furniture, pictures, and books belonged to the Carlyles—his hat is still on the hat-stand by the door. Go down into the kitchen and see the pump, the stone trough, and the wide grate where kettles boiled and into which Tennyson and Carlyle used to nip for a crafty cigarette, avoiding Mrs C.'s rebuke. Examine the rooms upstairs, with their four-poster beds, piles of books, mahogany cupboards, and dark Victorian wallpaper (which covers up 18th-century pine paneling). Look at the double-walled attic study, carefully designed

Carlyle's House

to keep out the noises of the house and the street (not a success), with the horsehair chair and reading shelf. The painting *A Chelsea Interior* (1857) hangs in the ground-floor sitting room and shows how little the house has changed. The tombstone in the small garden behind the house marks where Mrs. Carlyle's dog **Nero** lies buried. Carlyle was a famous Chelsea figure, and all his long life the *sage of Chelsea* took solitary walks along these streets. A bronze statue of Carlyle (by **Boehm** and erected in 1882) in the **Embankment Gardens** of Cheyne Row, is said to look very much like him. Here the essayist and historian sits surrounded by a pile of books and gazes sadly at the river through an invasion of juggernauts. ◆ Admission. W-Sa 11AM-5PM; Su 2-5PM, Apr-Oct. 5/24 Cheyne Row, SW3. 071/352.7087

36 Cross Keys ★★$ This small, friendly, and popular pub spills out onto the sidewalk in summer when the pretty walled garden in the back isn't big enough. The cold table—salads, meats, pâtés, cheeses—is always fresh and good. ◆ M-Sa 11AM-4PM, 5:30-11PM; Su noon-3PM, 7-10:30PM. 2 Lawrence St, SW3. 071/352.1893

37 King's Head and Eight Bells ★★$ Worth coming in for a drink just to raise your glass to a pub that is 400 years old. The pub has been modernized a bit—18th-century décor with engravings of Chelsea in those days. Gaze out at the river, enjoy the permanent buffet, and try the Wethered's or Flowers bitter. ◆ M-F 11AM-3PM, 5:30-11PM; Sa 11AM-11PM; Su noon-3PM, 7-10:30PM. 50 Cheyne Walk, SW3. 071/352.1820

Restaurants/Nightlife: Red	Hotels: Blue
Shops/Parks: Green	Sights/Culture: Black

38 Chelsea Old Church (All Saints) Founded in the middle of the 12th century. In spite of the heartless traffic outside, the German bombs that flattened it in 1941, and the unfortunate wooden Indian-style statue that sits impassively in front, this old church is spiritually intact and a glorious monument to its former parishioner **Sir Thomas More**. You feel his presence in the chapel, restored and designed in part in 1528 by **Holbein**, who was living with the Mores in their home nearby. And you feel the deep sadness of the story of the gentle man of conscience who could not recognize his friend **Henry VIII** as head of the Church of England and grant his blessing for divorce, and paid for this conscience with his life. More wrote his own epitaph (against the south wall to the right of the altar) 2 years before his death. The Gothic tomb doesn't contain the remains of the saint, which are believed to be buried in the Chapel of St. Peter ad Vincula, within the Tower of London. But Chelsea legend holds that his daughter **Margaret Roper** made her way back here with her father's head.

The ornate tomb with the urn is the burial place of Chelsea's next best-known citizen, **Sir Hans Sloane**. The chained books, including the *Vinegar Bible*, a 1717 edition that contains a printer's error converting the parable of the vineyard into the parable of the vinegar, are the only chained books still found in a London church. The square tower, made famous by so many artists, was a casualty of a German air raid in 1941, but it was rebuilt, and the careful restoration of the church is impressive. The **Lawrence Chapel** is supposedly where Henry VIII secretly married **Jane Seymour** a few days before their official marriage in 1536, a year after Sir Thomas More had ceased to be a conscience to the King. On summer days, the church is the setting for happier weddings, and each July a sermon written by More is read from the pulpit. A memorial wall stone commemorates the American writer **Henry James**, who lived in Chelsea and died near here in 1916. ♦ Tu-F, Su 11AM-1PM, 2-5PM; Sa 11AM-1PM. Old Church St, SW3. 071/352.5637

39 Roper Gardens This new (1965) garden on the site of part of **Sir Thomas More**'s estate is named after **Margaret Roper**, beloved eldest daughter of More. It replaced a garden destroyed in a German air raid. See the stone relief of a woman walking against the wind by **Jacob Epstein**, who lived in Chelsea from 1909 until 1914. ♦ Cheyne Walk, SW3

40 Crosby Hall (1466) Three hundred years after **Sir Thomas More** was executed, this splendid mansion was transported, stone by stone, from Bishopsgate in the City to Chelsea. The hall was originally built in 1407, then made into a royal palace by **Richard III**, and finally purchased in 1516 by More himself, so it is mere coincidence that in 1910 it made its way into More's Chelsea garden. It is now the dining room of the **British Federation of University Women**. The superb hammerbeam roof, the stunning oriel window, the long Jacobean table (a gift from **Nancy Astor**), and the **Holbein** painting of the More family, one of the 3 copies made by the painter for the 3 More daughters, are all worth seeing. The architecturally sensitive lament the postwar annex and neo-Tudor building of 1925 next door. ♦ Daily 10AM-noon, 2-4PM. Cheyne Walk, SW3. 071/352.9663

41 Beaufort Street One of the busiest crossroads in Chelsea, connecting the King's Road to Battersea Bridge.

42 Lindsey House (c. 1640–70) Remarkable for its beauty and its survival against all odds, this large country house is the only one of its date and size in Chelsea. It was built on the site of a farmhouse by the Swiss physician to James I and Charles I, **Theodore Mayerne**. In the 1660s it was sold to **Robert, 3rd Earl of Lindsey**, who substantially rebuilt it. In 1750, the house became the headquarters of the **Moravian Brethren**, whose ideas of Utopia

were rather grand and resulted in the house being sold and divided into separate dwellings. In the 1770s the remarkable cast of residents included painter **John Martin, Sir Mark Brunel**, who built the first tunnel under the Thames, and his son **Isambard**, who built many of England's suspension, and railway bridges and lived at **No. 98**. (**Brunel House**, 105 Cheyne Walk, is named after the father and son engineers.) **Whistler** lived at **No. 96** from 1866–79 (one of 4 Chelsea addresses), and it was here that he painted the famous portrait of his mother; and **Elizabeth Gaskell** was born here. The gardens connected to **Nos. 99** and **100** were designed by **Lutyens**. ♦ Nos. 96-100 Cheyne Walk, SW3

42 Turner's House England's greatest painter, **J.M.W. Turner**, lived in this tall, narrow house during his last years. In his attempt to remain anonymous he adopted his landlady's surname. He was known locally as *Puggy Booth*. Turner died here in 1851, uttering his last words, *God is Light*. ♦ 119 Cheyne Walk, SW3

43 Chelsea Harbour Where Cheyne Walk becomes Lots Road at its western end is a little enclave, once shabby and downmarket, now a fashionable place to live. Along a half-mile frontage between Lots Road and the River Thames a much sought after condo-minium development called Chelsea Harbour has attracted English television, pop, and sports personalities. It offers some of the best views and most expensive apartments in London. Crushed into this tiny area are houses, offices, shops, restaurants, landscaped gardens, and the **Conrad** hotel, all set around a 75-berth yacht marina. Hoppa buses (small red buses that supplement the regular bus system) from Earl's Court and Kensington High Street visit the area regularly, and the Thameslink riverbus service runs from here to Docklands and Greenwich via Charing Cross, Waterloo, and London Bridge.

44 Man in the Moon ★★$ This pub marks the beginning of World's End, that curve in

King's Road & Chelsea

the King's Road. It is a treasured institution—a first-rate theater club presenting mostly modern plays, as well as a distinguished pub with beautiful engraved glass, a real fire in winter, real ale year-round, and lunchtime fare as well. ◆ M-Tu 11AM-3PM, 5:30-11PM; W-Su 11AM-11PM. 392 King's Rd, SW3. Pub 071/352.5075, theater 071/351.2876

Antiquing
London is full of antique shops, but you have to know where to look to find them. While dealers scour the country, bargains are rare because even the sweetest little old lady living in the back of beyond knows that her furniture is worth good money. Even so, a mile or so beyond the World's End begins 2 miles of some spectacular antique shops housed in faded Victorian splendor in prettily painted but largely unrestored shops. Highlights include:

Furniture Cave One of the largest places to buy antique furniture. Twenty dealers work selling antiques and beautiful furniture from all over the world. ◆ M-Sa 10AM-6PM. 533 King's Rd, SW10. 071/352.4229

Christopher Wray's Lighting Emporium Actor-turned-shopkeeper and later millionaire, Christopher Wray gave up the lure of the bright lights for bright lights of his own, restoring and later manufacturing antique lamps, shades, and bulbs to be snapped up by a style-conscious middle class. His once-tiny shop is now the largest center of its kind in Europe selling restored antique and reproduction Georgian, Victorian, Art Deco, and Tiffany lamps and light fittings. For the Tiffanys, he imports hand-made opalescent glass from America. The shops themselves are Victoriana personnified, with old-fashioned cast-iron-and-glass awnings. ◆ M, W-Sa 9:30AM-6PM; Tu 10AM-6PM. 600 Kings Rd, SW6. 071/736.8434

45 Le Shop ★★★$ Formerly called **Asterix** after the French comic hero (the owners were asked to remove the name), this was London's first crêperie and the inspiration to its successors. The crêpes are made with buckwheat flour, and the winners include smoked salmon, chicken, mushroom, and corn, or mozzarella and spinach. Try fruit, ice cream, and sweet crêpes for dessert. The atmosphere is welcoming, the prices refreshing, and the possibility of an informal meal served with French cider or *bouche*, very tempting. ◆ Daily noon-midnight. 329 King's Rd, SW3. 071/352.3891

45 Natural Shoe Store Started by an American, this might be your salvation if you are beginning to feel weary of foot. Sensible brogues and half-brogues, loafers, lace-up boots (beautiful but they do require wearing in), clogs, Birkenstock sandals and shoes, Ecco walking shoes, and Grenson traditional English shoes. ◆ M-Sa 10AM-6PM. 325 King's Rd, SW3. 071/351.3721

45 Darlajane Gilroy Clever clothes that manage to be fun, fashionable, and classic, a kind of Audrey Hepburn '50s look made new. Reasonable prices, too. ◆ M-F 11AM-7PM; Sa 10AM-7PM. 327 King's Rd, SW3. 071/352.2095

46 Ed's Easy Diner ★$$ London's chic teenagers and 1950s Americana devotees can be found here in this chromium-plated New York-style coffee bar that could only have existed on a film set. It's open for coffee and donuts all through the day; delicious American food and good American beers are served, believe it or not, in an Anglo-American way. ◆ M-Th 11:30AM-midnight; F-Sa 11:30AM-1AM; Su 11:30AM-11PM. 362 King's Rd, SW3. 071/352.1956

47 Dome ★★$ A real brasserie, open all day, with French brasserie classics: *salade* niçoise, *croque-monsieur, crudités, assiette de charcuterie, mousse au chocolat,* espresso, *citron pressé.* You can get coffee and a croissant or a full English breakfast. Crowded at lunchtime, but no need to book. Service is a little on the slow side but it's made up for by the lively atmosphere. ◆ M-Sa 9AM-11PM; Su 10:30AM-10:30PM. 354 King's Rd, SW3. 071/352.7611

48 Rococo Chocolates Taste and imagination. This is the most eccentric and perhaps the most famous chocolate shop in the world. It is a chocoholic's paradise, where you can indulge both your palate and your eyes with the superb Belgian chocolates. The shop is a mixture of Baroque and contemporary—it looks like an art gallery. Indeed, in summer small exhibitions of art are held here. The windows are always worth a perusal. Take away a selection of chocolates, ranging from sardines to Venus' Nipples (white chocolate topped with coffee beans—enjoyed in *Amadeus*). ◆ M-Sa 10AM-6:30PM. 321 King's Rd, SW3. 071/352.5857

Restaurants/Nightlife: Red   Hotels: Blue
Shops/Parks: Green   **Sights/Culture: Black**

48 Chelsea Rare Books Now a Chelsea institution, with an excellent section of second-hand and antiquarian books on Chelsea in particular and London in general. It is also the place to come for handsome bound editions of **Dickens, Scott,** and once in a blue moon, **Jane Austen.** By all means, go downstairs and have a look at the English prints and watercolors, which are usually well-mounted and reasonably priced. To keep the yard of books you will inevitably buy standing in style, book ends, stands, and book slides are also for sale. ♦ M-Sa 10AM-6PM. 313 King's Rd, SW3. 071/351.0950

49 Thierry's ★★$$ You sometimes have to ring the bell to enter this vintage Chelsea restaurant, a great favorite of Chelsea dwellers, who like the honest, carefully prepared, and not overly original French dishes. The ambiance depends greatly on the warm and efficient **Di James,** who presides over the restaurant and charms newcomers and regulars alike with her interest in their meals and pleasure. ♦ M-Sa 12:30-2:30PM, 7:30-11:30PM. Closed last 2 wks August and September. 342 King's Rd, SW3. 071/352.3365

49 Avoir du Pois ★★★$$ Popular with Sloanes who otherwise play cricket when they aren't buying important English furniture at Christie's and Sotheby's. In the evenings and during Sunday lunch there's a live piano to serenade you through the menu, which is called *Private Pie,* a satiric gesture at the fortnightly magazine *Private Eye.* It offers an eclectic choice of nouvelle (a seafood pot-au-feu), American (eggs Benedict), and roast Scotch beef on Sunday. The desserts are sublime. The fixed-price lunch is a good value. ♦ M-Sa noon-2:45PM, 7-11:45PM; Su noon-1:45PM, 7-10:45PM. 334 King's Rd, SW3. 071/352.4071

50 Liberty A small and appealing outlet of the famous Regent Street department store selling mainly furniture and furnishings, including fabrics and wallpapers. Octavia furnishing fabric, William Morris print fabrics, and a few Liberty gifts like men's ties and ladies' silk scarfs. ♦ M-Tu, Th-Sa 9:30AM-5:30PM; W 9:30AM-6:30PM. 304A King's Rd, SW3. 071/352.6581

50 Osborne and Little Conveniently located just across the street from the Designer's Guild; if you like one shop you will probably like the other. The wallpaper and fabric in florals and clever trompe l'oeil marbles and stipples are all in very good taste. The shop is bringing out a range of Italian 15th-century-style wallpaper in subtle autumnal shades with golden stars. It is much cheaper to buy the paper here than to visit Juliet's house in Verona to see it. ♦ M-Tu, Th-F 9:30AM-5:30PM; W 10AM-5:30PM; Sa 10AM-4PM. 304 King's Rd, SW3. 071/352.1456

51 Manolo Blahnik Just off the King's Road on quiet Old Church Street is this museum of a shoe shop, often with one priceless shoe in the window. These are the shoes that **Sarah Ferguson** wore down the aisle on her walk to becoming a princess, and that **Princess Diana** has long worn, along with every genuinely glamorous lady in London. The shoes are beautifully designed and impeccably made in Italy in very limited numbers (12-15 pairs of each design), and they are worth every considerable pound you will pay. Particularly irresistible (and the price of the fare across the Atlantic) are the crocodile court pumps. ♦ M-F 10AM-6PM; Sa 10:30AM-5:30PM. 49 Old Church St, SW3. 071/352.8622

51 Hetherington How did you miss it? Simple, this shop has been here 12 years, but is so slim that it's easy to walk past without seeing it. But once it's caught your eye you will never forget the fabulous colorful dresses, evening wear, and wedding gowns that **Sasha Hether-**

ington has in her window. Once inside, you may see some of her illustrious clientele, perhaps an Italian contessa or a visiting European royal. Everything can be made to order (she will even turn dresses around in a week), and dresses are available for hire. ♦ M-Sa 10AM-6PM. 289 King's Rd, SW3. 071/352.0880

51 S. Borris ★★$ Ignore its dingy exterior and interior, this tiny sandwich bar has been here forever. Eat the food and you'll see why. Borris sells food to go, like scrumptious poppy-seed pastries, which they'll heat for you on the spot. But what makes this the most unusual deli in London is the cold display, with Beluga and Sevruga caviar, only. The contents of the fridge are worth more than the entire contents of the rest of the shop put together. When asked if he has ever sold any of the caviar, the proprietor explained it's for the ladies who host Chelsea's dinner parties and that he does a roaring trade, thanks. ♦ M-Sa 6AM-6PM; Su 9AM-2PM. 251 Kings Rd, SW3. 071/352.8729

52 Designer's Guild Outstanding design for the present and the future, with sofas, carpets, and fabrics that are modern, timeless, and country-house comfortable all at the same time. **Tricia Guild** goes from strength to strength with her fabrics, which look like brilliantly colored Impressionist watercolors of English gardens. Stunning accessories, especially the pottery, baskets, and lamps. If you really have no idea how to coordinate all the fabrics there is an interior design service, too. ♦ M-Tu, Th-F 9:30AM-5:30PM; W, Sa 10AM-5:30PM. 271, 277 King's Rd, SW3. 071/351.5755

You find no man, at all intellectual, who is willing to leave London. No, sir, when a man is tired of London, he is tired of life; for there is in London all that life can afford.

Samuel Johnson

They [the English] *are like their own beer: froth on top, dregs at the bottom, the middle excellent.*

Voltaire

52 David Tron Antiques Seventeenth- and 18th-century English and Continental furniture. A very classy shop that, along with **Jeremy** 2 doors down, gives a certain tone to the King's Road. ♦ M-F 10AM-5:30PM; Sa 11AM-4PM. 275 King's Rd, SW3. 071/352.5918

52 Green and Stone One of the few shops on the King's Road that has been here forever and still belongs to the original ethos of Chelsea. These dealers in art supplies carry beautiful sketchbooks and all you would ever want in oils and watercolors. For the un-skilled, there is a tempting collection of old and new silver and leather frames and a very good framing service. Green and Stone also stocks materials for doing your own decora-tive wall finishes and for gilding and frame restoration. ♦ M-F 9AM-5:30PM; Sa 9:30AM-6PM. 259 King's Rd, SW3. 071/352.0837

53 Jeremy Antiques Georgian and Continental 18th-century furniture and works of art. If you

have superb taste and can afford to indulge it, you will be quite happy here. ♦ M-Sa 8:30AM-6PM. 255 King's Rd, SW3. 071/352.0644

53 Chelsea Antique Market The most *flea market* in style of the various antique markets on the King's Road, the most likely to yield a bargain, and supposedly the first antique market in London. The stall owners still tend to be the friendliest. The strong point now is the books, and **Harrington Bros**. carries some of the best. The emphasis is on travel books, atlases and maps, natural history and color plates, children's books and fore-edge paint-ings. ♦ M-Sa 10AM-6PM. 245-253 King's Rd, SW3. 071/352.5689

53 Johanna Booth One of the nicest shops on the King's Road, and perhaps in all of Lon-don. Johanna Booth carries a fine collection of tapestries, Elizabethan and Jacobean furniture, and wood carvings. She is patient, knowledgeable, and nice, and her shop speaks of taste, simplicity, and imagination. One whole wall is lined with antiquarian books, also for sale. ♦ M-Sa 10AM-6PM. 247 King's Rd, SW3. 071/352.8998

54 Tiger, Tiger One of the best things about this toy shop is the price range. True, there are mu-seum-quality, hand-carved Noah's Arks, and stuffed seals and life-size (nearly) tigers that re-semble the real thing on the price tag, but there are also marbles, sheep hotwater bottles, hand puppets, and those wonderful farm animals and terrific mobiles that any doting grandparent can afford. ♦ M-Sa 9:30AM-6:30PM. 219 King's Rd, SW3. 071/352.8080

I love London. It is the most swinging city in the world at the moment.

Diana Vreeland, 1965

Restaurants/Nightlife: Red   **Hotels:** Blue
Shops/Parks: Green   **Sights/Culture:** Black

55 The Garage Fifties mobiles that'll plug into your memory banks are for sale outside on the forecourt. But there's more. Housed inside the old repair shop is a shopping complex that oozes '90s street cool and is proving the fashion shot in the arm the King's Road badly needs. Started by **Lauren Gordon** (of **Hyper Hyper** fame), there is a glittering array of England's fashion designers who are into the industrial and recycled looks—**Red or Dead's** Basic Unit, **Ray Matthew**'s house togs, **Richard Royal**'s recycled jackets, the **Scooby Doobies'** New Age house-hippy gear, and **Wigan**'s designer T-shirts. ♦ M-Tu, Th-Sa 10AM-6PM; W 10AM-8PM. 350 King's Rd, SW3. 071/351.5353

56 Givans A shop whose existence is a re-minder that the King's Road was not always trendy. Irish linen sheets, luxurious towel bathrobes, damask table linens, all of the kind of quality that is well worth searching out and taking home. ♦ M-Sa 9:30AM-5PM. 207 King's Rd, SW3. 071/352.6352

56 Henry J. Bean ★$ Fifties freaks, trendies, and the occasional punk join tourists and nuclear families in this Chelsea branch of yet another restaurant started by the industrious American **Bob Payton** (of **Chicago Pizza Pie** fame). He has figured out the formula for giv-ing the English fast food, American-style but better. Bean's is an English pub converted into an American saloon, with '50s and '60s rock 'n' roll music in the background. The all-star cast incudes potato skins, nachos, hamburgers, hot dogs, spicy chili, pecan pie, cheesecake, ice cream, brownies, and ice-cold American beer. The huge garden out back makes this a sunny-day favorite on the King's Road. Fashionable, friendly, and fun. ♦ M-Sa 11:45AM-11:45PM; Su noon-3PM, 7-10:30PM. 195-197 King's Rd, SW3. 071/352.9255

56 Chenil Galleries This has a worthy tradi-tion in Chelsea bohemia, including the dis-tinction of hosting the first public perfor-mance in 1923 of **Edith Sitwell**'s eccentric and original *Facade* to **William Walton**'s mu-sic, to the outrage of the critics. Such high artistic legacy in the dramatic arts has not been maintained; instead the static arts came into play. In 1979 it was established as an an-tique center specializing in Art Nouveau, Art Deco, and occasionally, fine art. Dealers sell an-tique textiles, furniture, silver, books, prints, and toys. Picture dealers and serious furniture deal-ers come here. Look for the mural depicting the gallery's artistic history. There is a garden res-taurant as well. ♦ M-Sa 10AM-6PM. 181-183 King's Rd, SW3. 071/351.5353

57 Chelsea Farmer's Market This collection of small food shops, open-air cafés, delicates-sens, and restaurants is a welcome addition for the residents of Chelsea, who drop in for quick and rather good cappuccino before div-ing into the **Chelsea Gardener** to replenish their window boxes and tiny patios. For the luncher and snacker there are fresh and delicious sandwiches, hot pizzas, a cold beer, or a glass of wine. Sit in the Astroturfed piazza and enjoy your repast in the English sun. There's even a homeopathic apothecary from Neal's Yard in Covent Garden. Some cafés stay open until 10PM. ♦ Market daily 10AM-6PM. Sydney St, SW3. 071/352.5600

58 Chelsea Town Hall On Saturday, busy shoppers trek in for the antique fairs and jumble sales that are a regular feature, as is the optimistic stream of wedding parties. Young brides in long white dresses, youngish brides in pale-pink suits, and various accomplices, ranging from 20 family members to 2 nervous witnesses, file in and out of the Chelsea Registry Office throughout the day. Formal photographs are usually taken on the steps outside, slowing traffic to a standstill. ♦ King's Rd, SW3

59 Edina Ronay The best fabrics—linens, silks, wools—with English *Brideshead Revisited* classicism, a French/Italian cut, and *je ne sais quoi*. The prices seem expensive when you walk in because the shop is small and on the King's Road. But the quality is Rue St.-Honoré, and you won't go wrong investing in an outfit. Ronay is famous above all for the handknit sweaters that established her name. ♦ M-Tu, Th-F 10AM-6PM; W 10AM-7PM; Sa 11AM-6PM. 141 King's Rd, SW3. 071/352.1085

59 David Fielden The designs are for brides who have a sense of daring as well as a tall body for the long, figure-hugging, Hollywood-style dresses. Customers include well-known glamour pusses like **Joan Collins, Elizabeth Taylor, Kim Basinger,** and **Morgan Fairchild.** Although the shop is tiny, contemporary daywear and eveningwear jostle happily next to the outrageous. ♦ M-Sa 10AM-6PM. 137 King's Rd, SW3. 071/351.1745

59 Antiquarius One of the earliest and best-known antique hypermarkets, and still one of the best. You will get agreeably lost in the maze of over 120 stalls, but you can find wonderful Georgian, Victorian, Edwardian, and Art Nouveau jewelry, antique lace, superb antique clocks, pictures, prints, and tiles, and if you shop carefully, you can expect to pay less than in a proper shop.

One of the longtime dealers at Antiquarius is **Trevor Allen,** who has irresistible antique jewelry and a good selection of Georgian and Victorian rings and earrings. Slide into a seat in the café, where you can renew your energies with coffee and chocolate cake. ♦ M-Sa 10AM-6PM. 135-141 King's Rd, SW3. 071/351.5353

59 Quincy Owned by **Jones** (at Nos. 71 and 129), a few doors down, but more traditional and classic, with very fine designs matched with quality fabrics. ♦ M-Sa 10AM-6:30PM. 131-133 King's Rd, SW3. 071/351.5367

60 Chelsea Potter ★$ A young, lively King's Road pub with an attractive interior, substantial lunches, and sidewalk chairs in spring and summer. ♦ M-Sa 11AM-11PM; Su noon-3PM, 7-10:30PM. 119 King's Rd, SW3. 071/352.9479

61 The Pheasantry ★$ This beautiful old building has been saved and restored, and now serves as home to a brasserie, restaurant,

and nightclub. On sunny days, summer and winter, sit outside and try the simple menu—stick to the pasta or steak, or have afternoon tea. ♦ Restaurant and brasserie: daily noon-3PM. Nightclub: M-Sa 6:30PM-2AM; Su 7:30-11:30PM. 152 King's Rd, SW3. 071/351.3084

62 Jones The window is worth a pause, and inside you will see *toute la Rue du Roi* trying on the latest creations by **Katherine Hamnett, Body Map, Jean-Paul Gaultier,** and Jones, of course, as well as unknowns who must be pretty proud to have gained admittance into the most popular and possibly best unisex shop on the King's Road. (One branch of Jones is, surprise, surprise, in Beverly Hills.) ♦ M-F 10AM-6:30PM; Sa 10:30AM-6PM. 71 King's Rd, SW3. 071/352.6899

63 Drummonds ★$ A good old-fashioned café with a varying menu and a buffet lunch that is served all day. Pub-style food in a café atmosphere. It is not easy to find such undemanding places. ♦ M-Sa 10:30AM-11PM; Su noon-3PM, 7-10:30PM. 49 King's Rd, SW3. 071/730.8180

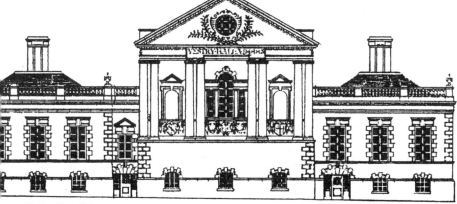

Chelsea Town Hall

More than 400 blue-ceramic plaques decorate the houses, or sites of houses, where the distinguished once lived in London. **English Heritage** decides who is qualified for the honor, following certain guidelines: the person must have died at least 20 years ago, been born more than 100 years ago, and made some important contribution to human welfare or happiness. The first plaque was placed in 1867 on the house where **Lord Byron** was born on Holles Street in Westminster.

David Ben Gurion lived at 75 Warrington Crescent, W9.

James Boswell lived and died on the site of 122 Great Portland St, W1.

Elizabeth Barrett Browning lived on the site of 50 Wimpole St, W1.

Charlie Chaplin lived at 287 Kennington Rd, SE11.

Sir Winston Churchill lived at 28 Hyde Park Gate, SW7.

Samuel Taylor Coleridge lived at 7 Addison Bridge Pl, W14, and at 71 Berners St, W1.

King's Road & Chelsea

Charles Darwin lived on the site of 110 Gower St, WC1.

Charles Dickens lived at 48 Doughty St, WC1.

Benjamin Disraeli was born at 22 Theobalds Rd, WC1, and died at 19 Curzon St, W1.

Sir Edward Elgar lived at 51 Avonmore Rd, W14.

George Eliot (Mary Ann Evans) lived at Holly Lodge, 31 Wimbledon Park Rd, SW18, and died at 4 Cheyne Walk, SW3.

T.S. Eliot lived and died at 3 Kensington Court Gardens, W8.

Benjamin Franklin lived at 36 Craven St, WC2.

Sigmund Freud lived at 20 Maresfield Gardens, NW3.

William Ewart Gladstone lived at 11 Carlton House Terrace, SW1, at 10 St. James's Sq, SW1, and at 73 Harley St, W1.

Joseph Grimaldi lived at 56 Exmouth Market, EC1.

George Frederick Handel lived and died at 25 Brook St, W1.

Thomas Hardy lived at 172 Trinity Rd, SW17, and at Adelphi Terrace, WC2.

William Hazlitt lived on the site of 6 Bouverie St, EC4, and died at 6 Frith St, W1.

Henry James lived at 34 De Vere Gardens, W8.

Jerome K. Jerome lived at 91-104 Chelsea Gardens, Peabody Buildings, SW1.

Amy Johnson lived at Vernon Court, Hendon Way, NW2.

Dr. Samuel Johnson lived at 17 Gough Sq, Fleet St, EC4, and at Johnson's Court, Fleet St, EC4.

John Keats was born on the site of The Swan and Hoop public house at 85 Moorgate, EC2, and lived at Wentworth Pl, Keats Grove, NW3.

Rudyard Kipling lived at 43 Villiers St, WC2.

David Herbert Lawrence lived at 1 Bryon Villas, Vale of Health, Hampstead Heath, NW3 in 1915.

T.E. Lawrence (Lawrence of Arabia) lived at 14 Barton St, SW1.

Katherine Mansfield lived at 17 East Heath Rd, NW3.

Karl Marx lived at 28 Dean St, W1.

W. Somerset Maugham lived at 6 Chesterfield St, W1.

Wolfgang Amadeus Mozart composed his first symphony at 180 Ebury St, SW1.

Napoleon III lived at 1c King St, SW1.

Lord Horatio Nelson lived on the site of 147 New Bond St, W1, and at 103 New Bond St, W1.

Sir Isaac Newton lived on the site of 87 Jermyn St, SW1.

Florence Nightingale lived and died on the site of 10 South St, W1.

Sir Robert Peel lived at 16 Upper Grosvenor St, W1.

Samuel Pepys lived on the site of 12 and 14 Buckingham St, WC2.

Sylvia Plath lived and died at 23 Fitzroy Rd, NW1.

Captain Robert Falcon Scott lived at 56 Oakley St, SW3.

George Bernard Shaw lived at Adelphi Terrace, WC2.

Percy Bysshe Shelley lived at 15 Poland St, W1.

William Makepeace Thackeray lived at 16 Young St, W8, at 2 Palace Green, W8, and at 36 Onslow Sq, SW7.

Anthony Trollope lived at 39 Montague Sq, W1.

Joseph Mallord William Turner lived at 23 Queen Anne St, W1, and at 119 Cheyne Walk, SW3.

Mark Twain (Samuel L. Clemens) lived at 23 Tedworth Sq, SW3.

H.G. Wells lived at 13 Hanover Terrace, NW1.

James Abbott McNeill Whistler lived at 96 Cheyne Walk, SW10.

Oscar Wilde lived at 34 Tite St, SW3.

P.G. Wodehouse lived at 17 Dunraven St, W1.

Virginia Woolf lived at 29 Fitzroy Sq, W1.

William Butler Yeats lived at 23 Fitzroy Rd, NW1.

Best Small Hotels

Abney Court $$ Sumptuous flower arrangements in the lobby, with elegant pale walls, lovely fabrics and antiques used throughout. Some rooms have four-poster beds, all have Jacuzzis and marble bathrooms. Light meals are served in your room. The drawback? Five floors and no elevator. ♦ 20 Pembridge Gardens, W2. 071/221.1518

The Beaufort $$ Pastel colors, fresh flowers, original watercolors, and comfy armchairs welcome guests. Inside your bedroom there's a Sony Walkman, a VCR, a teddy bear, access to a health club, room service, and drinks from a 24-hour bar, all included in the tariff. No hidden charges and no tipping! ♦ 33 Beaufort Gardens, SW3. 071/584.5252

Dorset Square Hotel $$ It's under the same management as the Pelham, but it's cheaper here. Two Georgian town houses have been spliced together—the décor is country house and all the rooms are different, with antique furniture and marble and mahogany bathrooms. Some rooms are small, and the double beds are remarkably slim. Traffic noise comes in from one side. ♦ 39 Dorset Sq, NW1. 071/723.7874

Dukes Hotel $$$ Two small lounges, a tiny restaurant, and a club atmosphere in the paneled bar famous for its vast selection of cognac. Bedrooms are simple and comfortable. The hotel overlooks a flower-filled, gaslit courtyard. ♦ 35 St. James's Pl, SW1. 071/491.4840

Eleven Cadogan Gardens $$ A gabled red-brick Victorian house with fine paneled staircases and sedate portraits hanging from the walls. Comfy sofas, a bridge table, and oil paintings greet the weary traveler in the lounge. Cozy bedrooms, but there's no restaurant or bar. ♦ 11 Cadogan Gardens, SW3. No credit cards. 071/730.3426

The Fenja $$ Marble busts and antiques greet you as you enter. Bedrooms are named after notable English artists and writers—the J.M.W. Turner Room has an enormous four-poster bed! No miniatures here; drinks in the rooms are in decanters. Service is very good: they carry your suitcases, polish your shoes, and help you with everything. Breakfast, light meals served in a small drawing room. ♦ 69 Cadogan Gardens, SW3. 071/589.7333

Fortyseven Park Street $$$$ A small lounge in the lobby is the only public room in this old Edwardian town house with high ceilings and a splendid staircase. If you're traveling on a budget you'll approve of the suites because they have kitchens, but it's really aimed at gourmets—the Roux brothers' **Le Gavroche** restaurant (Michelin 3-star) provides room service! ♦ 47 Park St, W1. 071/491.7282

The Halcyon $$$ The distant, thunderous roar of traffic disappears as you tuck into the nouvelle cuisine from the **Kingfisher Restaurant**. The hotel is painted cream and pink. Satellite TV and safes are in all the rooms; one suite has a conservatory. ♦ 81 Holland Park, W11. 071/727.7288

Hazlitt's $$ Three carefully preserved 18th-century terraced houses. Oak and pine furniture, baths with feet, and sloping floors add to the ambiance. Room service available at breakfast, only. Rooms are light and airy, though some are small, as are some beds. ♦ 6 Frith St, W1. 071/434.1771

The Knightsbridge Green Hotel $$ Friendly, efficient, and reasonably priced. The walls are whitewashed, and pretty fabrics are everywhere. Most of the bedrooms have sitting rooms. Tea and coffee are available all day in the one public room. ♦ 159 Knightsbridge, SW1. 071/584.6274

Pelham Hotel $$ It overlooks a busy street but has lovely décor, service, and a pretty, spacious restaurant with good cooking. ♦ 15 Cromwell Pl, SW7. 071/589.8288

Portobello Hotel $$ The rooms vary from tiny to palatial, with extraordinary features like a painted ceiling or a round bed. The lounge overlooks a lovely Victorian garden, which is out of bounds! The service is famous for its slowness. Twenty four hour service in the restaurant, but eat out if you can. ♦ 22 Stanley Gardens, W11. 071/727.2777

St. James's Club $$$$ This club is so special that we had to mention it again. See page 57 for complete details. ♦ 7 Park Pl, SW1. 071/629.7688

22 Jermyn Street $$ The rooms here are like tiny apartments filled with comfortable chairs and antiques. Breakfast and light snacks (but no restaurant), and a fridge stocked by Fortnum's across the street. ♦ 22 Jermyn St, SW1. 071/734.2353

George Lang
Owner Café des Artistes (New York), consultant, columnist for *Travel & Leisure*

A list of restaurants where you can eat well at a reasonable price, even with our dollar making a permanent home for itself in the subbasement:

Fox and Anchor. Being less than a block away from the Smithfield wholesale meat market (the largest in Europe), gets the choicest cuts each morning when the butchers open up at 5AM. Try the mile-high mixed grill of slices of pork, lamb, beef steak, sausage, fried egg, mushrooms, chips, and grilled ham.

Gurkhas Tandoori Restaurant. Sample the *Karang Shekuwa*, an assertive but not overpoweringly spicy lamb chop marinated and cooked over charcoal in a tandoori oven, as well as the vast variety of vegetarian dishes.

Phoenicia. Seven pounds for a good luncheon! Surely this must be the best buy in London, a city where you can

King's Road & Chelsea

easily spend twice as much on a single appetizer. For this you can select from a buffet of about 15 Lebanese *meze* and 3 or 4 main courses.

Geales Fish Restaurant. You surely don't come to this fish-and-chip place for atmosphere, but the fish here are always the prime specimens of the season, fried with crisp golden overcoats with a satisfying crunchiness that indicates very fresh oil and perfect timing.

Just Around the Corner. In a forlorn building a half-hour outside of the center of London, you can enjoy comforting, home-style food served at candle-lit tables, and at the end, the waiter presents no bill—he simply asks you to pay what you think the meal was worth.

Peter Jackson
President, British Topographical Society

Books about London

Ann Saunders, *The Art & Architecture of London* (1984, Phaidon). A huge guide covering the whole GLC area in great detail.

Edward Jones and Christopher Woodward, *A Guide to the Architecture of London* (1983, Weidenfeld & Nicholson). Exactly what it claims to be, in sections, with maps and a photograph of every building mentioned.

Malcolm Rogers, *Museums & Galleries of London* (1983, Ernest Benn). Every museum and gallery, from huge to tiny, carefully described.

Weinreb & Hibbert, *The London Encyclopaedia* (1983, Macmillan). Ideal for a quick reference, but not to be taken as the final word.

The Book of London (1979 and 1981, AA). Every beautiful page in color covering every aspect of London, both topographical and human.

Felix Barker and Ralph Hyde, *London As It Might Have Been* (1982, Murray). Amusing and amazing account of buildings that never were.

Hermoine Hobhouse, *Lost London* (1971, Macmillan). Wonderful but sad illustrated survey of what has gone forever.

Peter Nash
Creative Director

Penfriend. Typography runs in the family, so I've always had a soft spot for pens. This Art Deco shop is one of the few that sells everything from Mont Blanc to Waterman with handwritten descriptions of them in the window.

Bleeding Heart Wine Bar. Built in the cellars of the building above, it's in one of the oldest yards in London and is mentioned in the *Doomesday* book. The restaurant is a warren of oak-paneled archways with dark antique furniture and library books, even a grand piano in one of the rooms. The flagstone floor has trap doors, wheels, and cogs, winches and pulleys. It has a great atmosphere. There are bottles of wine stacked everywhere. The staff is French and so is the very good, cheap food. Book at lunchtime.

A walk in the early evening through the **Inns of Court** up Chancery Lane and **Lincoln's Inn**. It has a tremendous peace, serenity, and history from the oldest sur-

Bests

viving legal system in the world. On Chancery Lane walk past **Ravenscrofts**, the great robe makers, who make robes for the House of Lords and wigs for the judges. In the inn, with its Dickensian echoing alleyways, look up and you can see barristers in their rooms discussing cases. Careful through, don't linger too long; they lock the area up at night.

The Old Curiosity Shop nestling in the corner of Lincoln's is the oldest shop in London. It was frequented by Charles Dickens and is where little Nell and her grandfather actually lived. It's tiny, full of a mixture of antiques and curios and NO souvenirs of London. If he's not busy, the owner will tell you about the shop's history, and you can even buy a copy of a map dated 1600, which has the shop marked on it.

The Dove, at Hammersmith on the river. Very old pub (1796), right on the river in a very picturesque part of London. It's a particularly good place to have a drink on a summer evening. Next to it is a little row of old cottages; William Morris lived nearby. The whole area is very pretty.

Spread Eagle, near the *Cutty Sark*. It used to be Greenwich's coaching inn and is Georgian, if not older. Part restaurant, part antique shop, it's oak paneled and decorated in Victorian style with a spiral staircase and aspidistras on the columns. Upstairs is a nice old restaurant with a floor that's so bowed they turn the plates upside down and stick them under the table legs to straighten them up. Very good English/ French food, especially the game.

The Flask, at Highgate. The old inn at Highgate going out of London near the Great North Road. It was built in 1767, and its cellars, which are 100 years older, are where Dick Turpin used to hide. In summer you can sit outdoors.

Buster Edwards, the great train robber, selling flowers at Waterloo Station.

Valeries on Old Compton Street is an old-fashioned Italian pâtisserie where one can have breakfast—coffee, tea, and cakes—any time of day. Frequented by Soho's advertising and commercials people.

Gasworks is a small restaurant that's absolutely cram-packed with antiques. It's not the best food you'll ever eat but its probably the most interesting place you will ever eat in. Premeal aperitifs or after-dinner brandy and coffee must be taken in the drawing room among the risqué chess sets. You'll find it at the western end of the King's Road near the gasometers (massive cylinders for storing gas).

Paxton and Whitfield. You can smell this shop 4 doors along. One of the finest cheese shops in the world, it's also one of the oldest—nearly 200 years old. Ask nicely and they'll even cut you samples from among their 300 cheeses.

Jill Robinson Shaw
Novelist

My favorite thing about the Sloane Street area is the **Joseph** shops, watching the way Joseph skulks about casing his customers and staff like a wary, seductive general. *Are the troops slinky enough today? Don't want too much merriment here, are their legs long enough? Men's shoulders please, sloped forward so the jacket hangs as free as the zoot drape.* The look is Casablanca romantic, no matter how the season turns. Like Ralph Lauren, Joseph has his cast of characters—a maxi series—bringing his imaginery world to life. As Ralph Lauren has his New England, Santa Fe, and cruise ship, so Joseph has his Casablanca-cum-21st-century London.

Long before ornamentation became such a fuss in Paris, **Zandra Rhodes** was doing it here. Zandra Rhodes is one of a kind and her shop near Bond Street is a must. It's a great gallery of scarfs, sweatshirts, and jewels. Contemplate the gowns, the magic of their color and ornament—each one feels like a Gustave Klimt painting swirling through the fingertips.

Even without the legendary Victor, the **Gay Hussar** remains the warmest place to eat when you want to remember your grandmother's cooking, especially if she was Middle European. It's not just the brilliant goulash with serious paprika and dumplings, but a lovely white-fish salad starter with horseradish and cucumber and the best roast duckling served with red cabbage, apple sauce, and potatoes. Their Transylvanian cabbage shows just how Dracula got everybody to come over for a quick bite. The idea is not to eat for a week and go to the Gay Hussar with friends who like cranky conversations about politics; the food heats up opinions and adds savoury gusto to language. Half way through the meal, one begins to feel like one of the legendary political writers who dine here talking through epic lunches that you will never forget. Then struggle to decide between the chocolate-and-fresh-raspberry cake or the *rote grutze* (summer pudding).

Gordon Campbell-Grey's **Blue Coyote** in Oxford is a good, stylish Mexican restaurant.

If I can't get to a good Mexican in London, Indian is the next best thing. My favorite Indian restaurant is the **Bombay Brasserie**. They do a potato salad starter that resembles minature tortillas.

Everyone will tell you about their favorite Italian restaurant, but to me there is no comparison to **Santini**. It's expensive, but in a class entirely by itself. You can't miss with the salmon carpaccio (lightly grilled slivers of fresh salmon), whole sea bass, zucchini flowers, or the *quattro misto,* a selection of 4 exquisite pastas. The desserts and vegetables are irrelevant. The rest is luminous.

If one is getting into the realm of magic, then the great sorceror today is Raymond Blanc, and again, to muddle a phrase, if you have to ask or consider the cost, don't go. Price is irrelevant because his restaurant, **Le Manoir Aux Quat'Saisons**, is an entertainment of exquisite precision and has little to do with the business of fueling our bodies or gathering with friends to have something to eat. But it's divine.

Marta Eneguske, New York Architect
Howard Sandum, Literary Agent

Marta and Howard have been visiting London for 13 years. They love it, even if the food is expensive and the restaurants don't stay open late! Their favorite restaurants are **Brown's**, the **Ritz**, and the **Savoy**, but since they can't eat in those places every day, they started to search for what everyone looks for—good food, good service, and that extra something else that makes you feel wanted and special while you eat. Each year they update a secret list that is passed around to friends coming to London. Here are a few of their favorites:

Hodgson's. Since it was converted from a former auction room for antiquarian books 4 years ago, we have treasured our visits here. Crowded with barristers and clerks at lunch, at night it becomes a serene oasis where load-bearing columns lead the eye high into the ceiling and a skylight 3 stories up. They cook everything beautifully—like calf's liver in a raspberry *coulis* (sauce). We haven't seen anywhere better for quality and value.

Carvery at the **Hotel Russell**. For the ravenously hungry, even on Sunday and bank holidays, there's a wide array of hors d'oeuvres followed by Scotch beef, rare lamb, pork, or turkey. (You can have all of them if you wish.) Even with dessert it's a bargain.

Aldwych Brasserie at the **Waldorf Hotel** is the right place for after-theater suppers and snacks, when so many restaurants close early.

Over in South Kensington, **Daquise** stays open until 11:30 PM and is fun for after-theater Polish meals or afternoon snacks. We always like to stay in Kensington for a slower-paced week before moving to Central London.

Chanterelle, a happy place willing to serve gruff intellectuals in shirtsleeves; the **Bombay Brasserie**, serving a big menu of excellent Indian food in a fanciful Colonial setting and garden; or the more conventional **Vanderbilt Hotel**, with its good-value prix-fixe menu.

There are cheap restaurants dotted about all over London. Four favorites are: **Yialousa Greek Taverna**, where the *meyes*—8 or 10 different small dishes, from kabobs to deep-fried whitebait—are nibbled by mysterious international characters. At Marble Arch is **Il Boscaiolo**, an Italian restaurant filled with Italians behind the counter serving Italians in front of it with antipasto, canneloni, or spaghetti carbonara. Over in the City there's the **Barbican's Butler's Wine Bar**, which sells good, cheap ploughmen's lunches (meat or cheese here) to people who cannot see any fields to plough, just miles of vertical concrete. And far off in Greenwich opposite the Royal Naval College is a modest little fish-and-chip restaurant called **Macdonald's**. No, it's not the fast-food outlet.

The best place to drop in when you're well dressed is the **Hyde Park Hotel**'s downstairs bar if you're shopping in Knightsbridge, or the **Hotel Russell**'s lounge in Bloomsbury. If you're casual, then the **Paxton's Head** at 153 Knightsbridge is a good bet. **Jacques**, the pub in the **Hotel Tavistock** on Tavistock Square, does imaginative meat pies for lunch; the **National Gallery coffeeshop** is always reliable; but the **British Museum coffeeshop** is larger, more comfortable, and has a sumptuous choice of foods. Opposite is the **Museum Tavern**, an English pub with the best beefsteak and kidney pie in town. Reservations are in high demand at the **Tate Gallery Restaurant**, so the **Tate Cafeteria** is a quick and inexpensive alternative if you really mean business at the gallery. In Covent Garden we like the **Crusting Pipe** wine bar in the Piazza or the old wood-paneled pub, the **Green Man and French Horn** on St. Martin's Lane. Farther afield, try the upstairs dining room at **Toby's** pub, just where Fleet Street begins. If you visit **Kenwood House** in

Hampstead be sure to arrange for lunch at the coffeeshop in the former kitchen, a cavernous museum in itself.

Gerry Rosentswieg
The Graphics Studio, Los Angeles

Best Restaurants:

Alastair Little. High-tech décor. California cuisine prepared by owner/chef Alastair Little.

Langan's Brasserie. Very chic. Reservations essential.

Le Suquet. French seafood.

Sea Shell. Fish-and-chips. Take-away in front, restaurant behind.

Sweetings. Perhaps the oldest fish restaurant. Fish in a sea of pinstriped suits for lunch in the City.

Geales. Fish-and-chips in Notting Hill Gate. Located behind the Gate Cinema.

Arlecchino. Very good Italian food in Notting Hill Gate.

Red Fort. Indian food in elegant surroundings.

Khyber. Indian food.

La Brasseria. French brasserie that also serves English breakfast from 8AM.

Le Caprice. Theater-people chic, behind the Ritz.

Simpson's-in-the-Strand. Traditional English carvery. Frock-coat elegance—ties necessary—but worth it.

Peter's Restaurant. Taxi drivers' café. Great English breakfast.

The Knight in the triumph of his heart made several reflections on the greatest of the British Nation; as, that one Englishman could beat three Frenchmen; that we could never be in danger of Popery so long as we took care of our fleet; that the Thames was the noblest river in Europe; that London Bridge was a greater piece of work than any of the seven wonders of the world; with many other honest prejudices which naturally cleave to the heart of a true Englishman.

Joseph Addison

The Strand, Fleet Street & the City

It takes passionate pilgrims, vague aliens, and other disinterested persons to appreciate the points of this admirable country, wrote the never disinterested **Henry James** in *English Hours*. The Strand, Fleet Street and the City are for passionate pilgrims and vague aliens, those true and faithful lovers of London.

ven though the walk begins with the spruced up **Charing Cross Station** and
nds with Victoriana at its greatest in **Tower Bridge**, the area has become rather
ess obvious in its display of treasures since the days when **Boswell** insisted that
ery little was *the equal of Fleet Street*. For the curious, the city lover, the history-
ninded, and the Dickensian-spirited, the treasures of the Strand, Fleet Street, and
he City are many, worthy, and as Henry James himself said, *a tremendous
hapter of accidents.*

he Strand and Fleet Street and then Queen Victoria Street, a seamless thor-
ughfare echoing the path of the Thames, have been a main route connect-
ng Westminster to the City for more than 1000 years. These streets have wit-
essed 16 reigns, a sanctuary and university of English law, and *a street of ink,*

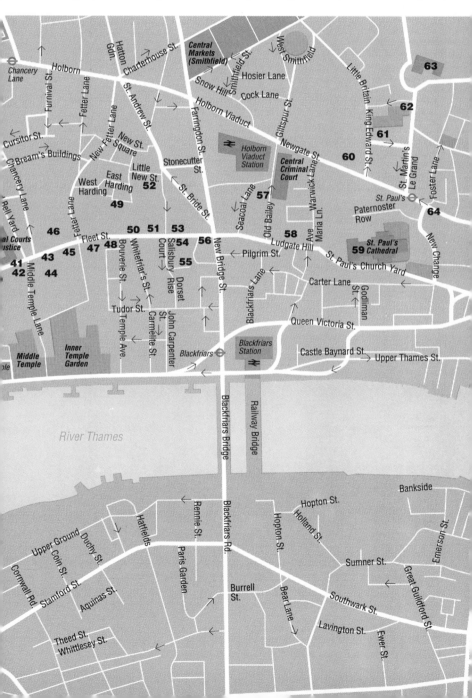

where events that transformed—or settled into—history were written and printed for millions of readers all over the world. Despite the computer age, these streets remain a well-trodden route from the world of government (Westminster) to the world of finance (the City), each deeply dependent on the other, each remarkably oblivious to the down-at-heel pathway that connects them.

Gone are the days when the mansions of the great bishops lined the Strand, entered by way of gardens that led down to the river. And gone also are the days when stupendous hotels, posh restaurants, and elegant theaters were constructed here to reflect in the glory of the newly opened Charing Cross Station. The Strand survived the Reformation, when aristocrats replaced the bishops in their great houses, but it failed to triumph over another kind of reformation, the building of the **Victoria Embankment** in 1867, which reclaimed land from the Thames but isolated the street from the river, removing the Thames from view and slowly wringing the life from the thoroughfare. Too many massive office blocks have since devitalized stretches of the long street, paving the way for humdrumness by day and desertion by night except by the vagrants who sleep here.

And now, Fleet Street has been deserted by the scribes, the reptiles, the diarists, the columnists, and the hacks, who have all dissipated to different parts of London. They return to their old watering holes on the *street of shame* with ever fonder memories and to gaze at the shells of the buildings they once occupied 24 hours a day, whose fronts remain but whose insides have been ripped out to make way for stockbrokers and computers.

This walk includes the oldest wine bar in London (**Gordon's Wine Cellar**), where you can fortify yourself with a glass of Madeira, and one of the oldest pubs (**The George**), where you can drink where that old London lover **Johnson** drank, after you examine the house (**Dr. Johnson's House**) in which he wrote the first English dictionary, an endeavor only partially inspired by his need to earn the money to pay for the drink. You can have a look in the **Law Courts**, and the criminally inclined can sit in on a case; buy silver ducks where businesspeople who meet the Queen Mum shop (**Searle & Co.**); put your cigars in a humidifier with a few thousand others in a traditional tobacconist (**S. Weingott**); and eat at the place where Mr. Pickwick was put on trial (**The George & Vulture**).

As you walk down the Strand and Fleet Street you are walking in the footsteps of an impressive list of walkers and talkers: **Sir Walter Raleigh**, **William Congreve**, **Sheridan**, **Johnson** and

Blackfriars Bridge

Boswell, **Coleridge** and **Lamb**, **Fielding**, **Thackeray** and **Dickens**. **Prince Charles** and **Lady Diana** drove this way en route to **St. Paul's Cathedral** when they got married. Nowadays, the singular figure of **J.P. Donleavy** can be seen striding along this ancient route. Along the way, you will be guided and amazed by glimpses of St. Paul's, masterpiece and monument to **Sir Christopher Wren** and beacon of hope and guardian angel for Londoners during the bombing of World War II, and once more in the 1990s as Prince Charles fights off the architects he feels are trying to despoil the city.

This is a fair-weather weekday walk. The Strand, Fleet Street, and the City hibernate on weekends, while St. Paul's is closed to passing visitors.

1 Charing Cross Station With the arrival of the railway at Charing Cross Station in 1863, the Strand became the busiest street in Europe, lined with enormous hotels, restaurants, and theaters built in the euphoria of the age. Recently, British Rail has reconstructed the cobbled driveway to the station and rebuilt the exterior walls as they were originally, adorned with 21 cast-iron lanterns. Charing Cross is the mainline station closest to the heart of London—and one of the busiest. More than 110,000 people use the station each weekday, and if you are here in the morning during rush hour, you will come face-to-face with nearly half of them. ♦ Strand WC2

2 Charing Cross Hotel $$ The hotel, designed by **E.M. Barry** in 1863-64, sits over the train tracks of Charing Cross Station and houses its waiting room. Railway hotels have a certain mystique, appealing to writers with vagabond souls and melancholy hearts. The trouble is, they always look better from the outside. Inside, you have to face hideous attempts at modernization, unmanageable legions of tour groups, and a tired, unhappy staff. The Charing Cross Hotel is no different, but it does have a few redeeming features: appealing Renaissance motifs on the facade, an old-fashioned and tranquil room on the 1st floor for morning coffee and

afternoon tea, an immense staircase that the insensitive converters of this hotel have not yet managed to demolish, and one of the better carveries in town. ♦ Strand, WC2. 071/839.7292; fax 071/839.3933

Within Charing Cross Hotel:

Charing Cross Hotel Carvery ★★$ If you are traveling on a shoestring with a large family this could be the answer to a few prayers: a set 3-course meal including coffee, dessert, and service. Children under 4 eat free, those 5-10 are charged half-price. The cafeteria-style service features all-you-can-eat helpings of roast beef, lamb, and pork. The vegetables tend to be overcooked and the desserts lacking in taste, but the place is full of foreigners enjoying English roast beef. ♦ M-Sa noon-3PM, 5-11:30PM; Su noon-3PM, 6-11PM. Reservations recommended. 071/839.7282

3 Coutt's Bank The bank of the royal family, established in 1692, has occupied this site of **John Nash** buildings since 1904. In a daring and skillful act of restoration in 1979, **Sir Frederick Gibberd** created an ultramodern building behind Nash's Neoclassical stucco facade and pepper-pot corner cupolas. ♦ 440 Strand, WC2

The Strand, Fleet Street & the City

4 Charing Cross Monument In 1290, a sad and devoted **King Edward I** placed 12 *Eleanor Crosses* along the route of the funeral cortege of his beloved consort, **Queen Eleanor**, from the north of England near Lincoln to Westminster Abbey. The final stopping place was a few yards from here, where the statue of **Charles I** now stands looking down Whitehall. But the marble-and-Caen-stone octagonal Eleanor Cross placed here was torn down by the Puritans in 1647. The Charing Cross in the forecourt of Charing Cross Station that you see today was designed by **E.M. Barry** in 1865, a year after he designed the Charing Cross Hotel. It is a memorial, not a replica of the original Charing Cross. ♦ Strand, WC2

The old **Charing Cross Hospital** at 28 Villiers St was moved to Fulham in 1973 but, confusingly, kept its original name, even though it is now nowhere near Charing Cross.

5 Craven Street The street forms the west border of Charing Cross Station with Villiers Street on the east, and reaches down to the Embankment. **Benjamin Franklin** lived at No. 36 (1757-62, 1764-72).

6 Sherlock Holmes Pub Stuffed to the gills with Sherlock Holmes memorabilia presented by the **Sherlock Holmes Society**, including the great detective's study; the sleuth was supposed to have met his adversaries from the underworld here. Although it seems to be a tourists' pub, it's frequented by local office workers who love the eccentricity of it all. ♦ M-F noon-2PM, 6-9PM. 10 Northumberland St, WC2. 071/930.2644

7 Playhouse Theatre (1882, **Sefton Parry**) In 1987, Londoners blinked in surprise when the Playhouse became light again after 12 years' darkness. In 1894, the first production of **George Bernard Shaw**'s *Arms & the Man* was staged here. In 1905, part of Charing Cross Station collapsed on the theater and killed 6 people. Actress/manager **Gladys Cooper** ran it until 1933; and it was taken over by the BBC as a radio sound studio from 1951-75, with the **Beatles**, among others, broadcasting from here. The theater is now owned by millionaire author **Jeffrey Archer** and has established itself as home of the one-(wo)man show. ♦ Seats 786. Northumberland Ave, WC2. 071/839.4401

8 Sir Joseph Bazalgette (**George Simonds**) It's sad that a man who had such a profound effect upon London and its people should be so totally forgotten, but such is the fate of the chief engineer. It was under Bazalgette that the solid granite Albert, Victoria, and Chelsea embankments were built between 1868 and 1874. The whole reclaimed 32 acres of mud, and unlike most new developments, was welcomed. Bazalgette had an even more important role, however: he built London's original 1300-mile sewerage system between 1858 and 1875. In doing so he saved London's citizens from utterly disgusting conditions, including an overpowering stench, regular sewage floods, and cholera epidemics. ♦ Embankment Pl, WC2

9 Villiers Street Named for **George Villiers**, Duke of Buckingham (also see Buckingham Street), whose fabulous York House covered the street. Villiers Street has a feeling of the past, with flower, fruit, and newspaper sellers, and 2 special attractions: the **Players Theatre Club** and **Gordon's Wine Cellar**.

George Villiers, Duke of Buckingham, was a clever opportunist, but not quite clever enough. A favorite of James I and his son Charles I, the Duke progressed from plain George Villiers to viscount, marquis, and, finally, Duke of Buckingham in less than 10 years. His ruthless behavior led to his assassination in 1628 and probably set the stage for Charles I's estrangement from Parliament and the Civil War—and the King's own execution.

10 Players Theatre Club The former site of Craven Passage (immortalized in the **Flanagan and Allen** song *Underneath the Arches* and in **George Orwell**'s *Down and Out in Paris and London*). In its place, the Player's Theatre has been built as part of the massive rebuilding program at Charing Cross. Victorian music hall at its best, with the same high-spirited sense of humor and fun that delighted audiences in the days before radio, television, and canned laughter. The only snag is that you must join and take a temporary membership out 48 hours before the show. (*Applause* and British Airways do have separate arrangements with the club.) It is well worth the effort and makes for a terrific evening under the auspices of **Mr. Reg Woolly**, who has been running the show since 1946. There are 2 bars and a supper room, and drinks and snacks are served during the performances. How civilized! (The homeless population that used to sleep in Craven Passage has been moved on as British Rail has sold the whole area, including the air above the station, to a pristine new offices and shops development called **Embankment Place**.) ♦ Seats 300. Dinner: Tu-Sa 6PM; Su 6:45PM. Shows: Tu-Sa 8:30PM; Su 8PM. Craven Passage, Villiers St, WC2. 071/839.1134

11 Gordon's Wine Cellar ★★★$ Slip through a curtain and you're here. Even though Gordon's looks every bit its 300 years, it feels very 1940s, like a film set of London during the War—camaraderie, warmth, and safety below. The bottles are stored behind a locked grill; the tables and chairs don't match; the food is exceptionally good and laid out the way it must have always been, with home-made terrines, smoked hams, roasted birds, first-class English cheeses (Stilton, Red Windsor), and a large choice of fresh salads. Hot meals are served in winter. Sherries, ports, and Madeiras come from the cask and are impressive, as are the house wines. Once discovered, this could be your favorite London haunt. It is closed between September 1990 and September 1991. ♦ M-F 11AM-11PM. 47 Villiers St, WC2. 071/930.1408

12 Embankment Underground Station The best route to **Hungerford Bridge**. Walk into the station from Villiers Street, out the other side, and up the flight of stairs to the bridge.

13 Hungerford Bridge (1863, **John Hawkshaw**) This bridge replaced one by **Brunel** of the 1840s, and the current paint job makes it a handsome red tapestry of trussed iron across the Thames. It is the only bridge in central London for trains and people and is a useful pedestrian walkway to the concert hall and theaters on the South Bank, with stunning views toward the City and Waterloo Bridge. ♦ Charing Cross, WC2

14 Victoria Embankment Gardens During the summer, office workers and tired tourists relax in deck chairs, children sprint along the grassy slopes, and bands play in the secluded and charming riverside garden. This is excellent picnic territory, with a considerable population of 19th-century statues among the dolphin lamp standards and camel and sphinx benches. One of the best statues is of **Arthur Sullivan**, who wrote the Savoy operas with Gilbert. The inscription *Is life a boon?* is from *Yeoman of the Guard*. Another favorite is the World War I memorial to the **Imperial Camel Corps**, complete with a fine miniature camel and rider. ♦ Victoria Embankment, WC2

But now behold in the quick forge
and working house of thought,
How London doth pour out her citizens.

Shakespeare, *Henry V*

15 Buckingham Street Parallel to Villiers Street and named after the same Duke of Buckingham whose mansion was built here in 1626 on land formerly occupied by the Bishops of Norwich and York. The street's most famous resident, philosopher **Francis Bacon**, was evicted by Buckingham during his expansionist building program. In place of the Duke's mansion stands **Canova House**, an 1860s Italian Gothic structure with red-brick arches built by **Nicholas Barbon**. The Duke of Buckingham's entrance to his gardens from the Thames at the bottom of the street is marked with the **York Water Gate**.

16 York Water Gate A fairly ironic monument for the corrupt Duke of Buckingham. Built in 1626 in the Italian style with Buckingham's motto in Latin, *Fidel Coticula Crux* (the Cross is the Touchstone of Faith), and the Duke's coronet, the gate marks where the Thames reached before the Embankment was built. ♦ Victoria Embankment, WC2

17 The Adelphi Parallel with the Strand is John Adam Street, the site of the late, lamented Adelphi, a stunning architectural and engineering achievement and London's first

grand speculative housing development. It was built between 1768 and 1774 by the **Adam brothers**, William, James, and Robert, with John as economic advisor. (*Adelphos* is Greek for brother.) The scheme was a testament to fraternal genius, but it proved a financial disaster. With brilliant vision and dreamy optimism, the brothers leased the land between the Strand and the Thames and built a quay above the river, with 4 stories of arched brick vaults for warehousing. On top of this structure they created 4 streets (**Adelphi Terrace, John Adam Street, Robert Street,** and **Adam Street**) and a terrace of eleven 4-story brick houses that faced the Thames, inspired by the 4th-century Palace of Diocletian at Spalato as well as by Pompeii and Athens. The project almost ruined the Adam brothers, and the houses were eventually occupied by a lottery sponsored by Parliament in 1773. In the 19th century, the Adelphi became greatly popular with artists and writers and home for such literary celebrities as **Thomas Rowlandson, Charles Dickens, John Galsworthy, Thomas Hardy, Sir James Barrie, H.G. Wells,** and **George Bernard Shaw. Richard d'Oyly Carte** lived at 4 Adelphi Terrace while producing the comic operas of Gilbert and Sullivan. In 1936, most of the Adelphi was demolished, a wanton act still lamented by architects and lovers of fine buildings. The legacy of the visionary speculation consists of the streets that the Adam brothers named after themselves and a few fragments: **1-3 Robert Street**, with the honeysuckle pilasters that were the trademark of the Adelphi; the offices of *The Lancet* at **7 Adam Street**, which are pure Adam; and **4-6 John Adam Street**, which contains excellent elements of the scheme. The Adam brothers remained sufficiently undaunted to go on to speculate and build Portland Place north of Oxford Street.

18 Royal Society of Art The most interesting building in the maze of once-Adelphi streets. Built by **Robert Adam**, it has all the noble tranquility, purity, and order that epitomize Adam architecture, complete with a Venetian window with a scalloped stone arch and acanthus-leaf capitals. The society was founded in 1754 with the aim of encouraging art, science, and manufacturing, and it employed talented artists and craftspeople of the day. The fine hall is decorated with 6 vast paintings by **James Barry** depicting the progress of civilization. Paintings can be seen by applying to the society after 9:30AM. ♦ 8 John Adam St, WC2. 071/930.5115

19 Adelphi Theatre Paternal devotion created the Adelphi, built in 1806 by **John Scott** to help launch his daughter's acting career. From 1837 to 1845, many of **Charles Dickens**' novels were performed here. But a real drama took place out front in 1897, when leading actor **William Terris** was shot by a

The Strand, Fleet Street & the City

lunatic. The theater's simple interior, with its straight lines and angles and deep-orange paneling, dates from extensive remodeling in 1930. Today the Adelphi is the home of popular musicals. See page 176 for seating plan. ♦ Seats 1500. Strand, WC2

20 Vaudeville Theatre (1870, **C.J. Phipps**) Completely refurbished in 1969, this is one of the most delightful theaters in London, with an elegant gold-and-cream décor, plum-covered seats, and a beautiful chandelier in the foyer. The Vaudeville has many long runs to its credit, including the first performances of **Ibsen**'s *Hedda Gabler*, **Barrie**'s *Quality Street*, and between 1954 and 1960, a record run of **Julian Slade**'s *Salad Days*. Also see page 177. ♦ Seats 694. Strand, WC2. 071/836.5645

20 Stanley Gibbons International The largest stamp shop in the world and, naturally, the shop for British and Commonwealth stamps. There are 2 huge floors of stamps, albums, hinges, magnifying glasses, and Stanley Gibbons stamp catalogs. Stamp auctions are held regularly. ♦ M 10AM-5:30PM; Tu-F 9AM-5:30PM; Sa 10AM-1PM. 399 Strand, WC2. 071/836.8444

21 Byron Dean, M&S, and G.B. Stamps Three stamp companies in one building, all nice to young collectors as well as those looking for the finest and the rarest. ♦ M-F 10AM-5PM; Sa 10AM-2PM. 79 Strand, WC2. 071/836.2341

Restaurants/Nightlife: Red   Hotels: Blue
Shops/Parks: Green   Sights/Culture: Black

21 Shell-Mex House (1931, **Messrs Joseph**) Beyond Adam Street, the vista changes dramatically to the cold-white bulk of Shell-Mex House and its mantelpiece clock, larger than Big Ben, ticking away the time. The immense building stretches from the Strand all the way to the Embankment. The Strand front of red brick and stone is all that remains of the **Hotel Cecil**, once the largest hotel in Europe (800 rooms). It was built in 1886 and demolished in 1930 to make way for this fortress of offices. The front is best seen from the other side of the river on the South Bank, a favorite view for theatergoers during intermissions at the National Theatre. ♦ Strand, WC2

22 Cleopatra's Needle The pink-granite obelisk, rising 68 feet high and weighing 180 tons, was created around 1500 BC by **Thotmes III** in Egypt on the edge of the Nile. Cleopatra had nothing to do with the obelisk, but it was named after the Queen when it was moved to Alexandria, the royal city of Cleopatra, during the Greek dynasty in 12 BC. The **Viceroy of Egypt** gave the obelisk to Britain in 1819. It was towed over in an iron pontoon like a giant cigar tube, but was very nearly lost in a gale off the Bay of Biscay. It was placed here by the river in 1878.

The Savoy

23 Savoy Hotel $$$$ In 1246, **Henry II** presented **Peter, Earl of Richmond** with a splendid piece of land overlooking the Thames. Here the Earl, who was also the Count of Savoy, built a magnificent palace where he entertained beautiful French women, organized politically advantageous marriages into the Anglo-Norman aristocracy, and created a feudal center of considerable power. The grand manor later came into the hands of **Simon de Montfort**, founder of the House of Commons, and the man who led the barons in their revolt against Henry III. The illustrious past of this palatial site reached a fiery climax when a mob of angry peasants under the leadership of **Wat Tyler** stormed the palace, destroying everything of value, ripping tapestries into shreds, flattening the silver and gold, and, finally, burning the palace to the ground. The flames were watched in the Tower of London by 14-year-old Richard II, who was planning a swift and ruthless repression of the peasant revolt. But the site seems to have been ripe for palaces, and in 1889 a luxurious hotel was built by entrepreneur **Richard d'Oyly Carte**, discoverer of Gilbert and Sullivan for whom he had built the still-existing Savoy Theatre on the same piece of land. The 7-story building took 5 years to complete and combined American technology with European luxury—the concrete walls, electric lights, and 24-hour elevators were all new to hotel construction in England. Tiny, bearded d'Oyly Carte outdid Peter of Savoy: he persuaded **Cesar Ritz** to be his manager and **Escoffier** his chef (his pots and pans are still at the hotel). **Johann Strauss**

played waltzes in the restaurant and **Caruso** sang. After having tea here, **Arnold Bennet** wrote his *Grand Babylon Hotel*. **Whistler** stayed here with his dying wife, sketching her and the river from his room. The first martini in the world was mixed in the **American Bar**, which has long been a favorite meeting place of Americans in London. The Savoy has fully recovered from its decline in the 1950s and 1960s, and now wins hearts with its Art Deco marble bathrooms and their dazzling chrome fixtures, afternoon tea in the Thames Foyer, and Edwardian riverside apartment suites, which are filled with antiques, arched mirrors, fine plasterwork, Irish linen sheets and a gracious atmosphere that even kings and queens cannot resist. (Illustrious names have lived in these apartments: earlier in the century, **Noel Coward**, and more recently, **Elaine Stritch**, who lived here until her husband died. Most of the apartments are now managed separately, although floor service is provided by the hotel. **Liza Minelli** and **Frank Sinatra** maintain apartments here.) These days, the restaurants at the Savoy serve more American tourists and English merchant bankers than dukes and duchesses, but the food is no doubt better for it. ♦ Deluxe ♦ Strand, WC2. 071/836.4343; fax 071/240.6040

Within the Savoy Hotel:

Savoy River Restaurant ★★★$$$ With fine views through the trees to the Thames, this spacious salmon-pink room rates as one of the prettiest places to dine in London. The elegant setting is matched with worthy cuisine, and if you have *le déjeuner au choix* (the set lunch) you can expect to eat well, feel rather grand, and survive the arrival of the bill. Even though you are surrounded by the daunting prospect of businesspeople and media folk lunching on expense accounts, it is well worth it. Under the auspices of chef **Anton Edelman** there are more choices than ever. For the healthy, or the saintly, there is a menu *de regime naturel* (simply cooked food) and even decaffeinated coffee. At dinner, as the menu changes so the prices rise; the nervous may work off their anxiety while dancing. One way to feel truly right with the world is to have breakfast in this sumptuous setting—freshly squeezed fruit juices, prunes, eggs, bacon, kippers, toast and marmalade, and the famous Savoy coffee in the company of cabinet ministers, opera singers, tycoons, and movie stars who have made this *the* place for the business breakfast in London. Breakfast and lunch must be booked at least a day or 2 ahead. ♦ M-Sa 7-10:30AM, 12:30-2:30PM, 7:30-11:30PM; Su 8-10:30AM, 12:30-2:30PM, 7-10:30PM. 071/836.4343

Savoy Grill Room ★★★$$$ Certain French food critics give the Grill Room a thumbs down, a mistake hard to comprehend. Under the talented guidance of **David Sharland**, this very English paneled room offers English classics prepared with a delicate touch and rare imagination. The daily lunch specialties are good, indeed—with farmhouse sausages,

creamed potatoes, and fried onions (bangers, mash, and onions) on Monday, steak kidney and oyster pudding on Wednesday, Irish stew or roast beef and Yorkshire pudding on Thursday. At supper, the menu is more expensive, richer, and just as traditional. Tuesday is fillet of beef Wellington, Friday is roast Norfolk duck with almonds and apples—and you can try roast pheasant, Dover sole, châteaubriand, roast partridge, or native oysters all week. More sophisticated palates may prefer the nouvelle dishes like *délice de saumon pére* St. Jacques (nut of salmon with vegetables and sauce *épicé*) or *suprême de pintada gastronome* (buttered breast of guinea fowl with button mushrooms and baby onions). The cooking is everything that you would expect from this, one of the premier hotels in the world. There are some excellent wines at the lower end of the price scale and special pre- and after-theater dinner menus that are a good value in theaterland. ♦ M-F 12:30-2:30PM, 6-11:15PM; Sa 6-11PM. 071/836.4343 ext 2149, 2150

Disheartening as it is to discover that hotels which endear themselves with their unique histories and strong characters are part of a hotel group, that is the way of the world. One can only hope that the groups are run with proper respect for the history, location, originality, and personality of each hotel within them. The most prestigious in the world is the **Savoy Group**, which in the capital alone owns the **Savoy Hotel** in the heart of theaterland and overlooking the Thames; **Claridge's** in Mayfair, which is a favorite of royalty and was acquired and rebuilt by **Richard d'Oyly Carte** in 1896; the **Connaught**, located on residential Carlos Place in Mayfair between Grosvenor and Berkeley squares, which was conceived as a London home for the landed gentry and has long been considered one of the world's most desirable hotels; and the **Berkeley**, off Knightsbridge, acquired by d'Oyly Carte in order to tempt the brilliant hotelier **George Reeves-Smith** into his company, and now the only hotel in London to boast its own rooftop swimming pool and cinema. In 1970, the Savoy Group acquired the Paris jewel **L'hotel Lancaster** on the Rue de Berri just off the Champs Elysées, a charming country château in the heart of Paris. Other members of the group include 2 quintessentially English restaurants: **Wilton's** on Jermyn Street (see page 56), managed by the Savoy since 1983, and famous for oysters, fish, lobsters, and game; and **Simpson's-in-the-Strand**, a bustling restaurant that has been serving Scotch beef and English lamb for 150 years (described below). And if seductive hotel living leaves you with signs of *mal du foie*, there is a health hydro, **Forest Mere**, an hour from London by train or car, which is an oasis of country scenery, swimming, tennis, and treatments located in an Edwardian mansion. The Savoy Group has been saved from the attack of the mighty conglomerate **Trust House Forte** until 1995.

SIMPSON'S
IN-THE-STRAND

23 Simpson's-in-the-Strand ★★★$$ Only a meal at Eton or Harrow could be more English than this, with tables arranged in long rows, dark-wood paneling, and, at lunchtime during the week, a sea of dark-suited men watching as joints of beef and lamb are wheeled to their tables on elaborate silver-domed trolleys and carved to their specifications. The quality of the beef is praiseworthy, but the vegetables are limp and rank somewhere between school and prison food, and the only way to avoid feeling rushed is to order one course at a time. If you want good service, tip the waiter before he gives you your beef (when he arrives with the trolley). Approach a meal here as an authentic English experience, and enjoy the Stilton, treacle tart, and house claret. ♦ M-Sa noon-2:45PM, 6-9:45PM. 100 Strand, WC2. 071/836.9112

The Strand, Fleet Street & the City

During Victorian times men were not allowed to smoke at home and used to go out to **divans** to smoke and drink. Their suspicious wives called such clubs *dives* from the word divan, which is just what **Simpson's** started out as.

24 Strand Palace Hotel $$ Opposite the Savoy, this hotel is more hotel than palace, but the location is hard to beat, the price makes it one of the best values in London, and with the money you save you can walk across the street and have an elegant lunch in the Savoy overlooking the Thames. The Strand Palace doesn't have room service, but does have those very English electric kettles in all 777 rooms, a coffeeshop open from 6:30AM-12:30AM, a pasta bar, and a cocktail bar. ♦ 369 Strand, WC2. 071/836.8080; fax 071/836.2077

25 Lyceum ★★★$ The tap room downstairs serves real ale and tranquility; the ground floor serves good salads, terrines, and tarts; and the bar upstairs has views over the Strand. A passage leads from the pub to a former disco, which was once the **Lyceum Theatre**, where theater history was furthered in great performances by **Henry Irving** and **Ellen Terry**. ♦ M-Sa 11AM-11PM; Su noon-3PM, 7-10:30PM. 354 Strand, WC2. 071/836.7155

Waterloo Bridge

26 The Russian Shop *Glasnost* comes to the Strand in the shape of this delightful shop bearing Russian gifts, like the nests of reasonably priced wooden dolls, pretty china, boxes encrusted with semiprecious stones, and brightly colored peasant shawls. The lacquerwork is something else, and so are th[e] prices. ♦ M-F 10AM-6PM; Sa 10AM-5:30PM 99 Strand, WC2. 071/497.9104

26 Smollensky's on the Strand ★$$ **Michael Gottlieb** must have designed this tongue in cheek, because the outside is exactly the same as Simpson's just up the street. Although it's underground, Smollensky's is on the side of a steep hill and you ca[n] see out to the delightful Queen's Chapel at th[e] Savoy, which is sometimes lit up at night. It'[s] a big Prohibition Era Deco-themed restauran[t] which offers American-style food, steak sand wiches, steaks, and corn-fed chicken, with matching US service and the guarantee of a good meal. Follow this up with a chocolate-peanut cheesecake or chocolate mousse, and finish your Pouilly Fuisse to the strains of a pianist at lunchtime or a band in the evening. Londoners love it and rumor has it that **Princess Di** takes the **Little Princes** to **Smollensky's Balloon** (Dover St) on Sunday because that's the day Smollensky does a kids' treat day with clowns, Punch and Judy, toys, and bedlam. ♦ M-Sa noon-midnight; Su noon-10:30PM. 105 Strand, WC2. 071/497.2101

27 Queen's Chapel of the Savoy (1820, **Sir Robert Smirke**) A haven of tranquility belong ing to the **Duke of Lancaster**, who is in fact the Queen. (The reigning monarch keeps this title, which goes back to **Henry IV**, who was Duke of Lancaster before he usurped the throne from Richard II.) Erected in 1505 in the late perpendicular style on the grounds of the Savoy Palace, the chapel has been used by royalty since the reign of **Henry VII**. The present building is almost entirely Victorian, rebuilt by Sir Robert Smirke in 1820 and restored by his brother **Sydney Smirke** after a fire in 1864. The original chapel was once part of the **Order of St. John** (1510-16), and since 1937 it has been part of the **Order of Chivalry,** the **Royal Victorian Order**. The heraldic plaque in the vestibule is made of gilded marrow seeds crushed into the seductive forms of the leopards of England. The stained-glass window commemorates **Richard d'Oyly Carte** (1844-1901), and another window is in memory of **Queen Mary**. The window with heraldic designs of the Royal Victorian Order was designed in part by **King George VI**. ♦ Tu-F 11:30AM-3:30PM. Closed August, September. Savoy Hill, WC2

Restaurants/Nightlife: Red   **Hotels:** Blue
Shops/Parks: Green   **Sights/Culture:** Black

28 Waterloo Bridge Designed by **Sir Giles Scott**, completed in 1939, and opened in 1945. The Regency bridge it replaced was opened on the second anniversary of the Battle of Waterloo, and the name of the bridge was changed in honor of the great battle. On the right of the bridge is the only floating police station in London, manned by the Thames Division, which patrols the 54-mile precinct of river in police duty boats 24 hours a day and deals with ship accidents, flood warnings, aimless barges, and bodies that make their way into the river. ◆ Victoria Embankment, WC2

Cruft's Dog Show, the world's most famous dog show, is held annually at Earl's Court in London. Its founder, **Charles Cruft**, entered the canine business in 1876, selling *dog cakes* in Holborn. In 1878, he was asked to run a dog stand at the Paris Exhibition. The first Cruft's Show opened in 1891 at the Royal Agricultural Hall in Islington. Now more than 90 shows later, 13,000 dogs enter the 3-day-long competition. The winner receives a *dogly* £250, Chum dog chow for life, and worldwide fame. The 1990 winner was **Olae Moonpilot,** a West Highland White Terrier.

---

29 Somerset House (1776-86, **Sir William Chambers**; 1830-35, **Sir Robert Smirke**; 1854, **Sir James Pennethorne**) One of London's premier Neoclassical buildings stands facing the Thames east of Waterloo Bridge. Beloved by Londoners, the stately Somerset is one of the few Georgian buildings still gracing the riverside. Like the old Adelphi, Chambers' Somerset House rose out of the Thames before the construction of the Embankment. The great palace of the **Protector Somerset** (1547-72), with its magnificent chapel by **Inigo Jones** and riverside gallery by **John Webb**, stood on this site and was at one time lived in by **Elizabeth I**, when she was a princess, and the queens of **James I, Charles I,** and **Charles II**. The present building has enjoyed a less illustrious existence, housing administrative offices and institutions and the Registry of Births, Deaths and Marriages.

It is particularly appropriate that the **Fine Rooms** (1776-80, **Sir William Chambers**) should now be occupied by the **Courtauld Institute**. The original inhabitants of this block were the Royal Society, the Royal Academy of Arts, and the Society of Antiquaries, who finally left in 1850 and were replaced by the Registrar General until the '70s. The rooms remained empty for 20 years. There is a bookshop and coffeeshop on the lower ground floors. Resist all temptations to use the lift; take the magnificent spiral staircase, dubbed the *Rowlandson* after a painting by **Thomas Rowlandson**, showing revelers falling down it at a party! The Courtauld is one of the galleries that most people mean to visit, but don't quite get around to. Yet it has the best Impressionist and Post-Impressionist collection in Britain, not to mention a fabulous classical collection. The major collections were assembled by **Samuel Courtauld** and **Viscount Lee** of Fareham (the British versions of the Guggenheims), who founded the institute in 1931.

The first 4 galleries contain Italian Renaissance and Dutch art from the 15th and 16th centuries given to the institute in 1978 by **Count Antoine Seilern**, now known as the **Prince's Gate Collection**. The range of art is extraordinary, from **Palma Vecchio**'s lush *Venus in a Landscape* to **Van Dyck**'s *Portrait of a Man in an Armchair* to **Botticelli**'s *Holy Trinity* and **Albertinelli**'s *Creation*. Gallery 2 contains **Rubens'** spectacular Baroque work *Descent from the Cross*, which was the model for the alterpiece in Antwerp Cathedral, while Gallery 3 is given over to the Rubens school entirely and *The Bounty of James I Triumphing Over Avarice*, a *modello* for the ceiling corners at Banqueting House, Whitehall. The haunting *Landscape by Moonlight*, at one time owned

The Strand, Fleet Street & the City

by **Sir Joshua Reynolds**, inspired both **Sir Thomas Gainsborough** and **John Constable**.

The Impressionist works are so familiar and frequently reproduced that they seem almost like icons of a world religion called 19th-century art. The surprise is that all the major Impressionist and Post-Impressionist artists are here, beginning with **Boudin, Daumier,** 3 **Manets, Monet, Degas, Renoir, Pissarro, Sisley,** 9 **Cézannes,** 3 **Gauguins, van Gogh, Seurat, Toulouse-Lautrec, Bonnard, Vuillard,** and **Modigliani**.

Exhibitions are changed regularly, but in Galleries 5 and 6 don't miss:

Modigliani's *Female Nude*, which even thousands of reproductions have failed to spoil.

Renoir's *La Loge*, with a man staring at the stage through opera glasses while the viewer stares with equal intensity at his voluptuous partner, her neck wound round with crystal beads, her boldy striped opera cloak falling open to reveal the rose tucked between her breasts.

Monet's *Vase of Flowers*, full of pink and mauve mellows and so evocative of summer light that it cuts through the grayest London day.

Gauguin's *Nevermore*. **Paa'ura** was Gauguin's 14½-year-old mistress, and this naked South Sea beauty somehow sums up his reaction against Impressionism. This painting and his *Te Rerioa* (The Dream) make you want to cut loose and fly to the islands.

Somerset House

The Strand, Fleet Street & the City

Van Gogh's *Peach Blossom in the Crau* and *Self Portrait of the Artist with a Bandaged Ear.* Together these 2 paintings sum up van Gogh somehow—at his happiest and at his most despairing. Van Gogh left Paris for Arles in 1888 and almost immediately the orchards of Provence became a foaming cascade of blossom. Here, he spent the happiest 8 months of his brief life. Nearby is the tragic self portrait, painted a few months earlier when he was recovering from a fit during which he had attacked Gauguin then cut off his own ear.

Manet's *A Bar at the Folies-Bergère.* Manet was an inspiration to the Impressionists and this is his last major work; his blond barmaid is instantly recognizable, and after looking at this work, no tawdry barroom can ever be quite the same again.

Cézanne's *Mont Ste-Victoire.* Cézanne was the artist who inspired **Braque** and **Picasso** during their Cubist period. In this painting the green, gold, and blue of the landscape form a geometric pattern so exquisite that you feel you could step into the landscape and walk away.

Upstairs on the 2nd floor is the **Portrait Gallery** (7), with Sir Thomas Gainsborough's lovingly crafted portrait of his wife and paintings by **Allan Ramsay** and **George Romney**.

Next door, Gallery 8, is for Bloomsbury lovers, with paintings by **Roger Fry** and the **Omega Workshops** collection, and some of the really huge pictures like **Oscar Kokoschka**'s *Prometheus Triptych.* Galleries 9 and 10 are more sedate with 19th- and 20th-century art by artists like **Sickert** and **Ben Nicholson**.

The gold treasures from the Italian and Netherlands collections of the 14th, 15th, and 16th centuries are found in Gallery 11, not jewels but tiny gold-ground panel paintings like the *Madonna* by **Fra Angelico**'s workshop and an exquisite triptych by **Bernardo Daddi** of 1338, the *Master of Flemalle Deposition*.

The Courtauld Collection also contains magnificent old master drawings by **Michelangelo, Rubens**, and **Rembrandt**, which can be seen on the ground floor. If you want to view some of the 25,000 old master prints, make arrangements in advance. If you need a moment to sit and contemplate all this wonderful art, there is a coffeeshop. There is a bookshop for mementos. ◆ M-Sa 10AM-6PM; Su 2-6PM. The Strand, WC2. 071/873.2777

Museum Bests

Dennis Farr
Director, the Courtauld Institute

Manet, *A Bar at the Folies Bergere*

Bernardo Daddi triptych

Cézanne, *Route Tournante*

Tiepolo, *The Immaculate Conception*

Rubens, *Descent From the Cross*

Toulouse-Lautrec, *Tête à Tête Supper*

---

30 The King's College Founded in 1829 by the **Duke of Wellington**, archbishops, and 30 bishops of the Church of England, and part of the University of London since 1898. Adjoins the east wing of Somerset House. ◆ Strand, WC2

Britons, who will never be slaves, must have that cup of tea; they will turn vicious for lack of it.

Jacques Barzun, *God's Country & Mine*

31 Statue of Isambard Kingdom Brunel
(1877, **Baron Marochetti**) Son of the equally famous **Marc Isambard Brunel**, he was the brilliant engineer who designed the Great Western Railway and built the *Great Western*, the first steamship to make regular voyages between Britain and America. ♦ Victoria Embankment at Temple Pl, WC2

32 Roman Bath Tucked away down Strand Lane along the east side of Somerset House under a dark archway, this 15-foot enigma is certainly not Roman, possibly Tudor, but more likely 17th century. Built over a tributary of the River Fleet, it fills each day with 2000 gallons of icy water that flow into a pipe and down into the Thames. **David Copperfield** used to take cold plunges here, but now the bath belongs to the National Trust and can be seen by appointment, although it is partially visible through a window. Be alert—this alleyway has become the home of a number of homeless people who wish to be left alone. ♦ Surrey Court, Surrey St, WC2. 071/633.5868

33 St. Mary-le-Strand (1718, **James Gibbs**) St. Mary-le-*Stranded* is the sadder, more apt name for this jewel of a church built on an island site and increasingly isolated by the widening of roads. The first major work by Scottish architect **James Gibbs** (St. Martin-in-the-Fields, the Redcliffe Camera at Oxford, the Senate House at Cambridge), St. Mary's dramatically combines styles—Ionic and Corinthian outside, Corinthian and Composite inside. As though in a self-fulfilling prophesy, the upper order contains the windows while the lower order is solid to keep out the noise from the street. In an act of continuing faith, the church is being restored. The splendid 5-stage steeple, weakened by wartime bombing, pollution, traffic vibration, and rusting iron clamps that bind the Portland stone, is being dismantled stone by stone. The hours are erratic because of the restoration, but if you get in, the barrel vault has ornate gilded and colored plasterwork. **Thomas Becket** was lay rector of the medieval church that stood here originally. The parents of **Charles Dickens** were married here. One-time poet laureate **John Betjeman** made it his life's work to save this beautiful church from being knocked down. ♦ Strand, WC2

34 Aldwych The crescent, identified mainly by the name on the street wall, sweeps around an immense stone fortress occupied by **Australia House, India House,** and **Bush House**. The word Aldwych is Danish and means *an outlying farm*. Its familiarity in London is enhanced by being the name of a tube station and a theater, the Aldwych, home of the Royal Shakespeare Company until 1982. ♦ Between the Strand and Kingsway, WC2

35 Waldorf Hotel $$$$ (1907-8, **A. Marshall Mackenzie**) Old-world charm, excellent service, and a refurbished interior, with marble floors, crystal chandeliers, coral-and-white walls, and palm trees and ferns. Tea in the **Palm Court Room** is one of London's greatest treats. You have a choice of Balijen India, Lapsang Souchong China, or the Waldorf's own blend of India Darjeeling, followed by an endless sequence of sandwiches, muffins, scones and clotted cream, pastries, and cakes. Tea dancing Friday-Sunday, smart dress preferred. ♦ Aldwych, WC2. 071/836.2400; fax 071/836.7244

36 Bush House (1935, **Harvey W. Corbett**) The American **Irving T. Bush** wanted a trade center with shops and marbled corridors, but it didn't work out that way. Today the **BBC World Service**, one of the most important broadcasting institutions in the Western world, uses the building for broadcasting across the world. *To the Friendship of English Speaking Peoples* is carved into the stonework of this vital building. The entrance for workers and shoppers alike is opposite St. Mary-le-Strand. Inside is **Penfriend**, a rather splendid pen shop offering the kind of personal service you just don't get in department stores. If you have a penchant for early radio recordings, there is a **BBC TV and Radio Shop** here, too. Access to the shopping arcade, only. ♦ Aldwych, WC2

The Strand, Fleet Street & the City

37 Statue of W.E. Gladstone (1905, **Sir Hamo Thronycroft**) The grand old man (1809-1898) looks out bravely onto the sea of uncaring traffic from the middle of the roadway where the Strand is rejoined by the Aldwych. Gladstone, a liberal statesman, was prime minister 4 times. He introduced educational reform (1870), the secret ballot (1872), and succeeded in carrying out the Reform Act of 1884. But he failed to gain support for a home rule for Ireland, which would no doubt have made the history of the 20th century in these islands more tranquil. ♦ Strand, WC2

38 St. Clement Danes (1680-82, **Sir Christopher Wren**) Now the church of the **Royal Air Force**. Wren's oranges-and-lemons church (so called because the church's bells play the tune from the nursery rhyme *Oranges and Lemons*), with its **James Gibbs'** steeple (1719), was blitzed during World War II and was skillfully rebuilt by **W.A.S. Lloyd** in 1955. The floor is inlaid with slabs of Welsh slate carved with the 735 units of the RAF, and the rolls of honors contain the 125,000 men and women of the RAF who died in World Wars I and II. The original pulpit by **Grinling Gibbons** was shattered in the bombing and painstakingly pieced together from the fragments. The organ was a gift from members of the US Air Force and there is a shrine to the USAF under the west gallery. Each March, oranges and lemons (*Say the Bells of St. Clements*) are distributed to the children of the parish in a special service. **Samuel Johnson** worshipped here and is now silenced in bronze behind the church, where he gazes nostalgically down the street he believed to be unequaled: Fleet Street. ♦ Strand, WC2

Royal Courts of Justice

39 Royal Courts of Justice (1874-82, **G.E. Street**) Better known as the **Law Courts**, this dramatic Gothic ramble of buildings, with a 514-foot frontage along the Strand, was built in a period of Victorian reorganization of the legal system and opened by **Queen Victoria** in 1882, with the power and glory of the law architecturally proclaimed. The main entrance is flanked by twin towers and slate roofs. Above the entrance on the left, **Solomon** holds his Temple and on the right is the founder of English law, **Alfred the Great.** The lofty **Great Hall** (23 feet long and 80 feet high) contains a monument to the architect **G.E. Street,** who, in the Victorian tradition of tutelage, was a pupil of George Gilbert Scott and teacher of Philip Webb and William Morris. There are 64 courts spreading over 7 miles of corridors and 1000 rooms. They are reached by way of the hall, and when the courts are sitting (weekdays 10:30AM-1PM, 2-4PM during legal terms), the public is admitted to the back 2 rows. The courts are worth a visit if you are interested in seeing the English justice system at work, visually enhanced by the wigged presence of judges and barristers and undisguised solicitors. Read the *Daily Lists* in the central hall to decide what appeals to you in the still faintly Dickensian world of probate, bankruptcy, and divorce. You are free to enter any court except those marked *court in camera* or *chambers.* ♦ Strand, WC2

It seems impossible to root out of an Englishman's mind the notion that vice is delightful, and that abstention from it is a privation.

George Bernard Shaw, *Mrs. Warren's Profession*

40 George Public House ★★$ Named after **George III** and once frequented by **Dr. Johnson** and **Oliver Goldsmith**, the author of the *Vicar of Wakefield*. The famous timbered tavern has one long-beamed and cozy room that serves buffet lunches, salads, tarts, and puddings. The excellent lunchtime restaurant upstairs is frequented by journalists, lawyers, the innocent, the guilty, and the tourist. Pantry snack bar downstairs. ♦ Tavern: M-F 11AM-11PM; Sa 11AM-3PM. Restaurant: M-F noon-2:30PM, 6-8:30PM. 213 Strand, WC2. 071/353.9238

40 Twinings Chinese Mandarins guard the Georgian entrance to London's narrowest shop and oldest business still on its original site. (Twinings has been paying taxes longer than any other business in Westminster.) The shop also contains the largest teapot in the world (3 feet high with a 13-gallon capacity). Queen Victoria and Prince Albert were the last to enjoy a cup from its depths. **Thomas Twining** opened the shop in 1716 as Tom's Coffee House, and the shop has been selling tea ever since it became the national drink. Alas, you cannot drink a cup of tea here; you can only buy it or find out about it in the small museum in the back of the shop. ♦ M-F 9AM-5PM and Lord Mayor's Saturday (2nd Sa in Nov) 216 Strand, EC4. 071/353.3511

40 Wig and Pen Club ★★$$ As the name indicates, this is a private club for lawyers and journalists, located in a modest 17th-century house that is the only building on the Strand that survived the Great Fire of 1666. You can have a look around before noon and, amazingly, if you produce your passport you can obtain a free temporary membership, which is especially nice for visiting lawyers and journalists. Foreigners are privileged, because Englishpeople cannot become instant members. Men must wear a jacket and tie, women must wear skirts. The club has an all-day alcohol license. ♦ 229-230 Strand, EC4. 071/583.7255

Summer in England means Wimbledon, the races at Ascot, the regatta at Henley, and **Pimm's Cup**, a favorite drink at all these events since **James Pimm** concocted the famous **Pimm's No. 1** in the 1840s. His confection of gin, fruit liqueurs, herbs, spices, and bitters is more popular than ever today. Pimm's Cup is simple to make: take one part Pimm's No. 1 and add 2 to 3 parts mixer, plenty of ice, a thin slice of lemon or lime, and a swirl of cucumber ring. You can alter the sweetness of the drink by using soda water, tonic, ginger ale, lemonade—even champagne. And to be perfectly proper, serve it in a frosted pewter or silver mug, as it's done in clubland.

41 Temple Bar Monument (1880, **Horace Jones**) The spiky griffin stands on the site of **Sir Christopher Wren**'s fine 3-arched gateway, which was here from 1672 to 1878. Sadly, it was dismantled because it was obstructing traffic and was moved to Theobald's Park in Hertfordshire. The griffin is a mythical beast famous for its voracious appetite and, appropriately, it marks the boundary between the City of Westminster, impelled by restraint, and the City of London, inspired by acquisition. The Temple Bar's griffin also marks the end of the broad, dozy Strand and the beginning of the congested and lively Fleet Street. The figures on either side of the griffin are **Queen Victoria** and **Edward VIII**, Prince of Wales. Periodic and welcome rumors that the gate by Sir Christopher Wren will return persist. ♦ Fleet St at Strand, EC4

41 Fleet Street This lively, crowded street has a glorious and eclectic mix of styles and levels and a tremendous skyline defined by the tower and pinnacles of the Law Courts, the tower of St. Dunstan-in-the-West, and the dome of St. Paul's Cathedral. Sadly, the editorial offices of the nation's newspapers have left here; the last to go was the *Daily Express* from the *Black Lubyjanka* at No. 123 in 1989, to a gray Lubyjanka crowded onto Blackfriars Bridge.

42 Royal Bank of Scotland (Formerly Child's Bank) The oldest bank in London (1671) and the inspiration for Tellson's Bank in **Dickens**' *A Tale of Two Cities*. The nonfictional roster of early customers includes **Charles II**, the **Duke of Marlborough**, **Nell Gwynn**, **Samuel Pepys**, **Oliver Cromwell**, and **John Dryden**. The bank is now part of **Williams' and Glyn's Bank**. ♦ M-F 10AM-3PM. 1 Fleet St, EC4

43 Prince Henry's Room Above the archway leading to the Temple. The timbered house containing Prince Henry's Room was built in 1610 as a tavern with a projecting upper story. The great treasure inside is the

Jacobean ceiling, one of the finest remaining enriched plaster ceilings of its date in London, with an equally enriched set of stories to go with it. The most persistant tale claims that the initials **P.H.** and the **Prince of Wales' Feathers**, which decorate the ceiling, commemorate the 1610 investiture of **Henry**, eldest son of **James I** and elder brother of the future and luckless **King Charles I**. The Prince died 2 years after his investiture from a chill caught after playing tennis, a game that can be said to have changed the entire course of British history. The room also contains mementos of one of London's most important figures, the diarist **Samuel Pepys**. Pepys was born in 1633 on nearby Salisbury Court, Fleet Street, baptized in nearby St. Bride's Church, educated at St. Paul's Cathedral, and lived most of his life close by Tower Hill. His remarkable shorthand diary, recording just over 9 years (1660-1669), fills many volumes and is the liveliest and fullest account of London life ever written, and includes the Plague (1665) and the Great Fire (1666). The wide oriel windows looking down over Fleet Street and across to Chancery Lane manage to frame London's timelessness in a

prism of light—the way one longs to see it. ♦ Admission. M-F 1:45-5PM; Sa 1:45-4:30PM. 17 Fleet St, EC4

44 The Temple An oasis of calm between the traffic of the Embankment and the bustle of Fleet Street. The Temple was originally the headquarters of the **Knights Templar**, a monastic order founded in 1119 to regain Palestine from the Saracens for Christianity. They settled at the Temple in 1160, but were suppressed by the pope, and all that remains of their monastery is the Temple Church and the Buttery. Since the 14th century, the buildings have been leased to lawyers and today house 2 of England's 4 **Inns of Court** (**Inner Temple** and **Middle Temple**), the voluntary legal society that has the exclusive privilege of calling candidates to the bar. Visitors are free to stroll through the warren of lanes, courtyards, and gardens and to admire the confidence of the buildings, each composed like an Oxford or Cambridge college, with chambers built around steep stairways, communal dining halls, libraries, common rooms, and chapels. The tranquility of the setting is accentuated by the speed with which the lawyers, either wearing their gowns or carrying them over their arms—loaded down with books and papers—race between their chambers and the Law Courts, the vast Gothic world that stretches from Temple Bar to the Aldwych.

The **Temple Church**, located within the precincts of the Inner Temple, was badly damaged during the Blitz, but has been skillfully repaired. The beautiful round nave, completed in 1185, is modeled after the Church of the

Holy Sepulchre in Jerusalem. It is the only circular nave in London, and one of only 5 in England, all connected with the Knights Templar. The chancel was added in 1240. The rib vaulting within the Gothic porch is original.

The **Middle Temple Hall**, also painstakingly restored after the Blitz, is a handsome Elizabethan building with a splendid double-hammerbeam roof and carved-oak screen. Here, aspiring barristers are called to the bar upon passing their examinations. Lunch and dinner are served in the hall, and though residence at the inns has become vestigial, the students must eat 3 dinners during each term here. **Shakespeare**'s *Twelfth Night* is said to have been performed in the hall in 1602. The round pond amid the mulberry trees outside in **Fountain Court** was featured in **Dickens**' novel *Martin Chuzzlewit*.

The **Inner Temple Gateway**, leading back to the Strand, is a half-timbered 3-story house that looks suspiciously stage set, but it is the real 17th-century thing, with **Prince Henry's Room** on the top floor. ♦ Temple, EC4

45 S. Weingott This tobacconist to the lawyers keeps a large humidifier on the premises that

contains a few thousand cigars. There are even cigars costing $20 each that come in their own polished box. It's been a traditional tobacconist since 1859 and very little has changed inside the shop or in its practices—S. Weingott will weigh tobacco or blend it; there are 119 brands and 50 loose varieties in old wooden drawers. The proprietor is also a wine merchant and you may be lucky enough to buy a bottle of Château d'Yquem from him. ♦ M-F 8:30AM-6PM. 3 Fleet St, EC4. 071/353.7733

45 L. Simmonds The journalists may have gone but this bookseller hasn't; it specializes in books to do with journalism from the UK, USA, and as far away as Nigeria. It has the best stock in the UK and is probably the slimmest shop on the street—reach out and both hands will touch the book-stacked walls on either side. ♦ M-F 9AM-5:45PM. 16 Fleet St, EC4. 071/353.3907

45 Ye Olde Cock Tavern ★★$$ Another illustrious role call of former regulars: **Nell Gwynn, Pepys, Goldsmith, Sheridan**, and **Garrick**—a theatrical lot of drinkers and thinkers who drank thoughtfully in this small tavern, which still serves tradition, an excellent bar lunch, and delicious roasts and puddings in the dining room. The original sign, carved by **Grinling Gibbons**, is happily preserved behind the bar upstairs, and the clientele is a civilized mix of journalists and barristers. ♦ M-F 11:30AM-3PM, 5:30-8:30PM. Reservations recommended for lunch in the restaurant. 22 Fleet St, EC4. 071/353.8570

Restaurants/Nightlife: Red   **Hotels:** Blue
Shops/Parks: Green   **Sights/Culture:** Black

45 Hoare's Bank The only private bank left in London, and still as old fashioned, discreet, and attractive as when it was founded in 1672. Well worth a peek inside. ♦ 37 Fleet St, EC4

46 St. Dunstan-in-the-West (1831-33, **John Shaw**) This architectural gem is the Romanian Orthodox patriarchal church in London and is beautifully situated on the north side at the curve in Fleet Street. Shaw's Victorian church, with its octagonal tower, open-work lantern, and pinnacles, was built at the beginning of the Gothic Revival on the site of an earlier church whose great treasures were saved when it was demolished to widen Fleet Street. The church is unusually placed, with the tower and entrance on the south and the brick octagon of the sanctuary and altar on the north. Treasures from the earlier church include the communion rail carved by **Grinling Gibbons** and the old wooden clock (1671) with 2 wooden giants that strike each hour. In 1830, the Marquis of Hertford bought the clock for his house in Regent's Park. Viscount Rothermere, a British newspaper proprietor, later bought the clock and returned it to the church in 1935 to commemorate King George V's Silver Jubilee. The statue of **Elizabeth I** over the door (believed to be the oldest outdoor statue in London) and the statues of **King Lud** and his sons came from the Ludgate when it was torn down in 1760. The bronze bust of **Lord Northcliffe** (1865-1922), newspaper proprietor and founder of the *Daily Mail*, was sculpted by **Lady Scott** in 1930. ♦ Fleet St, EC4

47 El Vino's ★★$ A lot of history has been written over bottles of wine in this haunt of boozy journalists. What starts as a piece of gossip, idle speculation, or a mischievous rumor and becomes an item in the *Standard Diary* or an article in *Private Eye* progresses to *something worth checking on* in more serious papers. Whoever said *in vino veritas* did not hang out at El Vino's on Fleet Street. This masculine institution is packed daily with journalists, lawyers, and City businessmen; women weren't allowed to drink at the bar until 1982, and few do it today. There's a long wine list and simple foods like Scotch salmon and Smithfield beef. Women must wear skirts and no denims are allowed. ♦ Bar: M-F 11:30AM-3PM; 5-8PM. Restaurant: M-F 12:30-2:30PM. 47 Fleet St, EC4. Reservations recommended 071/353.6786

48 Printer's Pie ★$ Famous for the Queen Victoria mixed grill and traditional English fare like shepherd's pie, sausages, mash, and onions. ♦ M-F 11:30AM-3PM, 5:30-11PM. 60 Fleet St, EC4. 071/353.8861

49 Dr. Johnson's House London is full of great men's houses, lovingly bought and preserved, restored, rearranged, and revitalized in the spirit of the departed. True, they usually possess an orderliness that the former inhabitants would find astonishing, especially in the houses of writers. But if the absence of chaos requires us to slightly suspend belief,

View From the Top

The Best Places to Look Down on London

St. Paul's Cathedral A 360-degree vista from the Golden Gallery at the top of the dome. Five hundred sixty steps to this 280-foot vantage point. ♦ Admission. M-F 10AM-4:15PM, Sa 11AM-4:15PM, summer; M-F 10AM-3:15PM, Sa 11AM-3:15PM, winter. Ludgate Hill, EC4. 071/248.2705

National Westminster Tower At 600 feet, Britain's tallest building. Not generally open to the public, but call to find out if they will organize a private viewing. ♦ 25 Old Broad St, EC2. 071/920.5555

Tower Bridge Fabulous views over the Tower of London and of the river life on the Thames. Ascend by the North Tower and traverse the river protected from the breeze in an enclosed 140-foot-high walkway before descending by the South Tower. ♦ Admission. Daily 10AM-6:30PM, Apr-Sep; daily 10AM-5:30PM, Oct-Mar. Tower Bridge, SE1. 071/407.092

The Monument Stone column built by Sir Christopher Wren between 1671-1677 to commemorate the Great Fire of London in 1666. It is 202 feet high and 202 feet west of the baker's shop on Pudding Lane, where the fire started. The steep spiral staircase with 311 steps offers stunning views of the City. ♦ Admission. M-Sa 9AM-6PM, Apr-Sep; Su 2-6PM, May-Sep; M-Sa 9AM-4PM, Oct-Mar. Monument St, EC3. 071/626.2717

Kenwod House The beautiful landscaped gardens of this 17th-century house offer 180-degree panoramic views of London. ♦ Daily 10AM-7PM, Apr-Sep; daily 10AM-5PM, Oct-Mar. Hampstead Ln, NW3. 081/348.1286

New Zealand House The view from the 18th floor is especially spectacular at night. It is used for private receptions and parties, so unless you are planning a party, it's not always possible to get in. ♦ Haymarket,SW1. 071/930.8422

Westminster Cathedral The 352-and -a-half-foot-high St. Edwards Tower allows a general 360-degree panorama over London. ♦ Admission. Daily 10AM-4PM, Apr-Oct. Ashley Pl, SW1. 071/834.7452

Royal Observatory In the Royal Park of Greenwich, the Royal Observatory looks over the Thames to London's east end and the Isle of the Dogs, with the National Maritime Museum and 17th-century Queen's House in the foreground. Unbeatable. ♦ Admission. M-Sa 10AM-6PM, Su 2-5:30PM, Apr-Oct; M-F 10AM-5PM, Sa 10AM-6PM, Su 2-5PM, Nov-Mar. Greenwich Park, SE10. 081/858.1167

we are ever grateful to the individuals and charitable trusts that preserve these houses for us, allowing us to snoop and speculate on those whose lives and letters add so richly to our own. One of the most tempting for the London lover is the house of **Samuel Johnson**, one of 3 of his London residences and the one where he produced the first complete dictionary of the English language, published in 1755. Until he came to Gough Square, Johnson had lived in miserable lodgings, taking whatever literary hackwork he could find. But with the advance he was given to write the *Dictionary*, he leased 4 Gough Square in 1748. On the day he signed the contract to write the *Dictionary*, he composed the following prayer: *Oh God, who hast hitherto supported me, enabled me to proceed in this labour, and in the whole task of my present state; that when I shall render up, at the last day, an account of the talent committed to me, I may receive pardon. For the sake of Jesus Christ, amen.* Johnson installed his assistants in the huge attic, and for the next 11 years they worked at their task. In March 1759, when his beloved wife, **Tetty**, 15 years his senior, died, he left his house, melancholy and impoverished, and went to live in Staple Inn. ♦ Admission. M-Sa 11AM-5:30PM, May-Sep; M-Sa 11AM-5PM, Oct-Apr. No. 17 Gough Sq, EC4. 071/353.3745

50 Dombey & Son No, there never was a Mr. Dombey, so there couldn't have been a son, either. No one is quite sure, but this tailor was believed to have been named after Charles Dickens' book. Here you can look through the window at the dying art of Savile Row-trained tailors cutting and sewing the bespoke suits they make for City workers. ♦ M-F 9AM-5PM. 151 Fleet St, EC4. 071/353.2940

The Strand, Fleet Street & the City

51 Ye Olde Cheshire Cheese ★★★$$ Probably the most profitable institution on Fleet Street. This cozy, firelit pub is one of the few remaining 17th-century chophouses in London, witnessing 16 reigns and hardly changing since it was rebuilt after the Great Fire of 1666.

The 14th-century crypt from Whitefriars monastery is beneath the cellar bar, and is available for private parties. The sawdust on the floor (changed twice daily) and the oak tables in *boxes* with benches on either side enchant foreigners, who long to have their England frozen in time. Considering the unrivaled popularity of the place, the food is pretty good, although the famous pudding of steak kidney, mushrooms, and game, which celebrated its bicentenary in 1972, no longer feeds 90 people or requires 16 hours to cook. Nor does it contain oysters and lark, but it is sustaining and flavorful. The biggest pies now serve 16-20 people with steak kidney, venison, and game packed under a delicious pie crust. There are rich game puddings in autumn and winter. Follow the pudding with Stilton or lemon pancakes and relish the Englishness of it all. ♦ Bar: M-F 11:30AM-11PM; Sa noon-3PM, 6-9PM. Restaurant: M-F noon-3PM, 6-9PM; Sa noon-3PM, 6-9PM. Reservations recommended. 145 Fleet St, EC4. 071/353.6170

51 Daily Telegraph Building (1928, **Elcock, Sutcliffe,** with **Tait**) This massive, modernish neo-Greek building once housed London's most sensible, conservative paper. The *Telegraph* was the capital's first daily penny paper, founded in 1855. The paper moved to Docklands but the building's facade remains. ◆ 135 Fleet St, EC4

52 Cartoonist ★★$ A Fleet Street *local* and headquarters of the **Cartoonist Club of Great Britain**, with every square inch of wall space covered in framed original cartoons. The telephones are used by the pressmen, who are the regulars here. ◆ M-Sa 11:30AM-3PM, 5-11PM. 76 Shoe Ln, EC4. 071/353.2828

53 Daily Express Building (1932, **Ellis Clarke** and **Atkinson,** with **Sir Owen Williams**) Nicknamed the *Black Lubyanka*, its black-glass tiles and chrome represent one of the finest examples—inside and out—of Art Deco in London. ◆ 121-128 Fleet St, EC4

54 Old Bell Tavern ★★$ An intimate and warm pub built by **Sir Christopher Wren** in 1670 to house and serve the workmen rebuilding St. Bride's nearby after it was destroyed in the Great Fire. ◆ M-Sa 11:30AM-3PM, 5:30-11PM; Su 11:30AM-3PM. 95 Fleet St, EC4. 071/583.0070

55 St. Brides (1670-84, **Sir Christopher Wren**; tower 1701-3) Wedged in between ponderous newspaper offices is Wren's *madrigal in stone*, one of his grander creations,

St. Brides Church

with the tallest of his steeples (226 feet), the origin and inspiration of the wedding cake, resting on a plain, squarish nave. The church was damaged in the Blitz and beautifully restored in the 1950s. Optimistic journalists marry and attend memorial services for fellow journalists here, the latter ceremony inevitably continued up *the Street* at El Vino in a boozy haze of memories about the departed. The crypt is now a museum established in memory of **Lord Beaverbrook.** ◆ Daily 9AM-5PM. Fleet St, EC4. 071/353.1301

55 Wynken de Worde ★★$$ Everyone's heard of Caxton, but Wynken de Worde was almost forgotten until now. A blue plaque calling him, rather unfortunately, the *Godfather of Fleet Street,* is just off Ludgate Hill o the Stationers Hall. This is the man who invented the printer's blocks without which th mighty Caxton presses would not have worked. Almost on the site where Wynken worked is this new restaurant and brasserie which has been decorated with antique ston church pews, a confessional box, and even an altar. It's frequented by City folk who appreciate good homemade cooking with a modern touch. The spinach-and-salmon rou lade is delicious, as are the traditional homemade pies and the smoked chicken. ◆ Brasserie: M-F 11:30AM-9PM. Restaurant: M-F noon-9PM. 1 St. Brides Passage, Bride Ln, EC4. 071/936.2554

56 Reuter's and Press Association (1935, **Sir Edwin Lutyens,** with **Smee** and **Houchin** Headquarters of 2 famous international new agencies. The genius of Lutyens comes through as always in this, his last commerci building in London. Located next door to Wren's beautiful St. Bride's, the Edwardian architect was wisely inspired by and respect ful of the wedding-cake church, conceiving his L-shaped plan as a backdrop and linking the building to the west door of the church b a high vaulted passage. ◆ 85 Fleet St, EC4

57 Le Gamin ★★★$$ For those who don't want to pay top whack at Le Gavroche, this cheaper, classy French café-style restaurant also owned by the inimitable brothers **Roux.** Needless to say, the food is divine—try the *boeuf* à la Bourguignonne; with a glass of Georges Duboef house red, life will be complete. All that's left is for you to overhear snatches of legal conversation from the lawyers and maybe even from the witnesses wh come here from the nearby Old Bailey Criminal Courts. ◆ M-F noon-2:30PM. 32 Old Bailey, EC4. 071/236.7931

Christopher Wren
Went to dine with some men.
"If anyone calls
say I'm designing St. Paul's."

Anonymou

Restaurants/Nightlife: Red   Hotels: Blue
Shops/Parks: Green   **Sights/Culture:** Blac

The City's Redevelopment

The controversy surrounding the wanton disregard of perspective, scale and skyline in the City's redevelopment, at its most stupefyingly insensitive during the 1960s and 1970s, prompted a letter to the London Times from one of the firemen who kept watch over St. Paul's Cathedral during World War II: *The climax of the Nazi fire raids on the City came on December 29, 1940. Churchill sent a message to the firemen—Save St. Paul's. The New Year dawned with most of the area north of the Cathedral as far as Moorgate a smoking ruin: 8 Wren churches gone; 2 City Livery Halls gutted; Paternoster Row, with its millions of books, in ashes. The Cathedral Chapter House was burnt, but the Cathedral stood scarred but safe. Now you tell us that, 600 feet high, a Seifert slab will overtop the Cross. The war memorial of the Fire Brigade Union carries lines from William Morris:*

There in the world new builded
Shall our earthly deeds abide
Though our names be all forgotten
And the tale of how we died.

Newbuilded? *Those of us with the fire service in the City on those winter nights of 1940-41 thought it would be so. Reading the* Times *(1 March 1975) I felt we might as well have let it burn. It would have saved the grabbers and developers a lot of trouble and money and make it much easier for their "architects." Certainly many a good fireman we lost in the City those nights might now be drawing his well-earned fire brigade pension.*

Prince Charles' Mansion House Speech

On Tuesday, 1 December 1987, a prince in shining armor galloped into the fray to suggest a return to what he considers a more humanly scaled architecture. He began with the proposed redevelopment of Paternoster Square at St. Paul's. Here are a few of his remarks:

St. Paul's is not just a symbol and a mausoleum for national heroes. It is also a temple which glorifies God through the inspired expression of man's craftsmanship and art.

Architecturally, I believe it has a character all of its own. What, then, have we done to it since the bombing? In the space of a mere 15 years, in the '60s and '70s, and in spite of all sorts of elaborate rules supposedly designed to protect that great view, your predecessors, as the planners, architects, and developers of the City, wrecked the London skyline and desecrated the dome of St. Paul's.

Paternoster was one of the very first of these CDAs—comprehensive development areas. [Postwar redevelopment areas] Praised by architects, it became the model for schemes that have destroyed the city centers of Bristol, Newcastle, Birmingham, Worcester—the list is endless. The Rape of Britain, it has been called.

Fortunately...today we have a second chance. As a result of technological change, places like Paternoster are obsolete. Here, surely, is a heaven-sent opportunity to build a model of real quality, of excellence, next to so great a building in the heart of our capital city. I, for one, would love to see the London skyline restored, and I am sure I am not alone in feeling this. If we wanted, we could use this "second chance" to rebuild a "City Without

Towers." So why don't we set that as a goal for the millenium year 2000?

Since this speech to the Corporation of London Planning and Communication Committee, **Prince Charles** has continued to fight hard to get his point of view across, using every means at his disposal—television documentaries, public speaking, and a book, *A Vision of Britain*. His influence is considerable—architects, developers, and planners have been forced to respond to the Prince's campaign.

---

58 St. Martin Ludgate (1677-87, **Sir Christopher Wren**) The sharp, dark obelisk spire is accent and prelude to St. Paul's Cathedral, a City prayer away. Wren's design centers around a cross inside a square, which is defined by 2 sets of stairs in the vestibule and 4 tall Corinthian columns that support 2 intersecting tunnel vaults. A magnificent brass candelabra hangs in the center of the crossing, and there is a pale, concerned pelican above the font.
♦ Daily 10AM-4PM, May-Oct; daily 11AM-3PM, Nov-Apr. Ludgate Hill, EC4

Sir Christopher Wren—he was knighted in 1672—was a remarkable polymath: brilliant Latinist, anatomist, astronomer, mathematician, engineer, and architect. His training as a mathematician and astronomer may have inspired his religious architecture: he liked clear glass; lots of light; pale, beautiful colors; patterned black-and-white floors; decorative touches of gold; space that allowed the worshipper to see and hear what was going on; and, above all, churches that emphasized man's power of reason as the foundation of faith. Wren was a deeply religious and humane man, son of a dean and nephew of a bishop. One of his great gifts was assembling and inspiring great craftsmen to work with him: **Grinling Gibbons, Jean Tijou** (ironwork), master masons like **Francis Bird**, and his clerk of works, **Nicholas Hawksmor**, an architect who was a genius in his own right.

After the Great Fire of 1666, Wren submitted his plan for rebuilding the City, but it was rejected. (His 18-foot-long Great Model for St. Paul's is preserved in the library of the cathedral.) But eventually, he did build 52 City churches and St. Paul's Cathedral, a contribution unparalleled in architectural history. During the

Second World War, over a third of the City was destroyed and nearly all of Wren's churches were severly damaged. But because elaborate plans still existed, many have been beautifully rebuilt and today 23 remain. Wren is buried in the crypt of St. Paul's Cathedral. Wren's famous epitaph, composed by his son and written in Latin in a vast compass design under the dome and on a black-marble slab in the crypt, translates *Beneath lies the founder of this church and city, Christopher Wren, who lived more than ninety years not for himself but for the public good. Reader, if you seek his monument, look around you.*

59 St. Paul's Cathedral (1675-1711, **Sir Christopher Wren**) Walking up Ludgate Hill, the glimpses of St. Paul's are inspiring, reassuring, and awesome. But when you are within a few yards, the cathedral grows smaller, the road veers too close, and the statue of **Queen Anne** (1866) seems dumpy and distracting. It pays to step back a moment when you realize you have reached Wren's greatest masterpiece to try and see what the architect himself intended: the slight curve of the road; the scale, monumental in the context of the medieval perspective; the magnificent dome, second only in Christendom to St. Peter's; and the skyline, uncluttered and harmonious. Even as late as 1939, before the German's chose St. Paul's as a main bombing site, the cathedral stood in a tapestry of streets, courts, squares, and alleys, and medieval London, which had spread far beyond the City's wall before the Plague of 1665 and the Great Fire of 1666, was still recognizable.

Three cathedrals have stood on this site. The first, founded by **Bishop Mellitus** in 604, was destroyed by fire in 1087 and was replaced by the gigantic and Gothic **Old St. Paul's**. But the magnificent cathedral, with one of the tallest spires in Europe, fell into desperate decay, and after the Great Fire of 1666, lay in ruins. Six days after the fire, Wren, then 31, submitted his plan for rebuilding the City and the cathedral. It was rejected, but Wren remained undaunted, and in May 1675, his design was approved. He laid the first stone on 21 June 1675, and the last was set by his son 33 years later. Wren managed to get an important concession attached to the design, which gave him the freedom to make *ornamental rather than essential* changes during construction. He took full advantage of the clause, modifying his design considerably—including deleting a tall spire—during the 3 decades spent building the church. But before Wren's masterpiece was finished, a kind of persecution began; his salary was withheld because progress was said to be too slow, and 8 years

after his triumph was completed he was dismissed from his post as Surveyor of Works. Another insult came a year later, when a balustrade was added around the top of the cathedral. Wren, retired and living in Hampton Court, would still come and sit under the dome of his monument: *If glory, it is in the singular mercy of God, who has enabled me to finish a great work so conformable to the ancient model.*

St. Paul's was the first building in London to have an exterior of Portland stone, and when it was cleaned in the 1960s, Londoners were astonished to discover a dazzling building of golden honey-colored stone. In front of the cathedral stands the statue of Queen Anne looking down Ludgate Hill. The original statue, carved in 1712 by **Francis Bird**, suffered from decay and occasional attacks—she lost her nose, orb, and sceptor—and was removed to the grounds of a girls' school in East Sussex in 1884. The Queen and the forecourt were originally inside a railing, which was sold at auction in 1874. At the same time, the road was expanded, bringing St. Paul's closer to the hellish stream of traffic en route to the City.

The spacious 78,000-square-foot interior incorporates tourist groups more readily than Westminster Abbey, and in spite of its 300 years and large population of statues and monuments, there is a lack of clutter, unique in cathedral design. The focal point is the huge dome-space at the crossing. The **dome** rises 218 feet above the floor and is supported by 8 massive double piers with Corinthian capitals. Wren actually created 2 domes; an inner dome covered in brickwork supports the outer dome and the lantern. The spandrels contain 19th-century mosaics executed by **Antonio Salviati**. *Matthew* and *John* were designed by **George Frederick Watts**; *Mark* and *Luke* by **W.E.F. Britten**; and *Isiah, Jeremiah, Ezekial,* and *Daniel* by **Alfred Stevens**. The surface of the dome is decorated with 8 large grisailles by **Sir James Thornhill**, depicting scenes from the life of St. Paul. The epitaph to Wren, who is buried in the crypt, is written in Latin on the pavement under the dome, and the plaque to **Winston Churchill**, also on the floor beneath the dome, was unveiled in 1974. If you are sound of wind and limb, it is well worth inspecting the dome more closely. For a small

Comparison of Cathedrals:

1. *St. Peter's Basilica*
2. *Florence Cathedral*
3. *St. Paul's Cathedral*
4. *St. Genevieve (Paris)*

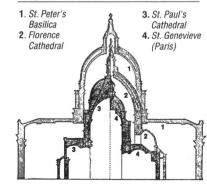

fee, you can climb the 259 steps to the **Whispering Gallery**, so called because if you stand at the entrance, you can hear what is being said in a normal voice on the other side 107 feet away. The gallery offers spectacular views of the concourse, choir, arches, clerestory, and the interior of the dome. If you are still feeling fit,

climb the steeper spiral to the **Stone Gallery**, which surrounds the top of the drum outside. From here you can see all over London. For the heartiest, the **Golden Gallery** at the top of the dome takes you to the lantern and the golden ball.

The best place to start a tour of the monuments in the cathedral is at the west entrance in the small **Chapel of All**

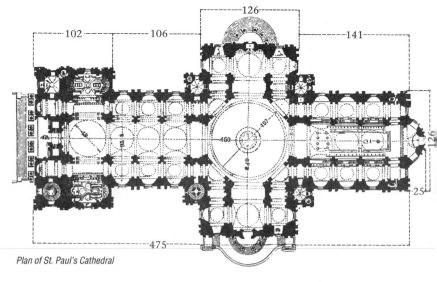

Plan of St. Paul's Cathedral

Souls, a 1925 memorial to **Lord Kitchener** (1850-1916) and *all others who fell in 1914-18*. Behind the splendid ornamented wooden screen—carved by **Jonathan Maine**, one of

The Strand, Fleet Street & the City

Wren's great craftsmen, in 1698—is **St. Dunstan's Chapel**, reserved for private prayer. Beyond the chapel in the main aisle are various monuments, though Wren did not want memorials in the cathedral and none were added until 1790. Most impressive is the monument to the **Duke of Wellington**, which fills the central bay. Painter and sculptor **Alfred Stevens** spent 20 years creating the huge equestrian statue of the Duke on top of a canopy, and it wasn't completed until 1912, nearly 40 years after Stevens' death. The third bay in the aisle contains an eerie Victorian monument to **Viscount Melbourne** (1779-1848), Queen Victoria's first prime minister. The inscription above the double doors guarded by 2 angels reads *Through the gate of death we pass to our joyful resurrection*. The **North Transept**, also called the **Middlesex Chapel**, is reserved for private prayer and contains a large marble font carved by **Francis Bird**. Beyond the crossing is the **North Chancel**, with a memorial screen that lists the names of former St. Paul's choristers who died in the 2 World Wars. The carved paneling on the right is the work of **Grinling Gibbons**. The marble statue, *Mother and Child*, by **Henry Moore** was presented to St. Paul's by the artist in 1984. The aisle terminates in the **Altar of the Modern Martyrs**, where the names of all known Anglican martyrs since 1850 are recorded in a book kept in a glass-topped casket. Pass through the fine **ironwork gate** by **Jean Tijou** and enter the **American Memorial Chapel**, paid for entirely by contributions of people all over Britain as a tribute to the 28,000 members of the American forces who lost their lives in Britain or on active service from Britain during World

War II. The names fill 500 pages of illuminated manuscript, bound in a red-leather volume and presented to St. Paul's by **General Eisenhower** on 4 July 1951.

The **choir** is enclosed by a low screen made from the original altar rail by Jean Tijou and contains the exquisite carved choir stalls made in the 1690s by Grinling Gibbons. The carved oak **baldacchino** (canopy) above the high altar was created from some of Wren's unused drawings by **Godfrey Allen** and **Stephan Dykes Bower**. It replaced the reredos damaged in 1941 and serves as Britain's memorial to the more than 324,000 men and women of the Commonwealth who died in the 2 World Wars.

The **Lady Chapel**, in the eastern end of the south choir aisle, contains the cathedral's original high altar. A life-size terra-cotta figure of *Our Lady with Infant Jesus*, sculpted by **Josephine de Vasconcellos**, stands in the south aisle. Nearby is a statue of **John Donne**, the poet who became one of the finest preachers the Anglican church has ever produced and the most famous dean of St. Paul's (1621-31). When Donne believed he was about to die, he called for sculptor **Nicholas Stone** to come and draw him in his shroud. It is the only effigy that survived the Great Fire intact.

On the second pillar in the south aisle hangs a version of **William Holman Hunt**'s most famous painting, *The Light of the World*, depicting a pre-Raphaelite Christ knocking at a humble door overgrown with weeds. The door has no handle and can only be opened from the inside; this is the door of the heart. Nearly life-size, it is the third and largest version of the painting Hunt produced and was presented to the cathedral by wealthy shipowner **Charles Booth** in 1908.

The **Chapel of the Order of St. Michael and St. George**, with its beautiful woodwork by **Jonathan Maine** and colorful banners, can only be entered on a 1½ hour **Supertour** (conducted from the **Friends' Table** near the west door). The order was instituted in 1818 for those who had given distinguished service to the Commonwealth. The chapel was dedicated in 1906 by **Bishop Henry Montgomery**, with the stirring words: *You who represent the best of the Anglo-Saxon race at work beyond the seas are now made the guardians of the west door of the cathedral.*

If you leave the chapel and continue westward along the aisle, you will reach the **Geometrical**, or **Dean's Staircase**, designed by Wren and built by **William Kempster**. Each stone step is set into the wall only a few inches, the weight at each level carried by the step below. The ironwork is by Jean Tijou.

The **crypt**, entered from the South Transept and covering the whole length of the cathedral, is probably the largest in Europe. Many famous people are buried here, including **Nelson** in the elegant black tomb Cardinal Wolsey had built for himself before he fell out of royal favor, Wellington, and Wren and his family. The artists' corner commemorates **Van Dyke, Blacke, Turner, Reynolds, Constable**, and many others. Noteworthy are the memorial to **John Singer Sargent** (1856-1925), designed by the artist himself, and the memorial to **George Frampton**, which includes a small replica of the statue of Peter Pan he sculpted for Kensington Gardens.

♦ Nominal donation requested. Cathedral: daily 7:30AM-6PM. Galleries, crypt, ambulatory: M-F 10AM-4:15PM; Sa 11AM-4:15PM. Services: Matins M-F 7:30, 8AM, 12:30PM, Su 7:30, 8, 10:30AM, 12:30PM; Evensong M-Sa 5PM, Su 3:15, 5PM; Holy Communion Sa 8AM, 12:30PM, Su 8, 11:30AM. Super tours: daily 11, 11:30AM, 2, 2:30PM. 071/248.2705

Something of the splendor of St. Paul's lies simply in its vast size, in its colorless serenity. Mind and body seem both to widen in this enclosure, to expand under this huge canopy where the light is neither daylight nor lamplight, but an ambiguous element something between the two.... Very large, very square, hollow-sounding, echoing with a perpetual shuffle and booming, the Cathedral is august in the extreme, but not in the least mysterious.

Virginia Woolf
The London Scene, a collection of 5 essays

---

60 London Chief Post Office and National Postal Museum (1907-11, **Sir Henry Tanner**) If you could save all your postcards and letters up and post them in just one spot it would be here: the most sumptuous place to stick a stamp on a letter in London. It makes such a minuscule task feel like an important occasion. This building was one of the first in London to have a reinforced concrete structure, which gives the tremendous white, marbled, and cavernous interior an immensely safe and reassuring feel. Part of the Roman City Wall can be seen here on request.

The National Postal Museum was started in 1965 by **Reginald M. Phillips** of Brighton. He wanted to create a national home for postal history, so he gave to the post office his own unique collection of 19th-century British postage stamps, documents, drawings, and proofs, together with a lot of money to get the whole thing going. The museum houses the **Phillips** and **Post Office Collections** and the **Berne Collection** of stamps from countries belonging to the Universal Post Union. Modern stamp history began with the penny-black, tuppeny-blue, and penny-red postage stamps on 6 May 1840, but the collections go back in history and forward to the present day, worldwide and maritime. The most popular countries' stamps are on display; those from more exotic locales are seen by prior arrangement as is the collection of letter boxes. Outside on the pavement stands the man who started it all, a granite **Rowland Hill** (1881, **R. Onslow Ford**), the founder of the **Penny Post**.
♦ M-Th 9:30AM-4:30PM; F 9:30AM-4PM. King Edward Building, King Edward St, EC. 071/239.5420

61 Postman's Park The City of London is long on big buildings and short on green spaces, so this tiny emerald enclave is all the more welcome. The park got its name because it is next to the Post Office. On one wall

The Strand, Fleet Street & the City

is a monument to heroic deeds, dedicated in 1900 and covered in plaques with stories that bring tears to your eyes: *William Fisher aged 9 lost his life on Rodney Road, Walworth, while trying to save his little brother from being run over. (July 12, 1886)*

62 St. Botolphs Without Aldersgate One of 4 churches in London built in the 10th century for the spiritual comfort of travelers and dedicated to St. Botolph, a 7th-century Saxon abbot, the traveler's patron saint. The church keeps its Saxon links to the present day: the priest in charge has the Saxon name, **Rev. Hereward Cooke**, and he can often be found inside the church. It has been rebuilt twice in its history, the last time by **Nathaniel Wright** in 1788-91, and again the interior is in urgent need of restoration. Despite its dull exterior, it is quite lovely inside because it is completely preserved 18th century, with big plaster rosettes covering the ceiling, 3 wooden galleries, a barrel-vaulted roof, and exquisite stained-glass windows (including the *Agony in the Garden*). Methodists will love this church because, close by in Little Britain, **John** and **Charles Wesley** were converted back in 1736, a fact that is commemorated outside the church and on a big bronze scroll outside the nearby Museum of London. ♦ M-F noon-3PM. Aldersgate St, EC2. 071/588.1053

63 Museum of London Two thousand years of London's history have been immortalized on this site, along the line of the old City wall. (The Romans took up residence in AD 43 and built a wall that was 3.25 miles long with 6 main gates; their wall was finally demolished as late as the 18th century, although bits of it still survive.) The explanation of how London

129

came to be as it is today can be found here, starting with a model Roman village and ending with the spectacular **Lord Mayor's Coach**, which is wheeled out on state occasions. There are 4 main themes within the museum: **Prehistoric and Roman**, which includes sculpture from the **Temple of Mithras**; **Medieval** spans a thousand years from the 5th century Dark Ages to the 15th century; **Tudor and Stuart** places these glittering eras against the Great Plague of 1665 and contains a re-creation of the Great Fire of 1666, which destroyed 80 percent of London, and in turn allowed Wren his prolific church-building career. In the **Modern** galleries (which cover Georgian and Victorian periods and the 20th century), the museum dubs London the world's first megalopolis and shows how the city is surviving (or not) the huge transition of the last 200 years. It is amusing to think that most of the artifacts have been dug up, either physically or metaphorically, around the city somewhere. Watch out for school parties—there are lots of them. The shop here is stacked with London paraphernalia, including over 400 different books on the mighty city. ♦ Free. Tu-Sa 10AM-6PM; Su 2-6PM. 150 London Wall, EC2. 071/600.3699

The Strand, Fleet Street & the City

Within the Museum of London:

Museum Restaurant ★$ In the summer you can sit outdoors here and a lot of Londoners do, but they arrive by 12:30PM to do so. The food is good enough, but it is the sun and fresh air that they are coming for, not the cold drinks, sandwiches, and salads. ♦ Tu-Sa 10AM-5PM; Su noon-5PM

64 Balls Brothers $ Judiciously avoid the sandwich bars at the front of St. Paul's. The sandwiches and coffee are okay, but the meals are everything that you'd expect from cafés that cater to tourists en masse. Instead, go around the back of the cathedral to what looks like an insurance office—this is Balls Bros., an underground bar where vast sandwiches (for England) are served, with at least 3 ounces of meat. This is a traditional-style bar, with wooden paneling, glass screens, and bric-a-brac. The only drawback: too few seats. ♦ M-F 11:30AM-7:30PM. 6 Cheapside, EC2. 071/248.2708

65 Le Poulbot ★★★$$$ Considering the amount of money sloshing around in the coffers of the Square Mile, the City is quite low on great eating establishments. This is one of the exceptions, and somehow most of the power-lunchers gravitate here to yet another **Roux** brothers' shrine, where they toy with such delicacies as the fricassee of turbot Bordelaise, followed by the *clafoutis de cerises*. Upstairs, for those who don't have limitless expense accounts, is a pub/café with cheaper French snacks. ♦ M-F noon-3PM. Reservations required. 45 Cheapside, EC2. 071/236.4379

66 Guildhall (1411-1440, **John Croxton**) The first mayor was installed in 1192. The Gothic porch, which is still the entrance to the hall from Guildhall Yard, was finished in 1430; the main structure was finished in 1439. The most extensive medieval crypt in London today still exists beneath the hall and it has one of the finest vaulted ceilings in London. The building is the largest hall after Westminster Hall and was used for treason trials in days gone by. Nowadays, it is used for state occasions. It survived (just) the Great Fire but was bombed out in World War II and repaired by **Sir Giles Gilbert Scott**, who also worked on the Houses of Parliament. The newer buildings were designed by **Sir Giles Scott, Son & Partners** and seem to match the Gothic classical front in a '60s way. It is open to the public, except when booked for state occasions, so ring and check. ♦ M-F 9:30AM-5:30PM. Aldermanbury, EC2. 071/606.3030

66 Guildhall Library and Clock Museum **Dick Whittington**, thrice lord mayor of London, left enough money to start this library in 1423. The entire contents was pilfered by the **Duke of Somerset** in 1549. (They say it was to furnish his newly built Somerset House.) The library is the greatest source of information on England's capital, with genealogical histories, parish registers, and heraldic histories of important Londoners. The Clock Museum, within the library's precincts, contains clocks and books dating back to 1814. There are now 3 clock collections under one roof, making it one of the foremost horological museums in the country. ♦ Library: M-F 9:30AM-5:30PM; Sa 9:30AM-4:45PM. Clock Museum: M-F 9:30AM-5:15PM; Sa 9:30AM-4PM. Guildhall, EC2. 071/606.3030

67 St. Lawrence Jewry On the wall of this church is one of the few remaining blue police phone boxes in London. The lord mayor and corporation worship here because it is close both to Mansion House and the Guildhall, not because it is particularly beautiful inside, having suffered great damage during World War II. ♦ Guildhall, EC2. 071/600.3699

68 St. Mary-le-Bow Every true Cockney is born *within the sound of Bow Bells*, which were smashed to smithereens never to ring again after a bombing raid in World War II. The church, on this spot since 1091, has a very bloody history: the tower collapsed killing 20, and people seeking sanctuary here got short shrift and usually death, too. Wren rebuilt it in 1670, and the exterior is rather splendid, but the interior, which was rebuilt in the late '50s, is not all that exciting. Its fame is its name. ♦ Cheapside, EC2. 071/248.5139

In order to appreciate England one has to have a certain contempt for logic.

Lin Yutang, *With Love & Irony*

Oh London is a fine town,
A very famous city,
Where all the streets are paved in gold,
And all the maidens pretty.

George Colman the Younger

Restaurants/Nightlife: Red **Hotels:** Blue
Shops/Parks: Green **Sights/Culture:** Black

69 Bow Lane and Watling Street One of the oldest parts of London. Watling Street was first mentioned in 1230, but it is believed to have been part of the main Roman Watling St between Dover and St. Albans, built nearly 1000 years earlier. The tiny streets here show graphically how chaotic the City is, lacking any formal plan. After the Great Fire of 1666 (which destroyed the plague rats as well as 80 percent of London's buildings) Londoners were desperate to get back to work and to make money. **Wren** and many others drew up spectacular plans for a beautiful city. But changing the street plan would have taken a long time and cost a lot of money, so to this day the medieval plan remains. The only difference is that the buildings are made of stone, not wood. Bow Lane is quaint and undeveloped, but the developers have moved in to make it look more kitsch. Still, ancient pubs like **Ye Olde Watling** (built from ships' timbers by Wren in 1668) and **Williamson's Tavern and Library Bar** (an old lord mayor's house dating back to the 17th century) still seem to be left intact; and the **Bow Wine Vaults**, the haunt of City businesspeople, and the old bookshop, **Jones & Evans** on Cannon St, haven't suffered, either—yet.

70 Mappin & Webb (1870, J. & J. Belcher) Rumbling away underneath this building is the District Line underground, which was built at the same time as the street. This Gothic-style building faces London's busiest crossing point and has become the subject of considerable controversy. Make the most of it; no one knows how long it will stay here. This building is both charming and eccentric, and makes a perfect place to buy discreetly beautiful jewelry in the company of some of London's most successful businesspeople. ♦ M-F 9AM-5:30PM. 2 Queen Victoria St, EC4. 071/248.2661

71 Mansion House (1739, Charles Dance) Lord mayors in London get just one year in office, and so a mere 365 days to live and work in the splendor of this Palladian mansion. There are a series of superb state rooms leading to an Egyptian banqueting hall with giant columns along each side on the 1st floor and the **Ball Room** on the 2nd. It is also one of the City's 2 magistrates courts. Closed for renovations from August 1990 until early 1992. ♦ Bank, EC2

On **Michaelmas Day**, 29 September, a new lord mayor of London is elected. On the second Saturday in November he celebrates by driving down to the Law Courts in the Strand to make a statutory declaration to the judges of the Queens Bench. He leaves Mansion House in considerable splendor in the Lord Mayor's Coach (an ornate affair built by Joseph Berry and Sir Robert Taylor in 1757), surrounded by a sea of similar carriages and modern floats in a carnival-like atmosphere. London has had a lord mayor since 1189, and King John, hoping to curry favor with the City, gave its citizens the right to elect a magistrate in 1215, just before the King was made to sign the Magna Carta. The title Mayor has never been granted, but he is still the head of the oldest municipal corporation in the world. Within the City he ranks before everybody except the sovereign, including princes of the Blood Royal; even the Queen asks his permission to enter the City. (Perhaps it's because he has the password to the Tower.) Unfortunately, the only mayor that anyone has ever heard of was **Dick Whittington**, who came to London in the 14th century believing that the streets were paved with gold. And discovering this was not the case, was leaving when he heard *Bow Bells* (St. Mary-le-Bow) chiming *Turn again, Whittington, thrice Lord Mayor of London*. The title nowadays confers a grant of around £80,000, but the mayor has to find at least £65,000 out of his own pocket to be able to fulfil his duties. Well Bow Bells didn't promise gold, did it?

72 Bank of England (1788, Sir John Soane) In 1797, **Richard Brinsley Sheridan** referred to *An elderly lady in the city of great credit and long standing* in the House of Parliament,

and the name stuck. The bank is still called the *Old Lady of Threadneedle Street* to this day, and looks after the nation's gold and the National Debt, issues bank notes, and acts as the government's and bankers' bank. The lady herself can be seen on the bronze doors, holding a model of the building on her knee. The outside walls of this massive structure have been left much as Soane had intended, but the inside, which was once a single story, now contains 3 stories below ground and 4 above. The bank has had a checkered history. The anti-Papist Gordon Rioters tried to storm the bank in 1780, one director embezzled £29,000, and it was still possible to break in through the sewers until 1836. The directors only discovered this when they were told by an honest sewerman. ♦ Threadneedle St, EC2

Courtesy Guardian Royal Exchange

73 Royal Exchange (1844, Sir William Tite) A building for merchants to meet and conduct business has been on this site since 1566 and received royal approval from both **Queen Elizabeth I** and, later, **Queen Victoria**. This classical building is the third Royal

Exchange (the other 2 were razed to the ground), although it hasn't been used for this purpose since 1939, and in a city of little sky-scrapers has become a rather ostentatious office block for **Guardian Royal Exchange Assurance**, which has been here since the 1800s. The pediment (**Richard Westmacott**) above the columns is carved in limestone and the central figure is Commerce. Outside is a rather tacky makeshift exhibition area, happily dwarfed by this giant building. The outside steps are used to proclaim a new sovereign. ♦ Bank St, EC2

73 Searle & Co. Clustered on the side of the Royal Exchange are a set of bijoux shops. This jeweler has been based in the City since 1893 and on this spot since 1932. The wooden exterior and interior are original and each evening the 60 tiny bejeweled gold and silver animals are lovingly tucked up for the night. City businesspeople come here to buy gifts, and Searle's ducks have even been seen swimming across the **Queen Mother**'s dining table from time to time. ♦ M-F 9AM-5:30PM. 1 Royal Exchange, EC3. 071/626.2456

73 Hermès A tiny branch of this chic Paris and Bond St store selling the classic women's

The Strand, Fleet Street & the City

scarfs and accessories that set its style apart. There are only imitators, but nothing quite as good. ♦ M-F 10AM-6PM. 3 Royal Exchange, EC3. 071/626.1120

73 Halcyon Days Charming enameled boxes and brooches decorate every available shelf in this offshoot of the **Mayfair** store. It says a lot about the area that Bond St has set up shop here. ♦ M-F 10AM-5:30PM. 4 Royal Exchange, EC2. 071/626.1120

73 Royal Exchange Art Gallery This little gallery specializes in marine art—watercolors and etchings from 1800 to the present day. It is hardly surprising when you realize that Lloyd's of London is no more than a quarter of a mile away. ♦ M-F 10:30AM-5:15PM. 14 Royal Exchange, EC3. 071/283.4400

74 George Peabody (1869, **William Wetmore Story**) This statue was erected in the year of the death of this American philanthropist who lived most of his life in Britain building 5000 homes for the poor, which still stand today. He is the only American buried in Westminster Abbey. ♦ Royal Exchange, EC2

75 Cornhill Once a grain market, this is the highest hill in the City. Today it is packed with office workers, bankers, and stockbrokers; a century ago these streets were traversed by authors like **Mrs. Gaskell, Thackery,** and the **Brontes**.

76 St. Michael's Alley One of the few places in London that makes you draw in your breath, for it is Dickensian London as you will rarely see it anywhere else. There's no need to rush along this alley, though—it ends where your eye rests and becomes modern London

again. Just 2 buildings, the **Jamaica Wine House** and the **George & Vulture**, lean across the street, sharing experiences of days gone by.

Within St. Michael's Alley:

Jamaica Wine House Not in the phone book; it's a regulars'-only pub, keeping strict City hours. It got its name from customers back in the 1670s who were trading in Jamaica. (You could get the best rum here.) See what you think now. ♦ Daily noon-3PM

George & Vulture ★★$$ This is a restaurant, not a pub, so book the day before at least, if you're thinking of coming here. Once a live vulture was used as a pub sign. **Charles Dickens** used the pub in the *Pickwick Papers* for the Bardell vs Pickwick trial. The brass plate outside is worn thin from its daily cleaning; inside it is just as pristine. And everything is old fashioned, from the excellent service to the rack of roast lamb, Stilton, and port at the end of your classic English meal. It is full of stockbrokers, bankers, and insurance magnates, and the wine list reflects its international clientele. ♦ M-F noon-2:45PM. 071/626.9710

77 Lloyds 1986 Building (1986, **Richard Rogers**) If you liked his Pompidou Center, this building will amuse as it is a much smaller version squashed into a confined space. Built around a central atrium and bedecked with oversize pipework, metal flooring, and glass, this zoo-style design allows the public to see the office workers busying about their day. The building caused a huge controversy when it was built, but it is a bold statement in a city packed with building blocks. Visitors' exhibition and gallery. ♦ M-F 10AM-2:30PM. 1 Lime St, EC3. 071/623.7100

78 Leadenhall Market (1881, **Sir Horace Jones**) A very pretty place crisscrossed with glass-roofed alleys. Highly decorated iron-and-glass facades cover over what is effectively the only place in the City for Londoners to buy any food at all. Cheese, butter, meat, fish, eggs, plants, even books can all be purchased here. ♦ Gracechurch St, EC3

79 Lombard Street In this, the center of banking, hang the medieval street signs banned during **Charles I**'s reign. (They regularly fell off of buildings, killing whomever happened to be standing or walking below.) They were hung up again after 300 years for **Edward VII**'s coronation. They're still here—the coronation never happened. Look for the giant gold grasshopper of old Martin's Bank, the castle of the TSB (Trustee Savings Bank), and even a gold cat and fiddle.

A famous nursery rhyme about the street sign:

Hey diddle diddle
The cat and the fiddle
The cow jumped over the moon
The little dog laughed to see such fun
And the dish ran away with the spoon.

Restaurants/Nightlife: Red   **Hotels:** Blue
Shops/Parks: Green   **Sights/Culture:** Black

80 St. Mary Abchurch Despite its gloomy interior, this is one of the best-preserved **Wren** churches in London, with almost everything left untouched by over-zealous attentions of renovators from bygone centuries. The war wreaked havoc here, but everything has been painstakingly restored to its former beauty. The reredos is by **Grinling Gibbons** (1686). There are churches dotted all over the City, but there are no conventional parishioners here. So the churches all busy themselves helping the working population of the Square Mile by running early morning and lunchtime Masses, self-help groups, relaxation classes, recitals, and concerts at lunchtime in this sea of activity. St. Mary Abchurch is a center for psychic research. ◆ Abchurch Yard, EC4

81 Fishmongers Hall (1834, **Henry Roberts**) The **Fishmongers Company** still performs its original function of checking all the fish that is sold in the City. The company historically organizes the **Doggetts Coat & Badge Race.** Peek in and you will see a giant wooden chandelier hung with candles. Sadly, it is not open to the public. ◆ King William St, London Bridge, EC4

82 The Monument It is getting quite difficult to see things from The Monument, since the buildings surrounding it are now rather taller than this block of Portland stone. If the column were laid down, it would touch the exact spot where the Great Fire began on 2 September 1666, in a baker's oven in Pudding Lane.

83 Southwark Cathedral This is the fourth church on this site and it's the earliest Gothic church in London. The oldest oak effigy (1275) is of a knight, ankles crossed, one hand on his sword, and even the ravages of time can't erase the eerie feeling that's he's just fallen asleep. **John Harvard**, founder of Harvard University, was born in Southwark in 1607 and baptized here. The reconstruction in 1907 of the Harvard chapel was paid for by the university in 1907. The area's more than a bit grim now, full of ugly warehouses, but once it thrived and had 4 theaters, including the **Globe** and the **Rose**. Every year a birthday service is held here in **Shakespeare**'s honor. ◆ M-F 9AM-5PM; Sa-Su hours vary. Services Su 9, 11AM choral, 3PM choral Evensong. London Bridge, SE1. 071/407.2939

84 The George $ As a child, **Charles Dickens** walked here every Sunday from Camden Town to visit his father in Marshalsea Prison; you'll even find the inn in *Little Dorrit*. This is an extraordinary survivor of bygone days. **Eisenhower** and **Churchill** drank beer here. It is the last timbered, galleried inn in London, rebuilt in 1676. The food is good, the beer not so bad, and it's well worth the walk. ◆ M-F 11AM-11PM; Sa 11AM-3PM, 6-11PM; Su noon-3PM, 7-10:30PM. 77 Borough High St, SE1. 071/407.2056

Annual income twenty pounds, annual expenditure nineteen pounds nineteen and six, result happiness. Annual income twenty pounds, annual expenditure twenty pounds ought and six, result misery.

Charles Dickens, Mr. Micawber in *David Copperfield*

Bests

Gillian Greenwood
TV Producer

Waterloo Sunset. The sunset over the River Thames during the winter months can be spectacular over the City skyline.

Lloyds Building. The architect Richard Rogers' magnificent building houses Lloyds of London in the City.

Highgate Cemetery. Beautiful but eerie, full of crumbling Victorian graves and Gothic monuments, including Karl Marx's tomb.

Luigi's. Old and well-established Italian restaurant in Covent Garden. Very friendly with theatrical connections.

London Library. Magnificent private lending library with overtones of a gentlemen's club.

Chiswick House and Gardens. An enchanting house built by Lord Burlington in the early 18th century. Set in splendid formal gardens, it is an oasis of cool classicism.

Notting Hill Gate. The Greenwich Village of London, with antique shops, Portobello market, and the Electric Cinema.

Boat trips to the **Tudor Hampton Court** or the maritime village of **Greenwich**.

A night walk over illuminated **Albert Bridge**.

The dome of **St. Paul's Cathedral**.

Mortimer Levitt
Chairman, The Custom Shop

Ah, London, my favorite city—clean, sweet smelling, elegant, and the world's most courteous citizens. My wife and I have been visiting for many, many years. We always stay at **Claridge's** and continue to consider it a treat. Our visits have always been in the spring or fall, and we have been lucky with the weather. Only once can I recall having to use umbrellas.

The splendid maintenance of homes and buildings in the West End is a continuing surprise. We even love **Oxford Street**, packed as it is with its double-decker buses. If the plays are not always 4-star, the actors are, and the theaters are venerable. And the taxis — in all the world they are the best. And the drivers, certainly the most agreeable. London never lets us down.

Bruce Banister
General Manager, Brown's Hotel

Browsing through the second-hand bookshops in **Cecil Court**.

Taking a glass of champagne in the **Crush Bar** during the interval of the ballet at the **Royal Opera House**.

I like meandering around the art galleries—like **Richard Green**—on Albemarle Street to find watercolors.

In the autumn I like to walk through **Berkeley Square** gardens, when the leaves are crunching and the trees are swaying.

A round sung by schoolchildren:

London's burning. London's burning.
Fetch the engines. Fetch the engines.
Fire! Fire! Fire! Fire!
Pour on Water. Pour on water.

High Holborn

High Holborn has the grimmest associations of any walk in the book, beginning with the largest meat market in the world (**Smithfield Market**) brilliantly juxtaposed with London's oldest hospital (**St. Bartholomew's**). It includes 2 sites where most London executions have taken place (**Smithfield** and **Newgate**) and the courthouse (**Old Bailey**) where the trials of many major British murderers of this century, including the **Yorkshire Ripper**, have been held. The road divides at the green oasis of **Lincoln's Inn**, and then moves on to the irresistible and eccentric **Sir John Soane's Museum**, a small-scale rehearsal for the grand finale, the **British Museum**. You can see where **Karl Marx** wrote *Das Kapital* (**British Library**), wonder at the Magna Carta and the **Rosetta Stone**, and end the day in the company of London's greatest writer (**Dickens House**).

Somewhere between the hanging geese of Smithfield, the inspired vision of **Thomas Rahere** (who built St. Bartholomew's in 1123), the secluded beauty of Lincoln's Inn, and the grandeur of the **Elgin Marbles**, you will see the real London: scholars, butchers, doctors, lawyers, writers, the innocent and the guilty, all drinking in the same pubs, all part of a London, ancient and ageless.

This authentic and Dickensian slice of London must be explored on a weekday, beginning at the crack of dawn at Smithfield Market and followed by the ideal breakfast at the **Fox and Anchor**. The courts at the Old Bailey are only in session during the week, and Sir John Soane's Museum and Dickens House are closed on Sunday, though the British Museum is open on Sunday afternoon.

1 Smithfield Market At midnight, the vans begin arriving at the oldest and largest dead meat and poultry market in Europe. Covering 10 acres and 2 miles of shop frontages, it is one of the few wholesale markets still on its original medieval site. Unloading, weighing, cutting, marking, and displaying all take place before selling begins at 5AM. Starting the day at dawn amid the bustle and ordered vivacity of early city life makes you feel like both an honorary and ordinary citizen, wherever you are. When you start a London day at Smithfield Meat Market, surrounded by white-coated butchers and *bummarees* (meat carriers) effortlessly carrying carcasses in imperious shades of pink, red, purple, and brown—calves by Georgia O'Keefe, piglets

by Mother Goose, anonymous rib cages by Francis Bacon—the surrealist artistry takes over. Feathered friends—chickens, geese, turkeys—smooth, sweet, and bloodless, hang alongside furry rabbits. The all-pervasive medieval feeling allows guilt and nausea to recede: life depends on death, markets depend on life. Signs announcing beef from Australia, New Zealand, and Scotland hang between the shining hooks, the hooks no competition for the arches, pillars, ornaments, and swirls of ironwork that are worthy of a City church. Though the animated atmosphere is pure medieval, the long iron-and-glass building, modeled on Paxton's Crystal Palace, is mid-Victorian, designed by **Horace Jones** and opened in November 1868 with a meaty banquet for

1200 people. With typical Victorian high-mindedness, a small park was built in the center of Smithfield where the *bummarees* can rest, but predictably, they choose now as

High Holborn

they chose then, the Smithfield pubs in the area, which have special licenses to open in the early-morning market hours.

The site has far more sinister associations than the slaughter of today. Originally, it was a *smooth field*, or level, of grassy expanse just outside the City walls for citizens' entertainment and exercise, and hence the name (a corruption of Smoothfield). Executions were held here as early as 1305, when **William Wallace**, the Scottish patriot, was executed on St. Bartholomew's Day. **Roger Mortimer**, who murdered **Edward II** and loved his queen, was executed here on the orders of **Edward III**, and it was here, in 1381, that the confrontation over a poll tax took place between **Wat Tyler** and his band of revolutionaries and the 14-year-old **Richard II**. The young king calmed the angry mob and promised them mercy and justice. The crowd took him at his word and peacefully dispersed, but Richard II delivered neither justice nor mercy, and Wat Tyler, stabbed by the lord mayor **(Sir William Walworth)** during the confrontation, died a few hundred yards away at St. Bartholomew's Hospital. From the 15th century onward, Smithfield was the execution place for all who were convicted of heresy, including most of the 277 Protestant martyrs who died for their faith during the cruel and tragic reign of **Mary I**, when they were burnt alive.

Smithfield's history is not totally grim. The great **St. Bartholomew's Fair** was held here every August, from Henry II's time until 1855. The 3-day event was the most important cloth fair in England, expanding as the export of wool and cloth grew. The **Royal Smithfield Show** (now held at Earl's Court) had its origins here in 1799, and as far back as medieval times there was a large horse-and-cattle market, with live animals being herded across the streets of London to get to market. The days of great fairs and exports have passed, but the area has been kept alive by the remarkable and ironic juxtaposition of its 2 principle institutions: the meat market and the hospital. However, plans are afoot to move the market to a less central site where costs would be lower, so see it while you can! ♦ M-F 5-10:30AM. Smithfield, EC1

2 Fox and Anchor ★★$ Full of bleary-eyed medical students, young doctors and nurses, and *bummarees* from the meat market eating huge platters of mixed grills: eggs, bacon, sausage, black pudding, kidneys, potatoes, tomatoes. Best appreciated after working up a greedy appetite. The special early-morning market license that allows alcohol to be served between 6 and 9AM is for bonafide market workers. Visitors get coffee. The facade is Art Nouveau, but the décor is unimpressive; the ambiance is the attraction. ♦ M-F 6AM-3PM. 115 Charterhouse St, EC1. 071/253.4838

3 Cloth Fair Here is the lingering feel of how the whole City of London was before it was destroyed by money, the Great Fire, and World War II. **No. 41** is the only house in the City built before the fire. **No. 43** was once home to **Sir John Betjeman**, one-time poet laureate and much-loved Englishman. Now the short terrace of houses is owned by the **Landmark Trust**, a charity devoted to rescuing minor buildings in distress before they are knocked down by vandals or developers. These simple 18th-century houses, facing **St. Bartholomew the Great**'s graveyard, are available for short self-catering holiday rentals in this, the heart of old London. ◆ Nos. 43, 45A Smithfield, EC1. Booking: Landmark Trust, Shottesbrooke, Maidenhead, Berkshire, SL6 3SW. 062/882.5925 (Book a year ahead)

4 St. Bartholomew the Great For lovers of antiquity and lovers of London, St. Bartholomew's is a kind of shrine, the oldest parish church in London. (Only the chapel of St. John in the Tower of London exceeds it in age.) It was built as a priory, along with St. Bartholomew's Hospital, as an act of gratitude by **Thomas Rahere**, a favorite courtier of **Henry I**, in 1123 after he had a vision during a fever in which St. Bartholomew saved him from a monster. The city's only surviving Norman church quickens the heart of all who enter by its simple majesty and ancient beauty and by the inexplicable power that comes from the stones, the strong pillars, the pointed windows, the tomb of Rahere, and the miracle of survival to which the church is witness. You do not see it quite as Rahere, first cannon and first prior, saw it. The massive nave was the choir of the original church; the original nave is part of the courtyard; and the 13th-century entrance gate was originally the west entrance to the south aisle. But the choir and vaulted ambulatories, crossing, apsed chancel, 2 transepts, and at least one bay of the nave are little changed since Rahere's time. The music sung during the choral service on Sunday seems to reach back in time, a heavenly complicity between stones, time, saints, and angels. The seats and pews face each other in the formation of collegiate churches.

The restored **Lady Chapel** dates from the 14th century. The font is the only medieval font in the city; **William Hogarth** was baptized here in 1697. The 5 bells in the tower are pre-Reformation, with the oldest peal left in London, rung before Evensong on Sunday. The crypt and cloister have been restored, and the large chamber is dedicated to the **City of London Squadron of the RAF**, which has a memorial service here each year.

During the Reformation, the church was sold and fell onto hard times. The cloisters became a stable, the crypt was used for storing coal and wine, and the Lady Chapel became a printer's office where a young printer named **Benjamin Franklin** worked in 1725. There was a blacksmith's forge in the north transept.

In the 1860s, architect **Sir Aston Webb** began the parliamentary restoration of the church. Along with his colleague **F.L. Dove,** he saved the reality and the spirit of St. Bartholomew's. The gateway was restored in memory of the 2 architects—notice the design of their coats-of-arms. The wooden figure of Rahere was carved from a beam taken from the church and placed here in memory of Sir Aston's son

Phillip, who was killed in action in France in 1916. ◆ Daily 8:30AM-4:30PM. Services Su 9, 11AM, 6:30PM. West Smithfield, EC1. 071/606.5171

5 St. Bartholomew's Hospital When **Wat Tyler** was stabbed by Sir William Walworth during his peasants' confrontation with Edward II, he was brought to *Bart's* and died in the emergency room. That was in 1331, and Bart's is still going strong, the oldest hospital in London and the only one of London's medieval foundations to remain on its original site to the present day. Like the church of St. Bartholomew the Great, the hospital was founded in 1123 by **Thomas Rahere**, although **Henry VIII** is regarded as a kind of second founder after he dissolved the priory during the Reformation and granted a royal charter refounding the hospital in 1546. The gateway, built in 1702 by **Edward Strong the Younger**, is topped by a statue of Henry VIII by **Francis Bird**. The collegiate-style buildings inside the great quadrangle were added by **James Gibbs** in 1730-70. Two large murals, *The Pool of Bethesda* and *The Good Samaritan* (1737), by **William Hogarth**, a governor of the hospital, line the staircase that leads to the Great Hall. The **Medical School**, which is a vital part of the hospital, is the oldest in London (1662). Now part of the University of London, Bart's has expanded in

recent years into a new building in nearby Charterhouse. ◆ West Smithfield, EC1

6 St. Bartholomew the Less A small octagonal church whose parish is St. Bartholomew's Hospital. The chapel was founded in the 12th century, rebuilt in the 15th century (two 15th-century arches survive under the tower), again in 1789 and 1820, and restored in 1951 following damage suffered during World War II. The register dates back to 1547 and records that **Inigo Jones** was baptized here in 1573. Open 24 hours for friends and family of patients in the hospital. ◆ West Smithfield, EC1

7 Bishop's Finger (The Rutland) ★★$ A good pub with 2 names and several devoted followings. It used to be called the Rutland, but Bishop's Finger is the name of one of the beers made by the brewery **Shepherd Neame**, to which the pub is tied, and the name stuck. *Bummarees* from the meat market, doctors and medical students from Bart's, lawyers and reporters from the Old Bailey, and money-makers from the City all drink together in the 2 bars, which spill over into the park opposite on sunny days. ◆ M-F 11:30AM-8:30PM. 9-10 West Smithfield, EC1. 071/248.2341

England is the paradise of women, the purgatory of men and the hell of horses.

John Florio, *Second Fruites*

8 St. Sepulchre The spacious church was originally dedicated in 1137 to East Anglican king **St. Edmund**. It was rebuilt in the 15th century, restored after the Great Fire (possibly but not certainly by **Sir Christopher Wren**), heavily Victorianized in 1878, and sensitively repaired after the war in 1950. Known as the *Musicians Church*, St. Sepulchre has a long tradition of memorial services honoring composers and singers, a **Musician's Chapel** with windows in memory of singer **Dame Nellie Melba** and composer **John Ireland**, and exquisite kneelers with names of great musicians, bars of music, and musical instruments worked in fine needlepoint. **Sir Henry Wood**, the founder of the **Promenade Concerts**, was baptized here, became assistant organist when he was 14, and is remembered in the central window of the north chapel, which is dedicated to **St. Cecilia**, patron saint

of music. Every year on St. Cecilia's Day, 22 November, a festival is held in her honor, with the choirs of Westminster Abbey and St. Paul's.

American associations with the church inspired the south wall stained-glass window of **Captain John Smith**, who led the expedition to Virginia in 1606-7. Taken prisoner by the Indians, he was saved by the chief's daughter **Pocahontas** just as he was about to be killed. The English captain became Governor of Virginia and Admiral of New England. His savior Pocahontas married another settler, **John Rolfe**, who brought her to England, the first in a long tradition of Englishmen marrying American women. Sadly, she suffered from the damp English winter and died.

Not all the associations of the church are as life-enhancing as the musical ones. To the right of the altar in a small glass case sits a handbell that was tolled outside the cell of a condemned man at midnight on the eve of his hanging. The bellman recited the following verses: *All you that in the condemned hole to lie; Prepare you, for tomorrow you shall die; Watch all and pray; The hour is drawing near. That you before the Almighty must appear; Examine well yourselves; in time repent. That you may not to eternal flames be sent. And when St. Sepulchre's Bell in the morning tolls. Lord have mercy on your souls.* All this, including the tolling of the great bell of St. Sepulchre on the morning of the execution, was

arranged and paid for by a request or endowment of £50 made by parishioner **Robert Dowe** in 1605. ♦ West Smithfield, EC1. 071/606.5171

9 Viaduct Tavern ★★$ A fascinating pub built over cells from the old Newgate Prison and named for Holborn Viaduct, the world's first flyover. Lavish interior with gold mirrors, an ornate metal ceiling, and large paintings. Light lunches. ♦ M-F 11:30AM-11PM; Sa 11:30AM-3PM, 7-11PM; Su noon-2PM, 7-10:30PM. 126 Newgate St, EC1. 071/606.8476

10 Old Bailey (1907, **Edward Mountford**; extension 1972, **McMorron and Whitby**) The figure of Justice, neither blind nor blindfolded, but with scales, stands atop the dome, gilded in bronze and prelude to endless TV and film thrillers. The carved inscription *Defend the Children of the Poor and Punish the Wrongdoer* over the main entrance proves as difficult a combination today as it was when Fagin went to the gallows on this very site in chapter 52 of *Oliver Twist*. The Old Bailey is the **Central Criminal Court**, serving Greater London and parts of Surrey, Kent, and Essex, and where the most serious, dramatic, and celebrated criminal court cases are heard. It was originally a medieval gatehouse used as a prison for murderers and thieves. **Newgate Prison**, as it was known, played an important and dreadful role in London life, especially during the late 18th and 19th centuries when it was London's chief prison. The conditions, despite numerous extensions and the installation of a windmill on the roof to improve ventilation, were notoriously barbaric. **Wat Tyler** led a successful assault and released all the prisoners in 1381. In 1750, a plague of jail fever swept through the prison, killing over 60 people, including the lord mayor, members of the jury, and 3 judges—the origin of a tradition still honored whereby judges carry nosegays on the first day of each session to ward off vile smells and diseases.

The first Old Bailey (or Sessions House) was built in 1539 as a hall for trials of the accused. The men who condemned **Charles I** were tried here in 1660; **Oscar Wilde** was tried here in 1895; and famous 20th-century murderers—**Dr. Crippen, Christie**, and **Peter Sutcliffe** (the Yorkshire Ripper) were also tried here. In 1973, a terrorist bomb went off in the building during a trial of members of the **IRA**, which led to fortresslike security during IRA trials. Public executions were held outside the Old Bailey from 1783 until 1868, replacing Tyburn as the site of the gallows. The road was widened to accommodate the large number of spectators.

The present building (1907), with its elaborate Edwardian frontage and extension (1972), accommodates 23 courts. Ten of them are in the old building, entered on Newgate Street, which has a very unassuming door with the words *Ring bell hard* written above a doorbell; the other 13 courts are in the new building entered from Old Bailey. Few experiences can be more fascinating than seeing the English judiciary at work during a trial here, with the judge and barristers in their white wigs and the accused in the dock. Major trials in courts 1-4 attract large numbers, so you may have to wait in line. No children under 14, cameras, or tape recorders. Free when court is in session. ♦ M-F 10:30AM-1PM, 2-4PM. Old Bailey, EC4. 071/248.3277

11 Magpie and Stump ★★$ Famous old pub with an illustrious reputation. The secret passage between the pub and the jail has now been bricked up and the windows upstairs are no longer hired out for viewing public hangings, but friends and family of the innocent and the guilty gather here to fortify themselves during the trials and to toast or console each other following commutations and acquittals. In the quiet bar in the back, crime reporters and barristers drink after a day's work at the Old Bailey, though presumably any conversation between the 2 professions is off the record. Pub lunch served. ♦ M-F 11:30AM-11PM. Old Bailey, EC4

12 Holborn Viaduct (1863-69, **William Haywood**) The world's first flyover, 1400 feet long and 80 feet wide, built to bridge the valley of the Fleet and to connect Holborn with Newgate Street, at a cost of 4000 dwellings. Its elaborate cast-iron work is best seen from Farringdon Street. Four bronze statues representing agriculture, commerce, science, and fine art grace the north and south sides. Before the viaduct was built, the steep banks of this part of the river were very difficult to negotiate. Steps lead down to Farringdon Street and **Holborn Viaduct Station**, a small railway station that serves commuters to the southern counties. ♦ EC1

13 Bubbs ★★$$$ Should you decide to go down the stairs to the side of the Holborn Viaduct, this bistro-style restaurant is close by, a series of connecting rooms packed with City ladies and gents. Take the plunge, try the fish specials, which change daily, or meat lovers can go for the entrecôte Béarnaise. Mont Blanc is the right pudding to follow. ♦ Daily noon-2PM. 329 Central Market, Smithfield, EC1. 071/236.2435

14 City Temple A congregational church opened by the famous preacher **Dr. Joseph Parker** in 1874. The church was totally gutted in an air raid in 1941 and lavishly rebuilt in 1950, incorporating the old facade by **Lord Mottistone** and **Paul Paget**. Not open to visitors. ♦ Holborn Viaduct, EC1

15 St. Andrew Holborn (1690, **Sir Christopher Wren**) Wren's largest parish church, built on the site of a church founded in the 13th century. In 1704, Wren refaced the medieval tower of the original church, which miraculously survived the 5 bombs that destroyed the interior of the church during World War II. In the 1960s the furnishings were replaced with treasures from the **Foundling Hospital Chapel** in Berhampstead, including the gilded 18th-century organ that **Handel** gave to the hospital and the 18th-century font and altar rails. The church records show the burial of

Thomas Chatterton in 1770, the young poet who committed suicide by poison at the age of 18 over the twin despairs of poverty and lack of recognition and became a symbol of the Romantic movement. Essayist **William Hazlitt** was married here in 1808, with **Charles Lamb** as his best man and **Mary Lamb** as a bridesmaid. **Benjamin Disraeli** was baptized here in 1817 at the age of 12. The tomb of **Captain Coram**, founder of the Foundling Hospital, survived the bombs of World War II, and a weeping cherub watches over the great, good man. ♦ Holborn Circus, EC1

16 Holborn Circus The statue of **Prince Albert** (1874) on a horse in the middle of a traffic island is unworthy of the prince who worked tirelessly for his adopted country, left a legacy of great museums, and introduced the Christmas tree. ♦ EC1

17 Ely Place A fascinating cul-de-sac of 18th-century houses still guarded at night by a watchman in a small gatehouse. Built on land belonging to the Bishops of Ely and officially owned by Ely Cathedral in Cambridgeshire, it remains legally under their jurisdiction, meaning London police cannot automatically enter, perhaps a more useful edict now that the lovely Adams doorways lead to offices of lawyers and accountants rather than to private houses. The developers' ax is waiting to fall over this charming street. ♦ EC1

18 St. Etheldreda (Ely Chapel) When this church was built in 1290, it was, of course, a Catholic church, and like all churches in England during the Reformation, it became Protestant or Anglican. In 1874, the Roman Catholics bought it back, the first pre-Reformation church to return to the fold. A masterpiece of 13th-century Gothic architecture (restored in 1935 by **Giles Scott**), the mood is one of great antiquity and warm everydayness. You enter to the smell of soup (from a small café in the adjoining church-run house, which provides morning coffee, lunch, and tea to nearby residents) and incense. (Mass is said daily at noon, and on Holy Days of Obligation both the crypt and the church are packed full.) The windows at the east and west ends are noted for their superb tracery; the west window (c. 1300) is one of the largest in London. Modern stained-glass windows by **Charles** and **May Blakeman** depict English martyrs. Very much a living church, St. Etheldreda's is active in Amnesty International and in the community. The vaulted crypt (1252) serves as a meeting room/Sunday school/storage area, irreverently and nicely chaotic. ♦ 24 hrs. Ely Pl, EC1

Hell is a city much like London—
A populous smoky city.
There are all sorts of people undone,
And there is little or no fun done,
Small Justice shown, and still less pity.

Shelley, 1819

19 Ye Olde Mitre Tavern ★★★$ Tucked away in the narrow alleyways off Ely Place, this 18th-century pub was originally built in 1546 as lodgings for the servants of the Bishops of Ely. The sign probably came from the bishops' gatehouse. Medieval tiles were discovered during roadworks in 1985. It is a perfect place for a half-bitter to quench your thirst after a salty breakfast at the Fox and Anchor. But it is a very small pub and you will have to get here early if you want to get in between noon and 3PM or 5:30 and 8PM. ♦ M-F 11AM-11PM. 1 Ely Court, Ely Pl, EC1. 071/405.4751

20 Hatton Garden The center of the diamond trade isn't what it used to be. Office blocks have descended and ascended and most of the shops look so vulgar or so impenetrable that you have to be pretty expert to shop confidently. The impressive building housing the **London Diamond Club** is not open to the public. But **R. Holt**, at No. 98, and **Andrew Ullman**, at No. 10, are open. **Mineral Stones**, at No. 111, cuts and mounts stones and minerals. Far more interesting value-wise are the **Hatton Garden** silver and jewelry auctions held every Thursday at 1:30PM, where you can buy and also sell your own valuable pieces, paying a commission of 10 percent if they are sold. Viewing for the next week's sale is Friday from 9AM-4:30PM, following each sale. ♦ M-F 9:30AM-5:30PM. 36 Hatton Garden, EC1. 071/242.6452

High Holborn

21 Bleeding Heart Yard Don't be put off by the name, Bleeding Heart Yard is featured in **Charles Dickens'** *Little Dorrit*. Bookshelves with the author's first editions and prints line the walls and the restaurant, which is underground, spooky, and lined with bottles of wine. One of the rooms even has a grand piano. Even though it's hard to find the wine bar and restaurant, they are well worth searching out because the wine bar is cheap and good (try the menu *rapide* with avocado, salami, and cheese with olive oil), and the restaurant, although a little pricier, is still a good value—tuck into a classic shoulder of lamb with mint sauce. In summer, there is a terrace, but you'll be jostling with lots of City workers. ♦ Bleeding Heart Yard, Greville St, EC1. 071/242.8238

22 Daily Mirror Building (1960, **Sir Owen Williams & Partners**; **Anderson, Forster and Wilcox**) An aggressive, vulgar newspaper has been translated into its architectural equivalent. Bad luck for Holborn. ♦ New Fetter Ln, EC1

23 Prudential Assurance (1879-1906, **Alfred Waterhouse**) This is what the late **Sir John Betjeman**, poet laureate and longtime resident of the neighborhood (Cloth Fair behind St. Bartholomew's), admired, defended, and fought hard to save: High Victorian architecture, massively confident. The Gothic red-brick immensity no doubt inspires confidence in those who pass by the large insurance company. It lies on the site of **Furnival's Inn**, where **Charles Dickens** wrote part of *Pickwick Papers*. Only the facade remains now. The rest of the building has been demolished and is currently being redeveloped. ♦ 142 Holborn Bars, EC1

24 Leather Lane Market A lunchtime street market reached by a passage down the east side of the Prudential Assurance Building. New clothes at bargain prices—lambswool sweaters (called *jumpers*), shoes, jeans—some plants, fruit, vegetables, and glassware are sold here. The only leather can be found at a stall that sometimes sells genuine chamois. Inexpensive **Colin's Nest** serves *pie and mash*—steak pies, mashed potatoes, etc. ♦ M-Sa noon-3PM. Leather Ln, EC1

25 Barnard Inn The oldest surviving secular building in the City, incorporating remains of the Inn of Chancery where Pip and Herbert Pocket shared rooms in *Great Expectations*. The 14th-century hall has 16th-century paneling and fine heraldic glass. From 1894 to 1958, this was the hall of **Mercer's School**. Now it is occupied by a restaurant called **School Dinners**, which features typical English public school fare. ♦ By appt only. Holborn, EC1. 071/405.5233

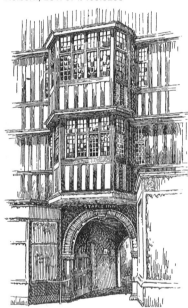

26 Staple Inn The pair of houses, dating from 1586, is the only survivor of pure, domestic Elizabethan London, with black-and-white timber and plaster, gables, overhangs, and oriels. Badly damaged in 1944 by a bomb and carefully restored, the inn now houses offices and old-world shops, including the **Institute of Actuaries**, which is now one of the Inns of Chancery affiliated with Gray's Inn. **Dr. Johnson** lived at No. 2 in 1759-60 following his wife's death and his departure from Gough Square. The silver griffin on the stone obelisk in the front marks the boundary of the City of London. ♦ Holborn, EC1

27 Cittie of Yorke ★★$ One of the largest pubs in London with the largest bar, this 17th-century establishment must have served most of Holborn in days gone by. The large 3-sided fireplace and little cubicles keep the place warm and intimate. The bar lunches are excellent and the real ales much appreciated by the legal clientele. ♦ M-F 11AM-11PM; Sa noon-3PM, 5:30-11PM. 22-23 High Holborn, WC1. 071/242.7670

28 Her Majesty's Stationery Office *HMSO*, as it is known to Londoners, carries a remarkable collection of maps, charts, guides, and travel books covering every inch of the British Isles. The shop also has the latest copies of laws passed in Parliament, museum replicas from the British Museum, and attractive copies of English country maps. ♦ M-F 8:15AM-5:15PM. 49 High Holborn, WC1. 071/276.0820

29 London Silver Vaults English silver has a richly deserved reputation: the silver content in silver marked with the hallmark of the British lion is the highest in the world and the tradition of design has been consistently strong. Unless you are familiar with hallmarks, makers, and dealers, buying silver is bound to be an unnerving experience, and coming to this underground prison with over 100 cells containing the highest concentration of silver dealers in London is not reassuring. You have to make your way through a lot of junk in the beginning and encounter diffident dealers once the silver becomes desirable. If you persevere and have a good idea of what you want, you will find lower prices than elsewhere. Study a simple hallmark card before you make a major silver purchase. ♦ M-F 9AM-5:30PM; Sa 9AM-12:30PM. Chancery House, 53-64 Chancery Ln, WC2. 071/242.3844

30 Hodgsons ★★$$ A 19th-century book auctioneers building-turned-restaurant. It is beautiful inside, with vaulting and a glass roof, and has become a favorite with lawyers who rush over from the nearby Courts of Justice for a lunch of sea bream with green-herb-and-Provençal sauce to discuss their case of the day all the while. Book lunch 2 days ahead. ♦ M-F noon-2:30PM, 5-10:30PM. 115 Chancery Ln, WC2. 071/242.2836

31 Lincoln's Inn Of the 4 great **Inns of Court** (Lincoln's Inn, Inner Temple, Middle Temple, and Gray's Inn), this is the most unspoiled and the only inn to have escaped World War II without major damage. (The inns were formed in the Middle Ages and were called inns because they provided lodgings for lawyers and students of law. They now belong to barristers' societies, which control the admission of students to the bar as well as finance, law reform, legal education, and the maintenance of professional standards in the legal profession. Lincoln's Inn was established on the site of the **Knights Templar**'s tilting ground after the dissolution of the order in the early 14th century. The rolls of the inn contain famous names—**Sir Thomas More, John Donne, Oliver Cromwell, William**

Penn, Horace Walpole, William Pitt, Benjamin Disraeli, Gladstone—reflecting the times when most people of education became lawyers. The brick-and-stone buildings, arranged in a collegiate plan, date from the 15th century. Enter through the **gatehouse** (1518) facing Chancery Lane, which bears the arms of **Sir Thomas Lovel**. The Tudor red-brick **Old Buildings** date from the early 16th century, and the **Old Hall** (1491), through the archway and small courtyard, has a superb wooden roof and **Hogarth**'s serious painting *St. Paul Before Felix* (1748). The hall was the **Court of Chancery** from 1737 to 1883; the case of Jarndyce vs. Jarndyce in *Bleak House* took place here. The red-brick **New Hall** and **Library** (1845, **Hardwick**) contain the vast mural by **G.F. Watts,** *Justice, a Hemicycle of Lawgivers*, and the oldest and most complete law library in England, with nearly 100,000 volumes. **New Square** (1697, **Serle**), toward Lincoln's Inn Fields, is on a tranquil and pretty courtyard of solicitors' offices, and is where 14-year-old **Charles Dickens** was once employed as a solicitor's clerk. The Gothic **chapel** was rebuilt in 1619-23. John Donne laid the foundation stone and gave the first sermon. ♦ Chapel and gardens M-F noon-2:30PM. WC2. 071/405.1393

Nos. 57, 58. Circular porch added by Sir John Soane.

32 Lincoln's Inn Fields Adjacent to Lincoln's Inn, the *field* was left open only after angry lawyers appealed to the House of Commons when property developers won the right to develop the space in 1620. The fine rectangular square is the largest in central London and is surrounded by tennis courts, flower beds, and a bandstand and is graced by many distinguished houses, including **Lindsey House** (Nos. 59-60) by **Inigo Jones** and its similar neighbor (Nos. 57-58) by **Henry Joynes**. ♦ Theobalds Rd, WC2

33 Sir John Soane's Museum Go out of the way to visit this museum! Sir John Soane (1753-1837), eminent architect of the Bank of England, chose the largest square in central London for the site of his house. He required an appropriate setting for his enormous collection of worldwide antiquities and art, and the result is a fascinating house unlike any other in London. In rooms of unusual proportions built on varying levels with spiral staircases and hundreds of mirrors, you feel that time has been suspended and that you have entered the mind of a brilliant and eccentric master builder. Incorporated within the house are **Monument Court**, an **Egyptian crypt**, and a mock-medieval ruin of a **monk's cloister**. In the **Picture Room** you can see **William Hogarth**'s paintings of *The Rake's Progress* (1732-33), ingeniously mounted by Soane so that they pull away from the wall, revealing hidden panels with subsequent paintings in the same series. A well-known highlight of the collection, found in the **Sepulchral Chamber**, is the magnificent **Sarcophagus of Seti I** (c. 1300 BC), discovered at Thebes in 1815 and snapped up by Soane when it was passed over by the British Museum. The collection contains many treasures and unpredictable juxtapositions of architectural fragments salvaged from buildings (such as the old House of Lords) that were destroyed during Soane's lifetime. Glancing through a window into the court known as the **Monk's Yard**, it is possible to catch a glimpse of a huge melancholy tomb inscribed *Alas, Poor Fanny*, a monument to **Mrs. Soane**'s favorite dog. ♦ Donations welcome. Tu-Sa 10AM-5PM. Free guided tour Sa 2:30PM. 13 Lincoln's Inn Fields, WC2. 071/405.2106

34 Great Queen Street Named in honor of **Henrietta Maria**, the devoted wife of **Charles I**. This once-fashionable street is now lined with restaurants, including the private advertising and media club **Zanzibar** at No. 30. ♦ WC2

High Holborn

35 Contemporary Wardrobe No, it's not for sale, but that fabulous little number *is* for hire, and with the opera close by, why not? This theatrical and screen costumier has one advantage over the competition—the clothes are so beautiful that they'd look good on a Paris catwalk, and all can be rented. Costumes designed from 1945 onward hang in glorious profusion on the rails, and have graced the backs of **Prince, David Bowie**, and the **Rolling Stones**, among many others, for the shop supplies films, videos, commercials, and TV. For ravers, fancy dress includes **Elvis, Marilyn Monroe, Madonna, beatnik, Dolly Parton, Mrs. Thatcher**, and the *Statue of Liberty* outfits. ♦ Carlton House, 66-69 Great Queen St, WC2. 071/242.4024

36 L'Opera ★$$ Popular with theatergoers and opera lovers who flock here after Covent Garden and English National Opera performances. The menu is nouvelle cuisine, where more attention is paid to the design on the plate than the quantity of food, and includes venison terrine, wild mushrooms, timbale (smoked-salmon ball stuffed with fish), and monkfish. Photographs of the history of opera decorate the walls. ♦ M-F 12:15-3PM, 6PM-midnight; Sa 6-11:30PM. 32 Great Queen St, WC2. 071/405.9020

37 Freemason's Hall (1933, **H.V. Ashley** and **F. Winton Smith**) Heavyweight headquarters of the **United Grand Lodge of England**, with a central tower rising 200 feet above the street. The building, a good example of '30s Art Deco, was conceived as a war memorial to masons who died in World War I and now houses an exhibition of the history of English freemasonry. A good idea as the British are very suspisious of the *funny handshake brigade*, as the Freemasons are called. This is the largest collection of masonic regalia, medals, art, and glassware in the world, but few of the sect's secrets are divulged. Look out for the angels and pyramids—both masonic symbols. ♦ M-F 10AM-5PM, Great Queen St, WC2. 071/831.9811

37 Bhatti ★★$$ Award-winning restaurant, popular with theatergoers. It serves good-quality food at reasonable prices in a 17th-century listed building that still retains much of the original paneling, stenciling, and fireplaces. (Listed buildings cannot be knocked down nor can the interiors be tampered with because they have been deemed important to England's heritage). Try the prawn tandoori (shrimp barbecued in clay ovens and served with onion-and-mint sauce) and the *peshawari nan* (leavened bread filled with dried fruit). ♦ M-Sa noon-3PM, 6-11:30PM; Su noon-2PM, 6-10PM. 37 Great Queen St, WC2. 071/831.0817

38 Anello & Davide The best ballet and tap shoes and very appealing old-fashioned leather lace-up boots with pointy toes. Though most of the women's shoes never look made to last more than the average run of a West End show, the more classic looking leather-lined shoes will last years and years. The Victorian-style button boots in soft leather are a great buy. This is now Anello & Davide's only London shop and well worth a visit. ♦ M-F 9AM-5:30PM; Sa 9AM-5PM. 35 Drury Ln, WC2. 071/836.1983

39 Mansfield A very chic shop specializing in antique luggage made mainly from endangered species like crocodile and alligator. It also contains what is believed to be the largest range of vintage pens in England, primarily from the '20s and '30s. Ring the bell. ♦ M-Sa 10AM-6PM. 30-35 Drury Ln, WC2. 071/240.7780

40 New London Theatre (1973, **Michael Percival**) The West End's newest theater sits on one of the oldest foundations—the site has held a place of entertainment since Elizabethan times. The New London is ultramodern, with moveable seats, lights, walls, and stage surrounded by lots of glass. The seating was expanded from 952 to 1102 to make room for the crowds for the feline phenomenon *Cats*. ♦ 167 Drury Ln, WC2. 071/404.4079

The chief advantage of London is that man is always so near his burrow.

Hugo Meynell

Restaurants/Nightlife: Red   **Hotels:** Blue
Shops/Parks: Green   **Sights/Culture:** Black

41 Last Days of the Raj ★★$$$ With its gleaming chrome, it looks much more like Upper East Side New York than India, but this Indian restaurant, run by a cooperative of first-rate chefs—6 Bangladeshis, an Indian, and a Nepali—has an imaginative menu and favorites like *nam lamb tikka*, prawn masala, and vegetarian *thali*. The menu hardly changes—it doesn't need to, it's so popular and highly rated. ♦ M-Sa noon-2:30PM, 5:30-11:30PM; Su 6-11:30PM. 22 Drury Ln, WC2. 071/836.5705

42 Stefania's Delicatessen ★$ Sandwiches, lasagne, and pizza to go in this Italian takeout. ♦ M-Sa 7AM-5:30PM. 184 Drury Ln, WC2. 071/831.0138

43 Museum Street Once you cross the broad intersection of New Oxford Street, High Holborn, and Bloomsbury Way, this narrow, friendly street is lined with some of the best antique-print dealers, bookshops, and jewelers in London.

43 S.J. Shrubsole Distinguished dealer in old English silver, with prices worthy of its neighbor, the British Museum. You will also find outstanding pieces of old Sheffield plate, with honest prices that reflect the integrity of the shop. ♦ M-F 9AM-5:30PM. 43 Museum St, WC1. 071/405.2712

44 Plough ★$ A literary pub with the feel of Bloomsbury about it, perhaps because it has remained popular with publishers and writers for so long—they appreciate the coziness in winter and the outdoor tables in summer. Bar lunch and wide selection of traditional ales. ♦ M-Sa 11AM-11PM; Su noon-3PM, 7-10:30PM. 27 Museum St, W1. 071/636.7964

45 Print Room Specializing in prints of London, Hogarth prints, and caricature prints of the 18th and 19th centuries, with a large, tempting, and reasonably priced collection of botanical prints. ♦ M-F 10AM-6PM; Sa 10AM-4PM. 37 Museum St, WC1. 071/430.0159

46 British Museum *Ennui*, wrote the lyricist of an old song, *was the day when the British Museum lost its charm*. It hasn't, as the hordes who head here daily will attest, and the only problem is managing to see the exhibitions through the crowds.

When **Sir Hans Sloane**, physician, naturalist, and collector, died in 1753, his will allowed the nation to buy his vast art, antiquities, and natural history collection for £20,000, less than half of what it cost to assemble. The collection grew rapidly and magnificently—and right out of **Montagu House**, where it had been on display since 1759. In 1823, **George II**'s huge library was given to the nation and a decision was made to build new quarters for the burgeoning collection. The architect chosen was **Robert Smirke**, who designed a large quadrangle with an open courtyard behind Montagu House, then surrounded the house with a fine Neoclassical facade with a portico decorated with figures representing the progress of civilization. The architect's brother **Sydney Smirke** converted the courtyard into the copper-domed **Reading Room** in 1852-57. Problems with space were alleviated in the 1880s, when the natural history exhibitions moved to the **Natural History Museum** (see page 68), and in 1970, when the ethnographic exhibitions were moved to the **Museum of Mankind** (see page 35).

Start with the **Egyptian Sculpture Gallery** on the ground floor (Room 25). The massive granite figures can be seen over the heads of any number of people. At the door is the **Rosetta Stone**, fascinating not in itself (it is an irregularly shaped, closely inscribed piece of black basalt), but because of the way it changed our understanding of history. Written both in Greek and in 2 forms of ancient Egyptian script, the stone's Greek translation provided the key to deciphering hieroglyphics unread for 1400 years. Inside the gallery is an overwhelming introduction to the ancient Egyptians—massive sculptures, intricate pieces of jewelry, and carvings. There is a haughty bronze cat from 600 BC, sacred to **Bastet** (an Egyptian deity); a large reclining granite ram with a tiny figure of **King Taharqa** tucked beneath his chin; and from the **Temple of Mut in Thebes**, carved in about 1400 BC, are 4 massive granite representations of the goddess **Sakhmet**, with the body of a woman and the head of a lion. The rest of the Egyptian exhibitions are on the upper floors (Rooms 56, 60-64, and 66).

Before climbing the stairs, visit Rooms 1 through 15, which hold the museum's collection of **Greek and Roman Antiquities**, including the hotly contested **Elgin Marbles** (Room 8), sculptures from the Parthenon that were brought to England in 1816 by **Lord Elgin** and which the government of Greece is seeking to have returned. Mostly fragments, they are described in the diary of an attendant who helped move them into the museum and who was assigned to the gallery where they were displayed. The diary of the attendant, **John Conrath**, can be

The British Library Reading Room during construction

seen in the **British Library Galleries**. *Northside*, he wrote, describing the frieze that had been inside the great colonnade, *a young man almost naked, putting a Crown on his head, another ready to mount, attended by his grooms, around the west corner a single person, a magistrate or director, two Chariots...South frieze, Seven more Bulls, a man Crowning himself*....Despite the disappointment of some early visitors at the eroded and broken state of the marbles, they have been an extremely popular exhibition since they were first installed, attracting such illustrious fans as the **Grand Duke of Nicholas**, later Czar Nicholas I of Russia, who spent 2 days looking at the marbles in 1817.

The upper floors hold **Medieval and Later Antiquities from Europe** (Rooms 41-47), with early examples of objects used in everyday life, including bronze weapons that look incapable of inflicting a mortal wound and the extraordinary **Lycurgus Cup**, a Roman goblet carved from a single block of green glass that shows the tortured face of the **Thracian King Lycurgus** as he is imprisoned by the tendrils of a vine. The rooms also contain remarkable displays of jewelry. The **Gallery of Clocks and Watches** (Room 44) shows a range of time pieces from the Middle Ages to the beginning of this century.

On the ground floor, to the right of the entrance, are the British Library

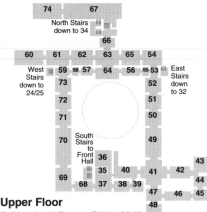

Upper Floor

Prehistoric and Romano-British **35-40**
Medieval and Lateral **41-48**
Special Exhibitions **49**
Coins and Metals **50**
Western Asiatic **51-59**
Egyptian **60-66**
Prints and Drawings **67**
Greek and Roman **68-73**
Oriental

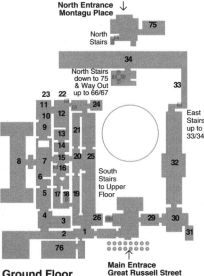

Ground Floor

Greek and Roman **1-15**
Western Asiatic **16-26**
Egyptian **25**
British Library **29-33**
Oriental **34, 75**
Special Exhibitions **76**

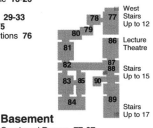

Basement

Greek and Roman **77-87**
Western Asiatic **88-90**

Objects of Special Interest

Assyrian Lionhunt Reliefs **17**
Clocks and Watches **44**
Egyptian Mummies **60, 61**
Egyptian Sculptures **25**
Hull Grundy Gift of Jewelry **47**
Indian Sculptures **34**
Lewis Chessman

Lindisfarne Gospels **30**
Magna Carta **30**
Mildenhall Treasure **40**
Parthenon Sculptures **8**
Portland Vase **14**
Rosetta Stone **25**
Sutton Hoo Treasure **71**

Galleries (Rooms 29-32a), where illuminated historical, musical, and literary manuscripts and maps are displayed in glass cases. Also here is the large, firm signature of **Elizabeth I** as she signs the order sentencing her favorite, **Essex**, to death by beheading. On permanent display are 2 of the 4 surviving copies of the Magna Carta issued in 1215 by **King John**; the **Lindisfarne Gospels**, written and illuminated in 698; a **Gutenberg Bible**; and **Shakespeare's First Folio**.

The **British Library Reading Room**, with its domed ceiling and 30,000 reference books, is on view to visitors every hour on the hour from 11AM Monday through Friday. The library has been used by readers as diverse as **Karl Marx, Lenin, Gandhi, George Bernard Shaw**, and **Thomas Carlyle**, though the latter was so irked at the amount of time it took for him to receive his books that he went off in a pet and helped found the London Library. For a fee, there are daily guided tours, lasting 90 minutes, of the highlights of the British Museum collections. Free gallery talks Monday-Saturday at 11:30AM; lunchtime lectures, Monday-Saturday at 1:15PM.

The British Museum, which abuts **Montagu House**, occupies the site of the house built by the first **Duke of Montagu**, who, needing to repair a fortune sadly rent by the extravagances of erecting his mansion, set out to win

High Holborn

the hand of the extremely rich and quite mad second **Duchess of Albemarle**. The Duchess, who insisted that she would only marry a crowned head of state, happily offered her hand when the Duke convinced her that he was the Emperor of China. The ghost of the erstwhile Empress must roam happily through the museum's collection of Oriental antiquities, located in Rooms 33 and 34 on the ground floor and Rooms 90-94 on the upper floor.◆ M-Sa 10AM-5PM; Su 2:30-6PM. Coffeeshop M-Sa 10:30AM-4:15PM, Su 3-5:15PM. Great Russell St, WC1. 071/636.1555

47 Westaway and Westaway The largest and most affordable dealer in cashmere, lambswool, Shetlands, Arans, Icelandics, scarfs, blankets, hats, suits, and socks—anything warm in wool. The Scottish cashmeres, woven in Scotland from the wool of cashmere goats in China, are considerably less expensive than anywhere else in London, with a far wider choice than you are likely to find in Scotland. ◆ M-Sa 9AM-5:30PM. 62-65 Great Russell St, WC1. 071/405.4479. Also at: 92-93 Great Russell St. 071/636.1718

The attitude of the English toward English; history reminds one a great deal of the attitude of a Hollywood director toward love.

Margaret Halsey, *With Malice Toward Some*

Restaurants/Nightlife: Red
Shops/Parks: Green

Hotels: Blue
Sights/Culture: Black

47 L. Cornelissen An old-fashioned shop with old-fashioned and very special art supplies: cobalt blues, British and French gold leaf, L. Cornelissen's own brand of violin varnish (Dragon's Blood—a transparent red coloring from the Middle East), pure-squirrel mop brushes, and quill brushes. Within Cornelissen you will also find **His Nibs, Philip Poole**, sadly now moved from his beautiful shop in Drury Lane due to the rent increases. The white-haired Mr. Poole himself still runs his spectacular scribbler's emporium, which sells every make and age of fountain pen—many of them collected when *biros* (ballpoint pens) became fashionable, as he was convinced they were a fad that wouldn't last)—every kind of ink, as well as beautiful pencils, paper, and objects related to fine writing. ♦ M-F 9:30AM-5:30PM; Sa 9:30AM-5PM. 105 Great Russell St, WC1. 071/636.1045

 48 Russell Square London's second-largest square, lined with huge plane trees and houses once favored by lawyers and merchants. Readers of **Thackeray**'s *Vanity Fair* may recognize this as the home of the Sedleys and Osbornes. The square was laid out in 1800 by **Humphrey Repton** and named after the Russells, Dukes of Bedford, who owned the land. The elaborate statue of **Francis, 5th Duke of Bedford** (1809, **Sir Richard Westmacott**) shows the land-loving

High Holborn

Duke leaning on a plow and holding corn. Some of the original houses by **James Burton** remain, including Nos. 25-29, which now contain the **Institutes of Commonwealth Studies** and **Germanic Studies**, branches of the University of London. The great law reformer **Sir Samuel Romilly** lived and died by his own hand at No. 2. **Sir Thomas Lawrence** had his studio at No. 67 (later demolished) from 1805 until his death in 1830. Here he painted his series of portraits of princes, generals, and statesmen who helped bring about Napoleon's downfall; it now hangs in the Waterloo Chamber at Windsor Castle. ♦ WC1

49 Hotel Russell $$ This rambling Bloomsbury monument looks and feels like it should be attached to the Great Western Railway. It was built by **Charles Fitzroy Doll** in 1898, with the Victorian appetite for size combined with modesty. The stairway is grand; the 320 rooms are not. Still, there is a certain uncomplicated comfort and a loyal following. ♦ Russell Square, WC1. 071/837.6470; fax 071/837.2857

50 Dickens House A Victorian row house jammed with Dickensiana, made all the more amazing because it is one of 4 Dickens houses open to the public. (The others are outside London, although he did live and work at other London addresses.) This is where Dickens lived from 1837 to 1839 and, wrote the latter parts of the *Pickwick Papers*, all of *Oliver Twist* and *Nicholas Nickleby*, and

Dickens House
Doughty Street

the beginning of *Barnaby Rudge*. He also wrote some 550 letters here. It was in the sitting room that Dickens' 17-year-old sister-in-law, **Mary**, died in his arms, an emotional blow that he never got over. You can see the writer's desk, the china monkey he kept on it for good luck, and the family Bible, as well as portraits, illustrations, autographed letters, and other personal relics. The 1st-floor drawing room has been reconstructed to appear as it did in Dickens' time, as have the study and basement, which is a reproduction of the *Dingley Dell* kitchen. You can still feel the presence of London's greatest writer. ♦ Admission. M-Sa 9:30AM-5PM. 48 Doughty St, WC1. 071/405.2127

John Stokes
Lecturer and Writer

London for me means **Bloomsbury**, which is no longer what it was in Virginia Woolf's day. It's much more interesting now. Bloomsbury is the home of students, of people who've just got off the train at King's Cross or Euston, of every ethnic group, and even a few Londoners. It's an area where tourists often stay, but rarely linger, which is a pity, but then Bloomsbury is for people who know what they are looking for. It has real bookshops: **Bernard Stone** (Lamb's Conduit Street) has the best range of poetry in London (conveniently close to some of the best beer at **The Lamb & Flag**), and **Gay's the Word** (Marchmont St, conveniently close to **Alora**, an inspirational health-food shop) with the most helpful assistants. More books can be found at the Sunday morning bookfair at the **Russell Hotel**. Bloomsbury has one of the most serious fish-and-chip shops in London (Leigh Street), and one of the most dedicated jazz record shops in the world, **Mole Jazz** (Grays Inn Road, conveniently next-door to a tatooist) will dig out all those rare releases you can't find in New York and Los Angeles. What it lacks in style Bloomsbury makes up for in expertise.

Barbaralee Diamonstein
Writer, Television Interviewer, Producer, and the longest-term Commissioner of the New York City Landmark Preservation Commission

Reading Room and **Egyptian Gallery** at the **British Museum**.

Anything at **Claridge's**, including the bathrooms.

Liberty fabrics and foulards.

Swaine & Adeney umbrellas.

Gate entrance to the **Victoria and Albert Museum**.

Tearoom and food department at **Fortnum & Mason**.

Antique shops on **Bond Street**, from **Mallet** to **Partridge's** to **Christopher Gibbs**.

Superb ham and 200 varieties of excellent cheeses at **Paxton and Whitfield**.

Sac Freres, dealers in amber for more than 80 years.

F. Sangorski and **G. Sutcliffe**, the most famous bookbinders in England (a by-product of the Arts and Crafts Movement).

Culpeper Ltd., named after the 17th-century herbalist Nicholas Culpeper. Soups, dried herbs, herbal cosmetics, and medicine.

Jane-Howard Hammerstein
Writer

Thanksgiving dinner at the **Connaught**.

A pre-breakfast walk along **Knightsbridge** (cutting in and out of South Carriage Drive) in front of the barracks just as the Household Cavalry comes out to head for work. Evocative of nursery rhymes, real bravery, and empire, it reminds me of how much I wanted a horse.

Shopping at **Lunn Antiques** in Parsons Green. An addiction once you realize that you can deal with them so nicely on the phone, that they'll get things off to Connecticut in a flash. Their beautiful shams only fit their own wonderful pillows, anyway. They have the best large square pillow for reading that exists: hard as a rock, and larger than the average *continental*.

The **Prince of Wales**. While the whole notion of royalty can be thought silly (at best) or delusive (at nearly worst), he does seem to want so badly to matter. And, anyway, if you didn't have him and his family, there wouldn't be people living in the palaces. Think of Buckingham P without Her standard running up its pole, or Kensington P without children and papparazzi.

Dining on Chinese food at **Tiger Lee** on the Old Brompton Road. The food is delicious, the décor isn't so relentless or precious as to imply a visit to a Hong Kong Disneyland, the service is lovely, and the wines are good. And the restaurant is the right size for humans to occupy while eating and talking. And I believe it is open every day but Christmas.

The **Imperial War Museum**. Interesting and enlightening; it makes one profoundly aware that war doesn't work, that it has never been a valid answer to a valid question. Neither stodgy nor pedantic, it intrigues and—for lack of a better word—entertains. Grand place.

The **Bombay Brasserie** isn't hard-line Moghul cuisine, and in no way insinuates the Real India. But going there is fun and attractive.

Burlington Arcade. It thinks it's the way it used to be, so it almost convinces you it is. *Almost* is something.

Moving about the city, in a car and on foot, over a period of days (if not weeks or months or years) so that you get a sense of how the place is laid out, how it is tended and regarded by its inhabitants, how it lives with its history. There are more sad pockets now then there used to be—more ugliness to assail the eye, more blight to shake the spirit—for we (in this whole world) don't seem perfectly equipped to live up to the notion of City. But for all that, London still can show off its own history and its own sense of itself, and that's worth a long look around.

Gwyn Headley
President of the Folly Fellowship and Coauthor of *Follies*, published by Jonathan Cape

In England, follies mean bizarre architecture, not a floor show. Here are 10 of London's finest to gape at or gulp in:

Severndroog Castle, Castlewood Park, SE18. Way off the tourist track, one of the finest triangular folly towers in Britain. Georgian architecture at its best.

Albert Memorial, Kensington Gore, SW7. Built to commemorate Queen Victoria's husband, using materials of Biblical sonority—cornelian, jasper, agate—and now nearing a state of collapse.

Hampton Court House Grotto, Hampton Court. The most spectacular grotto in the London area, recently

superbly restored. Note it's at Hampton Court House, not the palace.

Pagoda, Kew Gardens. One hundred sixty-three feet high—10 stories—no access to visitors, but a stunning building in a glorious setting.

Elizabethan Tool Shed, Soho Square, W1. Right in the middle of Soho Square, this half-timbered tool shed looks totally out of context, a refugee from Shakespeare's Stratford.

Crocker's Folly, Aberdeen Place, NW8. A real gin palace of a pub, built as the terminus hotel for the London & Midland Railway. Frank Crocker watched in horror as the navvies dug relentlessly past his palace to end up at Marylebone, a mile and a half away.

Langford Place, NW8. A private house in chichi St. John's Wood. If Chas. Addams had become an architect, this is what he'd have built.

The Rotunda, Repository Road, SE18. Built as a permanent tent in St. James's Park by the famous architect John Nash to celebrate The Year of Peace, 1814—the year before Waterloo. So they moved it to Woolwich. Now a museum, but may soon become a restaurant.

Stoke Newington Pumping Station, Green Lanes, NR. Almost worth going to Manor House tube for. Half a mile down the road, past a mock-Tudor row of houses, looms this gigantic sham castle.

Leinster Gardens, W2. Notice anything strange about Nos. 22-24 in this elegant street? They don't exist; one brick thick, they are mere facades put up to hide the tube line and to preserve continuity.

Covent Garden, Soho & Marylebone

The whole of **Covent Garden** revolves around the **Piazza**, modeled on Italian lines by **Inigo Jones** in 1627. But of the original, only **St. Paul's Church** survives. By 1830 it was fashionable for the rich to mingle here with farmers and flower girls, and this is where **Shaw** got his inspiration for *Pygmalion*. Walking around the streets you will tread in the footsteps of **Dickens** and **Chippendale**, who made their names here and lived and worked in the area for many years. Once the haunt of the poor, today's affluent media folk (designers, ad execs, and PR people) are the reason that so many of the restaurants around here are so very good. This tiny area is also full of quaint streets with designer shops aimed mainly at well-heeled kids to 30-somethings looking for the unusual. It can be expensive, even for the most obscure European designer gear, and the shops do come and go with monotonous regularity. Shopping starts here around 10:30AM and goes on until 6 or 7PM. If you're a theater buff don't come on Monday, as the **Theatre Museum** is closed.

 Soho, to the west of Covent Garden, was once a royal park, though from Victoria's time onward, Soho meant squalor, slums, and, more recently, sex shops. In the last 10 years, however, the cheap rents have attracted a new clientele—filmmakers, music companies (whose employees hang out in London's answer to Tin Pan Alley—**Denmark Street**), and designers—who have, in turn, attracted a new wave of excellent fashionable restaurants and brasseries. Sit down at virtually any table in these parts and you'll find yourself staring at a TV producer and perhaps even a star or 2. *So-ho!*, incidentally, was an ancient hunting cry.

The sedate line and relaxed, almost feminine feel to **Marylebone**—a shortened version of the church name **St. Mary by the Bourne** (stream)—is no surprise, as it has frequently been owned and passed on by women. The English love of titles explains how this area northwest of Soho and Covent Garden could be named after just one woman and her husband. **Margaret Cavendish Harley**, daughter of **Henrietta** and **Edward Harley**, Earl of Oxford and Mortimer, inherited the land. She married **William Bentinck**, 2nd Duke of Portland and Titchfield and owner of the Wigmore, Wimpole, and Welbeck estates. Marylebone is now owned by **Viscount Portman** and the **De Walden** family, Margaret and William's descendents, who have left most of the architecture untouched for everyone to enjoy.

Restaurants/Nightlife: Red   Hotels: Blue
Shops/Parks: Green   **Sights/Culture:** Black

1 Theatre Royal Drury Lane The present theater is the fourth on the site since 1662; 2 were destroyed by fire and one was demolished. *What sir*, said owner Sheridan, as his life's work went up in flames, *may a man not warm his hands at his own fireside?* Few London theaters have so illustrious or lengthy a past as Drury Lane. **Nell Gwyn** made her debut in *Indian Queen* in 1665 with **King Charles II** in the audience. **King George II** was shot at in the theater in 1716, and his grandson **George III** was shot at here in 1800. One of Gainsborough's favorite models, **Mary Robinson**, was discovered here by the **Prince of Wales** while playing Perdita in *A Winter's Tale* in 1779, and this is where the **Duke of Clarence**, later William IV, first saw **Mrs. Jordan**, the Irish actress who became his mistress and mother of his children. Drury Lane was also the scene of riots over higher admission prices and impromptu duels that spilled from the pit onto the stage. Today, it is the safer home of musicals, most recently *Miss Saigon*, *A Chorus Line*, and *Sweeney Todd*. **Benjamin Wyatt** modeled the present theater after the great theater at Bordeaux in 1811. The portico was added in 1820 and the pillars came from Nash's quadrant on Regent St. The shabby interior is a patchwork of styles. (See page 177 for seating plan.) ◆ Seats 2245. Catherine St, WC2. 071/836.8108

2 Luigi's ★★$$ After the show, this becomes a crowded Italian bistro full of actors and singers whose signed photographs line the wall. The atmosphere is lively, the food is authentic and mostly very good, especially the cannelloni. Booking for the late evening is essential. ◆ M-Sa 12:15-3PM, 5:45-11:30PM. 15 Tavistock St, WC2. 071/240.1795

2 Café du Jardin ★★★$$ A well-loved, busy, and unpretentious restaurant that serves simple but delicious French food. Try the English lamb with garlic sauce or steamed halibut with fish sauce. The cheese board includes the best of France and the pretheater supper (5-8PM) is the best value in the area. ◆ M-F noon-2:30PM, 5:30-11:30PM; Sa 5:30-11:30PM. 25 Wellington St, WC2. 071/836.8796

2 Taste of India ★★$$ Good-quality eating, cheap lunches, and a Sunday buffet. You'll find Indian snacks downstairs in the **Jewel in the Ground** wine bar. ◆ M-Sa noon-2:30PM, 5:30-midnight; Su 5:30-11:30PM. 25 Catherine St, WC2. 071/836.2538

3 Parker Brown's Beautifully designed women's clothes, party dresses, and evening wear for sale or rent. If you ring for an appointment they'll arrange to spend one hour with you while you choose your outfit. ◆ M-W, F-Sa 10:30AM-7PM; Th 10:30AM-8PM. 34 Tavistock St, WC2. 071/836.7436

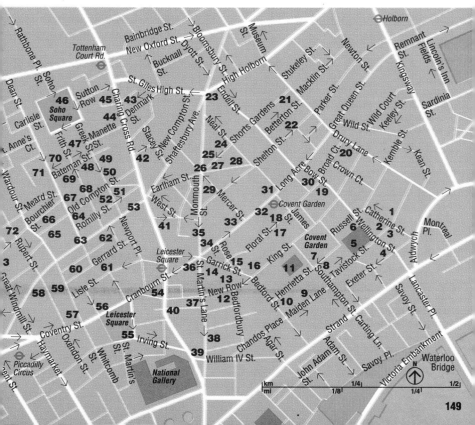

4 Joe Allen ★★★$$ Hidden behind an un-marked door; watch other diners suddenly dip out of sight then follow them in. This is London's favorite American restaurant, and the famous come here to spot and be spotted. Big burgers and salads, friendly staff (who actually act as if they are in America), good cocktails, and an extensive blackboard of unchanging favorites like chili. It's popular, so book ahead. ◆ M-Sa noon-1AM; Su noon-midnight. 13 Exeter St, WC2. 071/836.0651

5 London Transport Museum Outside it looks tiny, but inside you'll find old-fashioned buses, trams, trolley buses, and trains demonstrating how London's transport system works both above and below ground. Londoners will add that some of the exhibits are still in use on the Northern Line. (Outside are a set of public toilets that aren't as busy as those by St. Paul's Church). ◆ Daily 10AM-6PM. 39 Wellington St. 071/379.6344

6 Penhaligons Princess Di was recently spotted in this shop buying perfume. Who can blame her? Straight from the world of *Brideshead Revisited*, this darling perfume shop is filled with silver mirrors and dressing table treasures. The bottles are exclusive and as beautiful as the scents; you won't find them elsewhere. Bluebell is divine. ◆ M-F 10AM-6PM; Sa 10AM-5:30PM. 41 Wellington St, WC2. 071/836.2150

6 Orso ★★★$$ Much beloved by those in the know, this flourishing first-class Italian restaurant is a haven for good food and attentive service. The food is flown in fresh from Italy and

Covent Garden, Soho & Marylebone

varies from the extravagant to the homey, with some excellent Italian wines to boot. ◆ Daily noon-midnight. 27 Wellington St, WC2. 071/240.5269

6 Theatre Museum A 20-foot-high golden statue of *Gaiety* dominates the ground floor and gives a hint of what's to come. Here Britain proudly displays her theater collections, and the history of her stage from Shakespeare to now with regularly changing performing arts exhibitions. You can see theater, ballet, circus, music hall, opera, mime, puppetry,

rock, and pop. There's a tiny shop selling posters, postcards, and theater gifts and a tiny theater with regular shows. You can book tickets for the Barbican, West End shows, concerts, and the National Theatre. ◆ Tu-Su 11AM-7PM. 1e Tavistock St. 071/836.2330/1891, information 071/836.7624

Within the Theatre Museum:

Theatre Cafe ★★$ Theatrical types will feel at home here as the waiters are *resting* actors. It's full of theater machinery, like an ancient lighting console. Office workers come here at lunch because it's calmer and less crowded than the wine bar crush outside. So get here early for a quiet, relaxing, simple, and cheap meal of open sandwiches or salads; or in the afternoon try the teatime delectables like scones, cream, and jam. ◆ Tu-Su noon-7:30PM

7 Covent Garden Market Immortalized by **George Bernard Shaw**'s *Pygmalion* and the cockney flower girl Eliza Doolittle, who sold violets to rich operagoers here. Today the market has more in common with the luxury tastes of Henry Higgins than with the cockney vendors who can carry a tune. A brilliant example of urban survival, the restored central market is a tantalizing structure of iron-and-glass roofs covering a large square (1830, **Charles Fowler**). It was built because the market was full to bursting, but eventually the merchants had to leave and move to even bigger premises south in Vauxhall. Its revitalization has dramatically improved this part of London, providing shops, restaurants, cafés, and pubs. At the same time, it has freed the area of the wholesale fruit and flower market that, for all its sentimental charm, clogged this part of London mercilessly. Although the shops in the piazza are mainly boutique-size branches of existing chain stores, the surrounding shops are often one-offs (merchandise that is sold in one shop only, for a limited period). There is an antique market within the piazza on Monday, a crafts market Tuesday through Saturday, and a permanent fairground.

Within Covent Garden Market:

Opera Terrace ★★$$ Gazing out across the piazza is this glorious glass restaurant and café, a lovely escape from the crowds in spring and summer. There's a pianist in the restaurant, and during the evening opera music plays in the terrace bar. Great for the health conscious, as there's no high-cholesterol food on the menu. Try the steamed fingers of turbot and crayfish. For a formal meal try the restaurant, for lighter lunches and suppers go to the café. ◆ M-F noon-3PM, 6-11:30PM; Sa noon-3PM (café), 6-11:30PM (restaurant), Su noon-11:30PM, Apr-Sep; noon-7PM, Oct-Mar. 45 E. Terrace. 071/379.0666

Culpeper Mrs. C.F. Leyelfounded the **Herb Society** and Culpeper back in 1927, naming it after **Nicholas Culpeper**, an herbalist from 1616-1652. The products are natural and not tested on animals. ◆ M-Sa 10AM-8PM. No. 8. 071/379.6698

Puffin Bookshop Puffin is the children's imprint of **Penguin Books**, and there's everything here that you would expect from the publisher whose aim in life was to sell good-quality literature at a price anyone could afford. ♦ M-Sa 10AM-8PM. Unit 1. 071/379.6465

Penguin Bookshop Hard to resist—just avoid lunchtime, when it's packed to bursting. ♦ M-Sa 10AM-8PM; Su noon-6PM. Unit 10. 071/379.7650

Edwina Carroll Unique clothes in a unique shop specializing in collector's quality and hand-knit sweaters. ♦ M-Sa 10AM-6PM. Unit 16. 071/836.9873

Trivia Eccentric vases, flowers, clocks, and china. ♦ M-Sa 10AM-7PM. Unit 19. 071/379.7675

Crusting Pipe ★★$$ Candlelight, sawdust floor, and a limited menu. Treat yourself to the smoked salmon and salad or, if you are really hungry, the game pie and potatoes. Excellent English cheese and good wines. ♦ M-Sa 11:30AM-11PM. Unit 27. 071/836.1415

Doll's House The kind of dolls you dream about and see in Kate Greenwood books. Some look like museum pieces and some are. ♦ M-Sa 10AM-8PM. Unit 29. 071/379.7243

The Cabaret Mechanical Theatre Full of old toys and fascinating cardboard toy theaters. Also some pricey antique toys. ♦ M-Sa 10AM-7PM. Unit 33. 071/379.7866

Café Deli $ Pastrami sandwiches served under the beautiful wrought-iron canopy in the piazza. Light and inexpensive. Don't expect too much. ♦ Daily 9AM-7:15PM. Unit 5

Creperie ★$ Sweet and savory pancakes served at tables on the cobblestones around St. Paul's. ♦ Daily 10AM-11:30PM. Unit 21. 071/836.2137

Museum Store A bizarre collection of the best items from museum shops across the world. The Sissinghurst watering can sits next to an Egyptian cat from the British Museum and Charles Renee Mackintosh cards and prints. ♦ Unit 37. 071/240.5760

Cranks ★$ Reliable and popular chain specializing in vegetarian cooking with the best ingredients. Saintliness started with Cranks in the '60s and continues on today. There's a restaurant, takeout, and health-food shop here. ♦ M-Sa 10AM-8PM; Su 10AM-6PM. Unit 11. 071/379.6508

8 Jubilee Market One hundred eighty stalls where you can find homemade silk lingerie for a fraction of the price you would pay in a regular shop, hand-knit sweaters, pottery, hand-carved wooden salad bowls, etc. Poke around and the cream will rise to the top. The prices seem particularly good after shopping at the smart boutiques in the area. There are even a few fruit and vegetable stalls for old time's sake. ♦ Antiques: M 9AM-5PM. General: Tu-Sa 9AM-5PM

9 Rules ★★$$$ Nearly 200 years old, Rules is a museum of London's literary and theatrical beau monde, many of whom still come here today. The **Prince of Wales**, later Edward VII, and **Lillie Langtry** drank champagne behind a special door on the 1st floor and **Dickens** had a regular table across the room. Today the walls are covered with paintings, prints, and playbills. Rules is a compulsory stop for visitors to London. The secret to a good meal is selective ordering. Stick to very English dishes like Scotch beef with Yorkshire pudding, pheasant and grouse in season, and the weekday specials. ♦ M-Sa noon-midnight. 35 Maiden Ln, WC2. 071/836.5314

10 Porters ★★$$ Owned by **Richard**, the 7th Earl of Bradford, this deservedly successful restaurant is vast inside and serves high-quality, traditional English fare—pies, sausages, and delicious nursery puddings like jam *roly-poly* and sherry trifle. Honest prices, and fun for babies and toddlers, too. ♦ M-F noon-3PM, 5:30-11:30PM; Sa noon-11:30PM; Su noon-10:30PM. 17 Henrietta St, WC2. 071/836.6466

10 Boulestin ★★$$$ This restaurant is like an old gents' club gone strangely wrong. The pictures of cattle are painted in the George Stubbs style, but with huge bodies and tiny heads. The food is highly praised by **Egon Ronay**, as is the wine cellar, particularly the burgundies. Lunch is a good value. Try the rack of lamb with rosemary. ♦ M-F 12:30-2:30PM, 7:30-11:15PM; Sa 7:30-11:15PM. 1a Henrietta St, WC2. 071/836.7061

11 St. Paul's Covent Garden (1633, **Inigo Jones**) When the thrifty 4th Earl of Bedford was developing Covent Garden he asked Inigo Jones to design an economical church not much bigger than a barn. Jones complied, creating what he called the handsomest barn in Europe. The red-brick church with pitched roof, overhanging eaves, and the famous Tuscan portico was the setting for the opening scene in **Shaw**'s *Pygmalion*; it is now used by the daring street theater companies who shine in the summer. It was gutted by fire in 1795 and carefully restored by **Philip Hardwick**. Known as the actor's church because of its close association with the theater, there are numerous plaques inside commemorating actors, actresses, and playwrights. ♦ The Piazza, Covent Garden, WC2

In **St. Paul's Church, Claude Duval**, a highwayman hanged at Tyburn is buried.
Here lies Du Vall: Reader, if male thou art
Look to thy purse; if female to thy heart.

London! It has the sound of distant thunder.
James Bone, London Perambulator

12 Naturally British Hard-to-resist creations by British designers and craftspeople, including clothes, furniture, pottery, table linens, pewter, baskets, toys, and food. If you are looking for presents not to be found in department stores, this shop is a gold mine. ♦ M-Sa 10:30AM-7PM. 13 New Row, WC2. 071/240.0551

13 White Swan This rambling old Queen Anne pub is run by **Mr.** and **Mrs. England** (everybody's mum) and a staff that has been here for years. So have the regulars—local ad men, designers, and animators use it as a second office, and are all experts on local history. Draught Bass washes down the sandwiches. It gets very busy. ♦ M-Sa 11AM-11PM. 14 New Row. 071/836.8291

13 Scottish Merchant Every sweater in this shop is knit by hand in the Scottish Islands. There are fabulous one-offs, and the shop's design and the sweaters have been copied by every knitting shop across the British Isles, but without the quality. ♦ M-W, F 10:30AM-6:30PM; Th 10:30AM-7PM; Sa 10:30AM-5:30PM. 16 New Row, WC2. 071/836.2207

14 Garrick Club (1864, **Frederick Marrable**) **Dickens, Trollope, Millais,** and **Rossetti** met actors and *men of education and refinement* sitting in this gloriously ornate gentlemen's club. The walls are lined with portraits of famous actors and actresses from the British stage. Today's armchairs still hold writers—is that **Kingsley Amis** walking up the stairs over there? ♦ 15 Garrick St, WC2

15 Lamb & Flag (1623) The cobbled courtyard of this lovely pub is always full of office workers, who love its ancient charm. It wasn't always so nice; it used to be called the *Bucket of Blood* because local fighters came here. The poet **John Dryden** was beaten up near here in 1679 for writing nasty things about the Duchess of Portsmouth, Charles II's mistress. ♦ M-F 11AM-11PM; Sa-Su 7-11PM. 33 Rose St, WC2. 071/497.9504

15 Grimes ★★$$ Offbeat and modest cold-fish brasserie with some excellent seafood dishes. Try the mixed-seafood salad with walnut-and-fennel dressing, or the large *moules mariniére*. The specials reflect Billingsgate's offerings and shouldn't be missed. ♦ M-F noon-3PM, 5:30-11PM; Sa 5:30-11PM. 6 Garrick St, WC2. 071/836.7008

An Englishman is never so natural as when he is holding his tongue.

Henry James, *The Portrait of a Lady*

16 Palms Pasta on the Piazza ★★$$ Light, airy, and vastly superior to the pasta restaurants proliferating all over London. Everything is fresh and delicious. Start with the *bagna cauda* (raw vegetables served with a warm anchovy-and-walnut sauce). They don't take bookings, so get here early or after 2PM. ♦ M-Sa noon-11:30PM. 39 King St, WC2. 071/240.2939

16 Calabash ★★$$ Exotic and delicious African food in a laid-back atmosphere—distinctly appealing after the fashionable race of Covent Garden. Masks, headdresses, and batik cloths decorate walls and tables. Ghanaian ground-nut stew, Tanzanian beef stew with green bananas and coconut cream, and excellent Moroccan and Algerian wines. ♦ M-F 12:30-2:15PM, 6:30-10:30PM; Sa 6:30-10:30PM. 38 King St, WC2. 071/836.1976

16 Moss Bros. Hackett England's gentry held their breath when Moss Bros. closed its flagship store. Luckily, it only moved across the street to a space with a higher ceiling and thicker carpets and top designer labels. The rentals department, much beloved by Ascot and the charity ball set, bridegrooms and best men, still remains. ♦ M-Sa 10:30AM-6:30PM. 27 King St, WC2. 071/497.9354

17 Sanctuary One of the few drawbacks to traveling is the feeling that you are getting increasingly lumpish and unhealthy from the extra meals and lack of exercise. Some dedicated travelers continue to jog or swim, but for a woman in London, the Sanctuary is one of the most idyllic and essential indulgences. She can restore her spirits and health in the sauna, Turkish steam room, swimming pool, Jacuzzi, and sun bed. Shampoo, conditioner, towels, soap, body lotion, and cologne are provided free of charge. Indulge further with top-to-toe beauty treatments, including a massage, a facial, and a healthy lunch in the food bar. ♦ M-F 10AM-10PM; Sa 10AM-6PM; Su noon-8PM. 11 Floral St, WC2. 071/240.9635

18 Plumline Men's and women's highly individual shoes that you won't find anywhere else—classy, but not wild. A real find. Opposite is **Georgio Ferrari**, selling chic Italian designer shoes. ♦ M-F 10:30AM-6:30PM; Sa 10AM-6PM. 40 Floral St, WC2. 071/379.7856

18 Paul Smith This designer creates some of the best men's fashion clothing in town—eclectic waistcoats, the latest in accessories, sportswear, stylish suits, old-fashioned men's cardigans like Dad used to wear, superb shoes. Try lurking around until sale time, when the clothes become affordable. ♦ M-W, F 10:30AM-6:30PM; Th 10:30AM-7PM; Sa 10AM-6:30PM. 41-44 Floral St, WC2. 071/379.7133

18 Patricia Roberts Beware of the simple patterns here because they aren't. Mind-numbingly complicated patterns for expert knitters, or delightful hand-knitted sweaters from the doyenne of *tricoteuses*. The sweaters will set you back the price of a plane ticket. ♦ M-Sa 10:30AM-7PM. 31 James St, WC2. 071/379.6660

19 Bow Street Look again, this street really is bow shaped. Covent Garden's café society reads like a Who's Who of English history and literature. But most of it happened in just 2 spots—the **Garrick Club** and in Bow Street's **Will's Coffee House**, where you could expect to meet **Pepys, Dryden, Pope, Swift, Johnson, Boswell** and **Sheridan** or **Henry Fielding**, though not all together! When things got too unruly in the area (which was poor and dangerous by the late 18th century), Henry Fielding, the barrister and novelist, set up the forerunners of today's police force to catch thieves—they were called the *Bow Street Runners*. Today in **Bow Street Magistrates Court**, it's not thieves but illegal aliens who are put on trial.

19 Royal Opera House Three different theaters have stood on this site since 1732. The great dome and regal red, gold, and cream auditorium you see today is **Sir Edward Barry**'s 1858 design. The frieze, *Tragedy and Comedy* by **Flaxman**, under the portico was salvaged from a fire at the theater on the site in 1855. In 1946, Covent Garden became the national home of the Royal Opera and Ballet companies. Some of the great names who have played here are **Patti, Nellie Melba, Caruso, Gobbi**, and **Maria Callas**. The opera and ballet companies will be forced to move for 5 years while the site is being redeveloped. (See page 177 for seating plan.) ♦ Seats 2154. Bow St, WC2. Box Office 071/240.1066, 24-hr recorded information 071/240.1911

20 Fielding $$ A rare hotel in London: small, inexpensive, quiet, and family-fun. It attracts performers from the Royal Opera House, a stone's throw away, and celebrities like **Graham Greene**, who are drawn by the discreet charm and perfect location. The rooms are pretty modest—most have showers instead of baths—but the pedestrian street below spares you from the sounds of cars at night. Ideal if you are a music-lover or theatergoer. The hotel is named after **Henry Fielding**, the author of *Tom Jones* and a magistrate at Bow Street Court nearby. ♦ 4 Broad Ct. WC2. 071/836.8305

21 G Force Aggressive designer gear. That means you'll walk out equipped for the building site in heavy-duty, hard-wearing clothes with lots of stitching. ♦ M-Sa 11AM-6:30PM. 6 Shorts Gardens, WC2. 071/240.1048

*But English gratitude is always such,
To hate the hand which doth oblige too much.*

Daniel Defoe, *The True Born Englishman*

22 Ajimura ★★$$ Japanese food in London can be very expensive, but the Ajimura has kept its prices reasonable—hence the crowds. A versatile and relaxed restaurant that prepares sashimi, sushi, tempura, sukiyaki, *shabu-shabu*, and an endless variety of set meals and menu specials. Try the beef teriyaki. Book for supper. ♦ M-F noon-3PM, 6-11PM; Sa 6-11PM; Su 6-10:30PM. 51-53 Shelton St, WC2. 071/240.9424

23 Arthur Beale A yacht chandler who can trace his origins back to a company of ropemakers on the Fleet River at the start of the 16th century. Dream of the sea as you look at the bright-yellow macs and boots. ♦ M-F 9AM-6PM; Sa 9:30AM-1PM. 194 Shaftesbury Ave, WC2. 071/836.9034

24 Neal's Yard A quaint little courtyard jammed with tiny shops specializing in top-quality food popular with health nuts. There's even an apothecary selling herbal medicines quaintly packaged in old-fashioned blue-glass jars and bottles.

Within Neal's Yard:

Neal's Yard Dairy It's like walking into an edible map of England—Caerphilly, Wensleydale, Red Leicester, Sage Derby—all their own names and all from those parts of the country. Everything is British here, from the blue sheep's cheeses to the little round goat cheeses and the glorious well-matured cheddars. Move over France, the British cheesemakers are coming. ♦ M-W, Sa 9:30AM-5:30PM; Th-F 9:30AM-6PM. 071/379.7646

Covent Garden, Soho & Marylebone

Neal's Yard Bakery Co-operative A snack shop for the health conscious—quiches and salads can be eaten on the premises while the **Farm Shop** sells the only organic vegetable juice in London as well as Indian vegetarian curries to take home. ♦ M-Tu, Th-F 10:30AM-7:30PM; W 10:30AM-5PM; Sa 10:30AM-4:30PM. 071/836.5199

24 Sheep Shop Soay fleeces and naturally dyed wools for the die-hard knitter; spinning wheels for the truly dedicated! ♦ M-Sa 10AM-6PM. 54 Neal St, WC2. 071/836.4094

24 The Hat Shop A brilliant place to buy hats, and if it's too full they'll keep you outside while inside, everything from flying hats and straw boaters to picture hats pirouette and pout before the mirrors. ♦ M-Th 10AM-6PM; F 10AM-7PM; Sa 10:30AM-5:30PM. 58 Neal St, WC2. 071/836.6718

24 Natural Leather Bags, blousons, biker jackets, and leather accessories fill this shop to overflowing. Watch out for pigskin rucksacks and Alan Ladd-style trenchcoats. ♦ M-Sa 11AM-7PM; Su noon-6PM. 62 Neal St, WC2. 071/240.7748

Restaurants/Nightlife: Red	**Hotels:** Blue
Shops/Parks: Green	**Sights/Culture:** Black

24 Sam Fisher Men's wear shop packed with traditional English clothes like Aran sweaters and cashmere jackets at competitive prices. ♦ M-Sa 11AM-7PM. 76 Neal St, WC2. 071/836.2576

25 Mon Plaisir ★★$$ An authentic French brasserie and pretheater haunt, with good food and service to match. Get ready for French food the way you expect it, but better—garlic-laden frogs' legs, coq au vin, and escargots. ♦ M-F noon-2:15PM, 6-11:15PM; Sa 6-11:15PM. 21 Monmouth St, WC2. 071/836.7243

25 Monmouth Coffee House You can grab a cup of delicious fresh- ground coffee here and read the morning papers, or buy some to take away at very good prices. Monmouth keeps a limited range of top-quality coffees like Columbian Medelin, Kenyan, and Papua New Guinea mild. ♦ M-F 9:30AM-6:30PM; Sa 9:30AM-6PM. 27 Monmouth St, WC2. 071/836.5272

25 Ballabio Design Beautiful Italian elegance captured in a shoe. ♦ M-F 11AM-7PM; Sa 10AM-7PM. 29 Monmouth St, WC2. 071/836.0083

26 Seven Dials A tall column stood in the center here with sundials, each facing one street. Hence the name. As it was built by **Thomas Neale**, the Master of the Mint (where British coins are struck), a legend grew up that treasure was buried at the bottom of the column. It was dug up in 1773, but there was nothing there. The pillar went to Weybridge in Surrey, and it took until 1989 for some locals to band together to pay for a new Seven Dials to go in its place.

Covent Garden, Soho & Marylebone

Where famed St. Giles' ancient limits spread,
An inrailed column rears its lofty head;
Here to seven streets,
Seven dials count the day,
And from each other catch the circling ray.

26 Mountbatten Theater lovers flock to this hotel, named after **Lord Louis Mountbatten** of Burma, the much-beloved uncle of Prince Charles. It could almost be Broadlands, the family seat, because the Edwardian-style hotel is so full of Mountbatten's memorabilia, comfy sofas, chandeliers, and marble. ♦ 20 Monmouth St, Seven Dials, WC2. 071/836.4300; fax 071/240.3540

27 Joan Chatterley's Knitwear High-quality handmade knitwear, men's wear, and luggage. ♦ M-Sa 10AM-6:30PM. 38 Shorts Gardens, WC2. 071/379.5473

28 Smiths ★★★$$ The main restaurant is in the basement and is wonderful. The white walls are covered with fabulous highly colored modern art (for sale); the dark furniture is strewn with cushions in autumnal colors. The food is great, too; try the swordfish steak with tarragon mayonnaise and beurre blanc. Book ahead. ♦ M-F noon-11:45PM; Sa 6-11:45PM. 28 Neal St, WC2. 071/379.0310

28 Neal St. Restaurant Owned by **Sir Terence Conran** and managed by his brother-in-law **Antonio Carluccio**. Design is the thing here. Feast your eyes on Bauhaus chairs and menus designed by **David Hockney**. Try the *brandelli* of pasta with morel sauce or *taglioni* with wild mushrooms. ♦ M-F 12:30-2:30PM, 7-11:30PM. 26 Neal St, WC2. 071/836.8368

28 Head over Heels Up-and-coming Italian designer clothes and a helpful staff. ♦ M-F 11AM-7PM; Sa 10AM-6:30PM. ♦ 27 Neal St, WC2. 071/240.7737

29 Sheer Decadence Extravagant costume jewelry beckons customers from big glass cases. ♦ M-Sa 10:30AM-7:30PM. 44 Monmouth St, WC2. 071/379.4161

29 Dorin Frankfurt The black-and-white tiles and mirrors clash strangely with the feminine designer dresses. ♦ M-Sa 11AM-7PM. 46 Monmouth St, WC2. 071/836.4925

29 Dar & Dar The latest European designer labels aren't cheap, but they *are* wild. Well, rubber does keep Londoners dry. ♦ M-Sa 11AM-7PM. 53 Monmouth St, WC2. 071/240.7577

30 Café des Amis du Vin ★★$ Continental-style restaurant and wine bar. Upstairs is intimate and hushed, with formal lunches and good food; the ground floor is squashed together tables and a lot of noise; downstairs is *vrai parisienne*, with great atmosphere, lots of media folk, wine drinkers, and French snack eaters. It's vital to book. You must arrive very early to get a table downstairs. ♦ M-Sa noon-5PM, 6-11:30PM. 11-14 Hanover Pl, WC2. 071/379.3444

31 The Tea House If you like London policemen, you can buy one here and he will pour your tea forever. The shop is packed with eccentric and absurd teapots and over 40 teas, from jasmine to spiced Christmas teas, and decaffeinated teas and coffee. ♦ M-Sa 10AM-7PM. 15a Neal St, WC2. 071/240.7539

32 Blazer The British version of preppie clothes at reasonable prices. ♦ M-W, F-Sa 10AM-6:30PM; Th 10AM-8PM. 36 Long Acre, WC2. 071/379.6258

32 Frere Jacques ★★$$ The tiled floors and walls make you feel like you are in the south of France. The burgandies are good and the *fruit de mer* delectable. ♦ M-Sa noon-3PM, 6-11:30PM; Su 7-10:30PM. 38 Long Acre, WC2. 071/836.7823

32 Magno's Brasserie ★★$$ Not a brasserie at all, but a popular, well-run restaurant that boasts a highly original menu and a legion of faithful followers—media folk and theater buffs. The cooking can be uneven. There's a spectacular wine list, a set menu at lunch, and a highly recommended pretheater menu served between 6-7:30PM. ♦ M-F noon-2:30PM, 6-11:30PM; Sa 6-11:30PM. 65a Long Acre, WC2. 071/836.6077

London, a nation, not a city.
Benjamin Disraeli

32 Long Acre Once the medieval market garden (a place where people grew crops like potatoes or apples) of Westminster Abbey's monks, this street became the center of furniture-making by the middle of the 18th century. It's easy to imagine Chippendale walking from his home in St. Martin's Lane to start work each day in his Long Acre workshop.

33 Sabre High-quality Italian-style men's knitwear in beautiful colors, and not too expensive. ◆ M-W, F 11AM-7PM; Th 11AM-8PM; Sa 10AM-6PM. 120 Long Acre, WC2. 071/240.6897

34 Edward Stanford The largest collection of maps, guides, charts, atlases, and travel books in the world. **David Livingstone** had his maps drawn here, and that big chap over there is probably a mountain climber who's made a special trip here. ◆ M-W, F 10AM-6PM; Th 9AM-7PM. 12-14 Long Acre, WC2. 071/836.1321

35 St. Martin's Lane The furniture builder **Thomas Chippendale** may have lived here, but that didn't stop the city from knocking down the buildings to make way for Trafalgar Square. Unfortunately, they didn't renumber the street, so it starts at number 29!

36 Beotys ★★$$ An old Covent Garden favorite and one of the oldest Greek restaurants in town (it opened the year World War II ended). Charming, competent waiters, delicious *dolmades*, and succulent lamb. ◆ Daily noon-2:15PM, 5:30-11:30PM. St. Martin's Ln, WC2. 071/836.8768

36 New Shu Shan Divine ★★$$ You'll like this place if you crave hot Szechuan cooking. The fish in black-bean sauce is worth trying. ◆ 36 Cranbourn St, WC2. 071/836.7501

37 Sheekeys ★★★$$$ One of London's oldest and best-loved fish restaurants, tucked away on St. Martin's Court alongside Wyndham's and Albery theaters. Immaculate lobster, salmon, turbot, Dover sole—you name it, they serve it, even the humble fish cake tastes dreamlike here. Have a dozen oysters with a bottle of house wine or a full meal at the long oyster bar. ◆ M-F 12:30-2PM, 6-11:15PM; Sa 5:30-11:30PM. 28-32 St. Martin's Ln, WC2. 071/240.2565

38 Giovanni's ★★$$ A good old-fashioned Italian restaurant full of pictures of the West End stars who pop across the road to eat here after the show. Giovanni and the staff have been here for years. ◆ M-F 12:30-2:30PM, 6:30-11PM; Sa 6:30-11PM. 10 Goodwin's Ct, 55 St. Martin's Ln, WC2. 071/240.2877

38 London Coliseum Home of the English National Opera, which sings in English, only. A very splendid interior, complete with chariots and granite columns and 20 boxes. The globe on top was designed to move, but as this is illegal, the flashing lights are the next best thing. ◆ Seats 2358. St. Martin's Ln, WC2. 071/836.6131

Who now reads Bolingbroke? Who ever read him through? Ask the booksellers of London what is become of all these lights of the world.

Edmund Burke

38 Café Pelican ★★$$ A nice place serving good food, but it's expensive unless you stick to the brasserie menu. It keeps late hours, and if you do, too, you'll find yourself in the company of the actors and musicians working in the West End. You can have anything from *café complet* to sea trout in seaweed served with beurre blanc. ◆ Daily 11AM-12:30AM. 45 St. Martin's Ln, WC2. 071/379.0309

39 Droopy & Browns This fashionable wedding, ball gown, and party dress designer set up shop here recently. Opera and balletgoers smile knowingly at the window displays of next week's outfit. Lace, velvet, satin, silk—bliss at a price. ◆ M-W 10:30AM-6:30PM; Th 10:30AM-7:30PM; F 10:30AM-7PM; Sa 9:30AM-5:30PM. 99 St. Martin's Ln, WC2. 071/379.4514

Another street created as part of the massive slum clearance in Victoria's day, **Charing Cross Road** has been known for its antiquarian and secondhand bookshops for nearly a century. Dedicated bibliophiles may peruse the quaint pedestrian walkway

Covent Garden, Soho & Marylebone

of **Cecil Court** and **Bertram Rota** in Covent Garden during the work week, only; these old-fashioned antiquarian stores don't open to the sticky hands of the *hoi polloi* on weekends.

40 Pleasures of Past Times Showtime is captured forever in the books sold here for theater and ballet lovers, or you can buy printed Victoriana—the greeting cards are a real find. Nearby is the gracious **Dance Books** (836.2314). ◆ M-F 11AM-2:30PM, 3:30-5:45PM; 1st Sa of the month 11AM-2:15PM. 11 Cecil Ct, WC2. 071/836.1142

40 Bell, Book and Radmall Expensive first editions in locked glass cabinets tended by a knowledgeable staff—for the dedicated bibliophile, only. ◆ M-F 10AM-5:30PM. 4 Cecil Ct, WC2. 071/240.2161

40 Quinto and Francis Edwards Bookshop Look at the glorious leather-bound first editions and antiquarian books here, or gaze in awe at the old military maps and prints. There's every kind of secondhand book, too. ◆ M-Sa 9AM-10PM; Su noon-8PM. 48a Charing Cross Rd, WC2. 071/379.7669

Restaurants/Nightlife: Red   Hotels: Blue
Shops/Parks: Green   Sights/Culture: Black

40 Books of Charing Cross Road It's a wonder the floors don't give there are so many ancient books crammed into every conceivable cranny. There's a super-cheap bargain basement where you'll pay pennies (40p!) for a book. And a vast selection on the ground floor, where you can wax lyrical over the poetry and history or get hot under the collar in the political section. ♦ Daily 10:30AM-7:30PM. 56 Charing Cross Rd, WC2. 071/836.3697

41 Shipley Specialist Art Booksellers The helpful and knowledgeable staff will help you find any book on fine art and the working arts like design, graphics, and fashion. ♦ M-Sa 10AM-6PM. 70 Charing Cross Rd, WC2. 071/836.4872

41 Zwemmers Picasso, Mondrian, Warhol, Gainsborough—the art historian's bookshop selling the most fabulous, opulent art books; students at the nearby St. Martin's School can only gaze and start saving. ♦ M-Sa 9:30AM-6:30PM. 26 Litchfield St, WC2. 071/379.7886

42 No. 84 Charing Cross Road When **Helene Hanff** began writing letters here in 1945, this was the site of **Marks & Co's** bookshop. When the letters became a film, the bookshop disappeared!

43 Murder One With crime fiction and whodunnits in such profusion here, it's a relief to see Sherlock Holmes standing at the back of the store to reassure us that detectives really do know how to solve even the worst crimes that man thinks up. ♦ M-W, F-Sa 10AM-6PM; Th 10AM-7PM. 23 Denmark St, WC2. 071/497.2200

Covent Garden, Soho & Marylebone

44 W & G Foyle **Walt Disney** and **George Bernard Shaw** were just 2 of the illustrious customers of this British institution. It's crammed floor to ceiling with books, but they can be hard to find and the assistants aren't always knowledgeable. Don't knock it, though, the British defend this oddity to the hilt. ♦ M-F 9AM-6PM; Sa 9AM-5PM. 119 Charing Cross Rd, WC2. 071/437.5660

44 Waterstones Packed with all the latest books, and they're easy to find. ♦ M-F 9AM-6PM; Sa 9AM-5PM. 121-125 Charing Cross Rd, WC2. 071/434.4291

45 Break for the Border ★$ Mexicana comes to London. *Caramba!* If you suddenly long for some guacamole or chili, this is the place. It's loud, young, and packed. ♦ M-Sa 5:30-11:45PM; Su 5:30-10:45PM. 125 Charing Cross Rd, WC2. 071/437.8595

46 Soho Square Built in honor of **Charles II**; that's his statue in the center. The Elizabethan hut in the middle is actually a folly tool shed built in 1870. Look out for **Paul McCartney**, who occasionally visits his offices in the square.

47 L'Escargot ★★$$ London's adland comes here to gossip in public, and be overheard. ♦ M-F noon-3PM, 5:30-11:15PM; Sa 6-11:15PM. 48 Greek St, W1. 071/437.2697

47 The Gay Hussar ★★$$ Well-known politicians dive in here to gossip in private, and be seen. Try the goulash or roast duckling. ♦ M-Sa 12:30-2:30PM, 5:30-11PM. 2 Greek St, W1. Reservations required. 071/437.0973

47 Au Jardin des Gourmets ★★$$$ Ad people and politicians come here when they can't get into either of the above. Excellent Georges Duboeuf wines. ♦ M-F 12:15-2:30PM, 6:30-11:15PM; Sa 6:30-11:15PM. 5 Greek St, W1. 071/437.1816

48 La Bastide ★$$ The cooking varies here, but there are lots of delicious French casseroles from different regions of France, or ordinary brasserie food for the diner in a hurry. ♦ M-F 12:30-2:30PM, 6-11:30PM; Sa 6-11:30PM. 50 Greek St, W1. 071/734.3300

49 Ming ★★$$ Pekinese recipes inspired by the Ming dynasty are the specialty in this pale-blue restaurant. Live carp, eel, and lobster are delivered fresh daily. ♦ Daily noon-11:45PM. 35-26 Greek St, W1. 071/734.2721

50 Il Pollo ★$ The strongest spaghetti *vongole* in town. A haven for students. ♦ M-Sa noon-11:30PM. 20 Old Compton St, W1. 071/734.5917

51 Coach & Horses Most of Soho's pubs are hot, smokey, and cozy and have nothing much to distinguish them from one another. This one has cartoons all over the walls, London's rudest landlord, and lots of drunken journalists—the satirical magazine *Private Eye* holds regular lunches here. Last but not least, **Jeffrey Barnard** (who had a West End play written about him) is a regular. ♦ M-Sa 11AM-11PM; Su noon-3PM, 7-10:30PM. 29 Greek St, W1. 071/437.5920

51 Maison Bertaux ★★$ Don't be fooled by the spartan surroundings, Maison Bertaux has been here since 1871, and even when the ovens weren't working well (for about 5 years), it still turned out the lightest croissants in town. Only fresh butter and cream are used here, so cholesterol counters should avoid the scrumptious cream cakes and meringues. ♦ Tu-Sa 9AM-7PM; Su 9:30AM-1PM, 3:30-6:30PM. 28 Greek St, W1. 071/437.6007

52 Kettners ★$ Once **Oscar Wilde**'s favorite club, then **Frank Sinatra**'s. The dining rooms and piano bar are beautifully decorated and lovely to sit in; the fare is fairly standard with pizzas and burgers and salads. Don't let them put you upstairs unless you want cold food. Young, glittery advertising types froth and flutter in the champagne bar here, swallowing copious quantities of champagne cocktail. This room gets unbearable at lunchtime and from 6:30-7:30PM. ♦ Daily 11:30AM-midnight. 29 Romilly St, W1. 071/734.6112

Restaurants/Nightlife: Red   Hotels: Blue
Shops/Parks: Green   **Sights/Culture:** Black

If the British can survive their meals they can survive anything.

George Bernard Shaw

53 Shaftesbury Avenue For a British playwright to get a play *in the West End* is considered the pinnacle of success. Just walk down Shaftesbury Avenue at dusk when the hoardings light up and you'll feel the magic of the boards draw you in. There's just one intrusion of the modern age—the Cannon cinema in a modern block right in the middle. (See the Theater section, page 172, for a full description of the scene.)

54 Cork & Bottle ★★$ The best wine bar, with more than 140 different varieties, including the precious and rare, and a staff intelligent enough to appreciate it. The food is among the best in the wine bar category, with mainly cold dishes that taste beautifully fresh. ◆ M-Sa 11AM-2:45PM, 5:30-10:45PM. Cranbourn St, WC2. 071/734.7807

London's **Chinatown** is packed with restaurants that cater to the working Chinese and Westerners who want to taste Eastern cooking. Whichever one you choose, if going for dinner be sure to arrive early (around 8PM), as the best restaurants fill up fast.

55 Man Fu Kung ★★$$ This huge establishment claims to be the largest of London's Chinese restaurants. Dim Sum snacks are wheeled around until 6PM, when the full menu and matching prices suddenly appear. Try the chicken thighs wrapped in bean curd. ◆ M-Sa 11AM-11:45PM; Su 11AM-11PM. Leicester Sq, W1. 071/839.4146

56 Poon's ★★$ Wind-dried ducks, sausages, and bacon hang from the window. This restaurant is cheap, clean, attractive, and packed with a young crowd. ◆ M-Sa noon-11:30PM. 4 Leicester St, WC2. 071/437.1528

57 Jade Garden ★★$$ An elegant mirrored restaurant with a wide range of stir-fried, steamed, and roasted dishes served in clay pots. Try the mixed seafood noodles with squid and giant prawns. ◆ M-F noon-11:30PM; Sa-Su 11:30AM-11:30PM. 15 Wardour St, W1. 071/437.5065

57 Chuen Cheng-KU ★★$ Seats 400 but it still gets crowded. Dim sum at lunch, or try the lemon-sauced roast duck in the evening. ◆ Daily 11AM-11:45PM. 17 Wardour St, W1. 071/734.3281

58 Dragon's Nest ★★$$ The Szechuan cooking is spicy and hot here, but the quality can vary. Aubergine Szechuan-style, General Tsang's chicken is the specialty. ◆ M-F noon-3PM, 5-11:30PM; Sa-Su noon-11:30PM. 58-60 Shaftesbury Ave, W1. 071/437.3119

59 Wong Kei ★★$ The food is excellent, it's very cheap, and there's virtually no service. Offer a check or, even worse, credit cards and they get very angry. ◆ Daily noon-11:30PM. 41-43 Wardour St, W1. 071/437.3071

60 China ★$ China serves a delicious *char siu*. Good for snacks. ◆ M-Th, Su noon-midnight; F-Sa noon-1AM. 3 Gerrard St, W1. 071/439.7511

61 New Diamond ★★$ Hot pots are the speciality. Open incredibly late. ◆ Daily noon-3AM. 23 Lisle St, WC2. 071/437.2517

61 Mr. Kong ★★$$ Specializes in Cantonese food, but there are some unusual dishes. Try the *satay* eels and rainbow bean-curd broth. ◆ Daily noon-1:45AM. 21 Lisle St, WC2. 071/437.7341

61 Fun Shing ★★$$ Where you'll find Chinese eating. Devotees will travel a long way just to dine here. Try the stewed duck in preserved plum sauce. ◆ Daily noon-11:45. 15 Lisle St, WC2. 071/437.1539

62 New World ★★$ Like Man Fu Kung, this Chinese restaurant stakes a claim to be London's largest, with the same good quality and slightly lower prices. Dim Sum is the specialty. ◆ M-Sa 11AM-11:45PM; Su 11AM-11PM. Gerrard Pl, W1. 071/734.0677

63 Dean Street Mozart's father advertised his child prodigy here in 1763; he asked the public to test his son's ability to sight read. The 7-year-old boy and his 4-year-old sister gave a performance at **No. 21** (now the **Ben Uri Art Gallery**). Karl Marx lived at **No. 28**, above what is now **Leoni's Quo Vadis**.

63 Christopher New Unusual, ultrafashionable gear with quirky trimmings like coins and medals. ◆ M-F 10AM-7PM; Sa 10AM-6:30PM. 52 Dean St, W1. 071/734.5363

64 The French House (The York Minster) This pub was known affectionately as *The French* until *le patron*, **Gaston**, renamed it the French House, at which point all the regulars (or cog-

Covent Garden, Soho & Marylebone

noscenti) started calling it the York Minster. It was the official headquarters of the **Free French** in World War II, and the décor hasn't changed since then. There are still signed photos of famous Frenchpeople on the walls. **M. Gaston**, the landlord, who retired in 1989, had a policy of serving beer in half-pint measures, only. Dirty, dingy, and sleazy, this bar is, needless to say, packed to the gills with aging Soho reprobates and trendy young poseurs. ◆ M-F noon-9PM; Sa noon-3:30PM; Su noon-3PM. 49 Dean St, W1. 071/437.2799

64 Amalfi ★$ It still has Chianti bottles hanging from the ceiling and does a good plate of spaghetti (by London standards) with salad for a reasonable price. ◆ M-Sa noon-2:45PM, 6-11:15PM; Su noon-10:30PM. 29-31 Old Compton St, W1. 071/437.7284

65 Le Bistingo ★★$ You'll find a country-rustic look and solid portions of French food. No nouvelle cooking here. ◆ M-Sa noon-2:30PM, 6:30-11:30PM. 57-59 Old Compton St, W1. 071/437.0784

66 Algerian Coffee Stores One hundred years old in 1989, this shop doesn't seem to have changed at all, apart from the funny newfangled coffee makers in the window—try a rich house blend like Gourmet Noir. Interestingly flavored teas and tisanes outnumber coffees by 130 to 30. ♦ M-Sa 9AM-5:30PM. 52 Old Compton St, W1. 071/437.2480

66 A. Moroni & Son Homesick? Then dive into this 100-year-old shop for a copy of your favorite read—it's bound to be here. But no dallying; A. Moroni won't allow browsers because all of the stock leaves very little room. If you can, make up your mind before you go in. ♦ M-Sa 7:30AM-7:15PM; Su 8AM-1PM. 68 Old Compton St, W1. 071/437.2847

67 Burt's ★★$$$ Simple and stylish, the food is mainly vegetarian or fish. Decadent nouvelle-style dishes include oysters with black and red caviar, or more modest celeriac spring rolls to start. ♦ M-F 12:15-2PM, 5:30-11:30PM; Sa 5:30-11:30PM. 42 Dean St, W1. 071/734.3339

67 The Vintage House An enormous range of over 130 Scotch whiskies—there's even a single malt, the Spring Bank, that costs £6900. Also, a tremendous variety of wines. ♦ M-Sa 9AM-11PM; Su noon-2PM, 7-10PM. 42 Old Compton St, W1. 071/437.2592

67 Patisserie Valerie ★$ Packed with Soho wannabees and cussing regulars squashed for space—they all come for the cakes. Try the chocolate-truffle cake, but be prepared—there is never a time, day or night, when this pastry shop isn't packed. ♦ M-Sa 8AM-7PM; Su 10AM-6PM. 44 Old Compton St, W1. 071/437.3466

68 Frith Street (1680, **Richard Frith**) **John Logie Baird** brought the street into the 20th century when he gave the first public demonstration of TV at **No. 22**.

Covent Garden, Soho & Marylebone

68 Andreas ★$ Fans of Greek food will love the *kleftiko* here. ♦ M-F noon-3PM, 5:30-11PM, Sa 5:30-11PM. 15 Frith St, W1. 071/437.3911

68 Frith's ★★$$ A lovely modern restaurant with a garden outside in the summer and a diverse, constantly changing menu. Try the braised rabbit with dried woodland-mushroom sauce. ♦ M-F 12:30-2:30PM, 7:30-11:15PM; Sa 7:30-11:15PM. 14 Frith St, W1. 071/439.3370

69 Chiang Mai ★★$$ This black-and-white restaurant is a stylish place to eat delicious Thai cuisine. Try the hot-and-sour seafood salad in chili sauce. ♦ M-Sa noon-3PM, 6-11:30PM. 48 Frith St, W1. 071/437.7444

69 Alastair Little ★★$$$ Another haunt of London foodies, this is a restaurant where people go for serious eating. The décor is stark and there's an ever-changing Continental menu, a small Japanese menu, and a good selection of wines. As you tuck into your fish soup, try the Pouilly Fumé. ♦ M-F 12:30-2:30PM, 7:30-11:30PM; Sa 7:30-11:30PM. 49 Frith St, W1. 071/734.5183

69 Gopal's of Soho ★★$$ Spicy food, bright-pink tablecloths, and a friendly staff that serves the best meat/fish *thali* in town, plus

chicken *tikka*, shish kebab, king-prawn tandoori, *keema masala*, and heaps more. ♦ Daily noon-3:15PM, 6-11:45PM. 12 Bateman St, W1. 071/434.1621

70 Kaya ★★$$ Korean cooking par excellence with a friendly staff to guide you through one of the more exotic menus in London. If in doubt, stick with the spare ribs. ♦ M-Sa noon-3PM, 6-11PM. 22 Dean St, W1. 071/437.6630

71 The Red Fort ★★★$$$ Entrepreneur **Amin Ali** left **Last Days** to set up on his own, and Indian cooking went jet-set in the process. Now everyone copies him. The food is still the best, even if there are no megastars nibbling on *momos* at the Red Fort. ♦ M-Sa noon-2:45PM, 6-11:15PM; Su 6-10:45PM. 77 Dean St, W1. 071/437.2410.

Other Indian restaurants off the path which we had to mention:

Jamdani ★★★$$$ Another **Amin Ali** restaurant (see **The Red Fort** above), with delicious lamb *shabdegh*. ♦ Daily noon-2:45PM, 6-11:30PM. 34 Charlotte St, W1. 071/636.117

Lal Qila ★★★$$ If you've ever wondered where chefs go on their night off, come here and try the aubergines with tomatoes, ginger, and garlic, or lamb cooked in cream and yogurt. On Sunday there's a self-service buffet. ♦ Daily noon-3PM, 6-11:30PM. 117 Tottenham Court Rd, W1. 071/387.5332

Agra ★★$ Famous among curry lovers, it claims to be the oldest curry house in town. One of the few places where you can still get mutton curry. ♦ Daily noon-3PM, 6PM-midnight. 135-137 Whitefield St, W1. 071/387.4828

Diwan-E-Khas ★★$ A large restaurant on 2 floors serving divine Karahi and Kashmiri dishes. Try the excellent meat and vegetarian *thalis*. ♦ Daily noon-2:45PM, 6-11:45PM. 45 Grafton Wy, W1. 071/388.1321

Gurkha's ★★$ The chance to try a few Nepalese curries from the only people in the world who want to go into the army; there are all sorts of mementos on the walls to prove it. Try the *bhutawa* (stir-fried meat with chili). ♦ Daily noon-2:45PM, 6-11:45PM. 23 Warren St, W1. 071/387.2607

72 Berwick Street Market Lots of cheap fruits and vegetables on sale in this traditional London street market. Herbs are sold lower down, on Rupert Street . There's been a market here since the 1700s and a **Blue Posts** pub. ♦ M-Sa 9AM-3:30PM

72 Fratelli Camisa and Lina Stores Soho's Italian delis go on forever selling delicious fresh pastas, hundreds of cheeses, and panettones. Salamis hang from the ceilings, breads are stacked in baskets on the floor. ♦ Fratelli Camisa: M-W, F-Sa 9AM-6PM; Th 9AM-2PM. 1a Berwick St, W1. 437.7120. Lina Stores: M-W, F 8AM-6PM; Th 8AM-1PM; Sa 8AM-5PM. 18 Brewer St, W1. 071/437.6482

73 Melati A brisk, bustling café serving Malaysian and Indonesian food; the bean-curd omelet is the out and out favorite. ◆ M-Th, Su noon-11:30PM; F-Sa noon-12:30AM. 21 Great Windmill St, W1. 071/437.2745

74 Workers for Freedom No, it's not a Marxist Leninist plot (how passé!), it's a store selling outrageously bright clothes for people in search of the *look*. ◆ M-Sa 10:30AM-6PM. 4 Lower John St, W1. 071/734.3767

75 Brewer Street Buttery ★$ A friendly, clean café offering Polish and Slav fare. No alcohol is served here except in the ice creams and pastries. ◆ M-F noon-3:30PM. 56 Brewer St, W1. 071/437.7695

76 Beau Monde Women's power gear shares shelf space with hand-painted shirts in this tiny shop. ◆ M-Sa 10:30AM-6:30PM. 43 Lexington St, W1. 071/734.6563

77 Andrew Edmunds ★$ A homey little place with a friendly staff serving good soups and casseroles. Beware, it's hard to get a seat at lunch. ◆ M-F 12:30-3PM, 5:30-10:45PM. 46 Lexington St, W1. 071/437.5708

77 Sutherlands ★★$$$ Service is slow, but the food is divine. The ad people and the foodies wax lyrical about the painstakingly prepared, beautifully presented food. Try the John Dory with lemon sauce. ◆ M-F 12:15-2:15PM, 6:15-11:15PM; Sa 6:15-11:15PM. 45 Lexington St, W1. 071/434.3401

77 Ben de Lisi New York tries to wow impoverished Londoners in the shape of fashion designer Ben de Lisi. ◆ M-W, F 10:30AM-6:30PM; Th 10AM-7PM; Sa 10AM-6PM. 8 Silver Pl, W1. 071/734.0089

78 The John Snow In 1854, Londoners were dropping like flies from cholera until Dr. John Snow figured out that the bacteria was carried by water. The water pump he turned off, thereby saving countless lives, was near the site of this pub. There's a giant model of a steam train named after the good doctor and all sorts of memorabilia in the rather shabby pub. ◆ M-F 11AM-11PM. Lexington St at Broadwick St

79 Cranks ★$ Bastion of vegetarian eating. Takeout and sit-down meals. ◆ M-F 8:30AM-6PM; Sa 9:30AM-5:30PM. 8 Marshall St, W1. 071/437.2915

80 Phood ★$ Good sandwiches and cakes for the peckish on the move; there's a restaurant,

too. All the food is made on the premises. ◆ M-F 8AM-6PM; Sa 9AM-5:30PM. 29-31 Fouberts Pl, W1. 071/439.9330

81 West Soho Built on an old plague pit, it is now home to New Wave designer shops that hope to continue catering to radical chic kids and well-paid office workers. **Newburgh Street** boasts such delights as the daring young men's and women's clothes at **Academy Soho**; unusual women's wear at **Bond**; stylish and fun women's clothes at **Boyd & Storey**, where **Whitney Houston** has been spotted. The outrageous end is held up by **Jean Paul Gaultier**, while understatement is the keynote at **Giuseppina de Camillo at Duomo**. Last but not least, the No. 1 place to shop for fashion fans—**John Richmond**.

81 Liberty (1925, **E.T. and E.S. Hall**) This wonderful shop looks as if it stepped out of history, but it's much newer than you think. Before you go in, take your life in your hands and cross Regent Street to look at the main facade—above the 3rd story, carved in Portland stone, are **Doman & Clapperton**'s 3 strangely lifelike giant people gazing at the wealth of the Orient being carried by camel, elephant, and ship toward Britannia. The Great Marlborough Street shop was built from 2 men o'war, *HMS Hindustan* and *HMS Impregnable*, with beautiful Liberty stained glass and richly ornate Italian carving everywhere. **Arthur Lasenby Liberty** originally set up shop in 1875, and he used Oriental influences and the pre-Raphaelite look to good and lasting effect in England. Even though the unusual is commonplace in England now, Liberty still surprises with its unique collections of furniture, china, clothes,

and wallpaper from all over the world. ◆ M-W, F-Sa 9:30AM-6PM; Th 9:30AM-7PM. Regent St, W1. 071/734.1234

82 Chez Nico ★★★$$$ This is the restaurant where legend has it that if you complain about anything—the food, the table, the lighting—the chef may ask you to leave. The reason is that chef **Nico Ladenis** is a perfectionist and he expects his customers to appreciate this. Again, this is a shrine for foodies: one of the top 4 in *The Good Food Guide* and a *Michelin* 2-star holder. The menu is entirely in French. Try the consommé of langoustines, escalope of salmon in chive-cream sauce; for dessert, the lemon tart is voted the best in London. Book 2 weeks ahead for supper, 2 days ahead for lunch. ◆ M-F 12:15-2PM, 7-11:15PM. 35 Great Portland St, W1. Tube: Great Portland St. 071/436.8846

The following nursery rhyme—still sung by English children—was invented during the Great Plague of 1665, when sneezing was the first sign that someone was dying of the plague; the posies were introduced to keep the disease at bay.

Ring a ring o' roses
A pocket full of posies
A tishoo, A tishoo
We all fall down

83 St. Marylebone Parish Church This church is splendidly ornate on the outside, with huge gold statues on the steeple, and beautiful and tranquil within. **Elizabeth Barrett** and **Robert Browning**, the great Romantic poet, were married here. Today, it is an active holistic healing center as well as a church. ♦ M-Sa 10AM-7PM. Marylebone Rd, W1

84 Paddington Street Named after the station, not the bear. It has **James Taylor**, a fetching custom shoe shop where you can ask for anything—even shoes like Virginia Woolf might have worn. Nearby is the **Swedish Table**, owned by an intriguing couple selling beets, caraway potatoes, ebony rye breads, gravlax, candles, and gifts. If you're stuck for things to do in the area, they'll give you lots of ideas. You'll never hear a raised voice on **Chiltern Street**, a serene village in itself with musical instruments, heartwarming fireplaces, clothing stores, and its best-kept secret, **Chiltern Street Coffee Shop**, where you'll feel that you instantly belong while you eat the best club sandwich ever.

85 Le Muscadet ★★$$ The atmosphere and the food inspire the kind of intense conversation you always imagined you would have in a great French bistro. *Salade du mâche* with crisp bacon, impressive cheeses; if nougatine is available, have 2 slices. Do not miss the ginger sorbet. ♦ M-F 12:30-2:30PM, 7:15-10:45PM; Sa 7:15-10PM. 25 Paddington St, W1. Reservations required. 071/935.2883

Restaurants/Nightlife: Red
Shops/Parks: Green
Hotels: Blue
Sights/Culture: Black

86 Daunt Tall and effete, **James Daunt** was a Cambridge graduate-turned-New York City banker before he started this, a travel bookshop that makes it seem unnecessary to travel anywhere else. The shop takes you back in time to a turn-of-the-century Bloomsbury galleried studio, where books are arranged by nation—fiction, poetry, and nonfiction together. What you have is the soul and spirit of the land housed in the only original-purpose built bookshop left in London. ♦ M-Sa 8:30AM-8PM. 83 Marylebone High St, W1. 071/224.2295

86 Villandry **Jean Charles** and his wife, **Rosalind**, have brought St. Germain de Près to Marylebone with the charm and character of their French food shop. Selling delicacies that vary from 20 different kinds of bread—dried tomato to Parisien sourdough—to original salads, picnic baskets, and pastries from **Le Manoir aux Quat'Saisons**. The neighborhood gathers in its best tweeds every Wednesday when the fresh produce arrives from Paris. ♦ M-F 9:30AM-7PM; Sa 9:30AM-6PM. 89 Marylebone High St, W1. 071/487.3816

87 Maison Sagne ★★★$ Every day for 60 years **Miss Schultz**, a diminutive figure of great elegance in her black-veiled lady's riding hat, had tea at Maison Sagne. Now 98, her magic adds to the turn-of-the-century Viennese spell. One always imagined her at night, conducting the marzipan animals in a grand ballet whirling through the extraordinary variety of cream cakes and pastry flowers. A gathering place of great cachet—everyone is

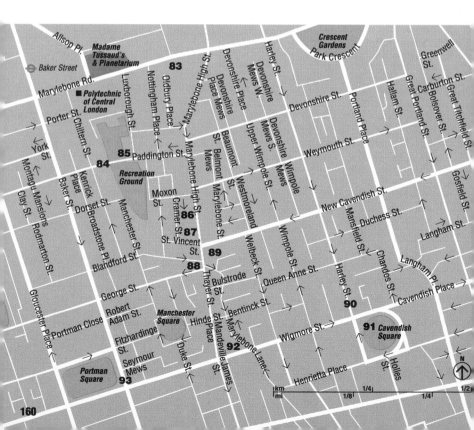

someone at Sagne on Saturday morning. **Stanley Comros** organizes his customers with care and diplomacy—it takes 5 years to be considered a regular. **Ray Hall** creates butterfly-light croissants and cakes of imaginative genius. ♦ M-F 9AM-4PM; Sa 9AM-1PM. 105 Marylebone High St. 071/935.6240

87 **Michaelangelo** **Paul Loizou** runs the kind of deli you'd imagine Jimmy Cagney ran in Chicago—nothing misses his glance, even when his back is turned. He puts together the only triple-decker New York deli sandwich in London—under protest, yes, but it's terrific. Everything's here—crisp potato pancakes, deep-dish pizza, challah. Anything you don't see he pulls out of a hat. ♦ M-Sa 8AM-7PM; Su 10:30AM-3:30PM. 102 Marylebone High St, W1. 071/486.5121

88 **Stephen Bull** ★★★$$ We first saw Stephen nipping swiftly down a street, dark eyebrows knit in furious concentration, undoubtedly over another fragrant, astonishing invention for the menu. Probably the most stylish, fresh-spirited restaurant in London, with innovative, no-nonsense food: masterful hamburgers, his vegetables are a celebration. If you could get a table you could eat here 3 or 4 nights a week without getting bored. Regulars are delighted that somewhere so good can be so cheap (by London standards). The wine list is superb. ♦ M-F noon-3PM, 6-11:30PM; Sa 6-11:30PM. 5-7 Blandford St, W1. Reservations required. 071/486.9696

89 **Marylebone Lane and High Street** It's still an old village at heart, despite the expensive shops that cater to the wealthy (and healthy) relatives of the ill who pay court to the good doctors of Harley Street close by. **Charles Dickens**, who lived all over London, wrote 11 books when he lived here.

London, that great cesspool into which all the loungers of the Empire are irresistibly drained.

Sir Arthur Conan Doyle, *A Study in Scarlet*

90 **Harley Street** This area is one gracious band of stately Georgian houses, all designed with the eye for proportion and attention to detail that this era left as its architectural legacy. Before the doctors came it was a fashionable street to live on, with residents like the **Duchess of Wellington** and **Prime Minister William Ewart Gladstone**.

91 **Cavendish Square** It's always so cold and windy in this stately square that it's almost possible to feel the tears of **Mrs. Horatio Nelson**, the woman the admiral didn't love, when she lived here in 1791. Standing among the trees you can see **Jacob Epstein**'s sculpture, the *Madonna and Child*, above the Convent of the Holy Child.

92 **Button Queen** A vision of an old sitting room filled with sewing boxes. Browsing for buttons can lead to endless inspiration: easy-to-transport gifts, magic refreshment for sweaters gone boring, buckles, and cufflinks. ♦ M-F 10AM-6PM; Sa 10AM-1:30PM. 19 Marylebone Ln, W1. 071/935.1505

93 **Baker Street** The street is named after **William Baker**, who built it, but everyone knows it as the home of the fictional sleuths Sherlock Holmes and Dr. Watson, who lived at No. 221b. The house doesn't exist anymore. Instead, there's the office block of the **Abbey National Building Society**, but they do employ someone full-time just to answer letters for the great detective! In 1951 they re-created his flat for the Festival of Britain; Holmes' flat can now be seen at the Sherlock Holmes Pub on Northumberland Avenue, WC2.

Covent Garden, Soho & Marylebone

Bests

Kate Beswic
Actress

To me, London means the endless possibilities of pottering. No other city can provide so many delectable ways to waste time. I have a collection of neighborhoods, streets within neighborhoods, and mews within streets that seduce, entertain, and pander to every mood and weather condition.

Monmouth Street, for instance, on the edge of Covent Garden, is a day trip in itself. I start at the top, at **Mysteries**, an Aladdin's Cave of crystals, exquisite *occult* jewelry, fortune-telling equipment—including crystal balls, pyramids, tarot cards, incense, and endless books and tapes telling you all you need to know about runes, pyramids, color therapy, healing, meditation, past-life regression, visualization, and for all I know, levitation. I like the charming Englishman in the white turban behind the counter, as well.

Having read up on, say, the Bach Flower remedies at Mysteries, the next stop is next door, into **Neal's Yard**, where I can do some subpottering in the pharmacy, which sells them. Its herbs and homeopathic remedies are set out in old-fashioned blue apothecary jars. I can also check out the latest scented soaps and bath oils.

Feeling peckish, I try either the *pan bagnia* at the bakery or a bowl of homemade soup from the soup stall, and add a piece of cheese from the dairy—all the cheeses are British and labeled with the name of the farm and the maker. I sometimes sit upstairs in the bakery, on one of the big floor cushions, and have some tea, herbal or industrial, but I usually prefer to sit outside, near the bike rack-cum-notice board and read the ads offering rooms and services and requesting rooms and services. I like the personal messages people leave—something simple like *Joe, we are in the Cave Mudge* provides a bit of innocent entertainment in between people-watching.

The coffee at Neal's Yard isn't very good, so I move on down to the **Monmouth Coffee House**, where they have every blend you can think of and offer a regular series of new and exotic flavors, or they will grind something special just for you. You can sit in one of the cozy wooden booths drinking large mugs of it, accompanied by coffee-bean-shaped chocolates and the morning papers, which hang, Continental style, on wooden rails.

Having made a god of my stomach, I move on rapidly past **Diskalides**, with its artistic arrangement of handmade white and dark chocolates, all decked out with ribbons and marzipan figures, past the **Seven Dials Monument**, recently and beautifully redone, and the **Mountbatten Hotel**, which has also been redone and looks like something from the raj, with its Indian chests, decorated elephants, bowls of potpourri, and general creamy, Imperial elegance, to **Dorin Frankfurt**, to try on her mad hats and jewelry, as well as her clothes, which manage to be utterly fashionable while at the same time looking like nothing you've ever seen before.

Bests

If I feel like some more coffee, I cut down **Shelton Street** for a cappuccino at the **Casbar**, which, being in the ballet school area, has the most beautiful clientele as well as the best cappuccino and the most interesting eavesdropping, second only to the Neal's Yard bakery.

Past Shelton Street, Monmouth St shades gently into Upper St. Martins Lane, then St. Martins Lane, with its little sister, New Row, leading off it. **Best of British** is a shop for presents, self-indulgence, or pure pottering. I like the Mr. Punch door stops, the old pub signs, the fantastic firescreens, and all the wonderful little things that one covets on sight, but that no one actually *needs*. In this shop, I live out my fantasy of being the sort of person who opens letters with a special silver opener, and whose pencil matches the letter holder matches the blotter matches the cushion matches the wastepaper basket matches the kleenex box matches the matches. And all handmade by British craftspeople. I also like the wreaths of flowers, and fruit made out of bread.

Exhausted by all this vicarious living I stumble across the road into **Cecil Court** for a little more. Cecil Court is a treasury of byegones: old prints, theater programs, ancient sheet music, papîer-mache theatrical jewelry, postcards, antique maps, rare and secondhand books, stamps, and best of all, there is **Dance**

Books, my personal oasis—peaceful, with soft music and absolutely the most attractive and knowledgeable assistants in London. It's a browser's paradise, with books on every aspect of every kind of dance or movement, plus magazines, tapes, posters, and cards. Did I say browse? It takes a stronger will than mine to leave Dance Books empty handed.

The last stop on this round of pleasure is **St. Martin-in-the-Fields**, for its crafts market, its lunchtime concerts, or yet more coffee or a meal in the crypt.

It's best to indulge in all this on a Tuesday, because I can work it off in **John O'Brien's** miraculous body-conditioning class at the **Pineapple**. Ninety minutes of his fast-paced mixture of ballet, modern dance, and yoga flash by and I invariably walk out feeling 2 inches taller and 10 pounds thinner. I'm always amazed by the "regulars" in this class, when I see how his technique has actually changed their body shapes. They're all so friendly and encouraging that I resolve to go regularly, too. But to get there, I have to walk down Monmouth Street...

Peter Davis
Composer and Writer

The **Gay Hussar Restaurant**. It has a great atmosphere—the food and wine are excellent. There's always a possibility of bumping into one of life's great bruisers, the Rt. Hon. Dennis Healey, MP, or for that matter the entire Labour Party.

The **Turner Gallery**. For the opportunity to be faced with genius and thus be inspired and to gain the inevitable *peace* one feels when in the presence of a master.

St. Paul's Cathedral. There's a superb echo; one hears choral music at its most magnificent.

Charlotte Street Studios. Perhaps one of the best-equipped studios of its kind, with a brilliant engineer who really enhances your work. A rare combination.

Ronnie Scotts. Ronnie's has everything: great music, dire jokes, and the guts to keep jazz alive (which isn't easy in the UK).

The Hippodrome. Kitsch elegance, the finest sound system in Europe, and a good place to go to at 2 in the morning.

Hungry's, Crawford Street. Simply the tastiest breakfast in London.

The **Rothko Room** at the **Tate**. Just to view that fabulous acreage of magenta and to know that Rothko, above all, changed the direction of so many aspirants.

King's Cross Station. An interesting mix of old and new architecture and the last vestiges of steam.

Singers. An intimate club close to the Astoria where one can hear some outstanding vocal talent, in the raw, before it's picked up and marketed.

Michael Fearnley
Journalist

Il Pollo. The ultimate Italian café spent years being a good, cheap, if grubby Italian nosherie before being discovered when the rest of Soho was. The spaghetti *vongole* and the carbonara are delicious. There's a trendy, lively atmosphere in the restaurant downstairs.

Bistingo. Part of a group of Bistingo restaurants, which will never be the pinnacle of eating but are reliable and fun to eat in. This one, like its South Kensington counterpart, is French, wooden, and homely.

Daquise. What's yummy in Polish?!

Market Bar. A neogothic bar with statuettes that look like bodies. Here you watch trendies like Richard Johnson from TV's 01 for London come here to sit 'round huge oak tables or spot other fashionable Londoners hiding behind the flowers or draped across the bendy wrought-iron furniture.

Efe's. It's the best Turkish in London. The restaurant's as fast moving as the clientele—BBC radio and ITN TV news journalists.

Sutherlands. It's very, very easy to spend loads of money here among advertising's bad boys.

Michael Gottlieb
An Anglophile Restaurateur from New York and Owner of Smollensky's Balloon

London taxis are the most comfortable taxis on earth and the drivers are the most knowledgeable.

Coming from a city like New York, where parks are at a premium, the parks here are great.

The weather is a wonderful mixture of cloudiness and unpredictability.

Even if I've had disagreements with them, I still like the police. They're probably the best of any large country in the world because they are unarmed.

The architecture is pretty and has history. I support Prince Charles and his views on architecture.

The British red bus—a marvel of design and engineering.

The old-style service in hotels like **Browns**, the **Savoy**, and the **Ritz.**

The crazy pattern of the streets means London's full of surprises and makes for distinctive areas and lovely small shops.

There are fewer potholes here than in other big cities.

The downside? There aren't enough cafés here, so there's not enough streetlife.

J.P. Donleavy
Writer

It was always my unfailing custom to perambulate to at least one of London's mainline stations every day. These included, in order of their attraction: **Paddington, Victoria, Charing Cross,** and **Liverpool Street.** In such places, I usually spent one-and-a-half hours around peak arrival time meeting trains off which no one ever came that I knew. But it is astonishing at how excited I could get in such hope. Next, I would snatch a taxi from in front of some intending, weary traveler and rush to teatime, usually at **Fortnum's** for their China Lapsang Souchong tea and Sacher torte chocolate cake. Over the years, as the **Jermyn Street** part of Fortnum's would get thronged, I also repaired to the emptier 4th-floor venue. **Christie's**, on King Street, was also a nice place to stop off to use the gents' convenience and to take pleasure in other

people's possessions, as well as to partake in the sad atmosphere of mature ladies depositing their pearls for appraisal.

Sometimes, on a variation of a theme of friendship, I would take tea with one William Donaldson (aka Henry Root) in either of 2 places: **Basil Street Hotel** or **Brown's**. These discreetly sedate places were chosen because there were often indiscreet matters to discuss. Mr. Donaldson was always a marvelous pleasure to see, and he was always as prompt to the split second as I was, which meant we would confront each other 2 minutes early. On occasions when our conversation was extremely indiscreet, the venue was changed to a suite at the **Grosvenor House**.

However, my most stable stand by, following a walk through **Mayfair** after tea, was champagne at **Claridge's**, followed by either a stroll under the massive plane trees in **Berkeley Square** or a visit to **Farm Street Church**. Then, with absolutely nowhere to go or no one to see, I would repair back to Victoria Station, meet the trains for a couple of hours, and then either take an apple out of my pocket to eat or go dine on game pie and beer at one of the Pall Mall clubs.

Jeannette Nelson
Singer and Voice Teacher

South Bank. There's always street theater in the foyer—everything from buskers to formal classical concerts.

For insomniacs, only. You can have a good greasy-spoon breakfast outside **Smithfield meat market** in your evening dress, or just go to the pub all night. You almost feel you are in the South of France, except for the roaring of the refrigerated meat lorries. Oh and, of course, the smell.

Bests

Chapel Market, Thursday-Sunday mornings. Markets like this are hard to find. It's a London market that has not been taken over by anyone else; you can hear the old street calls—*oranges, 5 for a pound, Mum!* and *Clear em up, 5 for a pound!* Just listen to that gradation.

Camden Passage, for its antiques.

Camden Lock, for bargain hunting, weekends only.

Clerkenwell Green, clockmaker's London, is a tiny triangle in the middle of the City that's almost like a country town.

The Good Food Guide, 1990
Best Restaurants

The Good Food Guide is the Anglo-Saxon answer to *Michelin*. But whereas *Michelin* uses the logic of symbols, *The Good Food Guide* revels in a love of language. Alert and learned palates, under the direction of **Tom Jaine**, rank the best out of 5. The top London 4 (scoring 5 out of 5) in 1990 are:

L'Arlequin ♦ 123 Queenstown Rd, SW8. 071/622.0555

La Tante Claire ♦ 68 Royal Hospital Rd, SW3. 071/352.6045

Chez Nico ♦ 35 Great Portland St, W1. 071/436.8846

La Gavroche ♦ 43 Upper Brook St, W1. 071/408.0881

Highlights

1 Tower Bridge London's most famous bridge became a museum in 1982. The original hydraulic machinery that operated the bridge until 1976 is on display, along with exhibitions that explain the Victorian genius behind the design. Built in 1894 by **Sir Horace Jones** and **John Wolfe-Barry**, the Gothic towered bridge represents Victorian architecture and engineering at its best. The twin towers of steel encased in stone support the 1000-ton weight of the bascules that were raised and lowered by the hydraulic machinery located in the piers of the towers. At the peak of London's river traffic and before steam replaced tall masts, the bascules rose as many as 650 times a month. Now they are operated by electricity and only open a few times a week. The glass-enclosed walkway, stretching majestically across the London sky 140 feet above the Thames, offers splendid views in every direction. From here you can step back and see the architectural variety of the city, from the Portland stone office buildings on Tower Hill to the brick and concrete of the postwar rebuilding to the glass and steel of the last 20 years. ♦ Admission; last tickets sold 45 min before closing. Daily 10AM-6:30PM, Apr-Oct; daily 10AM-4:45PM, Nov-Mar. Tower Hill, EC3. Tube: Tower Hill. 071/407.0922

2 Tower of London Though the crowds can be as thick and forbidding as the gray-brown stone, this medieval monument with its displays of armor and exquisite **Crown Jewels**, must be seen at least once in a lifetime. Nine hundred years of fascinating though brutal history are embraced within these walls, and even though the tower's violent years are long past, an atmosphere of impending doom still lingers. The tower has been used as a royal palace, fortress, armory, treasury, and menagerie, but it is best known as a merciless prison. Being locked up here, especially in Tudor times, was tantamount to almost certain death. **Anne Boleyn, Catherine Howard, Lady Jane Grey, Sir Thomas More**, and **Sir Walter Raleigh** are but a few who spent their final days, and in some cases years, in the tower.

The buildings of the **Royal Palace** and **Fortress of the Tower of London**, as it is officially known, reflect almost every style of English architecture, as well as the different roles the tower has played. **William the Conqueror** started the **White Tower** in 1078, and it was completed 20 years later by **William Rufus**. **Richard the Lionhearted** strengthened the fortress in the 12th century by building a curtain wall with towers, of which only the **Bell Tower** remains. **Henry III** and his son **Edward I** completed the transformation into the medieval castle of today. The 120-foot-wide moat, now covered with grass, was kept flooded with water by a series of sluice gates until 1843. Prisoners and provisions were brought in through the **Traitors Gate** when the Thames was still London's main highway. A gate in the **Bloody Tower** leads to the inner precincts. Once known as the **Garden Tower**, the Bloody Tower acquired its unpleasant name after the **Little Princes** mysteriously disappeared from it in 1485. Controversy still rages over whether **Richard III**, their uncle and protector, had them murdered so he could secure the throne. Sir Walter Raleigh was a prisoner in Bloody Tower from 1603 to 1615, and this is where he wrote *A History of the World*. Almost every stone in **Beauchamp Tower** contains desperately scratched messages from prisoners, pathetic reminders of those who perished. Nearby is the **Chapel Royal of St. Peter ad Vincule**, built in the 12th century and restored

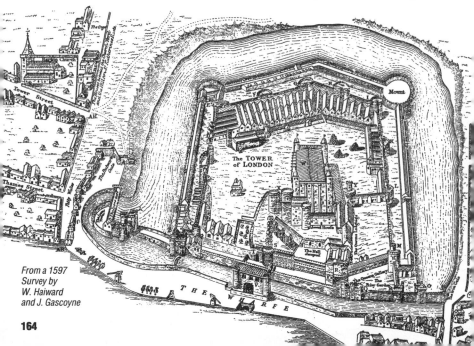

From a 1597 Survey by W. Haiward and J. Gascoyne

by **Henry VIII** in 1512 after a fire. The chapel is the burial place of the **Duke of Somerset, Duke of Northumberland**, Anne Boleyn, Catherine Howard, and Lady Jane Grey, all of whom were beheaded.

But glittering amid the historical doom and gloom are the Crown Jewels, the tower's most popular attraction. Dazzling and brilliant, almost breathing with fire, the spectacular collection far exceeds its reputation. The jewels were housed in **Martin Tower** until 1671, when the audacious **Colonel Blood** came very close to making off with them. They are now heavily guarded by yeoman warders in an underground strongroom in the 19th-century **Waterloo Building**. Here robes, swords, scepters, and crowns adorned with some of the most precious stones in the world are displayed. Most of the royal regalia was sold or melted down after the execution of **Charles I** in 1649. Only 2 pieces escaped: the **Annointing Spoon**, probably used in the coronation of **King John** in 1199, and the 14th-century **Ampulla**. The rest of the collection dates from the restoration of **Charles II** in 1660. **St. Edward's Crown** was made for Charles II, and has been used by nearly all of his successors, including **Queen Elizabeth II**. It weighs almost 5 pounds and is adorned with more than 400 precious stones. The priceless **Imperial State Crown**, originally made for **Queen Victoria**, contains some of the most famous stones in the world, including the **Second Star of Africa**, the **Stuart Sapphire**, and the **Black Prince's balas ruby**. Monarchs have worn this crown when leaving Westminster Abbey after coronation ceremonies, at the State Opening of Parliament, and at other state occasions. The exquisite **Koh-i-noor** diamond adorns the **Queen Mother's Crown**, made especially for the coronation of Queen Elizabeth II in 1937. But even grander is the 530-carat **Star of Africa**, believed to be the largest cut diamond, which is on the **Sovereign's Orb and Sceptre**. Most spectacular of the many swords is the **State Sword**, decorated with diamonds, emeralds, and rubies that form the national emblems of England, Scotland, and Ireland.

The imposing Kentish and Caen stone walls of the **White Tower** dominate the Tower of London. Built in 1078 for William the Conqueror by a Norman monk, the walls are 15 feet thick at the base, 11 feet thick at the top, and 90 feet above ground level. In 1241, Henry III, finding comfort within such dimensions, added a great hall and royal apartments and had the exterior whitewashed, hence the name White Tower. Today the tower houses the collection of **Tower Armories**, dating from the time it was the chief arsenal of the kingdom. The **Tudor Gallery** is the centerpiece of the collection. Here the personal armors of Henry VIII portray his massive presence more than any portrait ever could. On display are the armors made for foot combat when the King was young, slim, and charming, the famous ram's-horn helmet, and **King Henry's Walking Staff**, a spiked club with 3 gun barrels in the head.

St. John's Chapel, on the 2nd floor of the White Tower, is one of the finest examples of early Norman architecture, with simple columns, roundheaded arches, and beautiful tunnel vaulting. Apart from the windows, which were enlarged by **Sir Christopher Wren**, the chapel remains much as it was in 1080 when it was completed. It was here in 1503 that **Elizabeth of York**, wife of **Henry VII**, lay in state surrounded by 800 candles and Lady Jane Grey prayed before her execution in 1554.

The tower's great sense of history and tradition lives on through ceremonies that have been performed virtually unchanged for centuries. Most famous is the **Ceremony of the Keys**, perhaps the oldest military ceremony in the world. Every evening at precisely 8 minutes to 10PM, the chief yeoman warder, in a large scarlet coat and accompanied by 4 soldiers, secures the main gates of the tower. As the clock strikes 10, a bugler sounds the Last Post. On 21 May of each year, representatives from Eton College and King's College, Cambridge, place lilies and white roses in the oratory of **Wakefield Tower**, where **Henry VI** was murdered in 1471, forever remembering him as the founder of these 2 great centers of academe. This ceremony is not generally open to the public. However, one tradition that is open happens only every 3 years (1990, 1993, etc): the **Beating the Bounds**, which marks the boundaries of the tower's liberties. It takes 4 hours on Ascension Day and, unfortunately, isn't too exciting to watch but might be fun if you are passing. The yeoman warder and choir boys go around to each marker and beat it with a willow stick to establish the boundaries. (They used to beat one of the boys, not the stone!)

Tradition continues with the daily feeding of the ravens who live within the tower walls. Since Charles I decreed there should always be at least 6 ravens at the tower, there have always been 6 with 2 reserves. (In 1989 the tower managed to breed the birds successfully and now there are 9.) Their wings are clipped to keep them here because legend has it that if they leave, the tower will fall and the monarchy with it. Watch out, ravens are much bigger than crows and bite the ankles of unsuspecting tourists!

To attend the Ceremony of the Keys, write (suggesting alternative dates) to the Yeoman Clerk, the Queen's House, HM Tower of London, London EC3N 4AB. It is very popular, but only 70 people are allowed to watch, so write as soon as you book your flight.

The **Jewel House** is closed in January or February each year when the jewels are given a thorough cleaning. Ring and check before visiting during these months. ◆ M-Sa 9:30AM-5:45PM, Su 2-5:45PM, Mar-Oct; M-Sa 9:30AM-5PM, Nov-Feb. HM Tower of London, EC3. Tube: Tower Hill. 071/707.0765

And now the time returns again
Our souls exult, and London's towers
Receive the Lamb of God to dwell
In England's green and pleasant bowers

William Blake

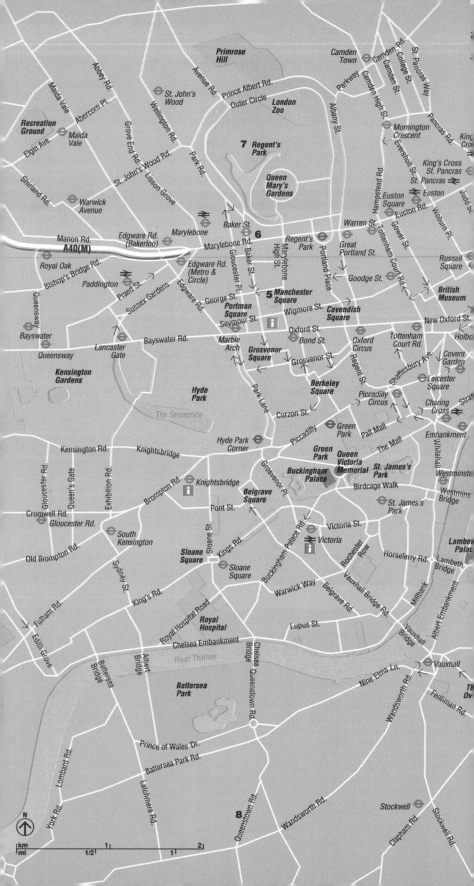

3 Docklands is like an architectural Toytown, especially when the easiest way into it is on the **Docklands Light Railway** (DLR), which floats above the whole scene giving the massive glass, chrome, and steel monoliths a peculiarly unreal air. Unless you go at lunchtime, the only people you will see are on the train itself, and they'll be fellow travelers because the trains run automatically. Even the skyscrapers under construction here don't seem to need human help as they go up. Bizarre when you think that they confidently expect 150,000 people to work here by the year 2000 and 100,000 people to actually live in this modern-age mausoleum to technology. It's 8 square miles and the largest urban redevelopment in the world. The area had a proud heritage as working dockyards from 1515, but around Victorian times became very poor and famous for criminals. (**Jack the Ripper** stalked the streets close by.) During World War II the area was bombed to smithereens and the docks never recovered, even though attempts were made to rebuild them. The **Royal Docks** were the last to close, in 1981. Miles of deserted and useless warehouses in bombed-out shells of streets were used as film sets by directors for about 10 years (you can see Gun Wharf, Wapping High Street, in the *Elephant Man*), and finally began to be converted in the early '80s. Though it is expensive and difficult for visitors or inhabitants to get to or around, the Docklands has become fashionable to live in. The locals who have been here for a long time receive no benefits from any of the new businesses that have arrived—in the way of jobs or shops (there aren't any useful ones)—and continue to complain. Eat before you come, the area is a desert for food. It is a purely visual feast for the eyes. The architect who built the World

Highlights

Financial Center in New York, **Cesar Pelli**, has come over to **Canary Wharf**, where he is constructing Britain's biggest building—modest by American standards, admittedly. It's 50 stories (800 ft) high, with a plaza as big as Trafalgar Square. Plans are underway for a new marina, an indoor stadium, two 400-bedroom hotels, shops, restaurants, and pubs.

At Docklands:

Tobacco Dock is a Georgian tobacco warehouse lined with malls and arches. It is quite beautiful, and when it's finished will be 3 times the size of Covent Garden. There are high street shops and some unusual designers here as well as street theater, puppets, and jazz. Outside are 2 replica 18th-century ships—one re-creates **Robert Louis Stephenson**'s *Treasure Island;* the other is a pirate ship. ♦ M-Th, Sa 10AM-8PM; F 10AM-10PM. The Highway, Wapping, E1. Tube: Shadwell or Wapping; DLR to Shadwell or Docklands Minibus from Tower Hill.

Hay's Galleria, next door to London Bridge, is a shopping mall with a magnificent, elegant sweeping glass roof. You can buy herbal body-care products and makeup, handmade Belgian chocolates, Italian shoes, and traditionally made teddy bears. It's also got cafés, restaurants, stalls, and classical musicians and clowns. Watch out for **David Kemp**'s *The Navigators*, a 60-foot-tall bronze moving sculpture with water jets and fountains. ♦ Tooley Street, SE1. Tube: London Bridge; British Rail or Riverbus to London Bridge City Pier

The Docklands Light Railway connects Tower Hill to the Isle of Dogs and the entire journey takes 16 minutes. As the road system around here is utterly inadequate even for the people who live and work here, use the DLR. It is fast, clean, and regular, but so tiny that during the rush hour many people can't get on—you shouldn't travel then unless you really have to. Do keep your wits about you on the return trip or you'll find yourself at Stratford, not Tower Hill. On weekends and after 9:30PM weekdays, the DLR is replaced by a bus service while maintenance takes place.

The **Thames Line Riverbus** uses a fast waterjet-powered catamaran to zoom from Chelsea Harbour to Greenwich every half-hour. It's supposed to take 20 minutes, but depends on the number of passengers, the tides (the Thames has the biggest tidal reach in the world), other river traffic, flotsam, and jetsam. There is no weekend service. Commuters tend to use the bus until 10:30AM and after 4PM, and as it only holds 62 passengers, it's a good idea to try and travel at other times. Don't get excited, London can never again become a city based around its river—150 years ago small boats plied the little river tributaries of the Thames, but the embankments put them underground. Now very few people live near the river on either shore, so there's no reason for the service to ever get really popular. Riverbus journeys from Chelsea Harbour, Cadogan Pier, Charing Cross Pier, South Bank Pier (Festival Hall), Swan Lane Pier. The Eastern section of the service goes from Charing Cross Pier, South Bank Pier, Swan Lane Pier, London Bridge City Pier (Hays Galleria), West India Pier (Isle of Dogs), Greenwich Pier. Buy your ticket on the boat. There's another hourly riverbus linking Charing Cross Pier with London City Airport in the Royal Docks, which uses short-range 50-seat Dash 7 planes to Paris, Brussels, Amsterdam, and the Channel Islands. Jets will be flying in here soon.

The Docklands is the only place in London where you can do watersports, and all of these places will teach you how to do it. For sailors, sailboarders, and canoers there's **Docklands Sailing Centre** (Kingsbridge, West Ferry Rd, Isle of Dogs, E14, 071/987.6097). Windsurfers can go to **Peter Chilvers Windsurfing** (Tidal Basin Rd, Royal Victoria Dock, E16, 071/474.2500). Waterskiers, wetbikers, and jetskiers should go to the **Royal Docks Waterski Club** (King George V Dock Gate No. 16, Woolwich Manor Wy, E16, 071/511.2000).

4 Thomas Coram Foundation for Children

Known as the **Foundling Hospital**, this is one of the most unusual small museums in London. It owes its origin to sea captain Thomas Coram (1668-1751), who made his name as a colonizer of America. Returning to London, Coram was shocked to see the number of abandoned infants. He enlisted *21 ladies of nobility and distinction, half dozen dukes and one short of a dozen earls* to petition George II for help in establishing a home for the foundlings.

The painter **William Hogarth** was one of the original governors and with his wife served as a foster parent to the children. Hogarth's major work, the *March to Finchley* (1746), and a superb, robust portrait *Captain Coram* (1740) are 2 treasures in the museum's picture collection, which includes works by **Gainsborough** and **Reynolds**. The composer **Handel** was also an early benefactor. He not only gave performances to aid the children, but also bequeathed his own copy of the *Messiah*, which is now on exhibit.

The collection that makes the museum unforgettable is found in a lovingly preserved 18th-century room known as the **Courtroom**. Here you can inspect the mementoes left by mothers in the baskets of their abandoned infants: coral beads, locks of hair, a black-wooden hand, a section of a map of England, earrings, watch seals, coins, a crystal locket, a single delicate lace glove, the letter A cut in metal, and a message scratched on mother of pearl: *James, son of James Concannon, late or now of Jamaica, 1757*. These tokens were the foundlings' only clues to parentage, the only hope of being able to answer the question *who am I?* Do ring in advance of visiting.
◆ Admission. M-F 10AM-4PM. 40 Brunswick Sq, WC1. Tube: Russell Sq or King's Cross. 071/278.2424

5 Wallace Collection (Hertford House) One

of the finest collections of French furniture, old master paintings, and *objets d'art* in the world. Visiting this grand townhouse built in the 1770s and seeing the owner's private art collection is much more intimate than going to a museum. The rich and varied collection was acquired by 4 generations of the Hertford family during the 18th and 19th centuries. The **second Marquis**, who added to the collection of English portraits with **Romney**'s *Mrs. Robinson* and **Reynold**'s *Nelly O'Brien*, bought Hertford House, then known as **Manchester House**, in 1797. But it was the **fourth Marquis** (1800-1870) who transformed the family's art collection into what you see today. An eccentric recluse in Paris who declared *I only like pleasing paintings*, the fourth Marquis amassed works by **Fragonard, Boucher, Watteau,** and **Lancret** for what can only be considered a paltry sum after the Revolution, when 18th-century art was unfashionable. He also made lavish purchases of 18th-century French furniture by **Boulle, Cressent,** and **Riesener,** including the chest of drawers made for **Louis XV**'s

bedroom at Versailles and pieces made for **Queen Marie-Antoinette**. Don't miss the exquisite collection of gold boxes, mounted with Sèvres porcelain and jewels, or the wrought-iron-and-bronze staircase balustrade, which was made in 1735 for the Palais Mazarin (now the Bibliothèque Nationale). It was sold in 1855 as scrapiron, but rescued by the fourth Marquis. Upon his death, the Marquis left his collection to his illegitimate son, **Sir Richard Wallace** (1818-1890), who had acted for him in all of his transactions and eventually added the European armor and the medieval and Renaissance works of art. Wallace brought the collection to Hertford House, and his widow left it to the nation. Public lectures are given on Tuesday and Thursday at 1PM. ◆ Free. M-Sa 10AM-5PM; Su 2-5PM. Hertford House, Manchester Sq, W1. Tube: Bond St. 071/935.0687

Helen McCabe
Art Historian and Writer

Best Paintings in the Wallace Collection:

Reynolds, *Miss Jane Bowles*. The adorable Miss Bowles, her pet in her arms, looks out at us with the innocence and pity of a madonna.

Watteau, *Fete in a Park*. Are Watteau's elegant figures creatures of the imagination who inhabit a world of everlasting pleasure, or are they real people in a real park, reluctant to leave?

Titian, *Perseus and Andromeda*. One of the great poesies Titian painted for Philip II of Spain in 1554-56.

Rembrandt, *Self-Portrait. The Artist in a Cap*. Painted in 1634-35, just after Rembrandt had moved to Amsterdam and married Saskia.

Proud of his newly acquired bourgeois status and confident in his talent as an artist, his face reveals intelligence, pride, and hope.

Elizabeth Louyise Vigée-Lebrun, *Madame Perregaux*. Dressed in black velvet trimmed with scarlet braid and ribbons, Madame Perregaux is bewitchingly pretty. Is she expecting someone as she draws back the curtain, or is she wondering what the future holds for her?

Peter de Hooch, *Woman Peeling Apples*. A celebration of the ordinary: mother and child absorbed in a simple household chore, bringing a sense of peace to their home.

François Boucher, *The Rising of the Sun*. Hung above a magnificent early 18th-century French rococo staircase, the painting echoes it's grace and elegance. Apollo, God of the Sun, prepares to embark in his horsedrawn chariot at the break of day.

Restaurants/Nightlife: Red	Hotels: Blue
Shops/Parks: Green	Sights/Culture: Black

6 Madame Tussaud's In Florence the queues go right around the block for 2 hours before opening at the fabulous Uffizi Gallery, filled with the Renaissance grand masters. In England the queues are the same length, but the grand masters (and mistresses) are made of wax. Forget whatever you may have against waxworks—there is nothing ordinary about Mme. Tussaud's. It has been a British institution since 1802, and once you see it you will understand why it attracts more than 2 million visitors a year. Part of the fun is watching the British themselves, who love to visit this museum and can be observed speaking their minds to the wax images of the controversial trade union leaders or standing with hushed respect before the figures of the royal family. Mme. T. learned her trade making death masks during the French Revolution, and those of **Louis XVI** and **Marie Antoinette** are displayed on spikes beside the actual blade that beheaded them. The oldest surviving

likeness (1765) is that of **Mme. du Barry** (known as *sleeping beauty*). A mechanism hidden in the bodice of her dress allows the figure to breathe. **Henry VIII** is surrounded by all 8 of his wives, and there is a full re-creation of the wedding party of the **Prince** and **Princess of Wales**. The wax likenesses are most often modeled from life and are never behind glass. They stand in small tableaux as figures from history, politics, literature, sports, and entertainment. There is a room devoted to **Contemporary Heroes** (**David Bowie**'s hair moves and **Elvis** talks; they have recently been joined by **Eddie Murphy** and English actor **Charles Dance**) and a **Chamber of Horrors** (Hitler, Jack the Ripper, **Charles Manson**). The newest areas are the **Garden Party** and **200 Years of Madame Tussauds**, where the great and the good are spookily immortalized. Culture buffs can admire the great **Luciano Pavarotti** while we lowbrows can smile at **Dudley Moore**. There are museum guards made of wax and an incredibly lifelike, exhausted tourist who dozes in a chair with guidebook in hand. The doors open a bit earlier on the weekend and during the summer.
◆ Admission. Daily 10AM-5:30PM. Marylebone Rd, NW1. Tube: Baker St. 071/935.6861

7 Regent's Park London is a city of parks and squares, and nowhere do nature and the built environment meet more gloriously than at Regent's Park. The essence of **John Nash**'s original plan of 1811 to turn 500 acres of farmland into a park survived through 8 years of government commissions. His spectacular terraces, iced with stucco and lined with columns, surround the park and make it look like a gigantic weddingcake, and are named after the titles of some of **George III**'s children. **Cumberland Terrace** (1826), with its magnificent pediment and 276-yard facade lined with Ionic columns, is the most splendid; **Chester Terrace** (1825) is the longest, stretching 313 yards with 52 Corinthian columns; and the elegant **Clarence Terrace**, designed by **Decimus Burton** in 1823, is the smallest. Many of

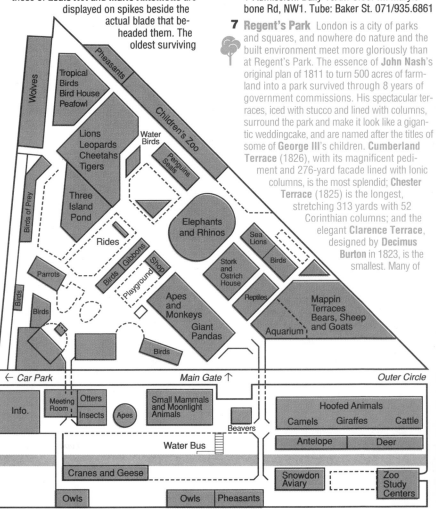

London Zoo

the terraces were tenderly restored after suffering bomb damage during World War II. The neo-Georgian **Winfield House**, now the residence of the US ambassador, is located on the site of **St. Dunstan's Lodge**, designed in 1825 by **Decimus Burton** for the legendary **third Marquis of Hertford**, who, it is said, used it as a harem. The curiously shaped boating lake, reaching out in every direction and surrounded by ash groves, is undeniably romantic. The exquisite **Queen Mary's Garden** contains 40,000 rose bushes laid out in large beds, each with a different variety. **Regent's Canal** skirts the northern boundary of the park and runs for 8 miles from Paddington to Limehouse and passes by the animals at London Zoo. One-and-a-half-hour cruises aboard the traditionally painted pair of canal boats, *Jason* and *Serpens* are available (071/286.3428). Between May and September you can visit the **Open Air Theatre** (071/935.5756); in August there are puppet shows and bandstand concerts. ◆ Daily 5AM-dusk. Regent's Park, NW1. Tube: Regent's Park, Baker St, Camden Town, or Great Portland St

Within Regent's Park:

London Zoo The oldest (created in 1828) and one of the most pleasant zoos in the world. The gardens of the **Zoological Society of London** were first laid out by **Decimus Burton** in 1828 and now spread over 36 enchanting acres of Regent's Park. Most of the 8000 animals have been released from those depressing iron cages that make them look bored and lethargic and are free to roam in settings similar to their natural habitats, separated from the public by moats. There are feeding displays, camel and llama rides, a **Moonlight World**, and Britain's largest aquarium, inhabited by 3000 creatures. The **Children's Zoo and Farm** is a thrill for kids, and a large crowd always turns up to watch the elephants take their baths. Two burrowing owls and a Persian leopard are among the newer residents; recent births include a giraffe, a zebra, and 21 inland bearded dragons. ◆ Admission. Daily 9AM-6PM, Mar-Oct; daily 10AM-dusk, Nov-Feb. Regent's Park, NW1. 071/722.3333. Tube: Regent's Park, Mornington Crescent, or Camden Town

8 **Arlequin** ★★★$$ When **Chez Nico** and Arlequin restaurants sat next to each other in South London's Queenstown Road, London foodies used to make regular pilgrimages to these shrines of good cooking. Chez Nico moved north, but Arlequin remains here and is still one of *The Good Food Guide*'s top 4 restaurants in London. It's a lot cheaper than others in its class, with lunch a positive bargain. The pretty, cozy restaurant is family run, with **Mme Delteil** fronting the house and chef **Christian Delteil** running the kitchens. The blissful menu changes slowly and there's an extensive wine list—French, of course. Try the scallops with mushroom-and-fennel ravioli or the *meli melo de foie gras frais* (fresh duck-liver salad). ◆ M-F 12:30-2PM, 7:30-10:30PM. Closed 3 wks in August. 123 Queenstown Rd, SW8. Bus: No. 137. Reservations required. 071/622.0555

Peter Jackson
President, British Topographical Society

The **Wallace Collection** in Manchester Square, because it seems like a privilege to be able to visit a grand townhouse to see the owners' private art collection rather than walking around a museum.

The **Blackfriar Pub** on Queen Victoria Street, because it is unlike any other pub in London, covered outside and in with carvings and mosaics of jolly monks being anything but monkish.

Sir John Soane's House in Lincoln's Inn Fields, because it has the most unexpected interior, with visual surprises around every corner—a labyrinth of curiously shaped rooms crowded with works of art.

The view of **St. Pauls** from **Cardinal Cap Alley, Bankside**, because this was my favorite view 30 years ago and in spite of all the rebuilding since then, it hasn't changed very much.

St. Bartholomew the Great Church in Smithfield, because, although the centuries have played about with it, you still get a feeling of medieval London among its massive Norman masonry.

The **Burlington Arcade** in Piccadilly, because each little shop has a personalized intimacy that is fast vanishing.

Wenceslaus Hollar (1607-1677) is my favorite artist because he was a superbly accurate draughtsman without whom we would have almost no idea of what prefire London looked like.

A Picturesque Tour Through the Cities of London and Westminster by Thomas Malton (1792) is my favorite book because it is, quite simply, the most beautiful London book ever published, and because I have never been able to afford a copy.

The statue of **Sir Sydney Waterlow** in **Waterlow Park**, Highgate, because he is the only London statue sensible enough to carry an umbrella.

Polly Hope
Sculptor, London

Cheshire Street Market, part of the Sunday-morning **Petticoat Lane** complex, is perhaps the last remaining view of Dickensian London and going fast. You will find excellent values in second-hand light bulbs, single-used boots, old tail coats, rusty fork-lift trucks, and, occasionally, such designer delights as second-hand Eames chairs and Deco crockery and light fittings. Plenty of '40s and '50s furniture. The market starts around 4AM. Bring a flashlight for finding things in the back of lorries. They pack up soon after midday. The terms are strictly cash, so keep your plastic cards well away in your inside pocket. Take the Aldgate or Algate East tube station, then walk up Brick Lane. The chaos starts under the railway bridge.

It is my belief, Watson, founded upon my experience, that the lowest and vilest alleys of London do not present a more dreadful record of sin than does the smiling and beautiful countryside.
Sir Arthur Conan Doyle,
Sherlock Holmes in *Copper Beeches*

Theater

Nowhere in the world does theater thrive as it does in London. Nearly 11 million people paid to see shows in the **West End** in 1988. Which means that every night some 35,000 people attended one of the 50 West End theaters, with stages ranging from the luxurious grandeur of **Covent Garden**'s 18th-century **Royal Opera House** to the comfort and advanced design of theaters in the **Barbican Center (Royal Shakespeare Company)** and the **South Bank (National Theatre)**, to revived and reverberating venues like the **Playhouse**. Another 15,000 saw alternative and fringe (Off Broadway) productions in smaller theaters, arts centers, clubs, and pubs, anywhere from **Hammersmith** to **Islington**. In 1988, nearly £139 million was spent on theater tickets in the West End, with well over a third of that coming from tourists, for whom theater has long been one of London's biggest attractions.

What makes English theater so exceptional? You not only see new theater on its way to the US, you can see revivals of the great plays by **Brecht, Chekhov, Ibsen, Miller, O'Neill**, and, of course, **Shakespeare**, presented by top directors and the finest actors and actresses. **Anthony Hopkins, Peter O'Toole, Jane Lapotaire, Stephen Berkhoff, Albert Finney, Janet Susman**, and **Maggie Smith**—one or more are usually treading the boards somewhere in the metropolis.

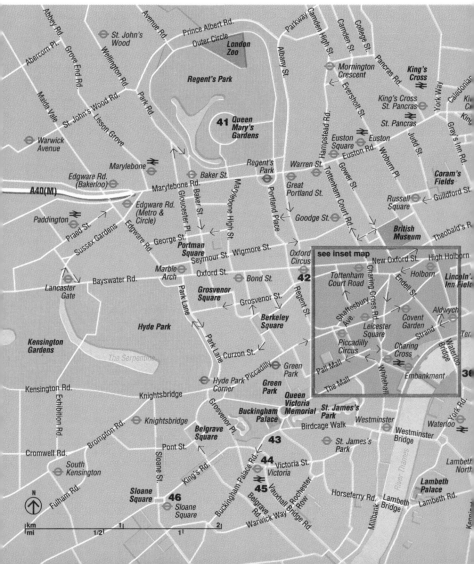

British theater has turned the tables on America. Whereas the early '80s saw many US imports on major London stages, they are now full of home-grown, but not homespun, shows that are themselves traveling the world; *Miss Saigon, Les Misérables, Phantom of the Opera*, and *Cats* have become the ambassadors for UK theater. In this inflationary age, the challenge is to maintain the quality and daring of British theater while avoiding the obvious financial temptation of producing the kinds of plays guaranteed to please the blander tastes of an international public.

London maintains an impressive stable of outstanding playwrights (**Harold Pinter, Tom Stoppard, Peter Shaffer, Alan Ayckbourn, David Hare, Caryl Churchill, Ronald Harwood**), a handful of theater geniuses (**Sir Peter Hall, Trevor Nunn, Jonathan Miller**), and many rising stars (**Nicholas Hytner, Elijah Moshinsky, Deborah Warner**).

Theatergoing is divided between the historic **West End** of **Shaftesbury Ave, Charing Cross Road**, and **Haymarket**; the **Strand**; and the subsidized modern powerhouses of British theater on the **South Bank** and at the **Barbican Center**. European and mold-breaking productions are usually seen at theaters away from the West End, like the **Royal Court, Almeida, Riverside**, and **Lyric, Hammersmith**. Details of West End

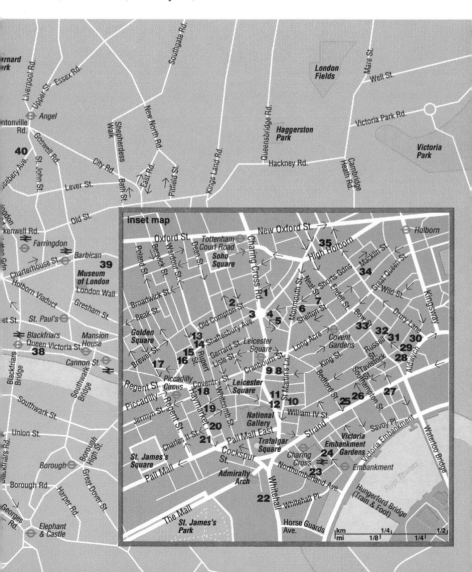

productions can be found in the national newspapers and in the *London Theatre Guide*, on racks in hotels or in *Time Out* or *City Limits*, which also include the avant-garde shows.

Ice cream is a vital part of the English theatergoing experience and so is queuing for drinks; it's the nearest that the English middle classes get to a rugby scrum. Bright people get to the theater early, have a drink before they go in, and order for the interval. It works. No one steals the drinks, and you don't have to wait in line. (By the way, programs are not free and can be quite expensive.)

There are restaurants to suit every appetite in theatrical London, whether you are looking for a drink, pub grub, or French cuisine. Many have special pre- and after-theater menus. The Covent Garden, Soho & Marylebone is a helpful guide to area dining.

1 Phoenix **Noel Coward** and his beloved **Gertrude Lawrence** starred here together in a number of shows, including Coward's own *Private Lives* on opening night. In 1969, Coward opened the bar, which is named after him. ♦ Seats 1000. Charing Cross Rd, WC2. 071/836.2294

2 Prince Edward This theater had been everything from a cabaret restaurant to a casino and cinema until **Tim Rice** and **Andrew Lloyd Webber** succeeded here with *Evita*. If the tickets you have say *limited viewing*, it means that only the lower half of the stage will be visible, which on spectacular shows is frightful, so watch out. ♦ Seats 1666. Old Compton St, W1. 071/734.8951

3 Palace A vast palace of a theater filled since 1891 with hits like *The Sound of Music, Cabaret, Jesus Christ Superstar*, and, of course, *Les Misérables*. It is now owned by composer **Andrew Lloyd Webber**, the 20th-century hero of the English musical. ♦ Seats 1480. Shaftesbury Ave, W1. 071/434.0909

4 Ambassadors Have you heard of *The Mousetrap*? That's the whodunnit by **Agatha Christie** that played at this theater for 22 years before transferring next door to St. Martin's. It

is both ornate and intimate inside. ♦ Seats 460. West St, Cambridge Circus, WC2. 071/836.6111

5 St. Martin's is the home of *The Mousetrap*. The show transferred here from the Ambassadors in 1974. It was written as a gift for **Queen Mary** by **Agatha Christie** and has never been made into a book, film, or TV play. As you leave you will be sworn to secrecy. No one has ever *told*, so the legend has been able to run successfully since 1952. There's a minimum 6-week waiting list. Remember, SSShhhh! ♦ Seats 550. West St, Cambridge Circus, WC2. 071/836.1443

6 Cambridge A wild mixture of styles inside, this theater was dark for most of the '80s, but with the current revival of interest in the theater, it's back in business. ♦ Seats 1273. Earlham St, WC2. 071/379.5299

7 Donmar Warehouse A nonprofit theater-in-the-raw located literally in a warehouse, with seats informally arranged around the stage. The Donmar was once used by the **Royal Shakespeare Company** for experimental productions (it is more comfortable nowadays) and now provides a venue for touring companies and its own fringe productions. ♦ Seats 200. 41 Earlham St, Covent Garden, WC2. 071/836.1071

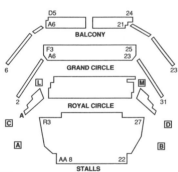

8 Albery Built behind Wyndham's Theatre in 1903, this elegant Edwardian theater moved effortlessly into the 1980s as the first theater to use electrical flying scenery. **Sir John Gielgud** made his first appearance here in *The Constant Nymph* in 1926, which ran for 587 performances. **Lionel Bart**'s musical *Oliver* holds the record run of 2618 shows between 1960 and 1966. The Albery was known as the **New Theatre** until 1973, when **Sir Bronson Albery**, a direct descendent of **Charles Wyndham**, became manager. There are good views from every seat and the original Louis XVI-style décor remains unchanged. ♦ Seats 879. St. Martin's Ln, WC2. 071/867.1115

9 Wyndham's Built back to back with the Albery in 1903 by **W.G.R. Sprague** for **Sir Charles Wyndham**. The 2 theaters are so close together that one spectator, invited onstage during *Godspell*, entered the wrong stage door and stumbled into a performance of *Pygmalion*. The bust over the proscenium is of actress **Mary Moore**, Wyndham's wife. This really is a lovely theater, cozy and quite beautiful inside. Every seat seems to be near the stage. ♦ Seat 759. Charing Cross Rd, WC2. 071/867.1116

10 Coliseum Home of the **English National Opera Company**. The Coliseum, with its signature globe on top, was built in 1902 for musical spectaculars, with luminaries **Ellen Terry, Dame Edith Evans, Lillie Langtry**, and **Sarah Bernhardt** appearing here in variety shows. Now many operagoers claim that the finest opera productions in the world take place here. All are sung in English, and if opera is your thing, it is worth a trip to London during their season (August–May). ♦ Seats 2558. St. Martin's Ln, WC2. 071/836.3161

11 Duke of York's **J.M. Barrie**'s play *Peter Pan* played here every Christmas for 11 years after the theater first opened back in 1904. Since then it's seen a lot of kids, mainly outside the stage door queuing for autographs from American stars like **Al Pacino**, who paced the boards here during the production of **David Mamet**'s *American Buffalo*. ♦ Seats 650.   St. Martin's Ln, WC2. 071/836.5122

12 Garrick This richly decorated Victorian playhouse is haunted, so beware! ♦ Seats 675. Charing Cross Rd, WC2. 071/837.6107

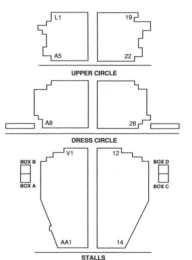

13 Queen's Built as a twin for the Globe next door by **W.G.R. Sprague**, the interior was once a salad of Italian, Georgian, and Edwardian styles, all impressively elegant. Sadly, the theater was bombed during WWII, and an unworthy exterior and foyer were added. But the excellent plays are by some of Britain's best playwrights: **Brian Westwood, Ronald Harwood, Alan Bennett**, and **Simon Grey**. ♦ Seats 979. Shaftesbury Ave, W1. 071/734.1166

14 Globe Baroque, French, and extravagantly decked out inside, the design makes going to the theater feel like a special evening out. ♦ Seats 983. Shaftesbury Ave, W1. 071/437.3667

15 Apollo (1901) One of the first theaters on Shaftesbury Avenue, the interior is ornate in pink, turquoise, and gold. ♦ Seats 780. Shaftesbury Ave, W1. 071/437.2663

16 Lyric This theater was built in the 19th century and refurbished in the '30s, so there's a very strong Art Deco feel about it. ♦ Seats 948. Shaftesbury Ave, W1. 071/437.3686

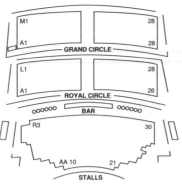

17 Piccadilly A large, comfortable theater with air conditioning, which is so rare in London and utterly vital in summer if you want to stay awake. ♦ Seats 1128. Denman St, W1. 071/867.1118

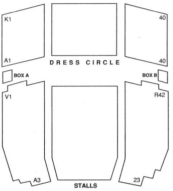

18 Prince of Wales Famous for its good family entertainment and television broadcasts. The Prince of Wales Theatre opened in 1884, and **Charles Hawtrey**'s *The Private Secretary* was first produced here, with **Beerbohm Tree** in the lead. In 1936 **Robert Cromie** redesigned the interior, leaving it starkly simple with one bonus—one of the largest bars in the West End. ♦ Seats 1122. Coventry St, W1. 071/930.8681

Theater

19 Comedy One-time home of the American import *Little Shop of Horrors*, this intimate little theater runs mainly modern productions. ♦ Seats 780. Panton St, SW1. 071/930.2578

20 Theatre Royal, Haymarket Built in 1820 by **John Nash**, the grand portico of 8 Corinthian columns over the sidewalk is still in place, along with the 9 decorated circular windows above the portico. This is the one theater in London whose outside makes you long to go inside. But the interior, which has been much altered over the years, is uncomfortable and hot; audiences and actors complain loudly and often. The theater puts on excellent independent productions with big stars in quality plays. Bars in most of the West End theaters are pretty bad, with expensive drinks and undrinkable wine, and this theater has one of the worst. Tuck a bottle and 2 small hotel

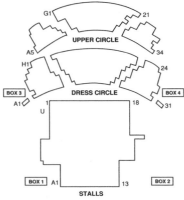

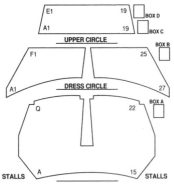

glasses in your bag and spend the intermission on the sidewalk outside, enjoying the night air and toasting to your foresight.
♦ Seats 906. Haymarket, W1. 071/930.9832

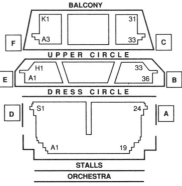

21 Her Majesty's The only theater that changes its name to fit the monarch—Her Majesty, for now. Popular Italian opera was performed here as early as 1705, when the first of 4 theaters was built on the site. After a fire in 1790, **Michael Novosielski** built the largest and most fashionable opera house in all of England, where evening dress was required even in the pit. The years that followed

Theater

were the golden age of the opera house. **Jenny Lind** made her debut in 1841 and *Fidelio* had its English premiere here in 1851. Another fire, another rebuilding, and competition from Covent Garden led to the demolition of the theater. Only the royal opera arcade, added by **John Nash** in 1816, remains. The present French Renaissance theater dates from 1897, built for **Beerbohm Tree** by **C.J. Phipps** (of the Savoy Theatre). Smash hits include *Chu Chin Chow* (2238 performances) in 1916, **Noel Coward**'s *Bitter Sweet* in 1929, and more recently, the *Phantom of the Opera*, which put this theater back in touch with its early operatic traditions. ♦ Seats 1209. Haymarket, SW1. 071/930.6606

Restaurants/Nightlife: Red   **Hotels:** Blue
Shops/Parks: Green   **Sights/Culture:** Black

22 Whitehall Built in 1930 to the designs of **Edward Stone** on the site of the original **Ye Old Ship Tavern**. The clean, simple design led one newspaper to comment that the theater made the government buildings in the area look as if they needed a shave. The Whitehall has been the home of light comedies, reviews, and farces, beginning with **Walter Hackett**'s *The Way to Treat a Woman* in 1930 and moving on to **Brian Rix**'s *Whitehall Farces* in the 1950s and '60s. ♦ Seats 662. Whitehall, SW1. 071/867.1119

23 Playhouse See page 112 for a complete description. ♦ Seats 786. Northumberland Ave, WC2. 071/839.4401

24 Players See page 112 for a complete description. ♦ Seats 300. Craven Passage, Villiers St, WC2. 071/839.1134

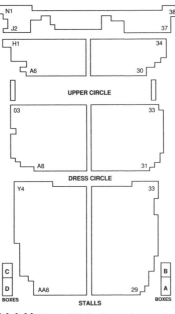

25 Adelphi Many of **Dicken**'s novels were staged here in the last century and musicals have taken over in the 20th. (See page 114 for a complete description.) ♦ Seats 1500. Strand, WC2. 071/836.7611

26 Vaudeville The productions are mostly straight theater, though the name suggests the music halls of earlier days. (See 114 for a complete description.) ♦ Seats 694. Strand, WC2. 071/836.9987

27 Savoy Built by **Richard D'Oyly Carte** as the permanent home of **Gilbert and Sullivan**'s comic operas, and more recently of the ingenius farce *Noises Off* by London playwright **Michael Frayn**. The Savoy was the first public building in the world to have electric lights. In early 1990, a fire gutted the entire building. Although the owners hope to restore the theater to its former glory, the process will take years. ♦ Seats 1122. Savoy Ct, Strand, WC2

28 Duchess One of the best-designed theaters in London, with excellent views from every seat. ♦ Seats 474. Catherine St, WC2. 071/836.8243

29 Strand The Strand and the Aldwych theaters sit like bookends on either side of the mighty Waldorf Hotel. Unusually, they were built as a pair, both quite magnificent. The proscenium above the arch is Apollo drawn by horses, with goddesses and cupids—the whole is so ornately decorated it's almost wanton to ignore it and rush out for that interval drink. ♦ Seats 925. Aldwych, WC2. 071/836.2660

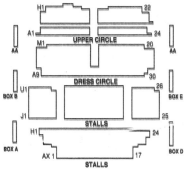

30 Aldwych Slums between Drury Lane and Lincoln's Inn were razed to make room for Aldwych and Kingsway roads, and in 1905 the Aldwych became one of the first theaters to take up residence. Designed by **W.G.R. Sprague** for **Charles Frohmant**, the Georgian theater is handsome and ornate, uncomfortable and wonderful. This was the home of the **Royal Shakespeare Company** from 1930 until 1982, when it moved to the Barbican, and its absence is much lamented. The smash hit *Nicholas Nickleby* began here. ♦ Seats 1089. Aldwych, WC2. 071/836.6404

London thou art the flower of cities all!
Gemme of all joy, jasper of jocunditie.

William Dunbar

At length they all to merry London come,
To merry London, my most kindly nurse,
That to me gave this life's first native source

Edmund Spenser

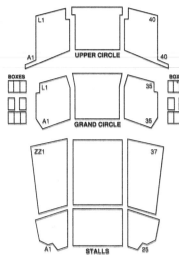

31 Theatre Royal, Drury Lane See page 149 for a complete description. ♦ Seats 2245. Catherine St, WC2. 071/836.8108

32 Fortune The immortal line *There is a time in the affairs of men which, if taken at the tide, turns to fortune* is embossed on a highly polished brass plaque in the foyer. Built after WWI, its delightful marble-and-copper foyer shows little evidence that money and materials were scarce. This is a lovely, intimate theater that puts on a wide selection of plays. But do watch out, there are pillars in the stalls, so be sure you aren't sitting behind one. ♦ Seats 432. Russell St, WC2. 071/836.2238

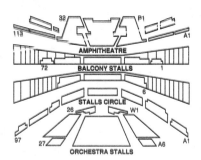

33 Royal Opera House See page 153 for a complete description. ♦ Seats 2154. Bow St, WC2. 071/240.1066, 24-hr information 071/240.1911

34 New London The home of *Cats*. (See page 142 for a complete description.) ♦ Seats 1102. 167 Drury Ln, WC2. 071/405.0072

35 Shaftesbury Massive public support prevented this beautiful theater from demolition. Recently renovated, it's easy to admire the rococo splendor and craftsmanship of the chandelier and statues. ♦ Seats 1358. Shaftesbury Ave, WC2. 071/379.5399

36 National Theatre The world-famous **National Theatre Company** was set up in 1962 under **Sir Laurence Olivier** and opened with **Peter O'Toole** in *Hamlet* in the **Old Vic**. In 1951, construction of a new concrete cultural

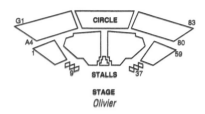

Olivier

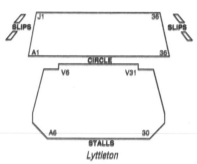

Lyttleton

paradise for the company, designed by **Denys Lasden**, was started on the South Bank. In 1976, the curtain was finally raised, with **Sir Peter Hall** as artistic director and Olivier as proud papa of the great company. Incorporated under one vast roof are 3 theaters, 8 bars, a restaurant, modern workshops, paint rooms, wardrobes, rehearsal rooms, and advanced technical facilities. The theaters differ in design, but all have first-class acoustics and site lines, ensuring good seats all around. The tickets are reasonably priced, with the added bonus of magnificent views of the Thames, the Houses of Parliament, and St. Paul's. **The Olivier** seats 1160 people in its fan-shaped auditorium; the dark-walled, rectangular **Cottesloe** (named after **Lord Cottesloe**, the chairman of the South Bank Board and Council) is the smallest and most flexible, with removable seating for 400. Experimental plays and fringe theater are performed here. The 890-seat **Lyttleton** is a proscenium theater, with roughly finished, shuttered concrete

Theater

walls for better acoustics. For a free tour of the building and backstage, call 071/633.0880. Buy tickets here at the main box office on the day of the performance or book ahead. The theater holds tickets for same-day sale. If you get in line by 8:30AM, you may be in luck when the box office opens at 10 for popular performances. You can also join the mailing list and reserve seats from anywhere in the world. Friday and Saturday nights are usually sold out, but inexpensive seats are often available for the rest of the week. Wednesday matinees are half-price. ♦ South Bank, SE1. 071/928.2252

37 Old Vic From 1962 to 1976, the Old Vic was the temporary home of the **National Theatre Company**, under the direction of **Sir Laurence Olivier**. Though the foundation stone, taken from the demolished **Savoy Palace**, dates from the theater's opening in 1818, the rest of

the Old Vic has changed interiors and owners many times, most recently in 1982, when Canadian entrepreneur **"Honest" Ed Mirvish** took over and gave the theater a 2.5-million-pound facelift. Now that Renaissance man **Jonathan Miller** has become director of the Old Vic, its great days have returned. ♦ Seats 1037. Waterloo Rd, SE1. 071/928.7616

38 Mermaid The most ignored theater in town; it's sad because this is the dream-come-true of **Sir Bernard Miles**, who had always wanted to build his own theater. It is modern, comfortable, with excellent views from every seat, and is easy to get to (next to Blackfriars tube). ♦ Seats 610. Puddledock, Blackfriars, EC4. 071/236.5568

39 Barbican Center When **Queen Elizabeth II** opened the Barbican in 1982, she called it one of the wonders of the modern world, and, as usual, the Queen was not exaggerating. Designed by architects **Chamberlin, Powell and Bon** on a site that was heavily bombed during the Blitz, this walled city within the City covers 20 acres, rises 10 levels, descends 17 feet below sea level, and caps it all with the most extensive flat roof in Europe. The **Royal Shakespeare Company**, which is Britain's leading subsidized company and is based in Stratford-upon-Avon, moved to the Barbican from the Aldwych in 1982. The theater, reached from levels 3 through 6, has 1166 seats with raked stalls and 3 circles that project toward the stage, putting every guest within 65 feet of the action. The 109-foot double-height fly-tower above the stage, used for scenery storage, is believed to be the tallest in the world. A remarkable stainless-steel safety curtain descends during intermissions. Small productions of **Shakespeare**, revivals, and new plays are performed in the **Pit**, which was originally a rehearsal space but has been redesigned as a flexible auditorium for 200 people. The **Concert Hall** (on levels 5 and 6) is the home of the **London Symphony Orchestra**. The area around the Barbican is slowly acquiring restaurants and cafés, but is still a windy wasteland at night, and the catering in the Barbican is appalling. (There *is* food at the **Waterside Café**. The cold buffet is quite good, but the hot food is dull, so eat before you come, because by the time you get back to the center of town all the restaurants will have closed.) Getting here can be a drag. One formula is to arrive by taxi and leave by the tube, but the most practical way is to take the tube both ways. It would help if the Barbican were better marked (en route and inside), but at least the tickets are now sold in central London at the Theatre Museum, Wellington Street, and Covent Garden. Do try and experience at least one of Shakespeare's plays by this brilliant company. There are some standby seats available. ♦ Recorded information 071/628.9760, box office 071/628.8795, credit card bookings 071/638.8891

Courtesy is not dead; it has merely taken refuge in Great Britain.

Georges Dunhamel

40 Sadler's Wells This is the home of the **Sadler's Wells Royal Ballet, London Contemporary Dance**, and the **Ballet Rambert**. It seems to be miles out, but it's easy to get here as long as the No. 19 or No. 38 bus from the West End is pointing in the right direction (toward Islington or Highbury Barn). It's hard to miss, but even so, conductors will always tell you when to hop off. (It's easier than finding your way around the Barbican!) ♦ Seats 1500. Rosebery Ave, EC1. 071/278.8916

41 Open Air This delightful outdoor theater presents a summer season (May-August) of **Shakespeare** and a musical. The food is barbecue and salads or bring-it-yourself (your Fortnum's hamper could come with you!). Divine on sunny days and starry nights. That old theater adage *The Show Must Go On* means what it says here, so take a *brolly* (umbrella), a mac, and galoshes if you think it will rain. Hay fever sufferers watch out! ♦ Seats 1187. Regent's Park, NW1. 071/486.2431

42 London Palladium On Sunday night during the 1950s most of Britain tuned in to *Sunday Night At The London Palladium*, broadcast from this luxurious 1910 music hall. This is the home of great variety shows—**Tommy Steele** sopping in *Singin' in the Rain*, a pantomime every Christmas, and the Royal Command Performance. ♦ Seats 2317. Argyll St, W1. 071/437.7373

43 Westminster The only major theater in London to occasionally allow the amateurs in. It shows a variety of plays throughout the year. ♦ Seats 585. Palace St, SW1. 071/834.0283

44 Victoria Palace Built as a music hall in 1910 by **Frank Matcham** for **Alfred Butt**, the theater retains much of its original style: classical outside and rich and atmospheric inside, with gray-marble walls, gold mosaics, and white Sicilian marble pillars. A statue of ballerina **Anna Pavlova**, who Butt introduced to London, stood atop the theater until WWII; the superstitious dancer pulled her car blinds down when she drove by. *Me and My Gal* played here until the outbreak of war in 1939. ♦ Seats 1565. Victoria St, SW1. 071/834.1317

45 Apollo Victoria It was originally designed as a cinema, but became a theater and is now known for the musical *Starlight Express*, in which roller skaters tear past the audience. ♦ Seats 2572. 17 Wilton Rd, SW1. 071/828.8665

46 Royal Court See page 90 for a complete description. ♦ Seats 401. Sloane Sq, SW1. 071/730.1745

London's Other Theater *by Sue Rolfe*

Some of the most stimulating drama at the heart of the British tradition is presented in the outer London theaters and studio spaces, all of which are managing, with low government subsidies, to produce work that is original enough to be snapped up by West End producers.

For the visitor interested in London's answer to Off Broadway, it is well worth consulting a weekly theater guide like *Time Out* to get a full picture of the range of drama available, as many of the smaller venues cannot afford to advertise in the classified sections of the national press. The most important things to remember are that the theater spaces are smaller, usually (but not always) modern, and the plays themselves are modern classics, avantgarde, or new plays. Outer London theaters within a half-hour from the West End:

The Royal Court at Sloane Square Famous for the work of **John Osborne, Edward Bond**, and **David Storey**, and dedicated to the work of new writers. Any production here is guaranteed to stimulate the imagination and challenge preconceptions. (See page 90 for a full description) ♦ Sloane Sq, SW3. 071/730.1745

The Lyric Theatre, Hammersmith A modern proscenium-arch theater. During the past decade it has established an unparalleled reputation for staging international classics, such as **Federico Garcia Lorca**'s tragedy *The House of Bernarda Alba* with leading British actresses **Glenda Jackson** and **Joan Plowright**. There's a restaurant and summer roof terrace on the premises. ♦ King St, Hammersmith, W6. 081/741.2311

Riverside Studio, Hammersmith An informal theater offering a variety of touring shows and avant-garde plays, with an art gallery, bars, and a cinema within the complex. ♦ Crisp Rd, Hammersmith, W10. 081/748.3354

The Bush Theatre An intimate modern theater where you can catch some of Britain's leading actors before they become famous. ♦ Shepherds Bush Green, W12. 081/743.3388

Greenwich Theatre Here you'll find a mixture of new and classic plays staged in a modern, steeply raked auditorium. Within the building are a restaurant, picture gallery, and jazz club. The theater is located in pleasant surroundings, just a short walk from the river. ♦ Crooms Hill, SEIO. 081/858.7755

The King's Head, Islington In the back room of this English pub, which still retains the old money system of pounds and pence, you can watch new plays and enjoy a delightful set supper cabaretstyle. After the show there are usually good modern jazz bands playing in the other bars. ♦ 115 Upper St, N1. 071/226.1916

Other studio theaters that have established firstclass reputations for exciting new drama are **The Orange Tree, Richmond; The Half Moon, Aldgate; Soho Poly; The Almeida in Islington; The Tricycle in Kilburn;** and the **Donmar Warehouse, Covent Garden.**

How to Buy Theater Tickets

You can go directly to the theater box office, usually open from 10AM until the start of the evening performance, and choose from what is left. The earlier you go, the better the selection. Wherever you go, always ask if it is restricted viewing, if there is air conditioning, and, if necessary, get the details regarding disabled access. (Every theater varies and some need advance warning.) Many have sound systems for the hard of hearing.

OPEN AIR THEATRE
REGENT'S PARK · LONDON, N.W.1

Monday JUNE 28
LOWER TIER £6.00

B 10

No money refunded. If performance is cancelled this ticket is exchangeable for any other performance of the season.

FEBRUARY 1986 at 7:30 PM
AMXC
£10.00
11-FEB-86
GRAND TIER
A14
GLC SOUTH BANK CONCERT HALLS

You can also call the box office and reserve your tickets with a major credit card; you must pay for them by post or in person within 3 days. If you pay for them in person, you'll need to show your credit card for identification purposes.

Ticket agencies that sell West End theater tickets are scattered throughout London and other large cities, including New York. Most charge an additional booking fee of 10-20 percent. **First Call**, a 24-hour credit-card service for London's top shows, concerts, and movies, offers a wide range of tickets at all prices and tries to provide a real choice of seating. Tickets are delivered by post or, if there isn't time, by courier to the box office for later collection. The booking fee is up to 70-percent less than the fee charged by most other services (071/ 240.7200). **Keith Prowse**, another ticket agency, doesn't charge a commission for certain theaters (081/741.9999; New York freefone 800/223.4446). **Ticketmaster** also offers some shows without any booking fee (071/379.4444).

For a real bargain, the **Leicester Square Ticket Booth**, in the heart of the theater district, sells half-price tickets the day of the performance—Monday-Saturday noon-2PM for matinees, 2:30-6:30PM for evening shows. Obviously, tickets for hit shows may not be available. There is a small booking fee and a 4-seat maximum per person.

Theatreline This is a new low-fee telephone service for essential West End theater information, including daily seat availability. There are 6 categories:

Plays 430959
Musicals 430960
Comedies 430961
Thrillers 430962
Children's 430963
Opera/ballet/modern dance 430964

American theater buffs who want to keep current on London theater happenings can subscribe to *London Theatre News*, a monthly newsletter that includes theater listings, reviews, interviews, backstage chatter, and restaurant tips. Subscriptions include access to a telephone ticket service. London Theatre News, Box 3000, Dept LTN A, Denville NJ 07834, 212/517.8608.

Most theaters are closed Sunday.

Scalpers In London, scalpers are called *ticket touts*, but they're the same the world over. They pose a major problem for London's theaters because they fuel the idea that tickets are expensive. Be careful; people have paid up to $200 for a ticket only to find out they have a seat behind a pillar. The **Society of West End Theatres** is collecting files on the touts and will prosecute, so do write to them if you lose out, but better still, either buy the tickets before you come to the UK or go and see another show; there are at least 50 to choose from in the West End. It is worth noting that London theater differs from New York in that last-minute booking for shows is often possible since some theaters reserve seats to be sold on the day of a performance.

Bests

Sue Rolfe
Theater Publicist

For quick meals before the theater or cinema, **Poons** original restaurant just off Leicester Square. (Authentic Chinese—try the garlic-grilled prawns.)

After-show leisure suppers, the **Gay Hussar** on Greek Street (Hungarian).

For strolling through London without the bustle, the City squares on a Sunday morning.

Looking at London from on high—take a boat from Westminster or Tower Bridge piers to Greenwich and climb up through the winding streets to Greenwich Park, where from the Observatory you can gaze down across the sweep of the Thames to the metropolis.

Take a boat the other way to Richmond and have lunch at **Mrs. Beetons** on the Hill. (Home cooking by neighborhood cooks.)

Explore the antique shops along the Hill and take in the magnificent view from the top before rambling down to the river, where you can hire boats or walk along the tow path past the meadows.

Brian Widlake
DJ on LBC (London's talk radio station)

Caprice for brunch
Tante Claire
The **Thames**
St. James's Park
The **Theater**
Royal Mid Surrey Golf Club
Greens in Duke Street, St. James's (oyster bar and seafood)
The **London Library**
Mayfair
King's Cross (Because when I'm there I couldn't be anywhere else in the world, which is worse.)

Francesca Simon
Writer

My Favorite Things about London

Brown's Hotel for tea, because they have big, comfortable sofas and bring the tea, cakes, scones, and sandwiches in one go, so you don't have to be demure about how many cakes you have.

Columbia Road Flower Market. On Sunday mornng, flower and shrub sellers line this Victorian street, selling a huge variety of plants and flowers, very cheaply. A great crush of people, but fun.

St. Pancras Station, for the way this beautiful, curving Victorian station sweeps you up to its entrance. Inside are splendid tiled ceilings.

The **Bush Theatre**. London's best fringe theater is located above a pub in Shepard's Bush and seats 100 squashed together. They produced the first plays of **Doug Lucie, David Edgar, Jonathan Gems,** and **Sharman MacDonald**, and it's the place to see young actors who will go on to great things. (Famous actors I've seen perform here include **Charles Dance, Julie Walters, Simon Callow,** and **Gayle Hunnicutt**.)

Walking across **Waterloo Bridge** at night, for the wonderful view of St. Paul's on one side and the Houses of Parliament on the other. Even the murky Thames manages to look inviting.

Sir John Soane's House for **Hogarth**'s *Rake's Progress* and the eccentricity of the rooms, all angles and curves and mirrors and arches—I always feel like Alice in Wonderland here. If you charm the guards they'll unfold painting behind painting behind painting.

Brick Lane. A bustling flea market on Sunday, selling everything from bicycles and lettuce to junk and antiques. (I bought an Art Deco fire screen for £1.) Brick Lane is in the heart of the immigrant area of Spitalfields, where first the Huguenots, then the Jews, and now the Bangladeshis live. Beautiful 17th-century Weavers houses line the nearby streets, plus old synagogues and Indian groceries. You'll find London's best Indian restaurants here, as well as the city's only decent bagels.

The **Bethnal Green Museum of Childhood**, where 19th-century teddy bears, dolls, and royal wedding dresses are all preserved. Fun for grown-ups, too.

Hackney City Farm. One of several working farms scattered around London; this one has pigs, sheep, goats, ducks, geese, rabbits, and hens.

John Gorham
Designer, London

Pasticceria Cappuccetto has smashing creamy cakes and fresh-fruit pastries.

Try **Gaby's** (next door to Wyndham's Theatre, for lovely hot salt-beef sandwiches and other Mediterranean specialities. My favorite is chicken liver on rye. The chicken liver comes about 2 inches thick, a meal in itself.

Rock and Sole Plaice is a good, old-fashioned, traditional English fish-and-chippy. They also do a very tasty banana or pineapple fritter. Yummy!

Patisserie Valerie is a good place for tea and overhearing *pseuds* gossip. It gets very crowded and you may have to wait awhile.

Rosamund Julius
Julius International Design Consultants

A walk in **Regent's Park** at any time of year.

Lunch at the **Connaught Hotel**.

Standing on **Westminster Bridge** in the evening, looking at the daggers of light reflecting onto the Thames.

Theaters—the old and the new.

The cosmopolitan mixture of people one sees and meets.

Dinner at **Langan's Brasserie**.

The book shops.

Leslie Julius
Julius International Design Consultants

The trees— everywhere.

A walk on **Hampstead Heath** on Sunday morning.

Drinks at the **Spainards** on Hampstead Heath.

A concert at the **Royal Festival Hall**.

English pubs.

Always exciting exhibitions.

The view from a Nash terrace looking north over **Regents Park**.

Hercules Bellville
Film Producer

Marianne North Gallery

Leighton House Gallery

The **London Library**

The **Criterion Brasserie** (the walls and ceilings, not the food, alas).

The **Whitechapel Gallery**

The **Michelin Building**

Glebe Place in Chelsea

The view from **Spur Road** across **St. James's Park** to **Whitehall** in the evening. (View can be obscured by foliage in the summer.)

Bests

Mavis Klein
Psychotherapist and Writer

Having a triumphal, celebratory cake in **Harvey Nichols**' coffee shop after buying a beautiful dress there at the first moment of their sale.

Having **John Lewis** all to myself at 9 on Monday morning.

Going to meetings of the **Astrological Lodge** at the **Artworkers Guild, Queens Square**, on Monday evening at 7.

Browsing in **Dillons** (Gower Street) or **Compendium** (Camden Town)—the best bookshops in London.

Going to any play at the **Hampstead Theatre**, Swiss Cottage.

Neale Birch
Actor

Barbican and the **Festival Hall**. There are always free concerts in the foyers.

Children's London

Bethnal Green Museum of Childhoood The country's largest collection of dollhouses and hundreds of toys for all ages. Artistic talent? Join an art workshop on Saturday. ♦ Admission. M-Th, Sa 10AM-6PM; Su 2:30-6PM. Cambridge Heath Rd, E2. 071/980.3204

The London Dungeon For little horrors everywhere. Britain's gory history is relived here, with painstakingly ghoulish attention to detail. Step into Pudding Lane and imagine what it was like in 1666 when the Great Fire was a conflagration all around. They boiled prisoners alive, they sewed on Charles I's head after he was beheaded. Here you can see how. Yuk! The squeamish shouldn't bother. ♦ Admission. Daily 10AM-5:30PM, Apr-Sep; 10AM-4:30PM, Oct-Mar. 23-34 Tooley St, SE1. 071/403.0606

The London Toy and Model Museum Toys down through the ages. See all the toys you could have bought for a penny at the turn of the century.

There are plenty of knobs to push to set mechanical toys in motion. But what kids really love is whizzing around on the garden railway and carousel rides. ♦ Admission. Tu-Sa 10AM-5:30PM; Su 11AM-5:30PM. 23 Craven Hill, W1. 071/262.7905

London Transport Museum London's underground system is the oldest in the world (detractors call it ancient), and some of the older trains are on show here. The way the whole system works was (and still is) a marvel and the whole thing is explained, with the chance to drive a London bus and a simulated driver's-eye view of a trip on the underground. It's a shame you aren't allowed to go aboard these trains, but the Northern Line is the best one if you still want to see and feel the oldest underground rolling stock in action. (See page 150 for more details.) (Next door is a very usefully placed set of public toilets.) ♦ Admission. Daily 10AM-6PM. The Piazza, Covent Garden, WC2. 071/379.6344

Madame Tussaud's Lifelike wax impressions of historical characters, famous people, pop singers, and film stars. Sleeping Beauty actually breathes. (See page 170 for more details) ♦ Admission. M-F 10AM-5:30PM; Sa-Su 9:30AM-5:30PM. Marylebone Rd, NW1. 071/935.6861

MOMI—Museum of the Moving Image The museum starts with precinema experiments, European cinema, cartoons, and goes through to the technical wizardry of a modern TV studio. The guides are all actors. You can be interviewed, fly across the Thames, read the news, and see how special effects are created. Get here early because everyone else does and you'll queue for hours to get in. Londoners rave about it. Okay, it's a bit like coals to Newcastle for Americans, but it's fascinating nonetheless.

MUSEUM OF THE

MOVING IMAGE

Allow 2 hours for a visit. ♦ Admission. Tu-Sa 10AM-8PM, Su, bank holidays 10AM-8PM, Jun-Sep; daily 10AM-6PM, Oct-May. South Bank Centre, Waterloo, SE1. 071/401.2636

Museum of London You can tell children like this place because it's always packed with them! Fascinating display of 2000 years of London's history, including Roman relics, royal treasures; the lord mayor's coach is here as well as a film of the Great Fire and an iron corpse cage where bodies of executed criminals were placed. (See page 129 for more details.) ♦ Free. Tu-Sa 10AM-6PM; Su 2-6PM. London Wall, EC2. Tube: Barbican, Moorgate, St. Paul's. 071/600.3699

Natural History Museum Meet Diplodocus in the entrance hall—this enormous monster has been extinct for 135 million years! Or gaze at the 90-foot-long giant Blue Whale suspended from the ceiling. There are now videos and exhibitions with buttons to push, especially in the human biology section, which are fun and educational at the same time. (See page 68 for more details.) ♦ Admission. M-Sa 10AM-6PM; Su 2:30-6PM. Cromwell Rd, SW7. 071/938.9123

THE LONDON PLANETARIUM

Planetarium Lose yourself in outer space watching films projected onto the vast copper dome. Star shows are held every 40 minutes. There are live laser shows set to rock music on most evenings. ♦ Admission. M-F 11AM-4:15PM; Sa-Su 10:15AM-5PM. Marylebone Rd, NW1. 071/486.2242

Rock Circus Imagine you are Michael Jackson. As you walk toward an electronically controlled model of yourself it comes to life. Creepy yes, tacky no. Madonna lies sexily on a couch, Bruce Springsteen plays to thousands of fans. These stars are lifelike, Bob Geldof is dressed forever as he was on the day of Live Aid. ♦ Admission. Daily 10AM-10PM. The London Pavilion, Piccadilly Circus, W1. 071/287.5474

Royal Britain The kings and queens of England have their individual stories told in this high-tech show. The more spectacular and grim moments come to life—much to the glee of the kiddies. ♦ Admission. M-Sa 9AM-5:30PM. Barbican EC2. 071/588.5858

Science Museum Head for the Children's Gallery and a den of working models. The original hands-on museum—little hands pull the levers and push the

buttons with glee. Mission control (parents) and even Mrs. Thatcher when she visited found it hard to step back so that the little ones could get in and try flying a plane on a simulator or going into the launch pad. (See page 69 for more details.) ♦ Free. M-Sa 10AM-6PM; Su 11AM-6PM. Exhibition Rd, SW7. 071/938.8000

Tower of London Built during the reign of William the Conqueror, the tower has been used as a prison, a mint, and even a menagerie. Don't miss the magnificent Crown Jewels or the Green where 17-year-old Lady Jane Grey was beheaded. (See page 164 for more details.) ♦ Admission. M-Sa 9:30AM-5PM; Su 2-5:30PM, Mar-Oct; M-Sa 9:30AM-4PM, Nov-Feb. Tower Hill, EC3. 709.0765

Zoo Waterbus These boats depart from Little Venice, at the end of Blomfield Road, W9, every hour on the hour, from 10AM-5PM, and travel to the zoo along Regent's Park Canal. The trip takes 40 minutes, and tickets include a special rate for the zoo. (See page 170 for more details.)

Pubs

In Britain it can be difficult to get a drink, although changes in the licensing laws in 1989 have meant longer hours, often all day on weekdays and Saturday (not Sunday). If you have children in tow, you will have to leave them outside unless they are over the age of 14.

The following pubs have gardens where children are welcome—if the weather allows, of course.

Admiral Codrington Haunt of yuppies and Sloanes, the affectionately called *Admiral Cod* welcomes children in both the restaurant and the conservatory. Even if it is raining, the perspex roof allows you to sit in this bright and cheery room surrounded by hanging plants. ♦ M-Sa 11AM-11PM; Su noon-3PM, 7-10:30PM. 17 Mossop St, SW3. 071/589.4603

Cross Keys Popular Cheyne Walk pub with an exceedingly pretty patio boasting a long list of horticultural prizes. In spite of the Russian vine, there is seating for 60. ♦ M-Sa 11AM-11PM; Su noon-3PM, 7-10:30PM. 2 Lawrence St, SW3. 071/352.1893

Dickens Inn After the lightships and sailing barges, a bit of dry land is just the ticket. Children are wel-

come in the snack bar and restaurant; Dickens will even make the portions that bit smaller and cheaper. ♦ M-Sa 11AM-11PM; Su noon-3PM, 7-10:30PM. St. Katherine's Dock, E1. 071/488.1226/2202

Duke of Somerset The only pub in the city of London with a paved patio. ♦ M-F 11AM-9:30PM; Sa noon-3PM, 7-11PM; Su noon-3PM, 7-10:30PM. Little Somerset St, Aldgate, E1. 071/481.0785

Earl of Lonsdale After a morning at Portobello Market, you can sit in the shade of an Iolanthus tree in the flag-stoned garden, or in the pretty conservatory. ♦ M-Sa noon-3PM, 5:30-11PM; Su noon-3PM, 7-10:30PM. 277 Westbourne Grove, W11. 071/727.6335

Restaurants/Nightlife: Red   Hotels: Blue

Shops/Parks: Green   **Sights/Culture: Black**

Scarsdale Arms A pretty patio surrounded by flower boxes and hanging baskets suspended from the plane tree branches. Children are catered to indoors in the restaurant. ♦ M-Sa noon-3PM, 7-11PM; Su noon-3PM, 7-10:30PM. 23a Edward's Sq, W8. 071/937.1811

Spaniard's Inn Highwayman **Dick Turpin** hung out in this ancient coaching inn. Rain or shine, the Spaniard's caters to kids, either in the large beer garden with a 100-bird budgerigar aviary or indoors in **Turpin's Bar** on the 2nd floor. ♦ M-Sa 11AM-11PM; Su noon-3PM, 7-10:30PM. Hampstead Ln, NW3. 081/455.3276

Clothing

Laura Ashley Smaller versions of the adult line. Floral cotton dresses for girls and sailor suits for boys. ♦ M-F 9:30AM-6PM; Sa 9AM-6PM. 9 Harriet St, SW1. 071/235.9796

Marks and Spencer With over 250 stores in the UK, the store's success lies in rigorous quality control and competitive prices. The knitwear and underwear are especially good. You can tell it's good because it's always packed with French and Italian customers. ♦ M-Tu 9AM-7PM; W-F 9AM-8PM; Sa 9AM-6PM. 458 Oxford St, W1. 071/935.7954

Mothercare Fashion garments as well as strollers and safety seats. ♦ M-F 9AM-8PM; Sa 9AM-6PM. 120 Kensington High St, W8. 071/937.9781

Peter Jones Wide range of children's clothes for all occasions at reasonable prices. (See page 91 for more details.) ♦ M-Tu, Th-Sa 9AM-5:30PM; W 9:30AM-7PM. Sloane Sq, SW1. 071/730.3434

Children's London

Scotch House You can find boy's trousers or girl's dresses in your own family tartan in the kids' department. Classic tailored coats with velvet collars and a good range of knitwear. (See page 85 for more details.) ♦ M-Tu, Th-Sa 9AM-6PM; W 9AM-7PM. 2 Brompton Rd, SW1. 071/581.2151

The White House Exquisite christening robes and traditional smocking, all embroidered in its own workshops. Silks and cashmeres for those special occasions. ♦ M-F 9AM-5:30PM; Sa 9AM-1PM. 51-52 New Bond St, W1. 071/629.3521

A proud mother said her baby looked liked **Churchill.** He replied: *Madam, all babies look like me.*

Bookstores

The Book Boat Housed on a barge on the river next to the *Gypsy Moth.* ♦ M-W, F-Su 10AM-5PM. Cutty Sark Gardens, King William's Walk, Greenwich, SE10. 081/853.4383

Children's Book Centre Giant bookshop with everything a parent could ever want to give a child from the world of literature. ♦ M-Sa 9:30AM-6PM. 237 Kensington High St, W8. 071/937.6314

The Children's Bookshop ♦ M-Sa 9AM-5:30PM. 66 High St, Wimbledon Village, SW19. 081/947.2038

Harrods A vast selection of children's books in the toy department on the 2nd floor; beware all ye who enter here, you'll find it hard to leave with just books. (See page 84 for more details.) ♦ M-Tu, Th-F 9AM-5PM; W 9:30AM-7PM; Sa 9AM-6PM. Knightsbridge, SW1. 071/730.1234

The Lion and the Unicorn ♦ M-Sa 9:30AM-5:30PM. 19 King St, Richmond, Surrey. 081/940.0483

Muswell Hill Children's Bookshop ♦ M-F 9:15AM-5:45PM; Sa 9:15AM-5:30PM. 29 Fortis Green Rd, Muswell Hill, N10. 081/444.5500

Puffin Bookshop (See page 151 for more details.) ♦ M-Sa 10AM-6PM. 1 The Piazza, Covent Garden, WC2. 071/379.6465

Top Ten English Children's Books

Gargling With Jelly by **Brian Patten**

The Hodgeheg by **Dick King-Smith**

The Lion, The Witch and The Wardrobe by **C.S. Lewis**

Matilda by **Roald Dahl**

Please Mrs. Butler by **Allan Ahlberg**

Rhyme Stew by **Roald Dahl**

The Snowman by **Raymond Briggs**

The Tale of Peter Rabbit by **Beatrix Potter**

The Very Hungry Caterpillar by **Eric Carle**

The Witches by **Roald Dahl**

Restaurants/Nightlife: Red	Hotels: Blue
Shops/Parks: Green	**Sights/Culture: Black**

Toy Shops

Beatties Wonderful selection of train sets and radio controlled toys. ♦ M-Sa 9AM-6PM. 202 High Holborn, WC1. 071/405.6285

Doll's House Exquisite dolls, straight out of a fairy tale. (See page 151 for more details.) ♦ M-Sa 10AM-8PM. Covent Garden Market, Unit 29. 071/379.7243

Dragons Beautiful hand-painted children's furniture and toys. (See page 82 for more details.) ♦ M-F 9:30AM-5:30PM; Sa 10:30AM-4:30PM. 23 Walton St, SW3. 071/589.3795

Hamleys of Regent Street A child's toy heaven, with 6 floors of dolls, stuffed animals, games, trains, robots. ♦ M-W, F 10AM-6PM; Th 10AM-8PM; Sa 9:30AM-6PM. 188-196 Regent St, W1. 071/734.3161

Just Games A variety of traditional and old favorites like Scrabble and Chess, plus the largest selection of imported European games on the continent. ♦ M-Sa 10AM-6PM. 71 Brewer St, W1. 071/734.6124

Kite Store Brightly colored kites, frisbees and boomerangs for all ages. ♦ M-F 10AM-6PM; Sa 10:30AM-5:30PM. 48 Neal St, WC2. 071/836.1666

Singing Tree New and antique doll houses plus all the accessories that go into them. ♦ M-Sa 10AM-5:30PM. 69 New King's Rd, SW6. 071/736.4527

Tiger, Tiger Everything from marbles and puppets to life-size stuffed animals. (See page 102 for more details.) ♦ M-Sa 9:30AM-6:30PM. 219 King's Rd, SW3. 071/352.8080

Virgin Games Centre The best place to shop in London for electronics and computer games. In addition, they offer a complete selection of Trivial Pursuit games. ♦ M-F 10AM-8PM; Sa 10AM-7PM. 100 Oxford St, W1. 071/637.7911

**Top Toys from Hamleys,
the largest toy store in the world**
188-196 Regent St, W1. 734.3161
Bedlam Cube
Diving Dolphin
Fluppets
Hamleys Chemistry Set
Jet Hopper RC Car
Junior Computer
Pictionary Board Game
Rock'n Flower
Rolling River

Best Homesick Diners

Henry J. Bean Favorite place for nighttime trendies, Saturday shoppers, and parents with kids, because of the huge garden. Juicy burgers with cheese, potato skins, nachos, and cheesecakes from London's Mr. America, **Bob Payton**. (See page 102.) ♦ M-Sa 11:45AM-11:45PM; Su noon-3PM, 7-10:30PM. 195-197 King's Rd, SW3. 071/352.9255

Break for the Border A busy Tex-Mex diner, great for satisfying chili and guacamole cravings. ♦ M-Sa noon-midnight. 8 Argyll St, W1. 071/734.5776. Also at: 125 Charing Cross Rd, WC2. 071/437.8595 (See page 156 for details.)

Ed's Easy Diner The perfect '50s retro diner, with good American-style diner food, including donuts, all reasonably priced. It's the place to be seen eating fast food; it is very good. ♦ M-Th 11:30AM-midnight; F-Sa 11:30AM-1AM; Su 11:30AM-11PM. 12 Moor St, W1. 071/439.1955. Also at: 362 King's Rd, SW3. 071/352.1956 (See page 100.)

5151 No, London isn't convinced that America is full of beer-swilling burger munchers, and this architect-designed restaurant proves it. The Cajun cooking—blackened and mesquite-grilled meats and fish dishes—requires a lot of ingredients to be flown across the Atlantic. Try the jambalaya. Half-price Sunday brunch. (See page 80.) ♦ M-Sa noon-3PM, 6:30-11:30PM; Su 11:30AM-4PM, 6:30-10:30PM; Su 12:30-3:30PM. Chelsea Cloisters, Sloane Ave, SW3. 071/730.5151

Gate Diner Burgers and fries, steak, and pecan pie. This is where the *ex-pats* hang out on Sunday. ♦ Daily 11:30AM-11:30PM. 184a Kensington Park Rd, W11. 071/221.2649

Joe Allen Baked-potato skins, great hamburgers, salads, brownies, actors, and opera singers. This is where everyone comes after the show—audience and stars. Conveniently located in Covent Garden and open late. (Also see page 150.) ♦ M-Sa noon-1AM; Su noon-midnight. 13 Exeter St, WC2. Reservations required. 071/836.0651

Smollensky's Balloon Two floors filled with Art Deco treasures, trompe l'oeil murals, girls in crinkled hair and leather, and men in Armani-clone suits. Bring the kids on Sunday, when Smollensky's brings out clowns, toys, and other treats for youngsters.

♦ M-Sa noon-midnight; Su noon-10:30PM. 1 Dover St, W1. 071/491.1199. Also: Smollensky's on the Strand, 105 Strand, WC2. 071/497.2101 (See page 116.)

Texas Lone Star Saloon The loud music and send-up décor don't overwhelm the food. The 1 1/4 lb T-bone steaks are tender, the salads are crisp, and the fries are crunchy. ♦ M-W 10AM-midnight; Th-Sa 10AM-12:30AM; Su noon-midnight. 117-119 Queensway, W2. 071/727.2980

TGI Friday's (Thank God It's) Tiffany lamps hang in this cavern of a place filled with dark, heavy tables. Big burgers, chunky chicken wings, and a special children's menu are featured. Sunday is kid's day; their menu is half price. High chairs are available for the very small. ♦ M-Sa noon-11:30PM; Su noon-10:30PM. 6 Bedford St, WC2. 071/379.0585

The Thames

The Thames winds a 215-mile course from the low, limestone Cotswold Hills of Gloucester eastward through London and into the North Sea, 50 miles ahead at Tilbury. It is a river full of variety, with many branches, backwaters, islands, and parklike landscapes, and some of England's most spectacular monuments along its banks. The upper reaches meander through a broad, flat basin, flowing past **Windsor Castle**, beautifully situated on the south bank, then around the 16th-century **Hampton Court** and on to **Kingston Bridge** and **Teddington Lock**, which marks the end of the tideway. It continues north to **Twickenham**, where **Ham House** and **Marble Hill House** face each other along its shores, through **Richmond, Old Deer Park**, and the banks of **Kew Gardens**, finally reaching the stone embankments that mark the start of **Central London**. It was here that the Romans built the first bridge over the Thames, spanning a shallow point from the south bank at Southwark to the north bank where the City now stands. Around this wooden bridge the settlement of *Londinium* grew up, quickly becoming a hub of communications and one of Europe's greatest ports. Many of London's historic landmarks reflect in the waters of the Thames: the **Houses of Parliament**, the **Embankment**, **St. Paul's Cathedral**, and the **Tower**. Downstream from the Tower are the **Docklands**; it is hard to capture their Dickensian spirit now that they have been converted into luxury apartments inhabited by yuppies. (Wait for a slightly misty day and you just may be able to visualize the time that Abel Magwitch tried to escape along these shores in **Dickens'** *Great Expectations*.) But some beautiful scenery is yet to come as the river rounds the bend between **Wapping** and **Rotherhithe**, passes beneath the **Old Thames Tunnel** (the first tunnel to be built beneath the river, completed in 1843), and loops around the **Isle of Dogs**. Suddenly, the tall masts of the *Cutty Sark* and **Sir Christopher Wren's Royal Naval College** at Greenwich come into view—a sublime spectacle not to be missed. Further downstream is the massive **Thames Barrier** at Woolwich Reach, designed to stop the surging tides that threatened to flood London (completed in 1982 at a cost of £64 million).

Twenty-eight bridges cross the Thames, from the **Tower Bridge** in London to Teddington Lock. There is one footbridge (Richmond), 9 rail bridges, and 18 road bridges. The oldest site is **London Bridge**. A bridge has crossed the river at this point from Roman times (AD 100),

Thames

with a bloody history to prove it. In the 1500s, Londoners expected to see 20 or so traitors' heads on poles above the bridge at any one time—until **King Charles II** banned the practice. **Sir John Rennie's** 1831 London bridge can be found in Lake Havasu City, Arizona—the old bridge was dismantled to make way for the new in 1987. A new road

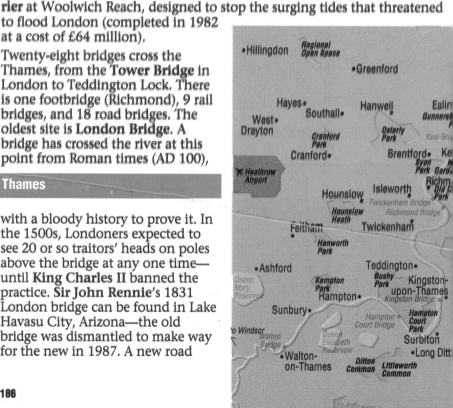

bridge is under construction at **Woolwich**. The Thames is navigable from the North Sea upstream to Lechlade, after which there are a series of locks. Passenger river cruisers and boats, even some old steam ships, travel during the summer between Oxford and Kingston, and from London upstream to Putney, Kew, Richmond, and Hampton Court, and downstream to Greenwich, Tilbury, Southend-on-Sea, and Margate. The river is at its best at dawn, when the sun shines through Tower Bridge; or at dusk, when you can see the sparkling lights of Albert and Chelsea. The trip along the river is lovely and makes the whole shape of London that much clearer. It is an ideal early-morning trip, although you do have to put up with inane commentary from the river boatmen, who, sadly, know nothing and couldn't care less about the history of the embankments, docks, quays, and shores they float past every day.

Forget six counties overhung with smoke,
Forget the snorting steam and piston stroke
Forget the spreading of the hideous town;

Think rather of the pack horse on the down,
And dream of London, small and white and clean
The clear Thames bordered by its gardens green.

William Morris (1834-1896), *The Wanderers*

The Thames by Boat

Boats leave from Westminster Pier, opposite Big Ben, and travel upstream to Kew (a one-and-a-half-hour journey) every 30 minutes, from 10:15AM-3:30PM. You can also go to Hampton Court via Richmond (a 3- 5 hour journey) at 10:30, 11:15AM, noon, and 12:30PM. Boats going downstream to Greenwich (a 45-minute journey) depart every 30 minutes from 10:30AM. (If you feel like it, the No. 1 bus can bring you back to the Strand from here.) There is even a trip to the **Thames Flood Barrier**, the world's largest movable flood barrier. This boat has a bar and food and leaves at 10, 11:15AM, 12:45, and 3:15PM. You can disembark at the **Flood Barrier's Visitor Centre** to learn how it works and how it was constructed.
♦ Information 071/730.4812

River Walk

Walking along the south side of the River Thames is bliss when it's sunny. Here London's famous skyline and many of her finest buildings crowd the water's edge. The views can't be beaten, although you will have to defy death by coming up and crossing some of the bridges by road. You can walk from Lambeth Bridge and Lambeth Palace, the home of the Archbishop of Canterbury, as far as Southwark Bridge, all along the water's edge. It's the best view you could hope for of the Houses of Parliament, the Savoy buildings, and the huge Shell Mex House clock. At the **Royal Festival Hall** dip in for lunch—one of the best cold buffets in town—take in a lunchtime concert in the **National Theatre** foyer, or art at the **Hayward Gallery**. To learn more about World Wars I and II, see the **Imperial War Museum**, just half a mile south of Westminster Bridge. Shakespeare lovers should go to **Bankside**, beneath Southwark Bridge. It's home of the **Shakespeare Globe Museum**.

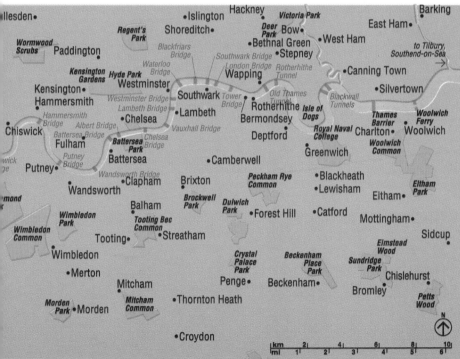

Day Trips

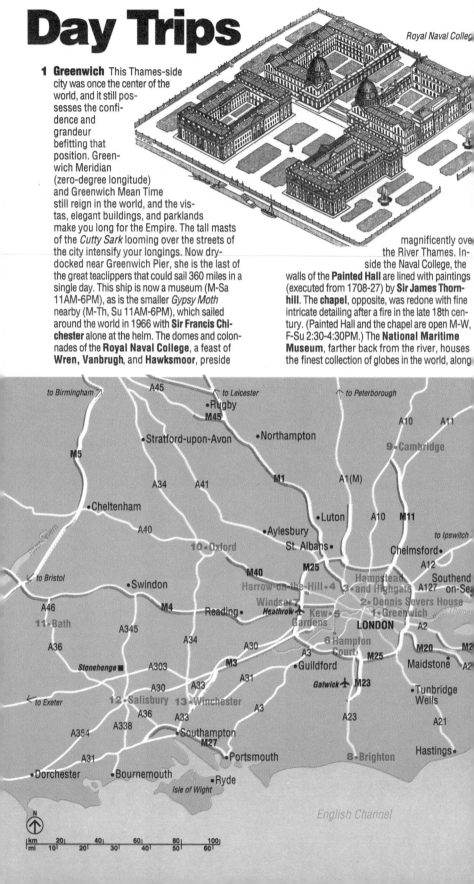

Royal Naval College

1 Greenwich This Thames-side city was once the center of the world, and it still possesses the confidence and grandeur befitting that position. Greenwich Meridian (zero-degree longitude) and Greenwich Mean Time still reign in the world, and the vistas, elegant buildings, and parklands make you long for the Empire. The tall masts of the *Cutty Sark* looming over the streets of the city intensify your longings. Now dry-docked near Greenwich Pier, she is the last of the great teaclippers that could sail 360 miles in a single day. This ship is now a museum (M-Sa 11AM-6PM), as is the smaller *Gypsy Moth* nearby (M-Th, Su 11AM-6PM), which sailed around the world in 1966 with **Sir Francis Chichester** alone at the helm. The domes and colonnades of the **Royal Naval College**, a feast of **Wren, Vanbrugh**, and **Hawksmoor**, preside magnificently over the River Thames. Inside the Naval College, the walls of the **Painted Hall** are lined with paintings (executed from 1708-27) by **Sir James Thornhill**. The **chapel**, opposite, was redone with fine intricate detailing after a fire in the late 18th century. (Painted Hall and the chapel are open M-W, F-Su 2:30-4:30PM.) The **National Maritime Museum**, farther back from the river, houses the finest collection of globes in the world, along

Royal Observatory

with marine paintings, navigational instruments, Nelson relics, and model ships. The centerpiece of the museum is the pure and classical **Queen's House**, designed by **Inigo Jones** in 1616-35. The great hall—a perfect cube—and the tulip staircase are both stunning. **Henry VIII** and his daughters **Mary** and **Elizabeth** were born here (Tu-Sa 10AM-6PM; Su 2-5:30PM). From the Queen's House, pass through **Greenwich Park**, with its delightful **flower garden**, to the buildings of the **Royal Observatory**, designed by Wren for **Charles II** in 1675-76. Inside is a fascinating collection of telescopes and astronomical instruments (M-Sa 10AM-6PM; Su 2:30-6PM). A river walk from the Naval College takes you to the extraordinary **Thames Flood Barrier**, comprised of 10 enormous movable gates between river piers and abutments on either bank. (The best place to eat is the **Spread Eagle**, 1-2 Stockwell St, 081/853.2333.) The best way to reach Greenwich is by riverboat. Boats depart from Westminster Pier every 20 minutes from 10:30AM to 3PM for the 45-minute journey. The last boat leaves Greenwich at 3:45PM in the winter and 5:45PM in the summer. Trains run from Charing Cross to Maze Hill every

half-hour and take 20 minutes. The bus route to Greenwich is dreary, but buses 177 and 188 run between Greenwich and Waterloo Station, making the journey in 35 minutes. If going by car, take A200.

2 Dennis Severs House Ninety-seven candles light this old, dilapidated house, which has no electricity, running water, or bathroom. You are visiting the home of a Hugenot silk-weaving family, **Jarvis**, who lived here from 1725–1919. The house is wedged solid with bric-a-brac from the past 3 centuries, all lovingly collected. But

Day Trips

this isn't a museum treat—Severs says that you use your soul, not your senses, when you visit his home and allow him to take you back 2 centuries. There is nothing like it in London. History lives here. Tours for up to a maximum of 8 people, 3 nights a week, 9PM-12:30AM. Book 3 weeks ahead. ♦ Admission. 18 Folgate St, Spitalfields, E1. 071/247.4013

Restaurants/Nightlife: Red   Hotels: Blue
Shops/Parks: Green   **Sights/Culture:** Black

3 Hampstead and Highgate Houses and cottages of every conceivable shape, style, and most periods ramble up and down the hills here. Hampstead is the prettiest London village and its residents are wealthy enough to keep it that way. (They refused to allow a MacDonalds on the High Street.) Above the village, close to **Jack Straw's Castle Pub**, there are misty views of London to be glimpsed across Hampstead Heath. Further along the top of the heath is the **Spaniard's Inn**, an Elizabethan coaching inn and gateway to London rumored to have been a refuge for highwayman **Dick Turpin**. ◆ M-Sa 11AM-11PM; Su noon-3PM, 7-10:30PM. Spaniard's Rd, NW3. 081/455.3276

Kenwood House grounds are idyllic for picnics and gazing across the beauty of Hampstead Heath toward an ornamental lake and concert bowl (where there are concerts on most summer weekends). Inside is the **Iveagh Bequest** of Grand Masters—works by **Gainsborough, Reynolds,** and **Vermeer**. The tea rooms are wonderful. ◆ Daily 10AM-5PM, Feb-Mar, Oct; daily 10AM-6PM, Apr-Sep; daily 10AM-4PM, Nov-Jan. Hampstead Ln, NW3. 081/348.1286

Highgate Cemetery Day or night, without doubt the spookiest place in London is the **Egyptian Avenue** dug deep into the ground at Highgate Cemetery. It is flanked by dark Egyptian columns—obelisks with catacombs built in between. At the top is the **Circle of Lebanon**, where the catacombs surround you. Above the whole scene is a cedar of Lebanon like you've never seen it before. **Christina Rossetti** is buried here; **Karl Marx** is buried in the eastern cemetery. Hourly tours year-round. ◆ Daily 10AM-5PM, Apr-Sep; daily 10AM-4PM, Oct-Mar. Swain's Ln, N6. 081/340.1834

4 Harrow-on-the-Hill Harrow was in existence by AD 767. In 1572 Harrow School was founded, clustering around the ancient parish church of St. Mary's. **Sir Winston Churchill** and **George Gordon, Lord Byron** (whose verses are forever immortalized in stone in the churchyard) are but 2 of an illustrious list of old boys. The school's gardens were landscaped by **Capability Brown**. London is pretty flat, so you can see for miles from the churchyard. Time has stood still here from the 17th century onward, as you will see when you walk past the tiny workmen's cottages, now pretty homes, which sit next to the palatial

Day Trips

Georgian villas of the fabulously rich. ◆ Tube: Metropolitan line from Baker St

5 Kew Gardens It began as a hobby for **Princess Augusta**, mother of **George III**, back in 1759, and blossomed into the most famous collection of flowers and plants in the world. Kew Gardens is a botanical paradise of more than 300,000 varieties, set in 300 lush acres along the east side of the Thames. Officially called the **Royal Botanic Gardens**, it was given to the nation by the royal family in 1841 and is, for all its pleasure-giving, a scientific institution where plants are studied, classified and cultivated. Kew Gardens offers a constantly changing display of flowers, as well as rock gardens, a stream with aquatic birds, a herbarium with more than 5 million varieties of dried plants, and stunning paths down to the river (with a sublime view of **Syon House** across the Thames). Amid the greenery is an array of 18th-century garden follies, designed by **Sir William Chambers** for Princess Augusta: classical temples, ruins of a Roman arch, a fanciful 10-story pagoda, and an orangery. The **Palm House**, with its sweeping curves of glass and iron, was built in 1844 by **Decimus Buron** and houses tropical plants from both hemispheres. All the greenhouses are architectural masterpieces, as are the grand entrance gates in the corner of Kew Green, also by Burton. Be sure to see **Queen Charlotte's Cottage**, the **Japanese Pagoda**, and if you are lucky enough to come in the spring, the **rhododendron dell**. The hurricanes of '87 and '90 have not affected this wonderful place too badly. The best way to get to Kew Gardens is by riverboat from Westminster Pier. Boats leave for the 75-minute journey every 30 minutes from 10:30AM to 3:30PM. You can also take a train or the tube to and from Kew. Trains leave from Waterloo Station for Kew Bridge; the tube to Kew Station is on the District Line. If driving, take the A30. ◆ Nominal admission. Gardens: daily 10AM-sunset. Greenhouses: daily 11AM-5PM. 081/940.1171

Maids of Honour Do try to visit Kew during the week, not just because it will be less crowded, but because the best tea shop in the area is open! Maids of Honour is the original home of the tarts, and was called that after one of **Henry VIII**'s maids of honor, who cooked such delicious pastries that he imprisoned her to ensure a constant supply. The recipe is still top secret. This quaint, rambling cottage is packed on the weekends and a must for cream teas. But you'll need patience to queue for a seat, although you can buy the cakes next door and eat alfresco in Kew Gardens itself. Book ahead for lunch. ◆ M 9:30AM-1PM; Tu-F 10AM-5:30PM; Sa 9AM-5:30PM. Tea Tu-Sa 2:45PM. 288 Kew Rd, Richmond. 081/940.2752

6 Hampton Court Not really out of town, but down the road 15 miles from London (and better still, down the river), Hampton Court is a must as far as day trips go. The palace was built in the 1500s by **Cardinal Thomas Wolsey**, minister to **Henry VIII**. Wolsey's wealth and lifestyle so exceeded the King's that, inevitably, the King pushed the Cardinal out of the court and took up residence himself. Henry VIII added a moat, a drawbridge, and a tennis court, amenities enjoyed by the 5 of his 6 wives who lived in the palace. **Elizabeth I** loved Hampton Court, and **Charles I** lived in it as king and as a prisoner of **Cromwell**. When **William** and **Mary** came to the throne in 1689

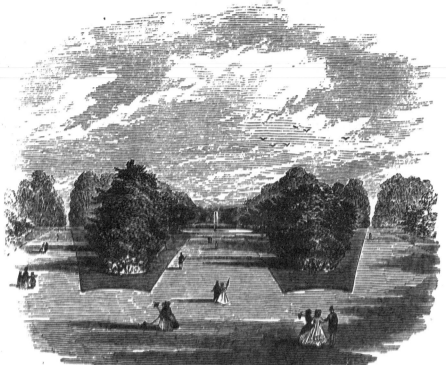

Hampton Court

they revamped the palace, with **Christopher Wren** and **Grinling Gibbons** in charge. The south front was severely damaged in a fire in March of 1986, but, luckily, most of the paintings and art treasures were saved. Signs marked with arrows are scattered throughout the palace to help you find the way to **Cardinal Wolsey's Apartments**; the **King's Dressing Room**, with works by **Holbein** and **Mabuse**; the **Great Hall**, which was the site of Henry VIII's famous banquets and performances of **Shakespeare**'s plays by the playwright's company; and the lower **Orangery**, with the 9 tempera paintings, *The Triumph of Julius Caesar* (1485–92) by **Andrea Mantegna**. The 50 acres of landscaped gardens are absolutely beautiful and the **maze** is irresistible. In summer, boats leave from Westminster Pier to Hampton Court at 10, 10:30, 11:30AM, and noon. The train from Waterloo Station takes 35 minutes. You can also hop a Greenline bus—No. 715A, 716, 718, or 725. ◆ Admission. M-Sa 9:30AM-5PM, Su 2-5PM, Jan-Mar, Oct-Dec; M-Sa 9:30AM-6PM, Su 11AM-6PM, Apr-Sep. 081/977.8441

7 Windsor Windsor lies on a pretty bend of the Thames just 21 miles from London and is home to a magnificent park, a famous boy's school, and the largest castle in the world still occupied by royalty—**Windsor Castle**. The castle has been a royal residence for more than 900 years. **William the Conquerer** first built a round keep made of timber in 1078 (now long gone), and over the centuries monarchs have enlarged the castle and constructed new buildings. **Edward IV** began **St. George's Chapel** in the 1820s. It is one of the best examples of perpendicular architecture, with its elaborately carved stone vaulting. **Henry VIII**, his third wife, **Jane Seymour**,

Windsor Castle

Charles I, and other monarchs are buried in the choir. The **State Apartments**, on the opposite side of the castle, are decorated with paintings by **Van Dyck** and **Rubens**. (**George III**, **George IV**, and **Queen Victoria** restored and beautified this, the present queen's favorite royal home.) Within the same complex is **Queen Mary**'s fabulous **Dolls' House**, designed by **Sir Edwin Lutyens**. The contents are a magical one-twelfth life-size, with one-inch books by **Kipling** in the library. The **Great Park** at Windsor is as fascinating as the castle, with 4800 acres of lawns, trees, lakes, herds of deer, ancient ruins, and **Prince Charles**—when he is playing polo on **Smith's Lawn**.

Across the cast-iron footbridge is **Eton College**, the best-known public school in Britain, founded in 1440 by **Henry VI**. It is best to visit the school when you can see the students in their Eton wing collars and tails. Etonians exude an air of confidence that is quite unrivaled, and it is no surprise that 20 British prime ministers are among the alumni. Schoolyard and Cloisters are open daily from 2-5PM. Windsor can be reached by train in 23 minutes from Paddington Station (change at Slough for Windsor and Eton Central); or in 50 minutes direct from Waterloo Station to Windsor Riverside. The Greenline bus from Hyde Park Corner takes 90 minutes. If you wish to drive, the M4 and then A308 will get you here in an hour. ♦ St. George's Chapel: daily 10:45AM-3:45PM, Feb-Dec. State Apartments (when the royal family is not in residence) and Dolls' House: M-Sa 10:30AM-5PM; Su 1:30-5PM, closes 3PM Oct-Mar. 07535/65538

The Cat Shop Cat lovers come from all over the world to buy from **Mr.** and **Mrs. Malcolm Nash**'s extraordinary collection of *catabilia*. They have around 3000 lines at any one time crushed into this teeny-weeny bow-fronted shop. Cat fire screens, roof cats, mantle cats, cushions, postcards, and plates. Next door is a rather good teashop, the **Court Yard Coffee Shop**, for cakes and buns. ♦ M-Sa 10:30AM-5:30PM; Su 11AM-5:30PM. George VP1, Thames Ave, Windsor. 753/860173

8 Brighton The first place to stop in Brighton is the **Royal Pavilion** (1815-1822, **John Nash**). Half a million pounds in real gold was the cost to the prince regent back in 1822. It is still as splendid today. It's built so like a fairytale Indian mogul's palace with its great onion-shaped dome, huge tentlike roofs, and lots of smaller ornate pinnacles and minarets you almost expect to see elephants carrying a rajah past you. Inside, it's pure Chinoiserie and filled with **Queen Elizabeth II**'s original furniture, chosen especially for this palace. It has a series of spectacular suites culminating in the banqueting room with brilliantly colored and gilt-painted walls and a ceiling like a huge palm tree with a bedragonned chandelier. There is nothing like it in Europe. ♦ Daily 10AM-5PM, Jan-May, Oct-Dec; daily 10AM-6PM, Sep. Pavilion Parade. 0273/603005

The rest of the town echoes the elegant proportions of Regency days with frequent and unexpected onion domes and roofs. For yet more inspiration, just behind the pavilion is the **Brighton Art Gallery and Museum** with its award-winning Art Nouveau and Deco collections. ♦ Free. Tu-Sa 10AM-5:45PM; Su 2-5PM. Church St. 0273/603005

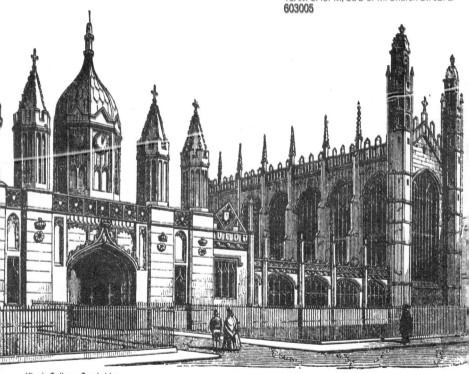

King's College, Cambridge

Magdelen College, Oxford

Brighton has 2 piers, but only the **Victorian Palace Pier** is open to the public. It's well worth visiting during the week. (Avoid the weekends as it's crowded with daytrippers.) Cream tea, buffeted by the waves at the pier's little **Palm Court Restaurant**, harks back to a long-forgotten time when breathing in sea air and promenading were the things to do. For lunch, try the crowded **Food for Friends** (17a-18 Prince Albert St, The Lanes, 0273/202310), an excellent vegetarian café. Then walk on because you are in deepest antiques land; the Lanes are 17th-century red-brick streets full of tiny shops selling everything old imaginable.

Brighton can be reached by train from Waterloo (1 per hour) or Victoria Station (2 per hour) in 50 minutes. Train is by far the best way to get here. By car, take the A23 or M23; it takes an hour or more. Express buses run all day from Victoria Coach Station (a 2-hour trip).

9 Cambridge If you can manage only one excursion to the *palaces of privilege and academe*, choose Cambridge. A few decades younger than Oxford, it is architecturally more cohesive, more beautiful, and less interrupted by the city itself. Cambridge is located in a part of England called East Anglia, on the edge of the Cam River, and the colleges back on to the river (hence the term *Backs*). The most interesting of the 29 schools at Cambridge is **St. John's Trinity** (founded by **Henry VIII**); **Clare; King's** (the chapel has beautiful stained-glass windows, fan vaulting, and lofty spires); **Corpus Christi; Queen's; Peterhouse**; and **Jesus**. The ideal time to visit is **May Week**, a 10-day period in June when graduating seniors receive their degrees. Festivities take place throughout the city, including a rowing competition on the Cam. Be sure to plan your day to include evensong in **King's College Chapel**, and however touristy it may seem, allow yourself to be punted on the River Cam along the Backs—it rivals the gondola in Venice in terms of sheer tranquility and beauty. Cambridge is not known for culinary

achievement, but you can get a good pub lunch at **Free Press** (7 Prospect Row, 0223/683337), which serves imaginative salads and excellent pies. If you can't get back to London for dinner, take a taxi to **Panos** (154 Hills Rd, 0223/212958), which serves a mixture of French and English food and has good grills. Try to book in advance. Cambridge, 54 miles from London, can be reached by train direct from Liverpool Street Station in 75 minutes, by bus from Victoria Station in a little under 2 hours, or by car on M11 to Junction 10 in 90 minutes.

10 Oxford The Gothic turrets, towers, and spires of famous colleges dominate the center of Oxford, which has been a university town since the 1200s. **Oxford University** (like Cambridge) is a collection of 30 colleges. **St. Edmund Hall, Merton**, and **Balliol**, built in the 13th century, are the oldest of the colleges. **Magdelen** (pronounced *maudlen*), the most beautiful, was once home to student notables from the likes of **Wolsey** to **Wilde**. A visit during the academic year (mid October to mid May) is most interesting; during the summer holidays, the colleges are deserted or filled with American students, although the buildings are open all day. Most of the colleges can only be visited in the afternoon during the school year. You won't eat better anywhere in Oxford—or perhaps in England—than at **Le Petit Blano** (272 Branbury Rd, Summertown,

865/53540), which serves regional French food with the finest English ingredients. Book now! Oxford is 56 miles from London and can be reached by train from Paddington Station in 60 minutes (trains leave hourly), or by bus from Victoria Station in 1 hour and 45 minutes. If you are driving, take M40 and A40 (90 minutes).

So poetry, which is in Oxford made an art, in London only is a trade.

Prologue to *University of Oxford*, 1984

11 Bath Elegantly proportioned Bath is as perfect as a novel by **Jane Austen**, who came here, sipped the water in the **Pump Room**, and captured its grace, elegance, and usefulness in *Northanger Abbey* and *Persuasion*. This Georgian city of terraces, crescents, and squares is the most famous spa in England, and worth a visit for its warm springs, Roman ruins, glorious architecture, and gentle Austenesque atmosphere. The Romans, nostalgic for the warm waters of home, founded Bath in AD 43 and stayed for 4 centuries. But it wasn't until the 18th century, when luminaries such as **Gainsborough, Queen Victoria**, and **Lord Nelson** were regular visitors, that Bath became the fashionable spa town that is remembered today. The Roman baths, among the most striking ruins in Europe, are still the city's major attraction. Excavations nearby have unearthed relics ranging from coins to a sacrificial altar. You can sample water from the fountain in the Pump Room (M-Sa 9AM-6PM; Su 11AM-5PM), which **Dickens** said tastes like warm flatirons. The Georgian perfection of the town is largely the work of two 18th-century architects—a father and son, both named **John Wood**. The modern architecture, well, close your eyes. After its heyday in the 18th century, the city's reputation went downhill. But the last 2 decades have brought new life to Bath. Today, smart Londoners come here for the city's renewed cultural life as well as the waters. One of the greatest achievements is the renovation of the **Theatre Royal**, which until a few years ago was a third-circuit theater. Now it hosts some of the country's top productions before they move on to London. The best place to eat in Bath is **Popjoys** (Sawclose, 0225/60494). But you absolutely must book in advance for the fabulous English food, served in the sumptuous house where **Richard Beau Nash** lived with his girlfriend **Juliana Popjoy**. Everything is fresh and delicious. Be sure to save room for the syllabub, which is as exquisite and English as Bath itself. One hundred sixteen miles from London, Bath can be reached in 70 minutes by high-speed train from Paddington Station, by bus from Victoria Station in 3 hours, or by car on M40 to Junction 18, then A46, in 2 hours.

12 Salisbury Wiltshire's country town of Salisbury, 83 miles from London, rests on a plain where the rivers Nadder and Bourne flow into the Avon, quietly expressing the calm beauty

of this charming medieval town and its famous cathedral. Salisbury's other major attraction is its convenient location, just 10 miles from **Stonehenge**, one of the most important prehistoric monuments in Europe.

Classic **Salisbury Cathedral**, consecrated in 1258, is the perfection of English cathedral architecture, made even more beautiful by its majestic spire (c. 1320) rising above the water meadows beside the Avon. At 404 feet high, it is the tallest spire in England, enchanting the eye with its deceptive lightness—the 6400 tons of stonework put such a strain on the 4 bearing columns that they are slightly bent. The Avon marks the western side of the cathedral's grounds, and a 14th-century wall of stone from **Old Sarum**, a cathedral that was razed in 1331 to provide building materials for the cathedral close, borders the other 3 sides. The interior of the cathedral is not as breathtaking as the exterior, due in part to the ruthlessness of **James Wyatt**'s renovations (1788-89), in which he removed the screens and chapels and rearranged the monuments in rows. Happily, the restoration by **Sir Gilbert Scott** in 1859 minimized some of the damage. The cathedral contains tombs of the Crusaders and those who died at Agincourt. Other treasures include exquisite lancet windows with patchworks of glass from the 13th and 15th centuries and a 14th-century wrought-iron clock that was restored to working order in 1956. The **Cloisters** and beautiful octagonal **Chapter House**, built from 1364 to 1380, were modeled after Westminster Abbey. Many of the cathedral's treasures are displayed in the Chapter House, including one of 4 existing copies of the Magna Carta, brought here for safekeeping shortly after 1265.

A couple of miles west of Salisbury and easily reachable by bus or car is the splendid **Wilton House**, the home of the **Earl of Pembroke** for more than 400 years, with 17th-century staterooms by **Inigo Jones**. The incomparable art collection includes 16 **van Dyck**'s, which are hung in the famous double-cube room (60 feet long by 30 feet high and 30 feet wide) where **General Eisenhower** planned the Normandy invasion. Wilton House is 2 miles west of Salisbury, and can be reached by bus every half-hour in 18 minutes or by car on A30. ♦ Admission. M-Sa 11AM-6PM; Su 1-6PM, Apr-Oct

Stonehenge Ten miles northwest of Salisbury on A345. The great, historic structure is one of the oldest and most important megalithic monuments in Europe, dating from between 1850 BC and 1400 BC. Though the fence around Stonehenge (added for its own protection) makes it look like a captive animal, and takes away from the initial impact, the sight of the long, eerie collection of stones is still breathtaking, and the way the monument interacts with the sun on certain days of the year is astounding. The stones are arranged in 4 series within a circular ditch 300 feet in diameter. The outer ring, with a diameter of 97 feet, is a circle of 17 sandstones connected on top by a series of lintel stones. The second ring is of bluestones, the third is horseshoe shaped, and the inner ring is ovoid. Within the ovoid lies the **Altar Stone**, made of micaceous sandstone. The great upright **Heelstone** is in the **Avenue**, the broad road leading to the monument. Some of the stones, weighing up to 4 tons each, have been shown to come from the Preseli Hills in Wales, a distance of some 135 miles. Stonehenge was at one time believed to be a druid temple, a theory contra-

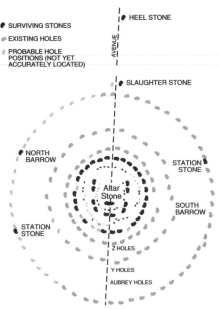

- ● SURVIVING STONES
- ◠ EXISTING HOLES
- ◜ PROBABLE HOLE POSITIONS (NOT YET ACCURATELY LOCATED)

HEEL STONE

AVENUE

SLAUGHTER STONE

NORTH BARROW

STATION STONE

Altar Stone

STATION STONE

SOUTH BARROW

Z HOLES

Y HOLES

AUBREY HOLES

Stonehenge plan showing the solstitial alignment of the axis of symmetry

dicted by the fact that the druids didn't arrive in Britain until c. 250 BC. In 1963, British astronomer **Gerald Hawkins** theorized that Stonehenge was a huge astronomical instrument used to accurately measure solar and lunar movements as well as eclipses.

Salisbury is 83 miles from London, and can be reached by way of a picturesque railway journey, leaving from Waterloo Station 10 minutes past every hour and arriving in Salisbury 90 minutes later. There are 2 bus trips daily from Victoria Coach Station that take 3 hours, but the bus service in the afternoon from Salisbury is often at awkward times—take the train! The station is a 10-minute walk from the center of Salisbury. If you are driving, take M3 and A30.

13 Winchester Ancient capital of England, graceful and unspoiled, and a perfect trip to combine with Salisbury and Stonehenge, only 20 miles away. Winchester was the capital of England for nearly 250 years, from 829 until the Norman Conquest, when the Normans gradually moved the capital to London. **King Alfred** and the Danes reigned here from 871 to 900, developing Winchester into a great center of learning. Picturesque **High Street**, the center of the city, is lined with a charming medley of buildings dating from the 13th century. Near the end of the street is the **Great Hall** (1235), all that remains of **Winchester Castle**, demolished in 1644-45. An early fake Round Table of the legendary King Arthur hangs in the hall, which was the scene of many medieval parliaments and notable trials, including that of **Sir Walter Raleigh** for conspiring against **James I**. The beautiful early Norman **cathedral** set in a peaceful close in Europe (556 feet), made to seem longer by its height (78 feet). The best view is from

Magdalen Hill, the approach road to Winchester from the east, which emphasizes its setting in the city. Begun in 1079, consecrated in 1093, and partially rebuilt in 1346-66, it contains a wealth of treasures, most striking of which are the 7 richly carved chantry chapels, especially **Bishop Wykeham's Chantry**, in the west end of the **nave**, which contains an effigy of the great builder, statesman, and founder of Winchester college and New College, Oxford. On the wall opposite are a brass tablet and window, dedicated to **Jane Austen** (1775-1817), who is buried here. The bronze statues of James I and **Charles I** are by **Hubet Le Sueur** (1685). Under the organ loft in the north transept is the **Chapel of the Holy Sepulchre** (12th century), with superb wall paintings (c. 1170-1205) of the *Life and Passion of Christ*. The oak screen separating the choir from the nave is by **Sir Gilbert Scott**, and the magnificent stalls (1305–10), with their misericords carved with human, animal, and monster motifs, are the oldest cathedral stalls in England, except for some fragments at Rochester. The **library**, over the passage between the south transept and the Norman arches of the old **Chapter House**, was built in the 12th century and reconstructed in 1668. It contains 4000 printed books and rare manuscripts, most important of which is the *Winchester Bible* (12th century), one of the finest medieval manuscripts.

If you walk about a mile south of the cathedral, you will come upon the ancient **St. Cross Hospital**, where the *Wayfarer's Dole* of a horn of beer and a portion of bread—once a handout to the needy—is still offered to visitors.

Winchester, 65 miles from London, can be reached by train from Waterloo Station in 65 minutes (trains leave 45 minutes past the hour), or by buses leaving Victoria Coach Station every hour for the 2-hour-and-10-minute journey. By car, take M3 and A33.

Bests

Peter Harrison
Designer, New York

Kew Bridge Pumping Station is an astounding and beautifully preserved example of Victorian high technology. Three truly huge steam engines used for over 100 years to pump water into London's water mains are on display. Amazingly, they run them on week-

Day Trips

ends, so you can see these colossal machines in action. There is also a museum with several smaller steam engines that they also run.

For Filofax nuts, try **Chisholm's** on Kingsway. They have more Filofax items than I have ever seen. An absolute *must* if you have the disease.

Restaurants/Nightlife: Red   Hotels: Blue
Shops/Parks: Green   **Sights/Culture: Black**

History

Event	Monarch
	BC
Julius Caesar invades Britain	**55-54**
	AD
Roman Conquest of Britain by Emperor Claudius. First London Bridge is built.	**43**
London is destroyed by Queen Boadicea.	**61**
Roman army withdraws from Britain to defend Rome.	**410**
The Vikings invade Britain and create havoc, sacking London as well.	**851**
	871 / **Alfred the Great** (871-901)
Alfred the Great occupies London.	**886**
	925 / **Athelstan** (925-40)
Canute captures London	**1017** / **Canute** (1016-35)
	1042 / **Edward the Confessor** (1042-66)
Consecration of first Westminster Abbey.	**1065**
William the Conqueror crowned at Westminster Abbey.	**1066** / **House of Normandy** / **Harold** (1066) / **William I** (1066-87)
Fire destroys most of the City and St. Paul's.	**1087** / **William II** (1087-1100; probably murdered)
White Tower is completed. William Profus	**1097**

History

begins to build the Great Hall at Westminster.

	1100 / **Henry I** (1100-35)
	1135 / **Stephen** (1135-54)

Event		Monarch
	1154	**House of Plantagenet**
		Henry II (1154-89)
Construction begins on London Bridge, the first stone bridge, completed in 1290.	**1176**	
	1189	**Richard the Lionhearted** (1189-99; killed in battle)
London establishes rule by mayor.	**1190**	
	1199	**John** (1199-1216)
King John signs the Magna Carta at Runnymede.	**1215**	
	1216	**Henry III** (1216-72)
First Parliament is summoned; English state begins.	**1265**	
Consecration of present Westminster Abbey.	**1269**	
	1272	**Edward I** (1272-1307)
Old St. Paul's Cathedral is completed, half as tall as the present building.	**1280**	
	1307	**Edward II** (1307-27; murdered)
	1327	**Edward III** (1327-77)
Edward III claims the French throne and the Hundred Years War begins.	**1337**	
Westminster becomes regular meeting place of Parliament.	**1338**	
Black death strikes Europe; about half of London's 60,000 citizens die.	**1348**	
	1377	**Richard II** (1377-99; deposed and murdered)
Wat Tyler's Peasant Revolt.	**1381**	

Event	Year	Monarch / House
	1399	**House of Lancaster.** **Henry IV** (1399-1413)
	1413	**Henry V** (1413-22)
Henry V's victory at Agincourt.	1415	
	1422	**Henry VI** (1422-61; deposed)
Joan of Arc is burned.	1431	
War of Roses begins.	1455	
	1461	**House of York** **Edward IV** (1461-83)
Caxton's printing press is set up at Westminster Abbey	1476	
Princes probably murdered in the Tower.	1483	**Edward V** (1483; probably murdered **Richard III** (1483-85)
Accession of Henry Tudor.	1485	**House of Tudor** **Henry VII** (1485-1509)
Henry VIII builds St. James's Palace.	1509	**Henry VIII** (1509-47)
Fall of Wolsey. Henry VIII moves into York Place (renames it Whitehall) and takes over Hampton Court.	1530	
Henry VIII's Reformation; dissolution of the monasteries, including Westminster Abbey.	1533	
Henry VIII divorces Catherine of Aragon.	1534	
Anne Boleyn is executed at the Tower of London.	1536	
Jane Seymour dies while giving birth to Edward VI.	1537	
Henry VIII marries Anne of Cleves.	1540	
Catherine Howard is executed in Tower of London.	1542	
Henry VIII marries Catherine Parr.	1543	
	1547	**Edward VI** (1547-53)
Mary marries Philip II of Spain and reinstates Catholicism. Citizens are martyred at Smithfield.	1553	**Mary I** (1553-58)
Elizabethan Age begins (45 years)	1558	**Elizabeth I** (1558-1603)
Mary, Queen of Scots, flees to England (executed 1587). Royal Exchange is set up.	1568	
Shakespeare arrives in London.	1585	
Spanish Armada tries and fails to invade Britain.	1588	
Wood from theater in Shoreditch is used to make the Globe of Bankside.	1598	
	1603	**House of Stuart** **James I** (James VI of Scotland; 1603-25)
Guy Fawkes tries to blow up Parliament in Gunpowder Plot.	1605	
Pilgrims sail on *Mayflower* and settle in New England.	1620	
Inigo Jones' Banqueting House is completed.	1625	**Charles I** (1625-49; beheaded)
Covent Garden is laid out.	1631	

History

Event	Year	Monarch / House
Quarrels between Charles I and Parliament lead to Civil War between the Royalists and Parliament. King is forced to leave London.	1642-6	

Charles I is executed at Banqueting House.	1649	
	1653	Commonweath: **Oliver Cromwell**, Protector (1653-58) **Richard Cromwell**, Protector (1658-59) **House of Stuart** (Restored)
	1660	**Charles II** (1660-85)
Great Plague; 100,000 die.	1665	
Great Fire destroys half of London; 9 die	1666	
Christopher Wren designs and builds St. Paul's and 51 London churches.	1666-1723	
	1685	**James II** (1685-88; deposed and exiled)
Glorious Revolution. William and Mary come to the throne.	1688	**William III** and **Mary II** (joint monarchs 1689-1702)
Bank of England founded.	1694	
Whitehall Palace destroyed by fire.	1698	
	1702	**Anne** (1702-14)
	1714	**House of Hanover** / **George I** (1714-27)
	1727	**George II** (1727-1760)
	1760	**George III** (1760-1820)

History

Dr. Johnson's Literary Club is founded.	1764	
Royal Academy of Arts is founded.	1768	
The Adelphi is built by Robert and John Adam.	1772	
America declares its independence from Britain.	1776	
Lord Nelson dies at the Battle of Trafalgar and is buried in St. Paul's.	1805	
Charles Dickens born in London.	1812	
Gas lighting is installed on Piccadilly.	1814	
Wellington defeats Napoleon at Waterloo. John Nash lays out Regent's Park, Portland Place, Regent Street, and the Mall.	1815	
	1820	**George IV** (1820-30)
National Gallery is founded.	1824	
First police force is founded. First London bus.	1829	
	1830	**William VI** (1830-37)
Barry and Pugin start the Houses of Parliament; completed in 1860.	1835	
London's first passenger railway opens, running from Southwark to Greenwich. London University receives Royal Charter.	1836	
Buckingham Palace becomes permanent residence of the sovereign.	1837	**Victoria** (1837-1901)
Nelson's statue is erected in Trafalgar Square. Brunel's Rotherhithe Tunnel (the first under the Thames) is built.	1843	

Event	Year	House / Monarch
British Museum is built on grounds of Montagu House.	1844	
Great Exhibition in the Crystal Palace at Hyde Park.	1851	
First mailbox on corner of Fleet Street and Farringdon Street.	1855	
Tooley Street fire; worst since 1666.	1861	
Opening of first underground railway.	1863	
Victoria proclaimed Empress of India.	1887	
Jack the Ripper strikes in Whitechapel.	1888	
Creation of London County Council, giving the city a comprehensive government for the first time.	1889	
First electric railway tube, from the City to Stockwell.	1890	
Tower Bridge, with double drawbridge, is built.	1894	
Queen Victoria's Diamond Jubliee.	1897	
	1901	House of Saxe-Coburg
		Edward VII (1901-10)
First fleet of horseless carriages.	1905	
	1910	House of Windsor
		George V (1910-36)
World War I; London is damaged from Zeppelin air raids.	1914-18	
Women win the right to vote.	1918	
General Strike.	1926	
	1936	Edward VIII (1936; abdicated)
		George VI (1936-52)
World War II; the Blitz; St. Paul's stands among ruins.	1939-45	
Rebuilding of London.	1945-55	
Festival of Britain. Southbank is built as culture center (Royal Festival Hall).	1951	
	1952	Elizabeth II
Clean Air Act ends fog and smog in Central London.	1956	
Post Office Tower is built.	1965	
New London Bridge and new Stock Exchange completed.	1973	
National Theatre is built.	1976	
Silver Jubilee of Queen Elizabeth.	1977	
Margaret Thatcher becomes first female prime minister.	1979	
Royal wedding of Prince Charles and Princess Diana. National Westminster Bank is built, at more than 600 feet, the tallest commercial building in London.	1981	
Greater London Council abolished.	1986	
The Times is the first newspaper to move to the Docklands.		
The Daily Express is the last newspaper to leave Fleet Street.	1989	
Introduction of Poll Tax in England	1990	

Essentials

Transportation

Airports Two airports serve London: **Heathrow** and **Gatwick**. You can get into London inexpensively and relatively quickly from either one. Heathrow is a lot closer to London, but the train service from Gatwick to Victoria Station is fast and easy, so if you can get a cheaper flight that goes into Gatwick, you'd be wise to take it.

Heathrow is 14 miles from central London. You can reach Hyde Park (Knightsbridge tube) by underground railway in about 40 minutes. If the prospect of taking public transportation seems too daunting, there are helpful **Travel Information Centres** in all terminals where you can find out where to go and how to get there. (Terminal 1: M-F 7:15AM-10:15PM; Sa 7:15AM-9PM; Su 8:15AM-10PM. Terminal 2: M-Sa 7:15AM-9PM; Su 8:15AM-10PM. Terminal 3: M-Sa 7:15AM-2PM; Su 8:15AM-3PM. Terminal 4: M-Sa 6:30AM-6:30PM; Su 8:15AM-6:30PM.)

There are 2 Heathrow tube (subway) stations, and both Heathrow Central and Terminal 4 are on the Piccadilly line and relatively new. Tubes leave Heathrow about every 2 minutes. The first train to Heath-row leaves King's Cross at 5:39AM Monday through Saturday and at 6:57AM Sunday. Departures start from Heathrow at 4:59AM Monday through Saturday and at 5:52AM Sunday. The last train into London leaves Heathrow at 11:47PM Monday through Saturday and at 11:43PM on Sunday. The **Airbus**, a bus service between Heathrow and London, costs a little more (dollars and francs are accepted) and takes a little longer (50 minutes), but you can see the sky and English cars and buses along the route into London. There are 2 Airbus routes: A1 to Victoria station via Hyde Park Corner, and A2 to Russell Square via Euston Station, Notting Hill Gate, Marble Arch, and Baker Street. If the bus seems too tiring, relax and take a black taxi into London and be prepared to pay handsomely for the spacious tranquility. There are frequent bus services (**Speedlink** and **Jetlink**) if you are transferring to Gatwick Airport that take about an hour, as long as the M25 isn't jammed up.

If you are booked on a charter flight like Virgin Airways you will probably arrive at Gatwick. But no matter how tired you are from the journey, don't take a taxi into London. Fast trains run every 15 minutes from Gatwick and reach Victoria Station in 30 minutes. Getting your cases down to the trains is a

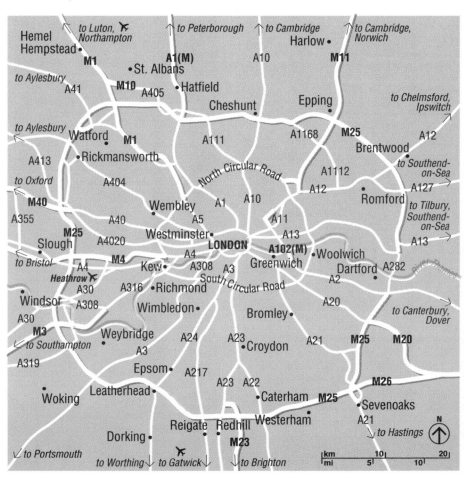

struggle but persevere. There is also a **Greenline** bus service that runs every half-hour from Gatwick Coach station and takes 70 minutes. ♦ Information desk 0293/28822

Bicycles For the stout-hearted only. An enchanting but exceptionally dangerous way to get around London unless you're an experienced cyclist. You must remember to stay on the left side of the street and lock your bike conscientiously. Try to avoid the main routes because, apart from the bus and car fumes being a drag, the lorries thunder past, often too close for comfort. But seeing London from a bike is one of the best ways to see it—slow enough to take in the beauty and find hidden ways through the backstreets and across London's parks, easy to park (lampposts and parking meters are free), and healthy, too. It's become very trendy—glamorous Londoners can be spotted cycling their Muddy Foxes to work, clad in skin-tight lycra gear and ski jackets, with their briefcases on the back, in all but the worst weather.

The London Cycling Campaign (3 Stamford St, SE1, 071/928.7220) is an excellent source of cycling information.

Bike Rental:

Dial-a-Bike ♦ 18 Gillingham St, SW1. 071/828.4040

F.W. Evans ♦ 77 The Cut, Waterloo, SE1. 071/928.4785

Portobello Cycles ♦ 69 Golborne Rd, W10. 081/960.0444

Savile's Cycle Store ♦ 97 Battersea Rise, SW11. 071/228.4279

Driving Try hard to avoid it, but if you are renting a car to drive into the English countryside be prepared for a few nerve-racking moments in London. One alternative is to call **European Chauffeurs Ltd.** (071/261.0069), which will drive you and your car to a site on your route, keeping you out of the worst of the city traffic. **Universal Aunts** (071/351.5767) will do the same, or you can drive and follow one of their guides. Otherwise, drive slowly and keep saying to yourself *left, left, left,* so you remember to drive on the left side of the road.

Car Rental A quicker and cheaper way is to take the tube or train to nearer your destination and hire a car outside central London. Renting a car in London is the same as renting a car anywhere in the world. Prices vary greatly and insurance and VAT add considerably to the cost. A credit card is just about as indispensable as a valid driver's license. You must be over 21, sometimes over 23, and have had your license for over a year.

Companies like Hertz and Avis give discounts of up to 50 percent if you book your car when you buy your ticket, so if you are planning to tour the country, arrange for a car in advance. It is now the law throughout the British Isles that drivers and front-seat passengers wear seat belts at all times.

Avis Locations throughout London. ♦ 081/848.8733

Camelot Barthropp Exclusively chauffeur-driver cars. ♦ Headfort Place Garage, SW1. 071/235.0234/0330

Europcar Locations throughout London. ♦ 081/950.5050

Godfrey Davis Chauffeur-driven and luxury cars. ♦ Davis House, 129 Wilton Rd, SW1. 071/834.6701

Hertz Locations throughout London. ♦ 081/679.1799

Parking Parking in central London is a nightmare, and police tow cars away and use wheel clamps (the Denver Boot) with infuriating regularity. If they tow you, it's a hefty fine and a trip to Marble Arch, Hammersmith, or Vauxhall to get your car back. If you are clamped, it will cost you somewhat less, plus a trip to a payment center and a wait of about 4 hours to get unclamped. Be sure to carry an ample supply of 10 and 50p pieces for meters and keep the things topped up; the police and traffic wardens do not respect the driver who has gone overtime. Use a car park if you can find one; it's much safer, although expensive.

London Transport The only way to become a citizen of a city, albeit a temporary one, is to use public transportation. Mastering the tube or the bus puts the city at your feet, eases the pressure on the wallet, and orients you in a way that taxi rides never will. Various passes are available that save time and money. Most are valid on buses and the underground, and can be purchased from underground station ticket offices, travel information centers, newsstands, and travel agents. The **Travelcard**, a combined bus/underground/British Rail ticket, is the best value for central London; it includes the Docklands light railway and suburban train systems. The Travelcard can be purchased for 1 or 7 days—you need a passport photo for the 7-day card. Travel and information centers are located in the underground stations at Heathrow Central, Euston, King's Cross, Piccadilly Circus, Charing Cross, Oxford Circus, Victoria, and St. James's Park. At the Travel Information Centre you can pick up free bus maps and guides.

The Big Red London Bus If speed is not a priority, take a London bus. Bus stops have signs showing the numbers of the buses that stop there, outlines of the bus route, and sometimes a map of the route. The view of London from the top of a bus is unbeatable, and the bus itself, fire-engine red, doubledecker, with its roller-coaster movements and friendly atmosphere, is one of those essential authentic experiences. People waiting in the queue will help you, but, regrettably, most buses are now one-man-operated and no longer have collectors. The collectors, whose rudeness was legendary, won't be missed as much as the mighty **Routemaster Bus** they patrolled so fiercely. Have your fare or Travelcard ready to show the driver as you board. And remember, you enter at the front of the bus. Like on the tube, the fare is tied to zones, but the bus is sometimes cheaper. You can buy a Travelcard for the bus only at tube stations or at sweet shops that have a sign saying that they sell them. These sweet shops are hard to find, so go to a tube station if you can. Strange but true: the bus driver cannot sell you a one-day bus pass.

Bus Etiquette is as follows:

1. Bus queues are not as sacred as they used to be, but do try and find the end.

2. You may be the only person at the stop waiting for your particular bus, so keep your eyes open. Buses do sail past, even when they're supposed to stop. Don't feel silly if you feel like flagging your bus down. If the stop is marked *Request*, wave the bus to stop.

3. Smoking is allowed at the back of the upper deck, so the pleasure of being on top has its drawbacks.

4. There is no standing on the upper deck or on the platform.

5. Even though the English do it, don't jump off—or onto—a moving bus.

6. Avoid bus trips at rush hour, 7:30-9:30AM, 5-6:30PM, as you may have to wait a long time to get one.

Three Scenic Bus Routes The numbers refer to bus routes and are displayed on the front of each bus.

11—King's Road, Sloane Square, Victoria Coach Station, Victoria, Westminster Cathedral, Westminster Abbey, Westminster, Whitehall, Horse Guards, Trafalgar Square, National Gallery, Strand, Law Courts, Fleet Street, St. Paul's.

53—Oxford Circus, Regent Street, Piccadilly Circus, National Gallery, Trafalgar Square, Whitehall, Horse Guards, Westminster, Westminster Bridge, Imperial War Museum, Elephant and Castle.

88—Bayswater, Hyde Park, Marble Arch, Oxford Street, Oxford Circus, Regent Street, Piccadilly Circus, Trafalgar Square, National Gallery, Horse Guards, Whitehall, Westminster, Millbank, Tate Gallery, Vauxhall Bridge.

Night Buses Special Night Buses (marked with the *N* sign) run from London to the suburbs through the night until 6 a.m. Buses leave from Trafalgar Square and the Central London restaurant, theater and cinema districts. One-day Travelcards are not valid.

The Underground The **tube**, as it is better known, is fast, clean (ish), and safe until about 9 at night, and easy to use (though not as fast and easy as the Paris Metro, as it is older and has greater distances to cover). Tube stations are indicated by the round red-and-blue **London Transport** signs. There are 11 lines, each marked by a different name and color to make recognition easier. Service starts at 5AM and ends around midnight. Buy your ticket before getting on the train, either from a vendor or machine. One-day Travelcards are available from large machines. Keep your ticket, which you put through a machine at both the start and end of your journey. Guards are on hand to help you through automatic exits, but getting packages through is difficult. Large-scale maps of the underground network are in each station, and each compartment of the train has a map of the route the train follows. Maddeningly, trains going to various destinations use the same platform, so look at the lit-up sign above the platform to verify the destination and route. Prices depend on the

length of the journey from one zone to another, not from station to station. (There are 5 possible zones in London and the one-day Travelcard covers the lot.) One ticket takes you to your destination, but always remember if you are doing   a few journeys in

a day to ask for a Travelcard. You can also ask for a free tube map and *Visitors Guide* when you buy your ticket. Smoking is not permitted anywhere on the underground.

Taxis Who has not been in love at one time with a black London taxi? Capacious, timeless, and honorable, these shiny black taxis (nearly all are Austins) are icons of English dependability and integrity. Great travelers consider London taxi drivers the best in the world, and rare is the experience of announcing your destination and getting a blank look. The drivers take tough exams to prove their knowledge of the streets, and have an honor code to take the shortest route, charging only what appears on the meter. There is a surcharge for large baggage after 8PM and on weekends and holidays. Tip between 10 and 15 percent. If you are suspicious beyond a doubt about route or price, take the driver's number and call the **Carriage Office** (071/278.1744). A taxi is for hire when the yellow *For Hire* sign is lit. The driver should stop if you flag him down, and if your destination is under 6 miles and within London borders, he must take you. Avoid using the car phones in taxis; they cost about £1 a minute to use whether you get through or not and can add a fortune to the price of your journey.

You can also call a 24-hour radio cab, pay for being picked up (the distance required to reach you), and avoid the pleading wait in the street (071/272.0272, 071/286.0286, or 071/253.5000).

Another option is a **minicab**. These are not black taxis but ordinary cars, available by telephone, only. Ask the price when you call and confirm it when the taxi arrives. Minicabs are the best value if you are going a long distance and can be a good value for getting to the airport when you are laden with packages and baggage. The rates for a trip to Heathrow are standard and reasonable. The drivers lack the incredible knowledge of London that London taxi drivers have, so they sometimes get lost. The quality and condition of the cars and the drivers varies greatly as the only requirement for the vehicle is that it has 4 doors! Only use recommended firms. ♦ Addison Lee 071/720.2161, Abbey Car Hire 071/720.2161, Greater London Hire 081/340.2450

Trains They're a great, civilized way to travel, and the sit-down breakfasts in the dining cars are both brilliant and more expensive than those at the Savoy. If you use the trains all the time you realize how unreliable they really are, but occasional travelers need not fear too much. The whole country is connected to London via British Rail, and there is a circular network of train stations that leads you into the English countryside, or as far as the suburbs. You can buy tickets at the **British Travel Center** (12 Lower Regent St, SW1, 071/846.9000) for all rail travel in Britain and rail and sea journeys to the Continent and Ireland. You can also get special deals on coaches here. Tickets are not inexpensive, so ask about cheap day returns, special-fare tickets, etc. Children under 16 pay half-price and those under 5 ride free. Buy your **British Pass** before you leave home. With a **Rover** ticket you can travel anywhere, anytime, from 4-22 days, and save considerably on fares. Look out for early-morning travel restrictions and avoid traveling on Friday, the busiest travel day in the UK.

Train information

Euston Station For the midlands, north Wales, the northwest, and the west coast of Scotland. ◆ 071/387.7070

King's Cross Station For northeast England and the east coast to Scotland. ◆ 071/278.2477

Liverpool Street Station For East Anglia—Cambridgeshire, Suffolk, Norfolk—and Essex. ◆ 071/928.5100

Paddington Station For western England—Oxfordshire, Cornwall—and South Wales. ◆ 071/262.6767

Victoria Station For the Continent, including the ultimate way to travel—the *Venice Simplon Orient Express* train, Victoria to Venice; Gatwick Airport. ◆ 071/928.5100

Waterloo, Charing Cross, and Victoria Station For southeast and southern England—Brighton, the coast. ◆ 071/928.5100

Sightseeing

Boat Trips The best way to see London if you are blessed with a warmish, sunny day. You can cover the entire 28 snaking miles of the Thames from Hampton Court to Greenwich Palace on one of the passenger boats that spend their days cruising up and downstream from central London. ◆ River trip information 071/730.4812

For the Disabled Artsline advises on theater, cinema, and museum access for those with disabilities and special needs. It also has minicom for the deaf, but is not a drop-in service. Most cinemas, theaters, and public places (including restaurants) do cater to the disabled. Always ring and check when booking or visiting, as this guarantees special help when you arrive and an appropriate seat. Telephone service, only. ◆ M-F 10:30AM-5PM. 071/388.2227

Evan Evans runs daily coach tours of London. It takes a number of disabled passengers, as long as someone able bodied travels with the disabled person. Advise on the nature of the disability before booking. ◆ M-F 9:30AM-5:30PM. 071/930.2377

Holiday Care Service This is a charity giving free information and advice on holidays for people with special needs—the elderly, the handicapped, and the disabled. It is not a booking service. Ring or write explaining the problem and what sort of holiday you are looking for, with an idea of your budget. Holiday Care has details on inclusive or specialized holidays, accommodations, transportation, publications, and guides for UK holidays. It can find holiday helpers who will drive elderly, handicapped, and disabled people around, too. ◆ 2 Old Bank Chambers, Station Rd, Horley, Surrey 9HW. 0293/774535

London Transport runs a daily **Carelink** service every hour on a clockwise circular route that goes past most of London's mainline stations (Waterloo, Victoria, Paddington, Euston, King's Cross, Liverpool St), starting at 8:30AM at Victoria. These buses connect with the wheelchair-accessible **Airbus** services to Heathrow Airport at both Victoria and Euston. Buses are specially designed and drivers specially trained. ◆ Carelink, LRT Unit for Disabled Passengers. 55 Broadway, SW1. 071/222.4600

National Trust owns places of historic interest or natural beauty all over the country, and has a booklet showing those accessible to people with disabilities, including scented gardens for the blind. ◆ 36 Queen Anne's Gate, SW1. 071/222.9251

Tours Bus tours are a good way to get a sense of the lay of the land. There are 2 basic types of tours: the panorama, which is a one-and-a-half to 2-hour 18- to 20-mile nonstop sightseeing tour; and the full- and half-day guided tours, which cover Westminster Abbey and the Changing of the Guard in the morning and St. Paul's and the Tower of London in the afternoon.

The **Harrods** tour is not recommended for panoramas, but is an excellent whole-day tour. It is expensive, but the fee includes all entrance tickets, a civilized 3-course lunch, a good guide, and sheer comfort. It leaves from Harrods 8:45AM daily (071/581.3603). Two-hour tours leave Harrods at 10AM, 1, and 4PM daily, and include tea, coffee, biscuits, and a taped commentary.

London Regional Transport is the best bet for the panorama. It's a traditional red double-decker bus, open-topped in summer. Tours depart on the hour from Piccadilly Circus, 10AM-7PM; Victoria, 9AM-6PM; Marble Arch (Speaker's Corner) and Baker St. Station, 10AM-5PM, every day except Christmas. There is no need to book; just get on the bus (071/227.3456).

Walking You only really know and love a city through your eyes and feet, and London offers stupendous rewards to the walker. Such distinguished feet as those of **Daniel Defoe, Samuel Johnson, James Boswell, John Gay,** and **Thomas Carlyle** made walking the streets of London part of their life's work. Some advice: Look both ways before crossing the street. Now there's the added hazard (and one not to be underestimated) of cyclists, both messengers and those fearful for their lives at the hands of motorists, cutting swathes through pedestrians on the pavement. Walking tours are listed in the back of the *Times* and in the weekly *Time Out* magazine, and include the City, the Great Fire and Plague, and the London of the Romans, Victorians, Shakespeare, and Dickens. It is now possible to walk from the Thames Flood Barrier back to the source in the Cotswolds—a very long walk, indeed!

Visitors Information

Afternoon Tea Civilized, refreshing, and much harder to come by than you would expect in the land of tea and sympathy. All the better hotels offer tea between 3:30-5:30PM, and trying to get a cup earlier or later can be difficult. In fact, trying to get a cup of a tea without the accompanying cakes and sandwiches is close to impossible. There is something to be said for skipping lunch or planning an after-theater supper and treating yourself to a traditional tea, which will include sandwiches, scones, cakes, and pastries. Try **Brown's Hotel**

(Dover St, W1, 071/493.6020), the **Waldorf** (Aldwych, WC2, 071/836.2400), or the **Ritz** (Piccadilly, W1, 071/493.8181), but book 2 weeks ahead and it's jacket and tie, only.

Beggars Britain has an estimated 250,000 homeless people and London has 5000 of them living on the streets, many in the Waterloo and Southbank area and along the Strand. In recent years, the numbers have increased as the mentally ill have been put out from institutions into the community for nonexistent care. At the same time, a lot of young people now beg on the streets of London and not all of them need to. None of them are dangerous. They won't take your money, but they will ask for it. It is wise, though, to carry some change in your pockets for the tube so that you don't need to search for your wallet when paying for a ticket in the central London stations late at night (Piccadilly, Leicester Square, Victoria, Charing Cross).

Climate Believe it or not, London's climate is moderate and mild. It does rain a lot, but the sun also shines a lot, and there hasn't been fog or smog in London for 20 years. Whatever the season, bring sweaters and jackets for evenings, and raincoats, umbrellas, and shoes that are kind to your feet and tolerate long distances and the odd puddle.

Fax and Telex At Westminster, there is a communications center with a walk-in fax and telex facility that is open M-Sa 9AM-7PM. You can send a fax or telex to the States and receive messages (1A The Broadway, St. James's, SW1, 071/222.4444). You will find an increasing number of small shops and newsstands offer fax facilities for a small charge. Look for a sign in the window. If you send a fax to the States at peak time (3-5PM), you can expect to pay $2 or more per sheet.

Health Take out health insurance before you come. Gone are the days when you could get free emergency treatment. Now you will be treated without questions, then charged at the private patient rate, which can be expensive. England and the US have no reciprocal health agreement. If you haven't arranged for medical coverage before arriving, do so as soon as you get here. Not all hospitals in London have 24-hour emergency rooms, but the following do.

Charing Cross Hospital ♦ Fulham Palace Rd, W6. 081/748.2040

Royal Free Hospital ♦ Pond St, NW3. 071/794.0500

St. Bartholemew's Hospital ♦ West Smithfield, EC1. 071/601.8888

St. Stephen's Hospital ♦ 369 Fulham Rd, SW10. 071/352.8161

St. Thomas Hospital ♦ Lambeth Palace Rd, SE1. 071/928.9292

University College Hospital ♦ Gower St, WC1. 071/387.9300

For emergency dental care, call 071/400.0400 or 081/677.6363 for 24-hour referral service.

Money Inflation has been sharply checked in the UK, but some things (hotels, gasoline, good restau-

rants) will always seem cruelly expensive, while others (woolens, books, antiques) make you feel personally prosperous. Sadly, theater tickets are not the bargain they once were, although they're still well below Broadway's top prices. The exchange rate varies daily and can be found in the *Times* each morning, but it is best to check with a bank because that is the rate you will actually get. Change your money and traveler's checks in one of the 4 main banks (Barclays, Midland, National Westminster, and Lloyds), not in shops or hotels, where the exchange rate will always punish you. The banks are working longer hours—some of the busiest now stay open until 5PM, and some Barclays Banks are open on Saturday morning. National Westminster has a Bureau de Change at Platform 8 in Victoria Station, which is open from 8AM to 9PM daily. American Express (6 Haymarket, SW1, 071/930.4411) is open M-F 9AM-5PM; Sa 9AM-noon; Su 10AM-4PM, and gives a fairly decent rate. You can cash a personal check for up to $1000 with an AMEX card. If you get seriously short of money, you can have money cabled to you at any post office, supposedly in less than 12 hours from the time it is sent. The post office will give you a Girobank check and cash it on the spot when you produce your passport. The English currency is pounds sterling (£). Check it out before you spend it. £1 is a small, thick goldish coin; 50 pence is a large hexagonal silver coin; 10p is large, silver, and round; 20p is tiny and hexagonal. There are 100 pence (p) in a pound. £5 notes are blue, £10 are brown, £20 are purple, and £50 are greenish gold. Credit cards are as popular here as they are in America, with Access (the English Mastercard) and Barclaycard (Visa) being the most widely used. Markets and antique dealers give better prices for cash.

Museums Famous, fabulous, but not always free. The **British Museum**, the **Tate Gallery**, the **National Gallery**, and the **Museum of London** have so far resisted the charges. Legislation to impose charges on all museums and galleries is currently being debated and, if it goes through, will deprive countless thousands of British and visitors alike from coming. The **National History Museum**, **Science Museum**, and **Victoria & Albert** already charge for access. Spend as much time in them as you can while you can. Most are open all day from Monday to Saturday and in the afternoon only on Sunday. Check to be sure. **Museum of London, Sir John Soanes**, and the **Dulwich Art Gallery** are all closed on Monday, for example.

Pickpockets The London that **Dickens** knew and wrote about has largely disappeared, but pickpockets remain. Watch your bag, keep cash tucked away in a pocket close to your body, and when sitting in cafés, don't put your handbag on the floor by your feet. Also, when trying on clothes, don't leave your bag in the dressing room if you go in search of a larger mirror or another size. Leave large amounts of cash and valuable jewelry in the hotel safe—you haven't thought of a hiding place that they haven't thought of. When checking in and out of hotels, keep your suitcases in view.

Post Offices There are main post offices, little newsstands, candy-shop post offices, and enormous branch post offices. Usually, the hours are M-Sa 9AM-5:30PM. A lot goes on in a post office, including the issuing of pension payments and TV licenses, so the queue to buy a stamp can take forever. The post office adds insult to injury by running ghastly video advertising while you wait. Either buy a lot and save time or allow half an hour and take a book and ear plugs. Happily, rescue has appeared in the shape of some newsstands that sell books of 1st- and 2nd-class stamps. Sadly, all letters abroad need weighing, so it's back to the post office. Rates are always going up. Ask for special-issue stamps and you will probably get something pretty.

Public Holidays New Year's Day, Good Friday, Easter Monday, May Day (first Monday in May), Spring Bank Holiday (last Monday in May), August Bank Holiday (last Monday in August), Christmas Day, and Boxing Day (December 26). Holidays in England are referred to as *bank holidays* because the banks are shut on those days. Confusingly, some shops now stay open, but you'll never know which ones unless you happen to wander past!

Pubs They are as much a part of the English way of life as cafés in France. You have to have at least one drink, and preferably a meal as well, in a pub in order to complete the English experience. The word pub is short for *public house*, and if you look above the doors of most of them, you will find the proprietors listed as landlords. Pubs are cursed with 2 drawbacks: they are smoky and have odd hours—generally, daily from 11AM-3PM, 5:30-11PM; although many of the busiest are now open M-Sa 11AM-11PM. In the outskirts of London, they tend to open and close a half-hour earlier. Ten minutes before closing, the barman calls *last orders*. Don't expect to get very exotic drinks in a pub. (Don't even aim for a dry martini.) The pub drink is beer, and if you want cold beer, ask for a lager. Ale should be served cellar temperature, like a red wine, and if you are in a real ale pub, ask for a Best Bitter, which is a not-really-bitter brew with a taste of malt and hops. Specify half or pint. There is no waitress service, even in pubs that serve food. You have to go to the bar and place your order, pay when you are served, and carry your drinks and food to a table. Pub food has a vocabulary all its own: *Bangers* are tasty cold or hot sausages; *bangers'n'mash* are hot sausages with mashed potatoes; *chips* are French fries; *crisps* are potato chips; *cornish pasties* consist of chopped meat and potatoes wrapped in dough and baked; *pork pie* is chopped pork flavored with spices and herbs; and *sausage rolls* are delicious meaty sausages rolled in dough.

Shopping Shopping is the single most popular activity among visitors to London, winning out over the theater, the Changing of the Guard, and the Elgin Marbles. Hours are generally Monday to Saturday from 9AM-5:30PM, but small boutiques and antique shops are open later and are often closed on Saturday. Many stores close at noon or 1PM on Saturday. Antique shops and shops outside the center of London sometimes close for lunch. The recent attempt to pass a law allowing Sunday trading failed, so there is almost no shopping on Sunday, except Petticoat Lane Market and Covent Garden.

The price marked on an item is the price you pay—no additional taxes are added on at the cash register. Major credit cards are accepted in most shops, though not in all antique shops. It is better to cash your traveler's checks at a bank and pay cash than to use them in a shop, unless they are in pounds sterling.

The main shopping shrines are the **West End**, which includes the famous **Oxford Street** with its large department stores, John Lewis and Selfridges; and

Regent Street with Liberty and Aquascutum. Just **north of Oxford Street** is **Christopher Place**, which has some of London's smartest shops (Paddy Campbell, Nicole Farhi, and, Mulberry), and **South Molton Street** (Browns, Jungle Jap). Bond Street, Burlington Arcade, Piccadilly, St. James's, and Jermyn Street are all in the West End shopping areas as well. **Covent Garden** is London's newest and liveliest shopping area, while Soho, famous for its food shops and fruit and vegetable markets, is chic and relatively cheap, the up-and-coming place once more. **Charing Cross Road**, in the same area, has the densest concentration of bookshops. **Knightsbridge** is chic and expensive and ranges from the vast and palatial Harrods to the minuscule boutiques on Beauchamp Place. **Chelsea** shopping is wonderfully relaxed and getting better all the time. The area includes the Fulham Road and the King's Road. Pimlico is the place to go for antiques, as are Camden Passage and Portobello Market.

VAT The Value Added Tax, at 15 percent of the marked price, can be substantial. But if you are leaving the UK within 3 months, you can claim back the VAT on many of the items you buy if you have spent over £100. Make sure the shop operates the over-the-counter export scheme, which involves filling out a VAT707 form. (The shop will give it to you along with a stamped, addressed envelope.) You must carry the goods for which you intend to collect a VAT refund as hand luggage and present them to UK customs as you leave the country. Customs will stamp the forms, and then you mail them back to the shop before leaving the country. If you forget and pack the goods, or simply cannot carry them, then you have to show them to the officials when you arrive in the US, get the form stamped there, and mail it to the shop. After about 6 weeks the shop will send you a check in sterling, which can end up costing a lot to process through your bank. The bigger the purchases, the more sensible this process is.

Telephones Red telephone booths have disappeared, replaced by nondescript Continental-style booths. The trouble is that the English think Americans are on the phone all the time. If you are planning to live up to the image, buy a **Phone Card** from a post office, newsstand, or sweet shop. These are particularly useful for international calls and come in units of 10, 20, 40, 100, or 200, at 10p a unit (£1 to £20). They do minimize frustration considerably, as more and more phone booths (called phone *boxes*) are converting to this vandal-proof method. Notices inside phone booths that accept phone cards only tell you the nearest place to obtain a card. An alternative is to find a phone that takes money (some take 10p and 50p, while others take only 10p). Pay phones that accept major credit cards are now being installed in central London and cost 50p minimum to use. Pay phones are twice as expensive as private phones; all calls in England cost about twice what

those in America cost. Avoid hotel phones; the charges are generally outrageous. You can call home collect by dialing the international operator at 155. If you are dialing across London, the old 01 telephone area has been divided. The inner part of

London (within a 4-mile radius of Charing Cross), north of the Thames (all the areas covered in the main chapters of this book), and the new Docklands area have been changed from 01 to 071. South of the river, and everywhere else that had an 01 number, has been changed to 081.

Useful phone numbers:

Al-Anon	071/403.0888
Alcoholics Anonymous	071/352.3001
America Direct	0101/area code/number
American Embassy	071/499.9999
American Express Travel Service	071/930.4411
Children's London (recorded info)	071/222.8070
International Operator	155
International Telegrams	193
London Directory	142
London Transport Lost Property	071/486.2496

Lost or Stolen Credit Cards:

American Express	(M-F 9AM-6PM) 0273/696933
	(24 hours) 071/222.9633
Diners' Club	(24 hours) 0252/516261
Mastercard	(toll-free, 24 hours) 0101/314/275.690
Visa (Barclaycard)	(24 hours) 0604/230230
Narcotics Anonymous	071/351.6794
Operator Services (if you can't get through)	100
Police, Fire, Ambulance (no coins needed)	999
Regional Directory	192
Release (legal help)	071/603.8654
Sportsline	071/222.8000
Taxi Lost Property	071/833.0996
Teledata	081/200.0200
(car trouble, lost keys, general help)	
Teletourist (daily events)	071/246.8041
	071/730.0791
Time	123
US Directory	153
Weather Forecast	071/975.900

(they won't tell you anything you don't already know)

Tipping In hotels and restaurants, a 10- to 15-percent tip is customary. Irritatingly, the service is often included in the bill, and not clearly marked. Check, and if you aren't sure, ask. If the service has been very good, you may wish to leave something on top, which should be left in cash. Taxi drivers expect between 10- and 15-percent. Porters, cloakroom attendants, and hairdressers also expect a small tip. If you are invited to a large house for a weekend in the country and there is a certain standard of grandeur

Essentials

(dressing for dinner) and evidence of a housekeeper or maid, you can leave money on your dressing table just before your departure. (A couple staying 2 nights usually leaves about £5.)

Toilets There are never enough public *loos*, and they never seem to be nearby. All public buildings (museums, department stores, cinemas, and theaters) have facilities, and if you are discreet and unobtrusive, you can take advantage of those in large hotels. Pubs and restaurants generally expect you to be a customer. More and more automated loos in the French style are appearing on streets and in parks.

Calendar

January Chinese New Year's, Gerrard St; January sales; International Boat show, Earl's Court; Rugby Union International, Twickenham, Middlesex; Benson & Hedges Masters Snooker Tournament, Wembley Conference Center, Wembley, Middlesex; Commemoration of execution of Charles I, Trafalgar Sq

February Cruft's Dog Show, Earl's Court; Clown Service, Holy Trinity Church

March Chelsea Antiques Fair, Chelsea Old Town Hall; Daily Mail Ideal Home Exhibition, Earl's Court; Oranges and Lemons Service, St. Clement Danes; Oxford and Cambridge Boat Race, from Putney to Mortlake; Camden Jazz Festival; Easter Monday, Westminster Abbey; London Harness Horse Parade, Regent's Park

April Grand National Steeplechase, Aintree; London Marathon; HM Queen's real birthday, Hyde Park and Tower Hill; Tyburn Walk, from Old Bailey to Tyburn Convent; Shakespeare's birthday, Southwark Cathedral; Shakespeare season opens, Stratford-upon-Avon; Cricket season opens; Polo season opens

May Whitbread Badminton Horse Trials, Badminton, Avon; Chelsea Flower Show, Royal Hospital grounds; Glyndebourne Festival Opera season opens, Glyndebourne, East Lewes, Sussex; Covent Garden Proms, Royal Opera House; Oak Apple Day, Royal Hospital; Royal Windsor Horse Show, Great Park, Windsor; American Memorial Day, Whitehall, Westminster Abbey, and Parliament Sq

June Summer Exhibition at the Royal Academy, Royal Academy, Burlington House; Beating the Retreat, Horse Guards Parade and Royal Artillery; Derby Day, Epsom Racecourse, Surrey; Grosvenor House Antiques Fair, Grosvenor House, Park Lane; Trooping the Colour, Horse Guards Parade; Royal Ascot, Berkshire Racecourse; Open Air Shakespeare season opens, Regent's Park; Second Test Match, Lord's Cricket Ground, St. John's Wood; Wimbledon Lawn Tennis Championships, All England Tennis Club, Wimbledon; Capital Radio Music Festival opens; London to Brighton bicycle race, from Hyde Park to Brighton

July Princess Diana's birthday; Henley Royal Regatta and Henley Festival of Music and the Arts, Henley-on-Thames, Oxfordshire; Royal Tournament, Earl's Court; Henry Wood Promenade Concerts, Royal Albert Hall; Doggett's Coat and Badge Race, from London Bridge to Chelsea; City of London Festival; Royal Garden Parties at Buckingham Palace; Cutty Sark Tall Ships Race, Plymouth Harbor and Tower Bridge; Parliament breaks for summer recess

August Edinburgh Festival; Bank Holiday Weekend, Hampstead Heath Fair and Nottingham Hill Carnival, Portabello Rd

eptember Autumn Antiques Fair, Chelsea Town
Iall; Battle of Britain Week, Westminster Abbey;
Ioyal National Rose Society Show, Vincent Hall;
arnborough International Air Show, Farnborough,
Iampshire; British International Motor Show, Bir-
ningham

Ictober Trafalgar Day, Trafalgar Sq; National Ser-
ice for Seafarers, St. Paul's Cathedral; National
Irass Band Championships, Royal Albert Hall; Horse
f the Year Show, Wembley Arena; Halloween

Iovember State Opening of Parliament, House of
ords, Westminster; Guy Fawkes Night; Lord
Iayor's Procession and Show, from Guildhall to
Ioyal Courts of Justice; Remembrance Sunday,
enotaph; London to Brighton Veteran Car Run,
om Hyde Park to Brighton; Beaujolais Nouveau Race

Iecember Royal Smithfield Show, Earl's Court;
Vorld Doubles Tennis Championships, Albert Hall;
nnual Ice Show, Wembley Arena, Middlesex;
Ihristmas Tree, Trafalgar Sq; Royal Choral Society
arol Concerts, Royal Albert Hall and Guildhall;
Vatchnight Service, St. Paul's Cathedral; Big Ben
himes the *Big 12*, Trafalgar Sq

Best Brunches

:aprice For those in the know, this is the best
runch in London. Blueberry muffins, the smoothest
ollandaise on eggs Benedict, and oh, delight!
reamy New England clam chowder. (Also see page
0.) ♦ Daily noon-3PM, 6PM-midnight. Arlington
Iouse, Arlington St, SW1. 071/629.2239

he Everyman Cafe ♦ Daily 11AM-11PM; Su
oon-5PM. Holly Bush Vala, NW3. 071/431.2123

151 Giorgio Armani now owns this stylish restau-
ant. Tasty Bloody Marys, but the Cajun-style eggs
enedict come on toast, not muffins, which is disap-
ointing. But they're made up for by the scrambled
ggs, which are wrapped in smoked salmon, and the
oominess of the tables—which are so large you can
ven read the papers if you get bored with the view of
rompton belles and beau strolling past. (Also see
age 80.) ♦ M-Sa noon-3PM, 6:30-11:30PM; Su
1:30AM-4PM, 6:30-10:30PM. Chelsea Cloisters,
loane Ave, SW3. 071/730.5151

Io's Bar & Grill ♦ M-Sa noon-3:30PM, 5:30-
1:30PM; Su 11AM-4PM, 5:30-11:30PM. 216
Iaverstock Hill, NW3. 071/794.4125

oe Allen London's best-known US restaurant of-
ers eggs Benedict and eggs Joe Allen (eggs on spin-
ch and mashed potatoes), the leading brunch fea-
ures, both available daily. The thirsty get free coffee
efills here. (Also see page 150.) ♦ M-Sa noon-1AM;
u noon-midnight. 13 Exeter St, WC2. 071/836.0651

Ianhattan It's hardly surprising that they serve
eal manhattans here, but if you're not up to full
trength don't ask for a mimosa—you need a Bucks
izz (the British translation for champagne and or-
nge juice)! ♦ Daily noon-11:30PM.175 Great Port-
nd St, W1. 071/436.0600

erendipity Brasserie & Bar ♦ Tu-Sa noon-
2:30AM; Su noon-3PM. The Mall, Camden Passage,
1. 071/359.1932

*he English winter—ending in July to recommence
I August.*
Lord Byron

It's a bit of a food desert here in Westminster, so
MPs do spend a lot of time in **Locketts**, although
they always hope they'll get taken elsewhere. The
food's the same as you'd expect to get at an English
public school.

Go in and listen to a debate, though it's often
difficult to get into the **House of Commons**. It's a lot
easier to get in the **House of Lords**, which is a much
nicer place to go as it's a riot of decoration and
plushness.

The **Tate Gallery** restaurant has one of the best wine
cellars in London—it has typical English food and an
Elizabethan menu.

When I'm not lunching someone, there's a really
good sandwich bar called the **Prêt-à-Manager** half
way up Victoria Street.

One of the best places around is the **Footstool** in the
Crypt of St. John's Smith Square. Legend has it that
the 4 towers on each corner were built like that
because Queen Anne wanted it that way. She kicked
over her footstool to show what design she
expected. *Build it like that!* she's supposed to have
snapped to architect Thomas Archer. And he did.

Judi Bevan
Freelance writer and columnist for
The Sunday Telegraph

Walking through **Russia Dock Woodlands**, a patch
of green by Surrey Quays. There is a surreal feeling
about emerging from the trees and seeing the Nat
West tower so surprisingly close.

Having a drink in the **Mayflower** on Rotherhithe
Street, from where the *Mayflower* is reputed to have
set sail for America. The pub is timbered and cosy
with a terrace at the back overlooking the river at the
back for warm weather.

Going to church at **St. Mary's**, 'round the corner
from the pub. Built in 1715, it is wonderfully solid
and extremely well kept. Lots of stained glass,
candles, and friendly greetings for visitors. Perfect
for those who like *bells, smells, and lace*.

Shirley Eskapa
Novelist

No matter how hectic my day, the delicious sense of
luxury of sinking into the seat of a London taxi is
unequaled. In a rainy rush hour it's as if I'm in a
private mobile safe haven, so very different from the
angst experienced in the taxis of other large cities.
However obscure my destination, I am sure the
cabbie will find his way, and faster, as the
camaraderie among cabbies means they let one

Essentials

another gracefully through the traffic. London taxis
are my greatest extravagance—where else can one
buy such bliss?

Restaurants/Nightlife: Red	Hotels: Blue
Shops/Parks: Green	**Sights/Culture:** Black

A

C

Index

U

V

W

Index

London Restaurant Index

Only restaurants with star ratings are listed below.
All restaurants are listed alphabetically in the main
index. Always telephone as far in advance as possible
to confirm your table and ensure that a restaurant
has not closed, changed its hours, or booked its
tables for a private party.

London Hotel Index

$$$$

$$$

$$

London BESTS Index

Index

Travel Notes

Since the publication of his first book in 1963, **Richard Saul Wurman** has distinguished his work with a singular passion: that for making information understandable. He has published over 50 books; **LONDON** ACCESS® remains faithful to the motivating principles found in his previous works. Each project has been based on the premise that you understand something only in relation to what you already understand.

Receiving both bachelor's and master's degrees from the University of Pennsylvania, Wurman graduated in 1959 with highest honors. In the course of his studies, he established a close personal and professional relationship with architect Louis I. Kahn. A fellow of the American Institute of Architects, FAIA, Wurman is also a member of the Alliance Graphique Internationale and was Vice President of the American Institute of Graphic Arts. He has been the recipient of several grants from the National Endowment for the Arts, a Guggenheim fellowship, two Graham fellowships, and two Chandler fellowships.

Wurman has applied his design expertise to the field of cartography, creating several revolutionary works that have culminated in the **US**ATLAS project. CITIES: A Comparison of Form and Scale, published in 1963, focuses on the relative size and scale of 50 cities, allowing the reader to compare them accurately to one another. In 1967, Wurman developed city maps with standardized scale and legends, coauthoring them in a volume entitled *URBAN ATLAS: 20 American Cities.* One of his most notable mapmaking experiences was as a member of an archaeological expedition during the first year of exploration (1958) of the Mayan city of Tikal, in Guatemala, where he surveyed one-third of the city. In 1988 he wrote the paper *Mapping and Cartography in Metropolitan Areas* for the XVII Triennale in Milan.

Currently, Wurman is the co-owner of **ACCESS**®Press with HarperCollins and of The *Understanding* Business. **ACCESS**® travel guides to London, Paris, Rome, New York City, Los Angeles, San Francisco, Tokyo, and other major cities answer tourists' questions, from the most common to the most obscure; the latest in the non- travel series is *The Wall Street Journal Guide to Understanding Money & Markets.* Wurman restructured and redesigned the Pacific Bell Yellow Pages directories into the more coherently organized product, the *SMART Yellow Pages*®. *INFORMATION ANXIETY* (1989), his breakthrough guide to handling the information glut, has been published in six languages.

Wurman, his wife, novelist Gloria Nagy, and their four children live in Manhattan and in Bridgehampton, New York.

Writing
Joan Plachta

Research
Cherry Park

Contributing Editor
Jill Robinson Shaw

Editing
Melanie Falick

Design
Lynne Stiles, *Senior*
Ellie Barrett

Maps
Julie Bilski
Michael Blum
Cheryl Fitzgerald
Kitti Homme
Patti Keelin
Michael Kohnke
Laurie Miller
Scott Summers

Text Styling
Jerry Stanton

Line Editing
Jean Linsteadt

Proofreading
Ann Dennehy
Karin Mullen
Caroline Scott

Scanning
Chris Middour

Cover Photograph
Reven T.C. Wurman

Printing and Otabind
Webcom Limited

Special Thanks
Mark Johnson
Ron Davis
Rajan Dev

ACCESS®PRESS

Creative Director
Richard Saul Wurman

Director
Jane Rosch

Editorial Director
Lise Friedman

Project Directors
Mark Goldman
Stuart L. Silberman

Writer's Thanks to:
Jane Anderson
Val Austin at British Tourist Authority
Eric Barr and David Pincott at British Telecom
Quentin Bell
S. Clark at Westminster City Council
Shirley Cowan at Guardian Royal Exchange
George Goodwin
Angela Heylin
Peter Nash
John Philips at the Greater London Records Office
Stewart Shaw
Colonel Trelawney at The Army
Susan Whiddington at The Society of West End Theatre

Previous Edition:
Carla Carlisle, Marlene Hamilton, Pippa Hayes, Writing and Research; Jean Linsteadt, J. Abbott Miller, Project Directors; Michael Everitt, Production Coordinator; Judy Cohen, Maria Giudice, Janice Hogan, Susan Pace, Naoto Sekiguchi, Lisa Victor, Daniel Wiley, Production; Kenneth Ludacer, Typesetting; Immanuel Ness, Word Processing; Reven T.C. Wurman, Cover Photography; Mary Pfister, Esther Allen, Proofreading; Bill Dorich, Printing Supervision; London Regional Transport 55 Broadway London SW1H 0BD (London Regional Transport Undergrouond Map, inside back cover), The Society of West End Theatres Bedford Chambers, The Piazza Covent Garden, London WC2E 8HQ, Thanks; Ken Brecher, Susan Dooley, Herbert Fry, Faustino Galan, David Gentleman, Ken Linsteadt, Colin Forbes, Rilchard Pilbrow, James Stirling, Michael Wilford and Associates, John Weale, Neil Saunders, Denise Silvester-Carr, Special Thanks.